Reading

Grade

Adaptin

PEARSON
Scott Foresman

scottforesman.com

Editorial Offices: Glenview, Illinois • Parsippany, New Jersey • New York, New York
Sales Offices: Boston, Massachusetts • Duluth, Georgia • Glenview, Illinois
Coppell, Texas • Sacramento, California • Mesa, Arizona

We dedicate Reading Street to
Peter Jovanovich.

His wisdom, courage,
and passion for education
are an inspiration to us all.

This work is protected by United States copyright laws and is provided *solely for the use of teachers and administrators* in teaching courses and assessing student learning in their classes and schools. Dissemination or sale of any part of this work (including the World Wide Web) will destroy the integrity of the work and is *not* permitted.

Accelerated Reader®

Cover Greg Newbold

About the Cover Artist
Award-winning artist Greg Newbold began drawing and painting at age three—and never stopped. His illustrated books for children include *Spring Song* and *Winter Lullaby*. Mr. Newbold also does illustrations for magazines, motion pictures, and food products, such as catsup and jelly. He creates his illustrations in a studio next to his house, snuggled in the Rocky Mountains of Utah.

ISBN-13: 978-0-328-24388-4

ISBN-10:   0-328-24388-4

Reading STREET

Where the Love of Reading Begins

Reading Street Program Authors

Peter Afflerbach, Ph.D.
Professor, Department of
Curriculum and Instruction
University of Maryland at
College Park

Camille L.Z. Blachowicz, Ph.D.
Professor of Education
National-Louis University

Candy Dawson Boyd, Ph.D.
Professor, School of Education
Saint Mary's College of California

Wendy Cheyney, Ed.D.
Professor of Special Education
and Literacy, Florida
International University

Connie Juel, Ph.D.
Professor of Education, School of
Education, Stanford University

Edward J. Kame'enui, Ph.D.
Professor and Director, Institute for
the Development of Educational
Achievement, University of Oregon

Donald J. Leu, Ph.D.
John and Maria Neag Endowed
Chair in Literacy and Technology
University of Connecticut

Jeanne R. Paratore, Ed.D.
Associate Professor of Education
Department of Literacy
and Language Development
Boston University

P. David Pearson, Ph.D.
Professor and Dean,
Graduate School of Education
University of California, Berkeley

Sam L. Sebesta, Ed.D.
Professor Emeritus,
College of Education,
University of Washington, Seattle

Deborah Simmons, Ph.D.
Professor, College of Education
and Human Development
Texas A&M University
(Not pictured)

Sharon Vaughn, Ph.D.
H.E. Hartfelder/Southland
Corporation Regents Professor
University of Texas

Susan Watts-Taffe, Ph.D.
Independent Literacy Researcher
Cincinnati, Ohio

Karen Kring Wixson, Ph.D.
Professor of Education
University of Michigan

Components

Student Editions (1–6)

Teacher's Editions (PreK–6)

Assessment
Assessment Handbook (K–6)
Baseline Group Tests (K–6)
DIBELS™ Assessments (K–6)
ExamView® Test Generator CD-ROM (2–6)
Fresh Reads for Differentiated
Test Practice (1–6)
Online Success Tracker™ (K–6)*
Selection Tests Teacher's Manual (1–6)
Unit and End-of-Year
Benchmark Tests (K–6)

Leveled Readers
Concept Literacy Leveled Readers (K–1)
Independent Leveled Readers (K)
Kindergarten Student Readers (K)
Leveled Reader Teaching Guides (K–6)
Leveled Readers (1–6)
Listen to Me Readers (K)
Online Leveled Reader Database (K–6)*
Take-Home Leveled Readers (K–6)

Trade Books and Big Books
Big Books (PreK–2)
Read Aloud Trade Books (PreK–K)
Sing with Me Big Book (1–2)
Trade Book Library (1–6)

Decodable Readers
Decodable Readers (K–3)
Strategic Intervention
Decodable Readers (1–2)
Take-Home Decodable Readers (K–3)

Phonics and Word Study
Alphabet Cards in English and Spanish
(PreK–K)
Alphabet Chart in English and Spanish
(PreK–K)
Animal ABCs Activity Guide (K)
Finger Tracing Cards (PreK–K)
Patterns Book (PreK–K)
Phonics Activities CD-ROM (PreK–2)*
Phonics Activities Mats (K)
Phonics and Spelling Practice Book (1–3)
Phonics and Word-Building Board and Letters
(PreK–3)
Phonics Songs and Rhymes Audio CD (K–2)
Phonics Songs and Rhymes Flip Chart (K–2)
Picture Word Cards (PreK–K)
Plastic Letter Tiles (K)
Sound-Spelling Cards and Wall Charts (1–2)
Strategies for Word Analysis (4–6)
Word Study and Spelling Practice Book (4–6)

Language Arts
Daily Fix-It Transparencies (K–6)
Grammar & Writing Book and
Teacher's Annotated Edition, The (1–6)
Grammar and Writing Practice Book
and Teacher's Manual (1–6)
Grammar Transparencies (1–6)
Six-Trait Writing Posters (1–6)
Writing Kit (1–6)
Writing Rubrics and Anchor Papers (1–6)
Writing Transparencies (1–6)

Practice and Additional Resources
AlphaBuddy Bear Puppet (K)
Alphasaurus Annie Puppet (PreK)
Amazing Words Posters (K–2)
Centers Survival Kit (PreK–6)
Graphic Organizer Book (2–6)
Graphic Organizer Flip Chart (K–1)
High-Frequency Word Cards (K)
Kindergarten Review (1)
Practice Book and Teacher's Manual (K–6)
Read Aloud Anthology (PreK–2)
Readers' Theater Anthology (K–6)
Research into Practice (K–6)

Retelling Cards (K–6)
Scott Foresman Research Base (K–6)
Skill Transparencies (2–6)
Songs and Rhymes Flip Chart (PreK)
Talk with Me, Sing with Me Chart (PreK–K)
Tested Vocabulary Cards (1–6)
Vocabulary Transparencies (1–2)
Welcome to Reading Street (PreK–1)

ELL
ELL and Transition Handbook (PreK–6)
ELL Comprehensive Kit (1–6)
ELL Posters (K–6)
ELL Readers (1–6)
ELL Teaching Guides (1–6)
Ten Important Sentences (1–6)

Digital Components
AudioText CDs (PreK–6)
Background Building Audio CDs (3–6)
ExamView® Test Generator
CD-ROM (2–6)
Online Lesson Planner (K–6)
Online New Literacies Activities (1–6)*
Online Professional Development (1–6)
Online Story Sort (K–6)*
Online Student Editions (1–6)*
Online Success Tracker™ (K–6)*
Online Teacher's Editions (PreK–6)
Phonics Activities CD-ROM (PreK–2)*
Phonics Songs and Rhymes
Audio CD (K–2)
Sing with Me/Background Building
Audio CDs (PreK–2)
Songs and Rhymes Audio CD (PreK)

My Sidewalks Early Reading Intervention (K)

My Sidewalks Intensive Reading Intervention (Levels A–E)

Reading Street for the Guided Reading Teacher (1–6)

UNIT
4

Unit 4
Adapting

Unit 5
Adventurers

Unit 2
Doing the Right Thing

Writing and Assessment WA1–WA18

Leveled Resources LR1–LR48

Differentiated Instruction . . . . . DI•1–DI•60

Teacher Resources TR1–TR42

Unit 3
Inventors and Artists

Writing and Assessment WA1–WA18

Leveled Resources LR1–LR48

Differentiated Instruction . . . . . DI•1–DI•60

Teacher Resources TR1–TR42

Adapting

*How do people and animals
adapt to different situations?*

Weslandia

A boy changes the world around him.

FICTION

connect to SOCIAL STUDIES

Stretching Ourselves

Young people make the most of their lives.

EXPOSITORY NONFICTION

connect to SCIENCE

Exploding Ants

Insects adapt to their environment.

EXPOSITORY NONFICTION

connect to SCIENCE

The Stormi Giovanni Club

A girl adapts to a new school.

PLAY

connect to SOCIAL STUDIES

The Gymnast

A boy tries to turn himself into an athlete.

AUTOBIOGRAPHY

connect to SOCIAL STUDIES

Unit 4
Skills Overview

		WEEK 1	WEEK 2
		396–411 **Weslandia/** **Under the** **Back Porch/** **Keziah** FICTION *How do people adapt to difficult situations?*	**416–435** **Stretching** **Ourselves/** **Helpful Tools** EXPOSITORY NONFICTION *How do people adapt to living with physical limitations?*
Reading	**Comprehension**	**T** ⊙ **Skill** Draw Conclusions ⊙ **Strategy** Answer Questions **T** REVIEW **Skill** Main Idea	**T** ⊙ **Skill** Generalize ⊙ **Strategy** Predict **T** REVIEW **Skill** Graphic Sources
	Vocabulary	**T** ⊙ **Strategy** Word Structure	**T** ⊙ **Strategy** Context Clues
	Fluency	Punctuation Clues	Emotion
Word Work	**Spelling and Phonics**	Words From Many Cultures	Prefixes *over-*, *under-*, *sub-*, *super-*, *out-*
Oral Language	**Speaking/Listening/ Viewing**	Demonstration Analyze Illustrations	Oral Presentation Listen to Oral Presentations
Language Arts	**Grammar, Usage, and Mechanics**	**T** Subject and Object Pronouns	**T** Pronouns and Antecedents
	Weekly Writing	E-Mail Writing Trait: Conventions	Journal Entry Writing Trait: Focus/Ideas
	Unit Process Writing	Story	Story
	Research and Study Skills	Instruction Manual	Technology: Telephone Directory
	Integrate Science and Social Studies Standards	*Time for* SOCIAL STUDIES Society, Culture, Government	*Time for* Science Human Body Systems, Physical Limitations, Disease

⊙ Target Skill   **T** Tested Skill

 **How do people and animals adapt to different situations?**

WEEK 3	WEEK 4	WEEK 5
440–457 **Exploding Ants/The Creature from the Adapting Lagoon** *How do animals adapt to survive?* EXPOSITORY NONFICTION	**462–483** **The Stormi Giovanni Club/Think Dress Codes Are a Drag?** *How do people adapt to a new school?* PLAY	**488–503** **The Gymnast/All About Gymnastics** *Why do people try to change themselves?* AUTOBIOGRAPHY
T ◉ **Skill** Graphic Sources ◉ **Strategy** Monitor and Fix Up **T** REVIEW **Skill** Author's Purpose	**T** ◉ **Skill** Generalize ◉ **Strategy** Story Structure **T** REVIEW **Skill** Draw Conclusions	**T** ◉ **Skill** Draw Conclusions ◉ **Strategy** Visualize **T** REVIEW **Skill** Generalize
T ◉ **Strategy** Context Clues	**T** ◉ **Strategy** Context Clues	**T** ◉ **Strategy** Word Structure
Tempo and Rate	Tone of Voice	Punctuation Clues
Homophones	Suffixes *-ible, -able*	Negative Prefixes
Description Listen to Poetry	Advice Listen to Advice	Informational Speech Analyze Media
T Possessive Pronouns	**T** Indefinite and Reflexive Pronouns	**T** Using *Who* and *Whom*
Tell a Story About an Animal Writing Trait: Word Choice	Advice Writing Trait: Voice	Tell How You Achieved a Goal Writing Trait: Word Choice
Story	Story	Story
Magazine/Periodical	Thesaurus	Graphs
Time for Science Animals, Environments-Biomes, Adaptations	**Time for Social Studies** Individual Development, Interactions, Groups, Communication	**Time for Social Studies** Individual Development and Identity, Sports

Predictors of Reading Success	WEEK 1	WEEK 2	WEEK 3	WEEK 4
Fluency (WCPM)	Punctuation Clues 120–128 WCPM	Emotion 120–128 WCPM	Tempo and Rate 120–128 WCPM	Tone of Voice 120–128 WCPM
Vocabulary/ Concept Development (assessed informally) (Vocabulary)	barren edible island livestock	dedication leg brace polio triumphant	African black mambas constrictors reptiles	count on settle in
Lesson Vocabulary	**Strategy** Word Structure blunders civilization complex envy fleeing inspired rustling strategy	**Strategy** Context Clues abdomen artificial gait handicapped therapist wheelchair	**Strategy** Context Clues critical enables mucus scarce specialize sterile	**Strategy** Context Clues cavities combination demonstrates episode profile strict
Text Comprehension (Retelling)	**Skill** Draw Conclusions **Strategy** Answer Questions	**Skill** Generalize **Strategy** Predict	**Skill** Graphic Sources **Strategy** Monitor and Fix Up	**Skill** Generalize **Strategy** Story Structure

Make Data–Driven Decisions

Data Management
- Assess
- Diagnose
- Prescribe
- Disaggregate

Classroom Management
- Monitor Progress
- Group
- Differentiate Instruction
- Inform Parents

Reading STREET

Success Tracker™

ONLINE CLASSROOM

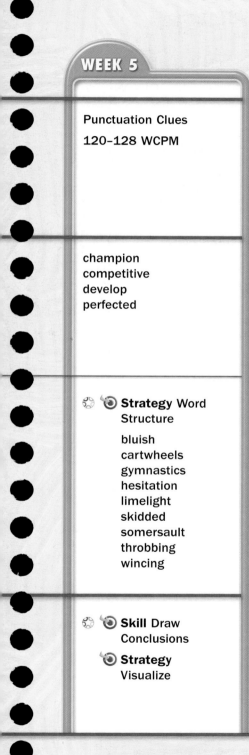

WEEK 5

Punctuation Clues
120–128 WCPM

champion
competitive
develop
perfected

◉ **Strategy** Word Structure

bluish
cartwheels
gymnastics
hesitation
limelight
skidded
somersault
throbbing
wincing

◉ **Skill** Draw Conclusions

◉ **Strategy** Visualize

◉ Manage Data

- Assign the Unit 4 Benchmark Test for students to take online.

- SuccessTracker records results and generates reports by school, grade, classroom, or student.

- Use reports to disaggregate and aggregate Unit 4 skills and standards data to monitor progress.

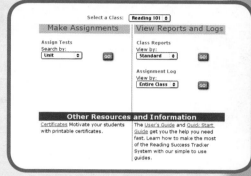

- Based on class lists created to support the categories important for AYP (gender, ethnicity, migrant education, English proficiency, disabilities, economic status), reports let you track adequate yearly progress every six weeks.

◉ Group

- Use results from Unit 4 Benchmark Tests taken online through SuccessTracker to regroup students.

- Reports in SuccessTracker suggest appropriate groups for students based on test results.

On-Level

Strategic Intervention

Advanced

◉ Individualize Instruction

- Tests are correlated to Unit 4 tested skills and standards so that prescriptions for individual teaching and learning plans can be created.

- Individualized prescriptions target instruction and accelerate student progress toward learning outcome goals.

- Prescriptions include resources to reteach Unit 4 skills and standards.

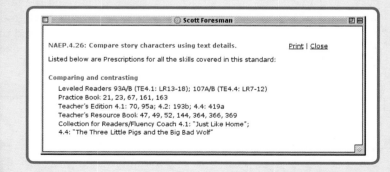

NAEP.4.26: Compare story characters using text details.   Print | Close

Listed below are Prescriptions for all the skills covered in this standard:

Comparing and contrasting

Leveled Readers 93A/B (TE4.1: LR13-18); 107A/B (TE4.4: LR7-12)
Practice Book: 21, 23, 67, 161, 163
Teacher's Edition 4.1: 70, 95a; 4.2: 193b; 4.4: 419a
Teacher's Resource Book: 47, 49, 52, 144, 364, 366, 369
Collection for Readers/Fluency Coach 4.1: "Just Like Home"; 4.4: "The Three Little Pigs and the Big Bad Wolf"

Unit 4
Grouping for AYP

Diagnose and Differentiate

Diagnose
To make initial grouping decisions, use the Baseline Group Test or another initial placement test. Depending on students' ability levels, you may have more than one of each group.

Differentiate

If... student performance is	**Below-Level**	**then...** use the regular instruction and the daily Strategic Intervention lessons, pp. DI·2–DI·50.
If... student performance is	**On-Level**	**then...** use the regular instruction for On-Level learners throughout each selection.
If... student performance is	**Advanced**	**then...** use the regular instruction and the daily instruction for Advanced learners, pp. DI·3–DI·51.

Group Time

On-Level
- Explicit instructional routines teach core skills and strategies.
- Independent activities provide practice for core skills and extension and enrichment options.
- Leveled readers (LR1–45) provide additional reading and practice with core skills and vocabulary.

Strategic Intervention
- Daily Strategic Intervention lessons provide more intensive instruction, more scaffolding, more practice with critical skills, and more opportunities to respond.
- Reteach lessons (DI·52–DI·56) provide additional instructional opportunities with target skills.
- Leveled readers instruction (LR1–45) builds background for the main selection and provides practice with target skills and vocabulary.

Advanced
- Daily Advanced Lessons provide compacted instruction for accelerated learning, options for investigative work, and challenging reading content.
- Leveled readers (LR1–45) provide additional reading tied to lesson concepts.

Additional opportunities to differentiate instruction:
- Reteach Lessons, pp. DI·52–DI·516
- Leveled Reader Instruction and Leveled Practice, LR1–45
- My Sidewalks on Scott Foresman Reading Street Intensive Reading Intervention Program

MY SIDEWALKS ON
SCOTT FORESMAN
READING STREET
Intensive Reading Intervention

Monitor Progress

STEP 2

- **Guiding comprehension questions** and skill and strategy instruction during reading
- **Monitor Progress boxes** to check comprehension and vocabulary
- **Weekly Assessments** on Day 3 for comprehension, Day 4 for fluency, and Day 5 for vocabulary
- **Practice Book** pages at point of use
- **Weekly Selection Tests** or **Fresh Reads for Differentiated Test Practice**

Assess and Regroup

STEP 3

- **Days 3, 4, and 5 Assessments** Record results of weekly Days 3, 4, and 5 assessments in retelling, fluency, and vocabulary (pp. WA16–WA17) to track student progress.
- **Unit 4 Benchmark Test** Administer this test to check mastery of unit skills.
- Use weekly assessment information, Unit Benchmark Test performance, and the Unit 4 Assess and Regroup (p. WA18) to make regrouping decisions. See the time line below.

YOU ARE HERE
Begin Unit 4

SCOTT FORESMAN ASSESSMENT

| Group Baseline Group Test | Assess | Regroup Units 1 and 2 | Regroup Unit 3 | Regroup Unit 4 (p. WA18) | Regroup Unit 5 | Assess |

| Week | 1 | 5 | 10 | 15 | 20 | 25 | 30 |

END OF YEAR

OUTSIDE ASSESSMENT

Initial placement → Outside assessment for regrouping → Outside assessment for regrouping

Outside assessments (e.g., DIBELS) may recommend regrouping at other times during the year.

Summative Assessment

STEP 4

- **Benchmark Assessment** Use to measure a student's mastery of each unit's skills.
- **End-of-Year Benchmark Assessment** Use to measure a student's mastery of program skills covered in all six units.

Unit 4
Theme Launch

Discuss the Big Idea

As a class, discuss the Big Idea question, *How do people and animals adapt to different situations?*

Explain that people and animals sometimes have to adapt to new situations or surroundings. Sometimes animals adapt to better protect themselves. Humans adapt to overcome physical limitations, or improve their lives.

Ask students to give examples of how people or animals might react to a new situation, such as a change in their environment.

One example of people and animals adapting to new situations is how they react to the changing of the seasons. When the weather gets colder, people wear different clothes and spend time doing different activities. Some animals might grow more fur or hibernate.

Theme and Concept Connections

Weekly lesson concepts help students connect the reading selections and the unit theme. Theme-related activities throughout the week provide opportunities to explore the relationships among the selections, the lesson concepts, and the unit theme.

UNIT 4

Read It Online
PearsonSuccessNet.com

Adapting

How do people and animals adapt to different situations?

390

 CONNECTING CULTURES

Use the following selections to explore the ways young people respond when they feel different from others or have to adapt to a new place.

Weslandia Have students discuss the reasons Wesley creates Weslandia and how others react to it. They can share their own experiences of feeling different from others and what they did in these situations.

The Stormi Giovanni Club Have students discuss how Stormi deals with moving to a new school. They can also share their ideas about adapting to new places.

Weslandia

A boy changes the world around him.

FICTION

connect to SOCIAL STUDIES

Paired Selection

"Under the Back Porch" and "Keziah"

POETRY

Stretching Ourselves

Young people make the most of their lives.

EXPOSITORY NONFICTION

connect to SCIENCE

Paired Selection

Helpful Tools

EXPOSITORY NONFICTION

Exploding Ants

Insects adapt to their environment.

EXPOSITORY NONFICTION

connect to SCIENCE

Paired Selection

The Creature from the Adapting Lagoon

EXPERIMENT

The Stormi Giovanni Club

A girl adapts to a new school.

PLAY

connect to SOCIAL STUDIES

Paired Selection

Think Dress Codes Are a Drag?

NEWSPAPER ARTICLE

The Gymnast

A boy tries to turn himself into an athlete.

AUTOBIOGRAPHY

connect to SOCIAL STUDIES

Paired Selection

All About Gymnastics

ONLINE REFERENCE SOURCES

391

Unit Inquiry Project

Adaptations

In the unit inquiry project, students each choose a group of people or animals and research how they have adapted to different situations. Students may use print or online resources as available.

The project assessment rubric can be found on p. 504a. Discuss the rubric's expectations before students begin the project. **Rubric** 4 3 2 1

PROJECT TIMETABLE

WEEK	ACTIVITY/SKILL CONNECTION
1	**IDENTIFY QUESTIONS** Discuss groups and situations students could research, such as how immigrants or refugees adapt to new locations or how bears adapt to humans moving into their habitats. Each student chooses a group and situation and browses a few Web sites or print reference materials to develop an inquiry question about it.
2	**NAVIGATE/SEARCH** Students conduct effective information searches and look for text and images that can help them answer their questions.
3	**ANALYZE** Students explore Web sites or print materials. They analyze the information they have found to determine whether or not it will be useful to them. Students print or take notes on valid information.
4	**SYNTHESIZE** Students combine relevant information they've collected from different sources to develop answers to their inquiry questions from Week 1.
	ASSESSMENT OPTIONS
5	**COMMUNICATE** Each student creates a graphic organizer that shows how a group of people or animals have adapted to a specific situation. Students may also give oral presentations based on their research notes.

CONCEPT DEVELOPMENT

Unit 4
Adapting

How do people and animals adapt to different situations?

Week 5

Expand the Concept
Why do people try to change themselves?

Connect the Concept

Literature

Develop Language
champion, competitive, develop, perfected

Teach Content
Gymnastics
Nadia Comaneci

Writing
Describe How You Achieved a Goal

Internet Inquiry
Gymnastics

TIME FOR SOCIAL STUDIES

Week 4

Expand the Concept
How do people adapt to a new school?

Connect the Concept

Literature

Develop Language
count on, settle in

Teach Content
Moving
E-mail
Friendship

Writing
Advice

Internet Inquiry
E-mail

TIME FOR SOCIAL STUDIES

Week 3

Expand the Concept
How do animals adapt to survive?

Connect the Concept

Literature

Develop Language
African black mambas, constrictors, reptiles

Teach Content
Biomes
Human Adaptations
Animal Experiments

Writing
Story About an Animal

Internet Inquiry
Animal Adaptations

TIME FOR Science

Week 1

Expand the Concept
How do people adapt to difficult situations?

Connect the Concept

Literature

Develop Language
barren, edible, island, livestock

Teach Content
Declaration of Independence
Amish Culture
African American Authors

Writing
E-mail

Internet Inquiry
Explore Civilizations

TIME FOR SOCIAL STUDIES

Week 2

Expand the Concept
How do people adapt to living with physical limitations?

Connect the Concept

Literature

Develop Language
dedication, leg brace, polio, triumphant

Teach Content
Animal Characteristics
Animal Survival
Food Web
Habitat

Writing
Journal Entry

Internet Inquiry
Adapting to Physical Limitations

TIME FOR Science

Unit 4
Adapting

Week 1

CONCEPT QUESTION
How do people and animals adapt to different situations?

Week 1
How do people adapt to difficult situations?

Week 2
How do people adapt to living with physical limitations?

Week 3
How do animals adapt to survive?

Week 4
How do people adapt to a new school?

Week 5
Why do people try to change themselves?

Week 1

EXPAND THE CONCEPT
How do people adapt to difficult situations?

Time for SOCIAL STUDIES

CONNECT THE CONCEPT

▶ **Build Background**
barren, edible, island, livestock

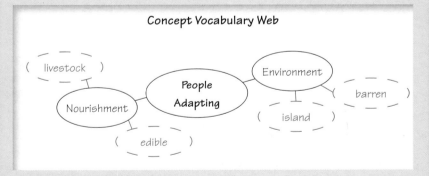

Concept Vocabulary Web

▶ **Social Studies Content**
Declaration of Independence, Amish Culture, African American Authors

▶ **Writing**
E-mail

▶ **Internet Inquiry**
Explore Civilizations

Preview Your Week

How do people adapt to difficult situations?

Why does Wesley take up the challenge of creating his own world?

Weslandia
by PAUL FLEISCHMAN   illustrated by KEVIN HAWKES

Genre **Fiction stories** are stories that the author has made up. As you read, notice how the character makes up his own world.

Student Edition pages 396–407

Audio CD

Genre	Fiction
🎧 **Vocabulary Strategy**	Word Structure
🎧 **Comprehension Skill**	Draw Conclusions
🎧 **Comprehension Strategy**	Answer Questions

Paired Selection

Reading Across Texts
Think About Poetry a Fictional Character Might Write

Genre
Poetry

Poetry

Genre
• A poem is a composition arranged in lines. Some poems have rhyme. Others do not rhyme.
• Many poems are written in the first person, with the speaker acting as a character.
• The poet creates images through the rhyme and rhythm of language.
• The poet also uses images to express thoughts and feelings.

Link to Writing
Think about your own favorite secret place and write a poem about it. Give the reader a picture of the place and an idea of when and why you go there.

Under the Back Porch
BY VIRGINIA HAMILTON

Our house is two stories high
shaped like a white box.
There is a yard stretched around it
and in back
a wooden porch.

Under the back porch is my place.
I rest there.
I go there when I have to be alone.
It is always shaded and damp.
Sunlight only slants through the slats
in long strips of light,
and the smell of the damp
is moist green,
like the moss that grows here.

My sisters and brothers
can stand on the back porch
and never know
I am here
underneath.
It is my place.
All mine.

Keziah
BY GWENDOLYN BROOKS

I have a secret place to go.
Not anyone may know.

And sometimes when the wind is rough
I cannot get there fast enough.

And sometimes when my mother
Is scolding my big brother,

My secret place, it seems to me,
Is quite the only place to be.

Reading Across Texts
Look back at *Weslandia* and ask yourself what kind of poem Wesley might write about the world he created.

Writing Across Texts Write a poem about *Weslandia* that you think Wesley might have written.

🎧 **Draw Conclusions** What makes the porch a secret place?

410

Student Edition pages 410–411

Audio CD

Read It
ONLINE
PearsonSuccessNet.com
- Student Edition
- Leveled Readers

Leveled Readers

◉ **Skill** Draw Conclusions
◉ **Strategy** Answer Questions
Lesson Vocabulary

Below-Level

On-Level

Advanced

ELL Reader
- Concept Vocabulary
- Text Support
- Language Enrichment

The Anasazi: The Ancient Builders

Integrate Social Studies Standards
- Society
- Culture
- Government

✓ Read

Weslandia,
pp. 396–407

"Under the Back Porch" and "Keziah,"
pp. 410–411

Leveled Readers

Below-Level **On-Level** **Advanced**
- Support Concepts
- Develop Concepts
- Extend Concepts
- Social Studies Extension Activity

ELL Reader

✓ Build Concept Vocabulary
People Adapting,
pp. 392l–392m

✓ Teach Social Studies Concepts
Declaration of Independence,
p. 399
Amish Culture, p. 405
African American Authors,
p. 411

✓ Explore Social Studies Center
Plan a Society, p. 392k

Weekly Plan

READING

45–90 minutes

TARGET SKILLS OF THE WEEK

Comprehension Skill
Draw Conclusions

Comprehension Strategy
Answer Questions

Vocabulary Strategy
Word Structure

LANGUAGE ARTS

30–60 minutes

Trait of the Week

Conventions

DAY 1
PAGES 392l–394b, 411a, 411e–411k

Oral Language

QUESTION OF THE WEEK *How do people adapt to difficult situations?*

Read Aloud: "The Black Stallion" 392m
Build Concepts, 392l

Comprehension/Vocabulary

Comprehension Skill/Strategy Lesson, 392–393

Draw Conclusions **T**

Answer Questions

Build Background, 394a

Introduce Lesson Vocabulary, 394b
blunders, civilization, complex, envy, fleeing, inspired, rustling, strategy **T**

Read Leveled Readers

Grouping Options 392f–392g

Fluency

Model Punctuation Clues, 392l–392m, 411a

Grammar, 411e
Introduce Subject and Object Pronouns **T**

Writing Workshop, 411g
Introduce E-mail
Model the Trait of the Week: Conventions

Spelling, 411i
Pretest for Words from Many Cultures

Internet Inquiry, 411k
Identify Questions

DAY 2
PAGES 394–403, 411a, 411e–411k

Oral Language

QUESTION OF THE DAY *Why do you think Wesley was such an outcast at school?*

Comprehension/Vocabulary

Vocabulary Strategy Lesson, 394–395

Word Structure **T**

Read *Weslandia,* 396–403

Grouping Options
392f–392g

Draw Conclusions **T**

Word Structure **T**

REVIEW Main Idea **T**

Develop Vocabulary

Fluency

Choral Reading, 411a

Grammar, 411e
Develop Subject and Object Pronouns **T**

Writing Workshop, 411g
Improve Writing with Refer to the Text

Spelling, 411i
Teach the Generalization

Internet Inquiry, 411k
Navigate/Search

DAILY WRITING ACTIVITIES

Day 1 Write to Read, 392

Day 2 Words to Write, 395
Strategy Response Log, 396, 403

DAILY SOCIAL STUDIES CONNECTIONS

Day 1 People Adapting Concept Web, 392l

Day 2 Time for Social Studies: Declaration of Independence, 399
Revisit the People Adapting Concept Web, 403

DAILY SUCCESS PREDICTORS

for Adequate Yearly Progress

Monitor Progress and Corrective Feedback

Vocabulary
Check Vocabulary, *392l*

- Practice Book, *pp. 151–160*
- Word Study and Spelling Practice Book, *pp. 61–64*
- Grammar and Writing Practice Book, *pp. 61–64*
- Selection Test, *pp. 61–64*
- Fresh Reads for Differentiated Test Practice, *pp. 91–96*
- The Grammar and Writing Book, *pp. 140–145*

Grouping Options for Differentiated Instruction

Turn the page for the small group lesson plan.

DAY 3   PAGES 404–409, 411a, 411e–411k

Oral Language

QUESTION OF THE DAY *Would you like to be Wesley's friend? Why or why not?*

Comprehension/Vocabulary

Read *Weslandia, 404–408*

Grouping Options 392f–392g

- 💿 Draw Conclusions **T**
- 💿 Answer Questions

Develop Vocabulary

Reader Response
Selection Test

Fluency

Model Punctuation Clues, 411a

Grammar, 411f
Apply Subject and Object Pronouns in Writing **T**

Writing Workshop, 409, 411h
Write Now
Prewrite and Draft

Spelling, 411j
Connect Spelling to Writing

Internet Inquiry, 411k
Analyze Sources

Day 3   Strategy Response Log, 406
Look Back and Write, 408

Day 3   Time for Social Studies: Amish Culture, 405
Revisit the People Adapting Concept
Web, 407

DAY 4   PAGES 410–411a, 411e–411k

Oral Language

QUESTION OF THE DAY *Where is a special, safe place you like to go when you want to be alone?*

Comprehension/Vocabulary

Read "Under the Back Porch," 410; "Keziah," 411

Grouping Options 392f–392g

Poetry
Reading Across Texts

Fluency

Partner Reading, 411a

Grammar, 411f
Practice Subject and Object Pronouns for Standardized Tests **T**

Writing Workshop, 411h
Draft, Revise, and Publish

Spelling, 411j
Provide a Strategy

Internet Inquiry, 411k
Synthesize Information

Day 4   Writing Across Texts, 411

Day 4   Time for Social Studies: African American Authors, 411

DAY 5   PAGES 411a–411l

Oral Language

QUESTION OF THE WEEK *To wrap up the week, revisit the Day 1 question.*

Build Concept Vocabulary, 411c

Fluency

Read Leveled Readers

Grouping Options 392f–392g

Assess Reading Rate, 411a

Comprehension/Vocabulary

- 💿 Reteach Draw Conclusions, 411b **T**

Idiom, 411b

- 💿 Review Word Structure, 411c **T**

Speaking and Viewing, 411d
Demonstration
Analyze Illustrations

Grammar, 411f
Cumulative Review

Writing Workshop, 411h
Connect to Unit Writing

Spelling, 411j
Posttest for Words from Many Cultures

Internet Inquiry, 411k
Communicate Results

Research/Study Skills, 411l
Instruction Manual

Day 5   Idiom, 411b

Day 5   Revisit the People Adapting Concept
Web, 411c

KEY 💿 = Target Skill   **T** = Tested Skill

Small Group Plan *for Differentiated Instruction*

Daily Plan AT A GLANCE

Reading
Whole Group
- Oral Language
- Comprehension/Vocabulary

Group Time
Differentiated Instruction

Meet with small groups to provide:
- Skill Support
- Reading Support
- Fluency Practice

Read

This week's lessons for daily group time can be found behind the Differentiated Instruction (DI) tab on pp. DI·2–DI·11.

Whole Group
- Fluency

Language Arts
- Grammar
- Writing
- Spelling
- Research/Inquiry
- Speaking/Listening/Viewing

Use *My Sidewalks on Reading Street* for Tier III intensive reading intervention.

DAY 1

On-Level
Teacher-Led
Page DI·3
- Develop Concept Vocabulary
- **Read** On-Level Reader *Adventure to the New World*

Strategic Intervention
Teacher-Led
Page DI·2
- Reinforce Concepts
- **Read** Below-Level Reader *Learning to Play the Game*

Advanced
Teacher-Led
Page DI·3
- **Read** Advanced Reader *Cheaper, Faster, Better: Recent Technological Innovations*
- Independent Extension Activity

ⓘ Independent Activities
While you meet with small groups, have the rest of the class...

- Visit the Reading/Library Center
- Listen to the Background Building Audio
- Finish Write to Read, p. 392
- Complete Practice Book pp. 153–154
- Visit Cross-Curricular Centers

DAY 2

On-Level
Teacher-Led
Pages 398–403
- **Read** *Weslandia*

Strategic Intervention
Teacher-Led
Page DI·4
- Practice Lesson Vocabulary
- Read Multisyllabic Words
- **Read** or Listen to *Weslandia*

Advanced
Teacher-Led
Page DI·5
- Extend Vocabulary
- **Read** *Weslandia*

ⓘ Independent Activities
While you meet with small groups, have the rest of the class...

- Visit the Reading/Library Center
- Listen to the AudioText for *Weslandia*
- Finish Words to Write, p. 395
- Complete Practice Book pp. 155–156
- Write in their Strategy Response Logs, pp. 396, 403
- Visit Cross-Curricular Centers
- Work on inquiry projects

DAY 3

On-Level
Teacher-Led
Pages 404–407
- **Read** *Weslandia*

Strategic Intervention
Teacher-Led
Page DI·6
- Practice Draw Conclusions and Answer Questions
- **Read** or Listen to *Weslandia*

Advanced
Teacher-Led
Page DI·7
- Extend Draw Conclusions and Answer Questions
- **Read** *Weslandia*

ⓘ Independent Activities
While you meet with small groups, have the rest of the class...

- Visit the Reading/Library Center
- Listen to the AudioText for *Weslandia*
- Write in their Strategy Response Logs, p. 406
- Finish Look Back and Write, p. 408
- Complete Practice Book p. 157
- Visit Cross-Curricular Centers
- Work on inquiry projects

① Begin with whole class skill and strategy instruction.

② Meet with small groups to provide differentiated instruction.

③ Gather the whole class back together for fluency and language arts.

On-Level

Teacher-Led
Pages 410–411

- **Read** "Under the Back Porch" and "Keziah"

Strategic Intervention

Teacher-Led
Page DI · 8

- Practice Retelling
- **Read** or Listen to "Under the Back Porch" and "Keziah"

Advanced

Teacher-Led
Page DI · 9

- **Read** "Under the Back Porch" and "Keziah"
- Genre Study

DAY 4

ⓘ Independent Activities

While you meet with small groups, have the rest of the class...

- Visit the Reading/Library Center
- Listen to the AudioText for "Under the Back Porch" and "Keziah"
- Visit the Writing/Vocabulary Center
- Finish Writing Across Texts, p. 411
- Visit Cross-Curricular Centers
- Work on inquiry projects

On-Level

Teacher-Led
Page DI · 11

- **Reread** Leveled Reader *Adventure to the New World*
- Retell *Adventure to the New World*

Strategic Intervention

Teacher-Led
Page DI · 10

- **Reread** Leveled Reader *Learning to Play the Game*
- Retell *Learning to Play the Game*

Advanced

Teacher-Led
Page DI · 11

- **Reread** Leveled Reader *Cheaper, Faster, Better: Recent Technological Innovations*
- Share Extension Activity

DAY 5

ⓘ Independent Activities

While you meet with small groups, have the rest of the class...

- Visit the Reading/Library Center
- Complete Practice Book pp. 158–160
- Visit Cross-Curricular Centers
- Work on inquiry projects

ELL

Grouping Place English language learners in the groups that correspond to their reading abilities in English.

Use the appropriate Leveled Reader or other text at students' instructional level.

TiP Send home the appropriate Multilingual Summary of the main selection on Day 1.

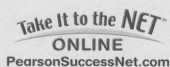

Take It to the NET ONLINE
PearsonSuccessNet.com

Jeanne Paratore
For ideas on using repeated readings, see the article "Using Repeated Readings to Promote Reading Success..." by Scott Foresman author J. Paratore and J. Turpie.

TEACHER TALK

An **Idiom** is a phrase that cannot be understood from the ordinary meaning of the words that form it, such as "hold your tongue." Idioms are especially difficult for English language learners.

Be sure to schedule time for students to work on the unit inquiry project "Adaptations." This week students develop inquiry questions about how groups of people or animals have adapted to different situations.

Looking Ahead

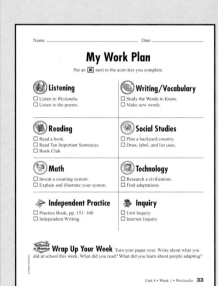

▲ **Group-Time Survival Guide**
p. 33, Weekly Contract

Customize Your Plan *by Strand*

ORAL LANGUAGE

SOCIAL STUDIES

Concept Development

How do people adapt to difficult situations?

CONCEPT VOCABULARY

barren   edible   island   livestock

BUILD

☐ **Question of the Week** Introduce and discuss the question of the week. This week students will read a variety of texts and work on projects related to the concept *people adapting*. Post the question for students to refer to throughout the week. **DAY 1** *392d*

☐ **Read Aloud** Read aloud from "The Black Stallion." Then begin a web to build concepts and concept vocabulary related to this week's lesson and the unit theme, Adapting. Introduce the concept words *barren, edible, island,* and *livestock* and have students place them on the web. Display the web for use throughout the week. **DAY 1** *392l–392m*

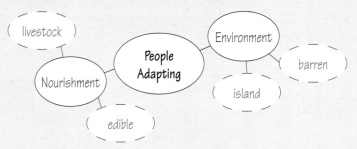

DEVELOP

☐ **Question of the Day** Use the prompts from the Weekly Plan to engage students in conversations related to this week's reading and the unit theme. **EVERY DAY** *392d–392e*

☐ **Concept Vocabulary Web** Revisit the People Adapting Concept Web and encourage students to add concept words from their reading and life experiences. **DAY 2** *403*, **DAY 3** *407*

CONNECT

☐ **Looking Back/Moving Forward** Revisit the People Adapting Concept Web and discuss how it relates to this week's lesson and the unit theme. Then make connections to next week's lesson. **DAY 5** *411c*

CHECK

☐ **Concept Vocabulary Web** Use the People Adapting Concept Web to check students' understanding of the concept vocabulary words *barren, edible, island,* and *livestock*. **DAY 1** *392l*, **DAY 5** *411c*

VOCABULARY

STRATEGY WORD STRUCTURE
An inflected ending is a letter or letters added to a base word. The endings *-ed, -ing,* and *-s* may be added to verbs to change the tense. You can use inflected endings to help figure out the meaning of an unfamiliar word.

LESSON VOCABULARY

blunders	fleeing
civilization	inspired
complex	rustling
envy	strategy

TEACH

☐ **Words to Know** Give students the opportunity to tell what they already know about this week's lesson vocabulary words. Then discuss word meaning. **DAY 1** *394b*

☐ **Vocabulary Strategy Lesson** Use the vocabulary strategy lesson in the Student Edition to introduce and model this week's strategy, *word structure*. **DAY 2** *394–395*

Vocabulary Strategy Lesson

PRACTICE/APPLY

☐ **Leveled Text** Read the lesson vocabulary in the context of leveled text. **DAY 1** *LR1–LR9*

☐ **Words in Context** Read the lesson vocabulary and apply *word structure* in the context of *Weslandia*. **DAY 2** *396–403*, **DAY 3** *404–408*

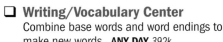

Leveled Readers

☐ **Writing/Vocabulary Center** Combine base words and word endings to make new words. **ANY DAY** *392k*

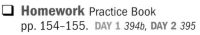
Main Selection—Fiction

☐ **Homework** Practice Book pp. 154–155. **DAY 1** *394b*, **DAY 2** *395*

☐ **Word Play** Have students work with partners to write the plural forms of *pizza, garage, tomato, peach,* and *history*. **ANY DAY** *411c*

ASSESS

☐ **Selection Test** Use the Selection Test to determine students' understanding of the lesson vocabulary words. **DAY 3**

RETEACH/REVIEW

☐ **Reteach Lesson** If necessary, use this lesson to reteach and review *word structure*. **DAY 5** *411c*

1 Use assessment data to determine your instructional focus.

2 Preview this week's instruction by strand.

3 Choose instructional activities that meet the needs of your classroom.

COMPREHENSION

SKILL DRAW CONCLUSIONS A *conclusion* is a decision you make after thinking about the details in what you read. Often prior knowledge can help you draw, or make, a conclusion. When drawing a conclusion, you need to make sure it makes sense and is supported by what you have read.

STRATEGY ANSWER QUESTIONS Answering questions can help you understand the text. Sometimes you must draw a conclusion to answer a question asked in a book, by a teacher, or on a test. The details or answers you need may be in one place or in several places.

TEACH

❑ **Skill/Strategy Lesson** Use the skill/strategy lesson in the Student Edition to introduce and model *draw conclusions* and *answer questions*. DAY 1 *392-393*

Skill/Strategy Lesson

❑ **Extend Skills** Teach about idioms. **ANY DAY** *411b*

PRACTICE/APPLY

❑ **Leveled Text** Apply *draw conclusions* and *answer questions* to read leveled text. DAY 1 *LR1-LR9*

Leveled Readers

❑ **Skills and Strategies in Context** Read *Weslandia,* using the Guiding Comprehension questions to apply *draw conclusions* and *answer questions*. DAY 2 *396-403*, DAY 3 *404-408*

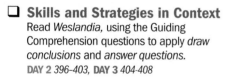

Main Selection—Fiction

❑ **Skills and Strategies in Context** Read the poems, guiding students as they apply *draw conclusions* and *answer questions*. Then have students discuss and write across texts. DAY 4 *410-411*

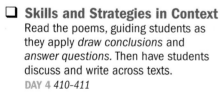

Paired Selection—Poetry

❑ **Homework** Practice Book pp. 153, 157, 158. DAY 1 *393*, DAY 3 *407*, DAY 5 *411b*

❑ **Fresh Reads for Differentiated Test Practice** Have students practice *drawing conclusions* with a new passage. DAY 3

ASSESS

❑ **Selection Test** Determine students' understanding of the selection and their use of *draw conclusions*. DAY 3

❑ **Retell** Have students retell *Weslandia*. DAY 3 *408-409*

RETEACH/REVIEW

❑ **Reteach Lesson** If necessary, reteach and review *draw conclusions*. DAY 5 *411b*

FLUENCY

SKILL PUNCTUATION CLUES Punctuation within text guides readers. Punctuation shows a reader where to pause (periods or commas), change inflection (question marks), and express emotion (exclamation marks).

TEACH

❑ **Read Aloud** Model fluent reading by rereading "The Black Stallion." Focus on this week's fluency skill, punctuation clues. DAY 1 *392l-392m, 411a*

PRACTICE/APPLY

❑ **Choral Reading** Read aloud selected paragraphs from *Weslandia* modeling changing inflections, expressions, and pauses. Then practice as a class, doing three choral readings of the selected paragraphs. DAY 2 *411a*, DAY 3 *411a*

❑ **Partner Reading** Have partners practice reading aloud, following punctuation clues, and offering each other feedback. As students reread, monitor their progress toward their individual fluency goals. DAY 4 *411a*

❑ **Listening Center** Have students follow along with the AudioText for this week's selections. **ANY DAY** *392j*

❑ **Reading/Library Center** Have students reread a selection of their choice. **ANY DAY** *392j*

❑ **Fluency Coach** Have students use Fluency Coach to listen to fluent readings or practice reading on their own. **ANY DAY**

ASSESS

❑ **Check Fluency** WCPM Do a one-minute timed reading, paying special attention to this week's skill—punctuation clues. Provide feedback for each student. DAY 5 *411a*

☑ Customize Your Plan *by Strand*

GRAMMAR

SKILL SUBJECT AND OBJECT PRONOUNS When a pronoun is used as the subject of a sentence, it is called a *subject pronoun*. *I, you, he, she, it, we,* and *they* are subject pronouns. Pronouns that are used after action verbs or as objects of prepositions are called *object pronouns*. *Me, you, him, her, it, us,* and *them* are object pronouns.

TEACH

❑ **Grammar Transparency 16** Use Grammar Transparency 16 to teach subject and object pronouns. DAY 1 *411e*

Grammar Transparency 16

PRACTICE/APPLY

❑ **Develop the Concept** Review the concept of subject and object pronouns and provide guided practice. DAY 2 *411e*

❑ **Apply to Writing** Have students review something they have written and apply subject and object pronouns. DAY 3 *411f*

❑ **Test Preparation** Examine common errors in subject and object pronouns to prepare for standardized tests. DAY 4 *411f*

❑ **Homework** Grammar and Writing Practice Book pp. 61–63. DAY 2 *411e*, DAY 3 *411f*, DAY 4 *411f*

ASSESS

❑ **Cumulative Review** Use Grammar and Writing Practice Book p. 64. DAY 5 *411f*

RETEACH/REVIEW

❑ **Daily Fix-It** Have students find and correct errors using grammar, spelling, and punctuation. **EVERY DAY** *411e-411f*

❑ **The Grammar and Writing Book** Use pp. 140–143 of The Grammar and Writing Book to extend instruction for using subject and object pronouns. **ANY DAY**

The Grammar and Writing Book

WRITING

CONVENTIONS Conventions are rules for written language such as proper punctuation and capitalization. Conventions are signals that writers use to make the meaning clear to readers.

TEACH

❑ **Writing Transparency 16A** Use the model to introduce and discuss the Trait of the Week. DAY 1 *411g*

❑ **Writing Transparency 16B** Use the transparency to show students how referring to the text can improve their writing. DAY 2 *411g*

Writing Transparency 16A   **Writing Transparency 16B**

PRACTICE/APPLY

❑ **Write Now** Examine the model on Student Edition p. 409. Then have students write their own e-mail. DAY 3 *409, 411h* DAY 4 *411h*

> **Prompt** In *Weslandia*, a boy decides to remake his world rather than accept it as it is. Think about someone you know who doesn't always "follow the herd." Now write an e-mail to that person reacting to something he or she has done.

Write Now p. 409

❑ **Writing/Vocabulary Center** Combine base words and word endings to make new words. **ANY DAY** *392k*

ASSESS

❑ **Writing Trait Rubric** Use the rubric to evaluate students' writing. DAY 4 *411h*

RETEACH/REVIEW

❑ **The Grammar and Writing Book** Use pp. 140–145 of The Grammar and Writing Book to extend instruction for using subject and object pronouns, referring to the text, and e-mails. **ANY DAY**

The Grammar and Writing Book

① Use assessment data to determine your instructional focus.

② Preview this week's instruction by strand.

③ Choose instructional activities that meet the needs of your classroom.

SPELLING

GENERALIZATION WORDS FROM MANY CULTURES Many words in English come from other languages and may have unexpected spellings: *khaki, ballet*. These words often do not follow the phonics rules students typically apply so other strategies must be applied for learning to spell them.

TEACH

❏ **Pretest** Give the pretest for words from many cultures. Guide students in self-correcting their pretests and correcting any misspellings. **DAY 1** *411i*

❏ **Think and Practice** Connect spelling to the phonics generalization for words from many cultures. **DAY 2** *411i*

PRACTICE/APPLY

❏ **Connect to Writing** Have students use spelling words to write an e-mail note to a friend or family member. Then review frequently misspelled words: *our, again*. **DAY 3** *411j*

❏ **Homework** Word Study and Spelling Practice Book pp. 61–64. **EVERY DAY**

RETEACH/REVIEW

❏ **Review** Review spelling words to prepare for the posttest. Then provide students with a spelling strategy—problem parts. **DAY 4** *411j*

ASSESS

❏ **Posttest** Use dictation sentences to give the posttest for words from many cultures. **DAY 5** *411j*

Spelling Words

1. khaki	8. canyon	15. barbecue
2. hula	9. yogurt	16. safari
3. banana	10. banquet	17. buffet
4. ballet	11. macaroni	18. stampede
5. waltz	12. polka	19. karate
6. tomato*	13. cobra	20. kiosk
7. vanilla	14. koala	

Challenge Words

21. papaya	23. sauerkraut	25. tsunami
22. artichoke	24. succotash	

*Word from the selection

RESEARCH AND INQUIRY

❏ **Internet Inquiry** Have students conduct an Internet inquiry on civilizations. **EVERY DAY** *411k*

❏ **Instruction Manual** Review the features and how instruction manuals are organized, and discuss how students can use manuals to learn how to do something. **DAY 5** *411l*

❏ **Unit Inquiry** Allow time for students to develop inquiry questions about how groups of people or animals have adapted to different situations. **ANY DAY** *391*

SPEAKING AND VIEWING

❏ **Demonstration** Have students choose one of Wes's *Weslandia* projects and prepare a how-to demonstration for the class. **DAY 5** *411d*

❏ **Analyze Illustrations** Have students study the illustrations on pp. 398-399 and p. 405 and answer questions. **DAY 5** *411d*

Resources for
Differentiated Instruction

LEVELED READERS

► **Comprehension**
- ◎ **Skill** Draw Conclusions
- ◎ **Strategy** Answer Questions

► **Lesson Vocabulary**
- ◎ Word Structure

blunders
rustling
complex
envy
inspired
fleeing
strategy
civilization

► **Social Studies Standards**
- Society
- Culture
- Government

Leveled Reader
Database
ONLINE
PearsonSuccessNet.com

Use the Online Database of over 600 books to
- Download and print additional copies of this week's leveled readers.
- Listen to the readers being read online.
- Search for more titles focused on this week's skills, topic, and content.

On-Level

ADVENTURE TO THE NEW WORLD
BY GRETCHEN MCBRIDE
ILLUSTRATED BY PHYLLIS POLLEMA-CAHILL

On-Level Reader

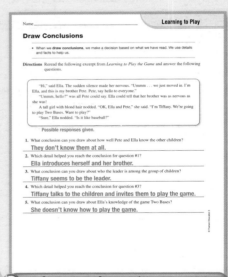

On-Level Practice TE p. LR5

On-Level Practice TE p. LR6

Strategic Intervention

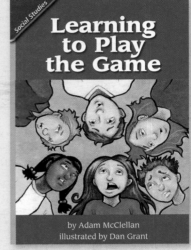

Social Studies
Learning to Play the Game
by Adam McClellan
illustrated by Dan Grant

Below-Level Reader

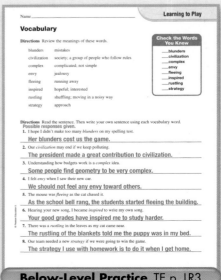

Below-Level Practice TE p. LR2

Below-Level Practice TE p. LR3

Advanced

Advanced Reader

Cheaper, Faster, **Better:** RECENT TECHNOLOGICAL INNOVATIONS

by Cynthia Swain

Name _____ **Cheaper, Faster, Better**

Draw Conclusions

- A **conclusion** is a sensible decision you reach after you think about the details or the facts in what you read.
- **Drawing conclusions** means to make sensible decisions or form reasonable opinions after thinking about the details or facts in what you read.

Directions Read the paragraph below, then answer the questions that follow.

Completing tasks we now do quickly was not nearly as easy in the 1970s, when Sally was growing up. If Sally wished to do research for a report, she had to ask her parents to drive her to the library. There, she used a large encyclopedia; her parents could not afford to buy her such a set. If Sally needed to type her report, she had to use a manual typewriter. Whenever she made mistakes, she had to use a special white solution to paint over the wrong letters. Then she could retype the correct letter. When Sally didn't remember the spelling for a word, she hauled out a huge dictionary to look it up. Sally was also a movie buff. To figure out which shows she would attend, she had to wait for the newspaper to be delivered. And if she wanted to shop, her only choices were to go to a mall and endure long lines and bustling crowds or to pore over heavy catalogues. If she wanted to shop at midnight, she was out of luck!

Possible responses given.

1. What conclusion can you draw about what it was like to do homework in the 1970s?
   Resources could be hard to get and time-consuming.
2. Give two facts or details to support your conclusion.
   Students had to go to libraries to use reference books and had to use manual typewriters.
3. What conclusions can you draw about what shopping was like in the 1970s?
   Shopping took more time and work, too.
4. Give two facts or details to support your conclusion.
   People went to malls or shopping centers or poured over catalogues.
5. Write a well-supported conclusion about how technology would have made life easier for Sally.
   Technology would have made shopping, studying, and selecting movies more convenient and less expensive activities.

Advanced Practice TE p. LR8

Name _____ **Cheaper, Faster, Better**

Vocabulary

Check the Words You Know
___CD-ROM
___Computer Age
___computer viruses
___email
___Industrial Revolution
___internet
___search engine
___telecommuting
___word processors
___World Wide Web

Directions Choose the word from the box that best matches each definition. Write the word on the line.

telecommuting — 1. when people work from home using their personal computers

computer viruses — 2. programs, designed by people, that do damage to computers or data

World Wide Web — 3. system that allows people to review, retrieve, and modify the websites found on the Internet

CD-ROM — 4. a compact disc that plays on a computer's CD-ROM drive

Industrial Revolution — 5. a term describing the changes in technology of the 1800s that changed how people lived

search engine — 6. a program that helps people find data on the Internet

email — 7. system of sending messages using computers linked by telephone wires

internet — 8. worldwide computer network, linked by telephone lines, that is used to send messages, data, and other services

Computer Age — 9. a term used to describe how computers have transformed modern life

word processors — 10. computer programs that edit, store, and retrieve documents and texts

Advanced Practice TE p. LR9

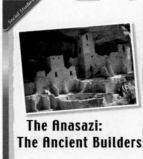

ELL Reader

The Anasazi: The Ancient Builders

by Zeke G. Ato

ELL Poster 16

Teacher's Edition Notes

ELL notes throughout this lesson support instruction and reference additional resources at point of use.

Teaching Guide pp. 106–112, 242–243

- Multilingual summaries of the main selection
- Comprehension lesson
- Vocabulary strategies and word cards
- ELL Reader 5.4.1 lesson

ELL and Transition Handbook

Ten Important Sentences

- Key ideas from every selection in the Student Edition
- Activities to build sentence power

More Reading

Readers' Theater Anthology

- Fluency practice
- Five scripts to build fluency
- Poetry for oral interpretation

Leveled Trade Books

Advanced
Below-Level
On-Level

- Extended reading tied to the unit concept
- Lessons in the Trade Book Library Teaching Guide

School + Home

Homework

- Family Times Newsletter
- ELL Multilingual Selection Summaries

Take-Home Books

- Leveled Readers

Family Times

Cross-Curricular Centers

Listening

Listen to the SELECTIONS

MATERIALS — SINGLES
CD player, headphones, AudioText CD, student book

LISTEN TO LITERATURE Listen to *Weslandia*, "Under the Back Porch," and "Keziah," as you follow or read along in your book. Listen to draw conclusions about what happens in the story and the poems.

If there is anything you don't understand, you can listen again to any section.

Reading/ Library

Read it AGAIN!

MATERIALS — SINGLES / PAIRS / GROUPS
Collection of books for self-selected reading, reading logs, student book

Select a book you have already read. Record the title of the book in your reading log. You may want to read with a partner.

Choose from the following:

- **Leveled Readers**
- **ELL Readers**
- **Stories Written by Classmates**
- **Books from the Library**
- *Weslandia*

TEN IMPORTANT SENTENCES Read the Ten Important Sentences for *Weslandia*. Then locate the sentences in the student book.

BOOK CLUB Look at "Meet Authors" on p. 770 of the student book. As a group, think of some questions you would like to ask the author, and write him a letter. Read other books by Paul Fleischman and get together with a group to share your favorites.

 Math

Invent a Counting System

MATERIALS — SINGLES
Writing and drawing materials

In *Weslandia*, Wesley adopts a new counting system based on the number eight. Design your own counting system, based on a number you choose.

1. **Choose a number for your counting system.**
2. **Write a paragraph explaining your counting system. Include the reasons you chose this number.**
3. **Draw a picture that illustrates how to count objects using your system.**

EARLY FINISHERS Divide a day into the same number of segments as the number you used for your counting system. Describe each segment of the day and decide what each is called.

My Counting System

My counting system is based on the number eight, because my birthday is on July 8th. To use my counting system, count by 8s.

8   16

Scott Foresman Reading Street Centers Survival Kit
Use the *Weslandia* materials from the Reading Street
Centers Survival Kit to organize this week's centers.

Writing/Vocabulary

Play with
Word Endings

MATERIALS `SINGLES`
Writing materials, index cards

Combine base words and word endings to make new words.

1. Write these four base words on separate index cards: *flee, blunder, inspire, rustle.* Put the cards face down in a pile. Write these word endings on separate cards: *-ing, -s,* and *-ed* and put them in a second pile, face down.
2. Choose one card from each pile. Combine the base word with the ending and use the word in a sentence that makes its meaning clear.
3. Time yourself. See how many words and sentences you can create in three minutes.

EARLY FINISHERS Combine the four base words with each of the three word endings and write them down. Remember spelling rules for adding endings to words.

"The mouse was fleeing from the hungry cat."

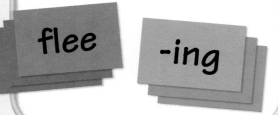

Social Studies

Plan a
Society

MATERIALS `SINGLES`
Writing and art materials

Plan your own backyard country the way that Wesley did in *Weslandia*.

1. Draw a picture of each plant you would grow in your backyard country and label it.
2. Think about the things for which Wesley used his plants. List things for which you would use your plants next to each drawing.

EARLY FINISHERS Name your backyard country. Create rules for your new country.

Shavonda's World

Fuzzy Flower

used for:
blankets,
socks, mittens

Canopy Leaf Tree

tree leaves
used for: fans,
umbrella, roof
for house

Technology

Explore
Ancient Cultures

MATERIALS `SINGLES`
Internet access, printer

Find out more about how ancient civilizations adapted to their environments.

1. Follow classroom rules to conduct an Internet search using a student-friendly search engine for information about an ancient civilization such as the Egyptians or Romans.
2. Narrow your search to focus on how the civilization adapted to its natural environment.
3. Print the information you find.

EARLY FINISHERS Underline the information you found that relates to food, clothing, and shelter.

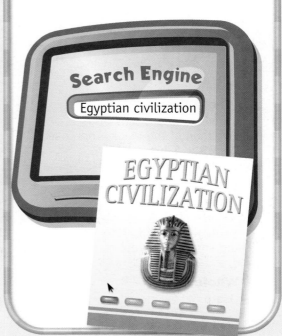

Search Engine
Egyptian civilization

EGYPTIAN CIVILIZATION

ALL CENTERS

OBJECTIVES

- Build vocabulary by finding words related to the lesson concept.
- Listen to draw conclusions.

Concept Vocabulary

barren not able to produce much

edible fit to eat

island body of land smaller than a continent and completely surrounded by water

livestock farm animals

Monitor Progress

Check Vocabulary

If...	then... review the
students are unable to place words on the Web,	lesson concept. Place the words on the Web and provide additional words for practice, such as *low tide* and *shellfish*.

SUCCESS PREDICTOR

DAY 1   Grouping Options

Reading

Whole Group
Introduce and discuss the Question of the Week. Then use pp. 392l–394b.

Group Time
Differentiated Instruction
Read this week's Leveled Readers. See pp. 392f–392g for the small group lesson plan.

Whole Group
Use p. 411a.

Language Arts
Use pp. 411e–411k.

Build Concepts

FLUENCY

MODEL PUNCTUATION CLUES As you read the excerpt from "The Black Stallion," model responding to punctuation while reading aloud by pausing for commas or periods or by raising your voice at the end of a question, as in the example, "Hadn't he called it carragheen?"

LISTENING COMPREHENSION

After reading an excerpt from "The Black Stallion," use the following questions to assess listening comprehension.

1. **How is Alec feeling in paragraph 1?** *(He is weak and hungry; willing to eat seaweed.)* **Draw Conclusions**

2. **Do you think Alec will survive? Why or why not?** *(Possible response: He will survive because he was clever enough to find food, and water from a spring.)* **Draw Conclusions**

BUILD CONCEPT VOCABULARY

Start a web to build concepts and vocabulary related to this week's lesson and the unit theme.

- Draw the People Adapting Concept Web.

- Read the sentence with *island* again. Ask students to pronounce it and discuss its meaning.

- Place *island* in an oval attached to *Environment.* Explain that an *island* is related to this concept. Read the sentences in which *barren, edible,* and *livestock* appear. Have students pronounce the words, place them on the web, and provide reasons.

- Brainstorm additional words and categories for the web. Keep the web on display and add words throughout the week.

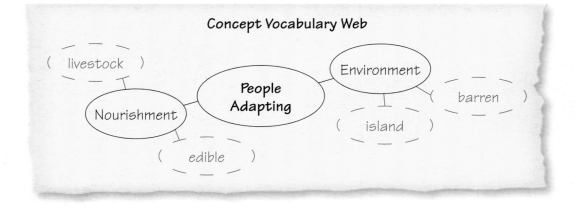

Concept Vocabulary Web

from THE BLACK STALLION

BY WALTER FARLEY

*On his way home from a visit with his
uncle in India, Alec is shipwrecked.
He is the only survivor of the accident, and
he must adapt to a strange island alone.*

One morning Alec made his way weakly toward the rocky side
of the island. He came to the huge rocks and climbed on top of
one of them. It was more barren than any other part of the island. It
was low tide and Alec's eyes wandered over the stony shore, looking
for any kind of shellfish he might be able to eat. He noticed the
mosslike substance on all the rocks at the water's edge, and on those
that extended out. What was that stuff the biology teacher had made
them eat last term in one of their experiments? Hadn't he called it
carragheen [KAIR ah jeen]? Yes, that was it. A sort of seaweed, he had
said, that grew abundantly along the rocky parts of the Atlantic coast
of Europe and North America. When washed and dried, it was edible
for humans and livestock. Could the moss on the rocks below be it?
Alec scarcely dared to hope.

Slowly Alec made the dangerous descent. He reached the water
level and scrambled across the rocks. He took a handful of the soft
greenish-yellow moss which covered them and raised it to his lips.
It smelled the same. He tasted it. The moss was terribly salty from the
sea, but it was the same as he had eaten that day in the classroom!

Eagerly he filled his pockets with it, then removed his shirt and
filled it full. He climbed up again and hurried back to camp. There
he emptied the moss onto the ground beside the spring. The next
quarter of an hour he spent washing it, and then placed it out in the
sun to dry. Hungrily he tasted it again. It was better—and it was food!

SKILLS ⟷ STRATEGIES IN CONTEXT

Draw Conclusions
Answer Questions

INTRODUCE

If you see clothes hanging on a line, you might conclude that someone is doing laundry. What might you conclude if you see a person leaning ladders against the house and opening paint cans? *(The person is going to paint the house.)*

Have students read the information on p. 392. Explain the following:

- To draw conclusions, or make inferences, you need to pull together and evaluate information while thinking about your prior knowledge.

- Sometimes you need to draw conclusions to answer questions posed by others.

Use Skill Transparency 16 to teach draw conclusions and answer questions.

Weslandia

Comprehension

Skill
Draw Conclusions

Strategy
Answer Questions

Draw Conclusions

- A conclusion is a decision you make after thinking about the details in what you read.

- Often your prior knowledge can help you draw, or make, a conclusion.

- When you draw a conclusion, be sure it makes sense and is supported by what you have read.

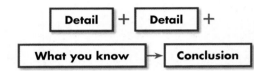

Detail + Detail +

What you know → Conclusion

Strategy: Answer Questions

Sometimes you must draw a conclusion to answer a question asked in a book, by a teacher, or on a test. The details you need for your answer may be in one place or in several places. Use those details plus what you already know to draw a conclusion that answers the question.

Write to Read

1. Read "The Go-Cart." Make two graphic organizers like the one above to help draw conclusions about why Jeff entered the go-cart race and how he felt about himself.

2. Answer this question and explain your answer: Was Jeff's family helpful and supporting?

392

Strategic Intervention

Draw Conclusions Show students a picture of a child who is crying. Ask students what they would say about the child. *(He or she is sad.)* Students should tell how they know the child is sad. *(The child is crying, and I know that I cry when I'm sad.)* Point out that they used details in the picture and their own knowledge to draw a conclusion about the child in the picture.

ELL

Access Content

Beginning/Intermediate For a Picture It! lesson on draw conclusions, see ELL Teaching Guide, pp. 106–107.

Advanced Before students read "The Go-Cart," ask them to share what they know about a go-cart. Have them study the picture carefully and name the characteristics they see. If necessary, provide them with additional information. Ask students how a ride in a go-cart would feel.

The Go-Cart

The summer had been downright boring. Nothing extraordinary had occurred. Then one day Jeff read the announcement in the local newspaper: "Go-Cart Race Next Month! First Prize $1,000!" He decided that he *had* to enter that race.

> **① Skill** Why do you think Jeff *had* to enter the go-cart race?

> **② Strategy** To answer that question, you need to draw a conclusion. The details in the paragraph can help you.

"But Jeff, you don't own a go-cart," his father said.

The newspaper noted that the go-cart had to be homemade, not factory-manufactured and bought. Jeff had been saving his allowance for what seemed like an eternity, and he had enough money to buy the plans and parts for a go-cart.

"But Jeff, you've never built anything," his mother said.

Jeff set about his building task. He read the instructions that came with his go-cart kit carefully. If something was confusing or hard to understand, he called the hardware store and asked for a clerk to explain. Every day he toiled on his go-cart, and every night it was that much closer to being finished.

Finally, the day of the race arrived. Jeff put on his helmet and revved his engine. The announcer roared, "On your mark! Get set! Go!" And Jeff, who had never raced a go-cart before, was off!

> **③ Skill** How do you think Jeff felt about himself as he revved his engine, waiting for the race to begin?

> **④ Strategy** To answer that question, think of details from throughout the story. Also think how *you* would feel if you were in Jeff's place.

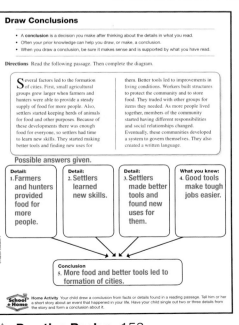

393

Available as **Skill Transparency** 16

Draw Conclusions

- A **conclusion** is a decision you make after thinking about the details in what you read.
- Often your prior knowledge can help you draw, or make, a conclusion.
- When you draw a conclusion, be sure it makes sense and is supported by what you have read.

Directions Read the following passage. Then complete the diagram.

Several factors led to the formation of cities. First, small agricultural groups grew larger when farmers and hunters were able to provide a steady supply of food for more people. Also, settlers started keeping herds of animals for food and other purposes. Because of these developments there was enough food for everyone, so settlers had time to learn new skills. They started making better tools and finding new uses for them. Better tools led to improvements in living conditions. Workers built structures to protect the community and to store food. They traded with other groups for items they needed. As more people lived together, members of the community started having different responsibilities and social relationships changed. Eventually, these communities developed a system to govern themselves. They also created a written language.

Possible answers given.

Detail: 1. Farmers and hunters provided food for more people.	Detail: 2. Settlers learned new skills.	Detail: 3. Settlers made better tools and found new uses for them.	What you know: 4. Good tools make tough jobs easier.

Conclusion
5. More food and better tools led to formation of cities.

School + Home **Home Activity** Your child drew a conclusion from facts or details found in a reading passage. Tell him or her a short story about an event that happened in your life. Have your child single out two or three details from the story and form a conclusion about it.

▲ **Practice Book** p. 153.

TEACH

① SKILL Use paragraph 1 to model how to draw a conclusion.

> **Think Aloud** **MODEL** The first paragraph tells me that Jeff is bored. Then it tells about a go-cart race with a big prize. I think Jeff wants to enter the race because he is bored and because he wants to win the prize money.

② STRATEGY Discuss how to draw a conclusion to answer a question.

> **Think Aloud** **MODEL** To answer the question, I needed to draw a conclusion. I used details in the paragraph and what I already knew to figure out why Jeff wanted to enter the go-cart race. I used inference to draw my conclusions.

PRACTICE AND ASSESS

③ SKILL Possible responses: nervous, excited

④ STRATEGY The story says that Jeff works hard to build a go-cart, so he must want to race. I know how I would feel, and I think Jeff would feel the same way.

WRITE Have students complete steps 1 and 2 of the Write to Read activity. You might consider using this as a whole-class activity.

Monitor Progress	
🔄 **Draw Conclusions**	
If... students are unable to complete **Write to Read** on p. 392,	**then...** use Practice Book p. 153 to provide additional practice.

Vocabulary Strategy

Use word structure and word endings to determine meaning.

INTRODUCE

Discuss the strategy for word structure using the steps on p. 394.

TEACH

- Have students read "Long-Ago Lives," using word structure to find meanings of words.
- Model using word structure to determine the meaning of *rustling*.

Think Aloud

MODEL I don't recognize a base word in *rustling*, but I do see an *-ing* ending. I remember that sometimes a base word drops the final *-e*. If I drop the *-ing* and add an *-e*, the base word is *rustle*, which is what leaves do in the wind. So *rustling* must mean "making a light, soft sound."

Words to Know

envy

fleeing

civilization

complex

strategy

blunders

inspired

rustling

Remember

Try the strategy. Then, if you need more help, use your glossary or dictionary.

Vocabulary Strategy
for Endings

Word Structure The endings *-ed*, *-ing*, and *-s* may be added to verbs to change the tense, person, or usage of the verbs. You can use endings to help you figure out the meaning of an unfamiliar word.

1. Examine the unfamiliar word to see if it has a base word you know.

2. Check to see if the ending *-s*, *-ed*, or *-ing* has been added to a base word. Remember that some base words drop the final *-e* before adding an ending. For example, *rustle* becomes *rustling*.

3. Reread the sentence and make sure the word shows action. (The ending *-s* may be added to nouns too.)

4. Decide how the ending changes the meaning of the base word.

5. Try the meaning in the sentence.

As you read "Long-Ago Lives," look for words that end with *-ed*, *-ing*, or *-s*. Use the endings to help figure out their meanings.

394

DAY 2 Grouping Options

Reading
Whole Group Discuss the Question of the Day. Then use pp. 394–397.

Group Time Differentiated Instruction
Read *Weslandia*. See pp. 392f–392g for the small group lesson plan.

Whole Group Use p. 411a.

Language Arts
Use pp. 411e–411k.

Strategic Intervention

Word Structure Have students circle the word endings for *fleeing*, *blunders*, and *inspired*.

ELL

Access Content Use ELL Poster 16 to preteach vocabulary. Choose from the following to meet language proficiency levels.

Beginning Use the Multilingual Lesson Vocabulary list that begins on p. 272 of the ELL Teaching Guide, as well as other home-language resources, to provide translations of the tested words.

Intermediate Ask students to share what they know about the words *civilization* and *complex,* based on home language cognates. (For example; Spanish: *Civilización*)

Advanced Teach the lesson on pp. 394–395. Have students select other vocabulary words and add them to their word meaning charts.

Resources for home-language words may include parents, bilingual staff members, bilingual dictionaries, or online translation sources.

Long-Ago Lives

We do not tend to think with envy about the lives of people who lived thousands of years ago. We are likely to imagine them fleeing for their lives from enemies or wild beasts. Any civilization without excellent shopping, television, and computers seems far too primitive for us.

However, we have learned much about early cultures. What we have learned shows us that their world was often complex, not simple. They were not all that different from us. For example, two thousand years ago the Mayan people played a ball game. The game was played by teams on stone courts with special goals. Players needed great strength and skill. The strategy was to send a heavy ball through a high stone ring using only hips, knees, elbows, and buttocks. Kings might play this game, for which the stakes were very high. No one wanted to make any blunders because the loser might lose his head!

This game may have inspired our modern game of soccer. Stand on one of these ancient ball courts and you can almost hear the rustling of a feather headdress and the yelling of the crowd.

Words to Write

Look at the pictures in *Weslandia*. Choose one to write about. Use as many words from the Words to Know list as you can.

395

Connect to Phonics

Word Study/Decoding Point out that the spelling of the base word often changes before adding an inflected ending. Model identifying the inflected ending and base word using *inspired* from p. 395, paragraph 3. Have students suggest other words they know with the inflected endings *-ed, -ing* and *-s*. Have them identify the inflected ending and base in each word. Then have them identify the meaning of each word with and without the inflected ending.

PRACTICE AND ASSESS

- Have students determine the meanings of the remaining words and explain the strategy they used.
- Point out that a base word sometimes is changed before an ending is added, such as dropping a final *e* or doubling the final consonant.
- If students made a word meaning chart on p. 394b, have them add a column for word endings.
- Have students complete Practice Book p. 155.

WRITE Students should use words from the list and other words with endings to describe their picture.

Monitor Progress

Word Structure

If... students need more practice with the lesson vocabulary,	then... use Tested Vocabulary Cards.

Vocabulary · Word Structure

- An **ending** is a letter or letters added to the end of a base word.
- Recognizing an ending will help you figure out the word's meaning.
- The endings *–s* and *–es* can be added to singular nouns to make them plural. The endings *–s, –ed,* and *–ing* can be added to verbs to change the tense. The endings *–er* and *–est* can be added to adjectives to use them to compare.

Directions Read the following passage. Then answer the questions below.

Lisa enjoyed camping with her brother and parents every autumn. In a way she felt they were fleeing civilization and their complex city life. She had noticed that life in the city often makes people anxious. She always felt happier while hiking through the woods and sleeping under the stars. There was no one to envy because the beauty of nature surrounded them. Even the blunders they made turned into games to play. Once they hiked down the wrong trail and got lost. Instead of worrying, they worked together to find the quickest way back. When she returned to the city, Lisa felt inspired by the beauty she had enjoyed.

Possible answers given.

1. In the word *fleeing*, how does the *–ing* change the meaning of the root word?
It changes the tense of the verb.

2. What is the difference between the *–s* in *blunders* and the *–s* in *makes*?
The first *–s* makes a noun plural, while the second *–s* puts a verb in the present tense.

3. How does the *–er* change the meaning of the root in *happier*?
It makes a comparison.

4. What does the *–ed* in *hiked* do to the meaning of the root word?
It puts the verb into the past tense.

5. Change some of the verbs in this sentence to put the verbs in the past tense: "Lisa calls out to her family, and then walks down the trail to meet them."
Lisa called out to her family, and then walked down the trail to meet them.

School + Home **Home Activity** Your child identified and used endings added to base words, such as *–s, –ed, –ing,* and *–est*. Read a newspaper or magazine article with your child. Change the endings of some of the words and discuss with him or her how the sentences' meanings change.

▲ **Practice Book** p. 155

Prereading Strategies

OBJECTIVES

- Draw conclusions to improve comprehension.
- Answer questions to help draw conclusions.

GENRE STUDY

Fiction

Weslandia is a fiction story. Explain that in fiction, characters and events may be realistic, even though they might be unusual or even unlikely in some way. *Weslandia* might also be called a modern-day fable, for the reader can infer a message at its conclusion.

PREVIEW AND PREDICT

Have students preview the title and illustrations and make predictions about the main character. Students should use lesson vocabulary words as they talk about what they expect to read.

Strategy Response Log

Ask Questions Have students make a list of questions they have about the selection based on the pictures. Students will answer these questions and ask others in the Strategy Response Log activity on p. 403.

Why does Wesley take up the challenge of creating his own world?

Genre

Fiction stories are stories that the author has made up. As you read, notice how the character makes up his own world.

396

ELL

Activate Prior Knowledge Have students talk about plants they know and ways different parts of the plants can be used. Provide vocabulary for the different plant parts, such as *leaves*, *stems*, *flowers*, *fruit*, *roots*, and *stalks*.

Consider having students read the selection summary in English or in students' home languages. See the Multilingual Summaries in the ELL Teaching Guide, pp. 110–112.

Weslandia

by PAUL FLEISCHMAN   illustrated by KEVIN HAWKES

397

SET PURPOSE

Discuss the picture on pages 396–397. Ask students where they think the boy is and what he is doing. Have them tell what they hope to find out as they read the story.

Remind students to draw conclusions and answer questions as they read.

STRATEGY RECALL

Students have now used these before-reading strategies:

- preview the selection to be aware of its genre, features, and possible content;
- activate prior knowledge about that content and what to expect of that genre;
- make predictions;
- set a purpose for reading.

Remind students to be aware of and flexibly use the during-reading strategies they have learned:

- link prior knowledge to new information;
- summarize text they have read so far;
- ask clarifying questions;
- answer questions they or others pose;
- check their predictions and either refine them or make new predictions;
- recognize the text structure the author is using, and use that knowledge to make predictions and increase comprehension;
- visualize what the author is describing;
- monitor their comprehension and use fix-up strategies.

After reading, students will use these strategies:

- summarize or retell the text;
- answer questions they or others pose;
- reflect to make new information become part of their prior knowledge.

Audio CD   AudioText

Guiding Comprehension

1 🎯 **Draw Conclusions • Critical**

On p. 398, Wesley's mother says, "He sticks out." What does this sentence tell you about Wesley?

Possible response: Wesley is different from other boys his age.

Monitor Progress
🎯 **Draw Conclusions**

If... students are unable to draw a conclusion,	**then...** use the skill and strategy instruction on p. 399.

2 **Setting • Inferential**

What do you think is the setting of this story? Why?

A neighborhood in a town. I think it is a town and not a city because the illustrations show yards, fences, and trees.

"Of course he's miserable," moaned Wesley's mother. "He sticks out."

"Like a nose," snapped his father.

Listening through the heating vent, Wesley knew they were right. He was an outcast from the civilization around him.

He alone in his town disliked pizza and soda, alarming his mother and the school nurse. He found professional football stupid. He'd refused to shave half his head, the hairstyle worn by **1** all the other boys, despite his father's bribe of five dollars.

Passing his neighborhood's two styles of housing—garage on the

398

ELL

Access Content Explain the idiom *sticks out* is the opposite of *fits in*. It means that a person is different and that people around him notice it. Ask students to name the ways in which Wesley sticks out.

left and garage on the right—Wesley alone dreamed of more exciting forms of shelter. He had no friends, but plenty of tormentors.

Fleeing them was the only sport he was good at.

Each afternoon his mother asked him what he'd learned in school that day.

"That seeds are carried great distances by the wind," he answered on Wednesday.

"That each civilization has its staple food crop," he answered on Thursday.

"That school's over and I should find a good summer project," he answered on Friday.

399

Declaration of Independence

Time for SOCIAL STUDIES

In this story, Wes breaks away from others so that he can develop his own way of life. This is similar to what the Thirteen Colonies did when they wrote the Declaration of Independence. The colonists decided to become an independent nation rather than remain under the rule of Great Britain. The Declaration stated the colonists had the right to "life, liberty, and the pursuit of happiness."

SKILLS ⟷ STRATEGIES IN CONTEXT

Draw Conclusions

TEACH

- Tell students that a conclusion is a decision you make after thinking about the details in a story. Prior knowledge can help them draw conclusions. Any conclusion must make sense and be supported by details.

- Model drawing a conclusion about Wes from p. 398.

Think Aloud **MODEL** This page tells us a lot about Wes. His mother says he sticks out, and Wes doesn't mind that he does. He doesn't like pizza, soda, or football. He refuses to wear his hair like the other boys. My conclusion about Wes is that he is not like the other boys.

PRACTICE AND ASSESS

Have students reread p. 399. Ask which conclusion is best supported by information on p. 399. *(Choice a)*

a) Wes is smart.

b) Wes likes to run.

c) Wes hates school.

EXTEND SKILLS

Repetition

Point out that one literary device that authors use to enhance language or emphasize ideas is repetition of sounds, words, thoughts, or sentences. Ask students to reread p. 399 and look for a phrase that is repeated. *("…he answered on Wednesday, …he answered on Thursday, …he answered on Friday.")*

Weslandia **399**

Guiding Comprehension

3 Figurative Language • Critical

What does it mean when the author says that "Wesley's thoughts shot sparks" in paragraph 2 on p. 400?

Possible response: It means that Wes was thinking and had come up with a good idea.

4 Main Idea • Inferential

Find a main idea and one supporting detail from pp. 400–401.

Main Idea: Wesley decides to grow his own staple food crop and begin his own civilization for his summer project. Detail: He turned over a plot of ground in his yard.

Monitor Progress	
REVIEW Main Idea	
If... students have difficulty finding a main idea and a supporting detail,	**then...** use the skill and strategy instruction on p. 401.

5 Characters • Critical

Text to Self **Think of a time when you felt like you were different from everyone else. How did it feel and what did you do about it?**

Answers will vary. Responses should include students' recollections of a time they've felt like they didn't belong and how they dealt with it.

As always, his father mumbled, "I'm sure you'll use that knowledge often."

3 Suddenly, Wesley's thoughts shot sparks. His eyes blazed. His father was right! He could actually *use* what he'd learned that week for a summer project that would top all others. He would **4** grow his own staple food crop—and found his own civilization!

The next morning he turned over a plot of ground in his yard. That night a wind blew in from the west. It raced through the trees and set his curtains snapping. Wesley lay awake, listening. His land was being planted.

400

ELL

Extend Language Reread aloud the phrase "and found his own civilization." Explain that in this example, *found* is a present tense verb that means to set up something. Tell students that *found* can also be a past tense verb that means something that is come upon by chance, as in the sentence, "I found a nickel on the sidewalk."

SKILLS ↔ STRATEGIES IN CONTEXT

Main Idea REVIEW

TEACH

- Remind students that the main idea is the most important idea about the topic.
- Details are pieces of information that support or tell more about the main idea.
- Model finding a main idea and a supporting detail from pp. 400–401:

 Think Aloud **MODEL** These pages discuss how Wesley decides to grow his own staple food crop and founded a new civilization for his summer project. This is the main idea. One detail that supports this idea is that "he turned over a plot of ground in his backyard."

PRACTICE AND ASSESS

- Have students find another detail on p. 401 that supports the main idea. *(seedlings appeared)*
- To assess, use Practice Book p. 156.

Five days later the first seedlings appeared.

"You'll have almighty bedlam on your hands if you don't get those weeds out," warned his neighbor.

"Actually, that's my crop," replied Wesley. "In this type of garden there are no weeds."

Following ancient tradition, Wesley's fellow gardeners grew tomatoes, beans, Brussels sprouts, and nothing else. Wesley found it thrilling to open his land to chance, to invite the new and unknown. **5**

The plants shot up past his knees, then his waist. They seemed to be all of the same sort. Wesley couldn't find them in any plant book.

401

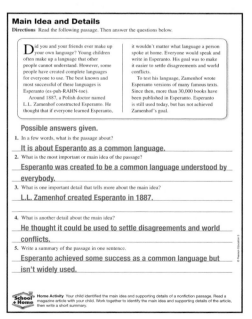

Main Idea and Details

Directions Read the following passage. Then answer the questions below.

Did you and your friends ever make up your own language? Young children often make up a language that other people cannot understand. However, some people have created complete languages for everyone to use. The best known and most successful of these languages is Esperanto (es-puh-RAHN-toe).

Around 1887, a Polish doctor named L.L. Zamenhof constructed Esperanto. He thought that if everyone learned Esperanto, it wouldn't matter what language a person spoke at home. Everyone would speak and write in Esperanto. His goal was to make it easier to settle disagreements and world conflicts.

To test his language, Zamenhof wrote Esperanto versions of many famous texts. Since then, more than 30,000 books have been published in Esperanto. Esperanto is still used today, but has not achieved Zamenhof's goal.

Possible answers given.

1. In a few words, what is the passage about?
   It is about Esperanto as a common language.

2. What is the most important or main idea of the passage?
   Esperanto was created to be a common language understood by everybody.

3. What is one important detail that tells more about the main idea?
   L.L. Zamenhof created Esperanto in 1887.

4. What is another detail about the main idea?
   He thought it could be used to settle disagreements and world conflicts.

5. Write a summary of the passage in one sentence.
   Esperanto achieved some success as a common language but isn't widely used.

Home Activity Your child identified the main idea and supporting details of a nonfiction passage. Read a magazine article with your child. Work together to identify the main idea and supporting details of the article, then write a short summary.

▲ **Practice Book** p. 156

Guiding Comprehension

6 **Vocabulary • Word Structure**

What is the base word of *blushing*? How does the ending -*ing* change the meaning of the base word?

The base word is *blush*, which means "to turn red." Adding -*ing* makes it mean "the act of turning red."

Monitor Progress

Word Structure

If… students have difficulty recognizing how the ending -*ing* changes the base word,	**then…** use vocabulary strategy instruction on p. 403.

---

7 **Main Idea • Inferential**

Besides growing a food crop, what else did Wesley do as part of his summer project?

He ate fruit from his plants, made a cup from half a rind, built his own squeezing device so he could make fruit juice, prepared tubers from his plants on the family barbecue, and wove a hat and a robe.

ONLINE

Have students type the keywords *backyard garden fruit* in a student-friendly search engine to learn about other types of fruit Wes could have grown in his garden. Be sure to follow classroom rules for Internet use.

"Are those tomatoes, beans, or Brussels sprouts?" asked Wesley's neighbor.

"None of the above," replied Wesley.

6   Fruit appeared, yellow at first, then blushing to magenta. Wesley picked one and sliced through the rind to the juicy purple center. He took a bite and found the taste an entrancing blend of peach, strawberry, pumpkin pie, and flavors he had no name for.

Ignoring the shelf of cereals in the kitchen, Wesley took to breakfasting on the fruit. He dried half a rind to serve as a cup, built his own squeezing device, and drank the fruit's juice throughout the day.

402

ELL

Extend Language Read aloud the phrase "and found the taste an entrancing blend of…" Pronounce the word *entrancing* clearly, putting stress on the second syllable. Explain that *entrancing* means delightful.

Pulling up a plant, he found large tubers on the roots. These he boiled, fried, or roasted on the family barbecue, seasoning them with a pinch of the plant's highly aromatic leaves.

It was hot work tending to his crop. To keep off the sun, Wesley wove himself a hat from strips of the plant's woody bark. His success with the hat inspired him to devise a spinning wheel and loom on which he wove a loose-fitting robe from the stalks' soft inner fibers.

Unlike jeans, which he found scratchy and heavy, the robe was comfortable, reflected the sun, and offered myriad opportunities for pockets.

403

Develop Vocabulary

PRACTICE LESSON VOCABULARY

Have students give a brief oral response to each question.

1. What kind of *blunders* might a baseball player make? *(A baseball player might drop the ball or strike out.)*

2. What kinds of things are painters *inspired* by? *(They are filled with feelings or influenced by the beauty around them.)*

3. What is a good *strategy* for passing a test? *(Studying is a good plan for doing well on a test.)*

BUILD CONCEPT VOCABULARY

Review previous concept words with students. Ask if students have found any words today in their reading or elsewhere that they would like to add to the People Adapting Concept Web, such as *outcast* and *alarming*.

VOCABULARY STRATEGY

Word Structure

TEACH

- Tell students that the endings *-ed*, *-ing*, and *-s* may be added to verbs to change the tense and the meaning of the word.

- Model using word structure to determine the meaning of *blushing*.

Think Aloud **MODEL** The word *blushing* has an *-ing* ending, and the base word is *blush*. I've heard of *blush* before. It means "to turn red." So, in this sentence *blushing* must mean the fruit was turning a shade of red.

PRACTICE AND ASSESS

Have students use word structure to determine the meaning of other verbs on pp. 402–403 that end in *-ed* or *-ing*. Ask them to identify verbs in which a final *e* is dropped *(squeezing, ignoring)* or a *y* is changed to *i (replied, dried, fried)* before adding the ending.

Answer Questions Have students review the questions they asked about the story earlier and answer any of those they can. (See p. 396.) Have them add any new questions they may have about the story.

If you want to teach this story in two sessions, stop here.

Guiding Comprehension

If you are teaching this story in two days, discuss any conclusions students may have drawn so far and review the vocabulary.

8 Graphic Sources • Inferential

What does the picture on p. 404 show about Wesley's method of telling time?

Possible response: It shows the sundial he created with a stalk and how he divided it into eight segments.

9 🎯 Draw Conclusions • Inferential

Why do you think Wesley's schoolmates went from being scornful to curious about his summer project?

Possible response: They probably saw that Wesley was doing some interesting things that they wanted to do too.

Monitor Progress

🎯 Draw Conclusions

If... students have difficulty drawing conclusions to answer questions,	then... use the skill and strategy instruction on p. 405.

DAY 3 Grouping Options

Reading
Whole Group Discuss the Question of the Day.

Group Time Differentiated Instruction
Read *Weslandia*. See pp. 392f–392g for the small group lesson plan.

Whole Group Discuss the Reader Response questions on p. 408. Then use p. 411a.

Language Arts
Use pp. 411e–411k.

His schoolmates were scornful, then curious. Grudgingly, Wesley allowed them ten minutes apiece at his mortar, crushing the plant's seeds to collect the oil.

This oil had a tangy scent and served him both as suntan lotion and mosquito repellent. He rubbed it on his face each morning and sold small amounts to his former tormentors at the price of ten dollars per bottle.

"What's happened to your watch?" asked his mother one day.

Wesley admitted that he no longer wore it. He told time by

404

ELL

Access Content Read aloud the phrase "and had divided the day into eight segments." Explain that *segments* are sections, or parts, into which a whole can be divided. Point out that in our civilization, days are divided into 24 segments, or hours.

the stalk that he used as a sundial and had divided the day into
eight segments—the number of petals on the plant's flowers.

He'd adopted a new counting system as well, based likewise
upon the number eight. His domain, home to many such
innovations, he named "Weslandia."

Uninterested in traditional sports, Wesley made up his own.
These were designed for a single player and used many different
parts of the plant. His spectators looked on with envy.

Realizing that more players would offer him more scope,
Wesley invented other games that would include his schoolmates,

405

Amish Culture

Traditionally, the Amish people live a self-
sufficient life that is different from much of American
society. They make their own clothing and live off their own
land. They travel by horse and buggy and do not use electricity in
their homes. They are a very religious people who respect tradition.

SKILLS ⟷ STRATEGIES IN CONTEXT

Draw Conclusions
Answer Questions

TEACH

Have students reread pp. 404–405. Model
drawing a conclusion about why Wes's schoolmates changed their minds, using both prior
knowledge and answers to questions raised
throughout the story.

Think Aloud **MODEL** Kids who are different are
often teased by others so that prob-
ably explains why Wes's schoolmates
were scornful at first. But once they saw the
interesting things he was doing, they became
curious. I think they changed their minds
because they wanted to have fun too.

PRACTICE AND ASSESS

Have students work in pairs to answer the
questions below to help them draw conclusions
about the story.

1) Why didn't Wes wear his watch anymore? *(He
used his sundial to tell time instead.)*
2) Why did he name his civilization "Weslandia?"
*(He named it after himself because he
created it.)*
3) Why did Wesley design sports for a single
player? *(He didn't have teammates when he
created them.)*

EXTEND SKILLS

Stereotype

A stereotype is an oversimplified idea about a
person or a group of people. *Nerd* and *dweeb*
are just two of the many words people find to
insult others who are unpopular or don't fit in. In
Weslandia, Wes's schoolmates torment him at
first because he is not interested in fitting into
their world (Wes may consider *them* stereotypes),
but later they are curious and finally even
envious of his individuality.

Guiding Comprehension

10 🎯 **Draw Conclusions • Inferential**

How do Wes's parents feel about his summer project?

Possible response: They are pleased with it because it makes Wes happy.

11 **Author's Purpose • Critical**

How do you think the author feels about independent thinking and creative kids like Wes?

Possible response: He probably thinks that it's a good idea for kids to be creative and not always follow what the crowd does.

12 🎯 **Draw Conclusions • Critical**

Text to World **What would our world be like if no one was like Wes and everyone lived the same way?**

Possible response: Our world would be pretty boring and no one would come up with new ideas.

Strategy Response Log

Summarize When students finish reading the selection, provide this prompt: Recall all of the things Wesley does to create his own civilization in *Weslandia*. Then write down only the most important points.

games rich with strategy and complex scoring systems. He tried to be patient with the other players' blunders.

August was unusually hot. Wesley built himself a platform and took to sleeping in the middle of Weslandia. He passed the evenings playing a flute he'd fashioned from a stalk or gazing up at the sky, renaming the constellations.

His parents noted Wesley's improved morale. "It's the first
10 time in years he's looked happy," said his mother.

Wesley gave them a tour of Weslandia.

"What do you call this plant?" asked his father. Not knowing

406

its name, Wesley had begun calling it "swist," from the sound of its leaves rustling in the breeze.

In like manner, he'd named his new fabrics, games, and foods, until he'd created an entire language.

Mixing the plant's oil with soot, Wesley made a passable ink. As the finale to his summer project, he used the ink and his own eighty-letter alphabet to record the history of his civilization's founding.

In September, Wesley returned to school . . . He had no shortage of friends.

11
12
407

 STRATEGY SELF-CHECK

Answer Questions

Have students answer these questions: Why did Wesley feel miserable at the beginning of the story? Why did Wesley feel happy at the end of the story? What conclusions can you draw about Wes at the end of the story? Use Practice Book p. 157.

SELF-CHECK

Students can ask themselves these questions to assess their ability to use the skill and strategy.

- Did I use my own experiences to draw conclusions about the story?
- Did I use the answers to questions to help me draw conclusions about the story?

Monitor Progress	
Draw Conclusions	
If... students have difficulty drawing conclusions,	**then...** use the Reteach lesson on p. 411b.

Draw Conclusions

- A **conclusion** is a decision you make after thinking about the details in what you read.
- Often your prior knowledge can help you draw, or make, a conclusion.
- When you draw a conclusion, be sure it makes sense and is supported by what you have read.

Directions Read the following passage. Then answer the questions below.

When Kyoung first arrived in the United States, he saw all the tall buildings and cars and people. It looked just like he'd seen in the movies. Everyone and everything moved very quickly. There also was so much more of everything than in his village in his old home. It wasn't until he got to his new home in Maryville that time seemed to slow down.

At school, the other students didn't talk to him much because they had trouble pronouncing his name. His teacher suggested they call him "Bill." So Bill became his nickname. The other students talked to him more, asking questions about his country or what he had gone through before he came to the United States. He tried to explain, but it was not always easy. The cultures were very different and he was still learning English. Nevertheless, he told them a little each time they asked.

Possible answers given.

1. How do you think Kyoung felt when he first reached the U.S.?
   He may have felt excited, and a little frightened and homesick.
2. What parts of the text helped you reach the conclusion you described above?
   The passage describes how the U.S. seems like a movie, and how everything is big and fast-moving.
3. What things that you already knew helped you reach the conclusion you described above?
   Big cities are often amazing to people from the countryside.
4. Do you think Kyoung using the nickname "Bill" was a good idea? Why or why not?
   Yes; it made students more willing to try talking with him.
5. How do you think Kyoung felt when other students asked him about his past? Is your conclusion based on the passage, on your own experience, or both?
   Happy to be asked; I based my answer on the text and on how I would feel if I were Kyoung.

Home Activity Your child drew conclusions from the details of a brief story. Read an article or story with your child about a faraway place. Ask him or her questions about how someone from there of your child's age might adapt to life in the United States.

▲ **Practice Book** p. 157

Develop Vocabulary

PRACTICE LESSON VOCABULARY

Students orally respond *yes* or *no* to each question and provide a reason.

1. Could you build a *complex* model without the directions? *(No; I could not build a very difficult model without directions.)*

2. Would a modern *civilization* include a government? *(Yes; a modern civilization needs leadership and rules.)*

3. Can a snake make a *rustling* sound? *(Yes; snakes can move with quick, small, rubbing sounds.)*

BUILD CONCEPT VOCABULARY

Review previous concept words with students. Ask if students have come across any words today in their reading or elsewhere that they would like to add to the People Adapting Concept Web, such as *patient* and *morale*.

Reader Response

Open for Discussion **Personal Response**

Think Aloud

MODEL I would love to visit a place like Weslandia, but not live there. I think it would be lonely there without friends and family to share it.

Comprehension Check **Critical Response**

1. Possible response: He must have had fun describing new fruit and thinking about how to make a flute from a stalk. *Author's Purpose*

2. Responses will vary, but should include that the illustrations show the boy is curious and imaginative. *Draw Conclusions*

3. Possible response: I would admire anyone with that much creativity and courage to be different. *Answer Questions*

4. Possible response: Wesley's *strategy* to change things was to invent his own *civilization*; this made others feel *envy* and *inspired* them. *Vocabulary*

Look Back and Write For test practice, assign a 10–15 minute time limit. For assessment, see the Scoring Rubric at the right.

Retell

Have students retell *Weslandia*.

Monitor Progress
Check Retelling [4 3 2 1] Rubric

If... students have difficulty retelling the story,	**then...** use the Retelling Cards and the Scoring Rubric for Retelling on p. 409 to assist fluent retelling.

SUCCESS PREDICTOR

Check Retelling Have students use the story illustrations to guide their retellings. Be sure to focus on comprehension and overlook any mistakes in English. For more ideas on assessing students' retellings, see the ELL and Transition Handbook.

Reader Response

Open for Discussion Would you like to live in Weslandia or a land of your own making? What is your opinion about making a new civilization? Use *Weslandia* as support for your opinion.

1. *Weslandia* shows that you can find a fun idea for a fantasy tale just beyond your own back door. How can you tell that Paul Fleischman had fun inventing this story? Use examples from the text. **Think Like an Author**

2. Pretend you have never read *Weslandia*. Look only at the illustrations, from start to finish. Then draw conclusions about the plot and characters. Use examples from the art to support those conclusions. **Draw Conclusions**

3. Would you say that Wesley is a person you could admire? Support your answer with details from the story. **Answer Questions**

4. Wesley sees himself as an outcast from civilization. What do you think he meant? What did he do to change his situation? Answer using words from the Words to Know list. **Vocabulary**

Look Back and Write Look at the picture on pages 404–405 and read the story's final sentence. Explain how they make a surprise ending to *Weslandia*.

Meet author Paul Fleischman on page 770.

Scoring Rubric | **Look Back and Write**

Top-Score Response A top-score response uses the picture on pp. 404–405 and the final sentence to conclude that schoolmates who once made fun of Wesley now want to play his games and be his friends.

Example of a Top-Score Response In the picture, the students who used to make fun of Wesley are playing the games he has invented. Now they admire Wesley for all his inventions. It is surprising that he has become popular over the summer. Wesley has not changed, but his classmates have come to appreciate him.

For additional rubrics, see p. WA10.

Write Now

E-mail

Prompt

In *Weslandia*, a boy decides to remake his world rather than accept it as it is.

Think about someone you know who doesn't always "follow the herd."

Now write an e-mail to that person reacting to something he or she has done.

Writing Trait

In e-mail, use **conventions**, such as proper punctuation and capitalization, so that your message will be clearly understood.

Student Model

E-mail heading contains important information.

E-mail can use informal language and tone.

Conventions of capitalization and punctuation help make writer's meaning clear.

Subject: Explain, please
Date: 3/31/07
From: Jimmy Tuff
To: Wesley
cc: Biff, Travis, Kirk

Hey, Wesley, what are you doing in that weed patch? Mom says the seeds might blow into our garden plot. Then we'd have weeds too!

That straw hat and robe thing you wear make me laugh. But I wouldn't mind trying that tasty-looking fruit. How about sharing some?

We kids can't figure out what you're up to. Please meet us in the park this afternoon and tell us what's going on.

Jimmy

Use the model to help you with your own e-mail writing.

409

Write Now

Look at the Prompt Explain that each sentence in the prompt has a purpose.

- Sentence 1 presents a topic.
- Sentence 2 suggests students think about the topic.
- Sentence 3 tells what to write.

Strategies to Develop Conventions

Have students
- write complete sentences with correct end punctuation.
- use apostrophes in contractions correctly.
- use capital letters for the pronoun *I* and to begin proper nouns and sentences.

NO: here's what i think, wesley.
YES: Here's what I think, Wesley.

For additional suggestions and rubric, see pp. 411g–411h.

Writer's Checklist

☑ **Focus** Does the subject line name the topic?
☑ **Organization** Does the e-mail have a clear beginning and ending?
☑ **Support** Do details support the main idea?
☑ **Conventions** Are pronoun forms correct?

Scoring Rubric | Narrative Retelling

Rubric 4 3 2 1	4	3	2	1
Connections	Makes connections and generalizes beyond the text	Makes connections to other events, stories, or experiences	Makes a limited connection to another event, story, or experience	Makes no connection to another event, story, or experience
Author's Purpose	Elaborates on author's purpose	Tells author's purpose with some clarity	Makes some connection to author's purpose	Makes no connection to author's purpose
Characters	Describes the main character(s) and any character development	Identifies the main character(s) and gives some information about them	Inaccurately identifies some characters or gives little information about them	Inaccurately identifies the characters or gives no information about them
Setting	Describes the time and location	Identifies the time and location	Omits details of time or location	Is unable to identify time or location
Plot	Describes the problem, goal, events, and ending using rich detail	Tells the problem, goal, events, and ending with some errors that do not affect meaning	Tells parts of the problem, goal, events, and ending with gaps that affect meaning	Retelling has no sense of story

Retelling Plan

☑ **Week 1** This week assess Strategic Intervention students.
☐ **Week 2** Assess Advanced students.
☐ **Week 3** Assess Strategic Intervention students.
☐ **Week 4** Assess On-Level students.
☐ **Week 5** Assess any students you have not yet checked during this unit.

Use the Retelling Chart on p. TR16 to record retelling.

Selection Test To assess with *Weslandia*, use Selection Tests, pp. 61–64.

Fresh Reads for Differentiated Test Practice For weekly leveled practice, use pp. 91–69.

SUCCESS PREDICTOR

Poetry

OBJECTIVES

- Examine features of poetry.
- Practice a test-taking strategy.
- Compare and contrast across texts.

PREVIEW

Ask students to preview the poems by looking at the pictures and reading the title and first few lines of each poem. After they preview ask:

- **What do you think these two poems will be about?** (Possible response: Places around the house that kids use to play or hide in.)

Link to Writing

Before students begin to write, have partners describe their secret places. Encourage them to ask each other questions about how the place looks, sounds, smells, and feels.

 **AudioText**

DAY 4 Grouping Options

Reading

Whole Group Discuss the Question of the Day.

Group Time Differentiated Instruction
Read "Under the Back Porch" and "Keziah."
See pp. 392f–392g for the small group lesson plan.

Whole Group Use p. 411a.

Language Arts
Use pp. 411e–411k.

Poetry

Genre

- **Poetry is meant to appeal to the senses, emotions, or mind.**
- **Sensory words in a poem help the reader understand what the writer smells, sees, and feels.**
- **Some poems rhyme; others do not.**
- **Sometimes, the writer repeats words or phrases to emphasize a point or create rhythm.**

Link to Writing

Think about your own favorite secret place and write a poem about it. Give the reader a picture in words of the place and an idea of when and why you go there.

Under the Back Porch

BY VIRGINIA HAMILTON

Our house is two stories high
shaped like a white box.
There is a yard stretched around it
and in back
a wooden porch.

Under the back porch is my place.
I rest there.
I go there when I have to be alone.
It is always shaded and damp.
Sunlight only slants through the slats
in long strips of light,
and the smell of the damp
is moist green,
like the moss that grows here.

My sisters and brothers
can stand on the back porch
and never know
I am here
underneath.
It is my place.
All mine.

410

Keziah

BY GWENDOLYN BROOKS

I have a secret place to go.
Not anyone may know

And sometimes when the wind is rough
I cannot get there fast enough.

And sometimes when my mother
Is scolding my big brother,

My secret place, it seems to me,
Is quite the only place to be.

Reading Across Texts

Look back at *Weslandia* and ask yourself what kind of poem Wesley might write about the world he created.

Writing Across Texts Write a poem about *Weslandia* that you think Wesley might have written.

Draw Conclusions What makes the porch a secret place?

411

African American Authors

Time for SOCIAL STUDIES

Both Virginia Hamilton and Gwendolyn Brooks wrote about the everyday life of African Americans. Brooks grew up in Chicago and wrote poems about being female and black. Hamilton, on the other hand, tried to stay away from writing about life's problems and instead recorded traditional African American riddles and stories. Hamilton wrote folk tales, novels, biographies, and picture books. Brooks also wrote novels, a book for children, and an autobiographical collection of memoirs, interviews, and letters.

POETRY

Use the sidebar on p. 410 to guide discussion.

- Explain to students that poetry is the arrangement of words in lines having rhythm or a regularly repeated accent, and, often, rhyme.
- Ask students to tell how they know these are poems by looking at them.

Draw Conclusions

Possible response: No one knows about it.

CONNECT TEXT TO TEXT

Reading Across Texts

Have students find words and details about Weslandia. Then discuss how the details could be used to write a poem.

Writing Across Texts Students can describe all of Weslandia or concentrate on one feature of it. Their poems may rhyme or not.

Weslandia 411

Fluency Assessment Plan

☑ **This week assess Advanced students.**

☐ **Week 2** Assess Strategic Intervention students.

☐ **Week 3** Assess On-Level students.

☐ **Week 4** Assess Strategic Intervention students.

☐ **Week 5** Assess any students you have not yet checked during this unit.

Set individual goals for students to enable them to reach the year-end goal.
- Current Goal: 120–128 wcpm
- Year-End Goal: 140 wcpm

Oral fluency depends not only on reading without halting but also on word recognition. After students read passages aloud for assessment, help them recognize unfamiliar English words and their meanings. Focus on each student's progress.

Fluency Coach CD To develop fluent readers, use Fluency Coach.

DAY 5 Grouping Options

Reading
Whole Group
Revisit the Question of the Week.

Group Time
Differentiated Instruction
Reread this week's Leveled Readers. See pp. 392f–392g for the small group lesson plan.

Whole Group
Use p. 411b–411c.

Language Arts
Use pp. 411d–411l.

PUNCTUATION CLUES

Fluency

DAY 1

Model Reread "The Black Stallion" on p. 392m. Explain that as you read, you will use punctuation as a guide, for instance pausing at commas and raising your voice slightly to indicate a question. Model for students as you read.

DAY 2

Choral Reading Read aloud p. 400. Have students notice how you use an excited tone of voice when reading sentences that end with exclamation points and pause at the dash. Have students practice as a class doing three choral readings.

DAY 3

Model Read aloud p. 402. Have students notice pauses for commas and periods, and how your voice changes when reading the question. Practice as a class by doing three choral readings.

DAY 4

Partner Reading Partners practice reading p. 402, three times. Encourage them to read with pauses and expression, using punctuation as a guide. Have them offer each other feedback.

Monitor Progress | Check Fluency wcpm

As students reread, monitor their progress toward their individual fluency goals. Current Goal: 120–128 words correct per minute. End-of-Year Goal: 140 words correct per minute.

If... students cannot read fluently at a rate of 120–128 words correct per minute,
then... make sure students practice with text at their independent level. Provide additional fluency practice, pairing nonfluent readers with fluent readers.

If... students already read at 140 words correct per minute,
then... they do not need to reread three to four times.

SUCCESS PREDICTOR

DAY 5

Assessment
Individual Reading Rate Use the Fluency Assessment Plan and do a one-minute timed reading of either selection from this week to assess students in Week 1. Pay special attention to this week's skill, punctuation clues. Provide corrective feedback for each student.

RETEACH

Draw Conclusions

TEACH

Review the definition for *conclusion* on p. 392. Complete Practice Book p. 158 as a class. Point out that students need to complete sentences 1–3, and explain what they know about playing games, before drawing a conclusion in sentence 5.

ASSESS

Have students reread "Keziah" on p. 411 in their books and draw conclusions about why the speaker likes his secret place. *(Possible response: He likes to be away from problems, in a quiet place sometimes.)*

For additional instruction on drawing conclusions, see DI·52.

EXTEND SKILLS

Idiom

TEACH

An idiom is a group of words that cannot be understood by the ordinary meaning of the words. Examples include "pulling your leg" or "bury the hatchet."

- In idioms, words take on non-literal meanings.
- Often the meaning of idioms can be understood by figuring out what makes sense in context.

Reread p. 400, paragraph 3 together as a class and point out the idiom: "(the wind) set his curtains snapping." Explain that Wesley's curtains don't actually snap, but they make a noise that sounds like snapping when the wind blows them hard.

ASSESS

Have students brainstorm and write down other idioms they know as well as their meaning.

OBJECTIVES

- Draw conclusions to improve comprehension.
- Recognize and interpret idioms.

Skills Trace	
Draw Conclusions	
Introduce/Teach	TE: 5.4 392–393, 484–485; 5.6 634–635
Practice	Practice Book: 153, 157, 158, 186, 193, 197, 198, 253, 257, 258, 276, 296
Reteach/Review	**TE: 5.4 411b, 467, 503b, DI•52, DI•56; 5.6 653b, 683, 687, 735, 745, DI•52**
Test	Selection Test: 61–64, 77–80, 101–104; Benchmark Test: Units 4, 6

ELL

Access Content Reteach the skill by reviewing the Picture It! lesson on draw conclusions in the ELL Teaching Guide, pp. 106–107.

Draw Conclusions

- A **conclusion** is a decision you make after thinking about the details of what you read.
- Often your prior knowledge can help you draw, or make, a conclusion.
- When you draw a conclusion, be sure it makes sense and is supported by what you have read.

Directions Read the following passage. Then complete the diagram.

People have played games throughout history. There are all kinds of games—card games, board games, sports games, children's games, and problem-solving games. People have invented games that can be played by one person, a few people, or by whole teams. Games give people a chance to challenge their minds and bodies. They also give people the thrill of winning. Best of all, games are fun.

Possible answers given.

Detail:	Detail:	Detail:	What you know:
1. People have played games **throughout recorded history.**	2. There are many different **kinds of games.**	3. Games challenge people's **minds and bodies.**	4. **I like playing games.**

Conclusion
5. People everywhere **love to play games.**

School + Home Home Activity Your child drew conclusions from facts or details found in a reading passage about games. Read a story or an article with your child. Work with him or her to draw conclusions from the details in it.

▲ **Practice Book** p. 158

Vocabulary and Word Study

VOCABULARY STRATEGY

🎯 Word Structure

ENDINGS Remind students that *-ed, -ing,* and *-s* may be added to verbs to change the tense. The endings can also be used to help determine the meaning of an unfamiliar word. Have students examine words with these endings from *Weslandia.* Ask students to identify base words and meanings and then see if they can make new words with the other two endings.

Word	Base Word	Meaning	New Words
moaned	moan	made a long, low sound of pain	moaning, moans
listening			
replied			
adopted			

Plural Nouns

The ending *-s* can also be added to nouns to make them plural. Some plural nouns require an *-es* ending. Nouns ending in a consonant and *y* change the *y* to *i* before adding *-es.* Have students work with partners to write the plural forms of these five nouns from *Weslandia.*

1. pizza: pizzas
2. garage
3. tomato
4. peach
5. history

BUILD CONCEPT VOCABULARY

People Adapting

LOOKING BACK Remind students of the question of the week: *How do people adapt to difficult situations?* Discuss how this week's Concept Web of vocabulary words relates to the theme of adapting. Ask students if they have any words or categories to add. Discuss whether the words and categories are appropriately related to the concept.

MOVING FORWARD Preview the title of the next selection, *Stretching Ourselves.* Ask students which Concept Web words might apply to the new selection based on the title alone.

Put a star next to these words on the web.

Display the Concept Web and revisit the vocabulary words as you read the next selection to check predictions.

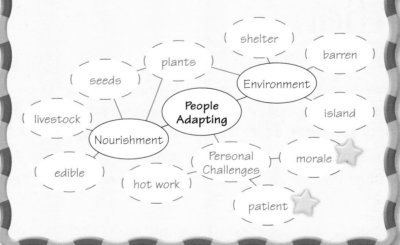

Monitor Progress

Check Vocabulary

If... students suggest words or categories that are not related to the concept,	**then...** review the words and categories on the Concept Web and discuss how they relate to the lesson concept.

SUCCESS PREDICTOR

Speaking and Viewing

SPEAKING

Demonstration

SET-UP Have students choose one of Wes's Weslandia projects and prepare a how-to demonstration for the class.

TOPICS Students can choose to demonstrate weaving cloth, crushing seeds to make oil, creating a sundial, adopting a new counting system, devising an 80-letter alphabet, building a flute, or making up sports and games. Encourage them to choose something that they are comfortable with and can get the materials they need. Students may work in pairs.

PLANNING Provide these planning tips for students:

- Make sure you have all of the materials you need before you begin your demonstration. Plan how to lay them out and in what order.

- Try out your project to see if it works.

- Practice your demonstration to make sure you can do it in the time allotted.

ADAPTATION Advise students to think of ways they will handle any problems that may come up during their demonstrations, such as running out of materials or dropping something. Encourage them to allow extra time in case they need to correct any errors or redo a step.

VIEWING

Analyze Illustrations

Have students study the illustrations on pp. 398–399 and p. 405 then answer these questions orally or in writing.

1. **What is happening in the illustrations on pp. 398–399? Describe Wes's surroundings.** *(Possible responses: He's being chased by bullies. His surroundings are messy, disorganized.)*

2. **What do you think the illustrator wants to convey about Wes based on the illustrations on pp. 398–399?** *(Possible responses: He's awkward, unhappy, a misfit, unpopular.)*

3. **Look at the illustration on p. 405. Compare Wes in that illustration to Wes in the illustrations on pp. 398–399.** *(Responses will vary but may include how Wes became happier and more confident, and his surroundings appear more orderly.)*

the stalk that he used as a sundial and had divided the day into eight segments—the number of petals on the plant's flowers.

He'd adopted a new counting system as well, based likewise upon the number eight. His domain, home to many such innovations, he named "Weslandia."

Uninterested in traditional sports, Wesley made up his own. These were designed for a single player and used many different parts of the plant. His spectators looked on with envy.

Realizing that more players would offer him more scope, Wesley invented other games that would include his schoolmates,

405

ELL

Support Vocabulary Use the following to review and extend vocabulary and to explore lesson concepts further:
- ELL Poster 16, Days 3–5 instruction
- Vocabulary Activities and Word Cards in ELL Teaching Guide, pp. 108–109

Assessment For information on assessing students' speaking, listening, and viewing, see the ELL and Transition Handbook.

Vocabulary

SUCCESS PREDICTOR

Grammar Subject and Object Pronouns

DAY 1 Teach and Model

DAILY FIX-IT

1. Caleb told we about a book he red. *(us; read)*

2. It were about islands with natives and bannana trees. *(was; banana)*

READING-GRAMMAR CONNECTION

Write this sentence on the board:

He was an outcast from the civilization around him.

Explain that *he* is a subject pronoun, and *him* is an object pronoun. *He* is the subject of the sentence, and *him* is the object of the preposition *around*.

Display Grammar Transparency 16. Read aloud the definitions and sample sentences. Work through the items.

Subject and Object Pronouns

A **subject pronoun** is used in the subject of a sentence. Singular subject pronouns are *I, you, he, she,* and *it.* Plural subject pronouns are *we, you,* and *they.* When you use a person's name and a pronoun in a compound subject, be sure to use a subject pronoun.

   We invented an imaginary country. It is far away. She and I planned a trip there.

An **object pronoun** is used in the predicate of a sentence after an action verb or with a preposition, such as *for, at, into, with,* or *to.* Singular object pronouns are *me, you, him, her,* and *it.* Plural object pronouns are *us, you,* and *them.* When you use a person's name and a pronoun in a compound object, be sure to use an object pronoun.

   That story reminds me of him. Leon told them. He helped Jenny and me.

Directions Write *S* if the underlined word is a subject pronoun. Write *O* if the word is an object pronoun.

1. I would like a treehouse. — S
2. Will you help me with the project? — O
3. Dad and we can get lumber and nails. — S
4. Use this rope to lift materials to Dad and him. — O
5. You and I have done a fine job. — S
6. They'll climb up the ladder with us. — O
7. It will make a great clubhouse. — S
8. Let's invite Danny and her to join. — O
9. She and Jamahl brought sandwiches. — S
10. This lunch in the branches tasted great to them. — O

Directions Underline the correct pronoun in ( ) to complete each sentence.

11. Sometimes (us, we) pretend the treehouse is a fort.
12. Both Brian and (I, me) want to be in charge.
13. Larry and (them, they) will be the troops.
14. Janmarie made a cool flag for (us, we).
15. We made (her, she) an honorary member of our club.
16. Because Dad helped us, we made (he, him) an honorary member too.

Unit 4 Weslandia   **Grammar 16**

▲ **Grammar Transparency** 16

DAY 2 Develop the Concept

DAILY FIX-IT

3. The natives had lived on the iland for centurys. *(island; centuries)*

4. Them ate the roots, leaves, and fruits of a plant that growed there. *(They; grew)*

GUIDED PRACTICE

Review the concept of subject and object pronouns.

- When a pronoun is used as the subject of a sentence, it is called a **subject pronoun.** *I, you, he, she, it, we,* and *they* are subject pronouns.

- Pronouns that are used after action verbs or as objects of prepositions are called **object pronouns.** *Me, you, him, her, it, us* and *them* are object pronouns.

HOMEWORK Grammar and Writing Practice Book p. 61. Work through the first two items with the class.

Subject and Object Pronouns

A **subject pronoun** is used in the subject of a sentence. Singular subject pronouns are *I, you, he, she,* and *it.* Plural subject pronouns are *we, you,* and *they.* When you use a person's name and a pronoun in a compound subject, be sure to use a subject pronoun.

   He has many original ideas. They are exciting and unusual.

   Mom and I made bird feeders.

An **object pronoun** is used in the predicate of a sentence after an action verb or with a preposition, such as *for, at, into, with,* or *to.* Singular object pronouns are *me, you, him, her,* and *it.* Plural object pronouns are *us, you,* and *them.* When you use a person's name and a pronoun in a compound object, be sure to use an object pronoun.

   The teacher asked him about his project. It seemed brilliant to me.

   This project was fun for James and me.

Directions Write *S* if the underlined word is a subject pronoun. Write *O* if the word is an object pronoun.

1. Some kids don't know what to think about him. — O
2. They can't understand someone who is different from them. — O
3. She praised his project for its originality. — S
4. Rainelle and I invited him to set with us. — S
5. We were fascinated by his ideas. — S
6. He has become a valued friend to her and me. — O

Directions Underline the correct pronoun in ( ) to complete each sentence.

7. Most people choose friends who are like (them, they).
8. (Them, They) feel comfortable with people who agree with them.
9. You and (I, me) have different points of view.
10. A friend with original ideas always surprises (I, me).
11. (Us, We) need to think about what we do and say.
12. (I, Me) prefer independent thinkers.
13. Jose and (her, she) agree with me.
14. We have many exciting conversations with (he, him) and (she, her).

Home Activity Your child learned about subject and object pronouns. Read a magazine article with your child. Ask him or her to identify several subject pronouns and object pronouns in the article.

▲ **Grammar and Writing Practice Book** p. 61

DAY 3 · Apply to Writing

DAILY FIX-IT

5. If I went to a jungle I would take a safarie. *(jungle,; safari)*

6. Help! There's a crockodile in the pool. *(crocodile; pool!)*

AVOID REPETITION

Subject and object pronouns allow writers to avoid repeating nouns.

Repetitive: The twins said that the twins would help in the garden.

Better: The twins said they would help in the garden.

• Have students review something they have written. They may be able to improve it by replacing nouns with subject and object pronouns.

HOMEWORK Grammar and Writing Practice Book p. 62.

Subject and Object Pronouns

Directions Use a pronoun from the box to complete each sentence. Write the sentence.

| they | he | I | us |
| them | she | me | you |

1. My mom and **I** plant a garden every summer.
2. **She** lets me pick out the seeds we will plant.
3. Some new flowers surprised **us** both this season.
4. **They** looked very strange among the roses and daisies.
5. As we watched **them** grow, we became more and more amazed.
6. Their enormous leaves and huge white flowers puzzled **me** and Mom.
7. Finally, Dad confessed. **He** had planted moonflower seeds to surprise us!
8. Would **you** have fallen for his joke?

Directions Write a paragraph about a unique person you know. Use subject and object pronouns correctly.

Possible answer: My friend Carrie is one-of-a-kind. She leaves me funny phone messages in rhyme. They always make me laugh. One time she convinced a group of us to try to make the world's biggest doughnut. It was a doughy disaster! Carrie also competes in the race-walk. For her, an Olympic gold medal in this sport is a serious goal.

Home Activity Your child learned how to use subject and object pronouns in writing. Ask your child to write a description of something he or she did with a friend or a group. Remind your child to use subject and object pronouns correctly.

▲ **Grammar and Writing Practice Book** p. 62

DAY 4 · Test Preparation

DAILY FIX-IT

7. Paul and him wrote a book on finding food in the wild! *(he; wild.)*

8. The section on edible Flowers are interesting. *(flowers is)*

STANDARDIZED TEST PREP

Test Tip

You may be asked to identify the correct pronoun in a phrase such as *Jane and I* or *Terry and her*. Decide whether the subject pronoun or object pronoun is correct by saying the sentence with just the pronoun and not the rest of the phrase. *Example:* I climbed the mountain. Jane and I climbed the mountain. Jane showed her our pictures. Jane showed Terry and her our pictures.

HOMEWORK Grammar and Writing Practice Book p. 63.

Subject and Object Pronouns

Directions Mark the letter of the pronoun that correctly completes each sentence.

1. ___ like to find wild foods.
   A Them
   B I
   C Me
   D She

2. You can make a meal of ___.
   A we
   B they
   C them
   D he

3. Dana and ___ found wild strawberries.
   A he
   B him
   C us
   D them

4. In the fall ___ harvest cattails.
   A me
   B her
   C us
   D they

5. ___ can grind the roots to make flour.
   A Him
   B We
   C Them
   D Her

6. Papa and ___ hunt for mushrooms in the woods.
   A her
   B me
   C she
   D us

7. Have ___ ever picked wild asparagus?
   A you
   B it
   C them
   D him

8. Uncle Dick and ___ found hickory nuts.
   A us
   B her
   C them
   D they

9. Dad asked Phil and ___ to shell the nuts.
   A she
   B he
   C me
   D I

10. He and ___ agreed it is a messy job.
    A them
    B I
    C it
    D her

Home Activity Your child prepared for taking tests on subject and object pronouns. Have your child write subject pronouns and object pronouns on index cards. Then mix the cards and sort them into subject pronoun and object pronoun piles.

▲ **Grammar and Writing Practice Book** p. 63

DAY 5 · Cumulative Review

DAILY FIX-IT

9. The tamato was an early food of South american natives. *(tomato; American)*

10. Chocolate also comed to us, from Native Americans. *(came; us from)*

ADDITIONAL PRACTICE

Assign pp. 140–143 in The Grammar and Writing Book.

EXTRA PRACTICE Grammar and Writing Practice Book p. 137.

TEST PREPARATION Grammar and Writing Practice Book pp. 155–156.

ASSESSMENT

CUMULATIVE REVIEW Grammar and Writing Practice Book p. 64.

Subject and Object Pronouns

Directions Write the letter of each pronoun next to the correct category.

B 1. Singular subject pronoun   A we
E 2. Plural object pronoun   B she
C 3. Singular object pronoun   C me
A 4. Plural subject pronoun   D you
D 5. Singular and plural, subject and object pronoun   E them

Directions Write S if the underlined word is a subject pronoun. Write O if the word is an object pronoun.

6. We learned about the Anasazi people. **S**
7. They built a civilization in the Southwest. **S**
8. Like many civilizations, it depended on crops. **S**
9. Maize and pumpkins provided the staple foods for them. **O**
10. Little rain fell, but the Anasazi hoarded it to water crops. **O**
11. The teacher asked Lia and me to report on cliff dwellings. **O**

Directions Underline the correct pronoun in ( ) to complete each sentence.

12. My family and (I, me) visited Chaco Canyon.
13. (Us, We) learned about the pueblos the Anasazi built there.
14. Their skill in building with adobe amazed Sara and (I, me).
15. The people who lived here disappeared 800 years ago and took little with (them, they).
16. Why they left is a mystery to (us, we).
17. Scientists and (they, them) agree that drought may have forced them to migrate.

Home Activity Your child reviewed subject and object pronouns. Challenge your child to write sentences using you, he, she, it, him, her, and them correctly.

▲ **Grammar and Writing Practice Book** p. 64

Writing Workshop E-mail

OBJECTIVES

- Identify the characteristics of an e-mail.
- Write an e-mail that refers to a text.
- Focus on conventions.
- Use a rubric.

Genre E-mail
Writer's Craft Refer to the Text
Writing Trait Conventions

Conventions In assessing the writing of language learners, remember that a consistent grammatical error may reflect the writing conventions of the home language. Address the skill by using the appropriate Grammar Transition lessons in the ELL and Transition Handbook.

Writing Traits

FOCUS/IDEAS All details are focused on ideas about the story.

ORGANIZATION/PARAGRAPHS The e-mail contains several paragraphs, each developing its own topic.

VOICE The writer's personality and interest come through. The language brings the topic to life.

WORD CHOICE The writer engages the reader with precise, colorful words.

SENTENCES The writer uses questions and exclamations for interest.

CONVENTIONS Spelling, punctuation, capitalization, and grammar (including subject and object pronouns) are accurate.

DAY 1 Model the Trait

READING-WRITING CONNECTION

- *Weslandia* tells about an unusual, inventive character.
- Students can refer to the text for examples of Wesley's creativity and a model of conventions.
- Students will write an **e-mail** using details from the text and correct spelling, punctuation, capitalization, and grammar.

MODEL CONVENTIONS Discuss Writing Transparency 16A. Then discuss the model and the writing trait of conventions.

 Think Aloud I see that the writer has filled in the subject and names of the sender and receiver. These headings are a convention of e-mail messages. The writer uses complete sentences with correct capitalization and punctuation.

E-mail

An **e-mail** is an electronic letter (usually a brief, friendly message) sent by computer. Although an e-mail is often informal, you should still use correct grammar, spelling, and punctuation.

This is standard heading information for every e-mail.

From: Student Chris
To: Wesley
cc:
Subject: Weslandia

Body paragraphs each develop a separate topic.

You don't know me, but I feel as though we could be brothers. I just finished reading about your civilization called Weslandia. Like you, I am excited by the idea of discovering the new and unknown.

References to the story create connection between the sender and receiver.

I thought the staple crop you discovered was fantastic! The way you used every part of the plant for clothing, food, and other needs was resourceful. Using the plant's oil for a suntan lotion and mosquito repellant was especially clever. When I read how you sold it back to the kids who had once teased you, I laughed! How did you ever come up with the idea of pressing oil from the seeds?

The game that you play on stilts looks like a blast. What do you call it? What are the rules? By the way, congratulations on turning your enemies into playmates.

Chris Student

Unit 4 Weslandia   Writing Model **16A**

▲ **Writing Transparency** 16A

DAY 2 Improve Writing

WRITER'S CRAFT
Refer to the Text

Display Writing Transparency 16B. Read the directions and work together to use the text to locate supporting details.

 Think Aloud **REFER TO THE TEXT FOR DETAILS** Wesley is a unique character. Tomorrow we will write about someone we know who is unique. Who can I use as my subject? I have a friend who likes to mix all sorts of foods together to make new recipes. He is unique. I can think about my friend and recall examples that show his creativity and unusual approach.

GUIDED WRITING Some students may need more help shaping text references. Have them page through *Weslandia* and point out details they enjoyed. Help them state these details in sentences that could be added to the writing model.

Refer to the Text

You may be asked to write an essay about a story you have read. **Refer to the text**— specific people, things, or incidents in the story— to support your ideas.

Directions Imagine you are writing a letter to a story character. Match the letter of the text with the character in the story.

D 1. Goldilocks
A 2. Jack
E 3. Hansel and Gretel
B 4. Sleeping Beauty
C 5. Cinderella

A Trading the cow for beans sounded like a stupid move, but it was actually brilliant. How did you know the beans were magic?
B What I'd really like to know is did you have any dreams while you were asleep all that time? Did you mind missing out on so many years?
C My stepmother makes me do a lot of work around the house too. My little sisters just play. No fair!
D Furthermore, our son's bed must be replaced. Didn't your parents teach you to respect other people's property?
E You two were very clever to outwit that nearsighted witch. How did you get the courage to shove her in the oven?

Directions Write a note (or an e-mail) to a character in one of your favorite stories. Refer to things that happen in the story. **Possible answer:**

Dear Harry, My heart went out to you when you had to live with your mean aunt and uncle after your parents were killed. Your cousin was such a spoiled brat! It was really great when you got to go to Hogwarts Academy for Witchcraft and Wizardry. Quidditch is an awesome game! What is it like to ride a broomstick? Sincerely yours, Charlene Student

Unit 4 Weslandia   Writer's Craft **16B**

▲ **Writing Transparency** 16B

DAY 3 Prewrite and Draft

READ THE WRITING PROMPT

on page 409 in the Student Edition.

In Weslandia, *a boy decides to remake his world rather than accept it as it is.*

Think about someone you know who doesn't always "follow the herd."

Now write an e-mail to that person about something he or she has done.

Writing Test Tips

- Make direct references to the story to create a connection between you and the recipient of your e-mail.
- Don't stray—focus on two or three interesting actions of the character.
- Remember to use correct spelling—even in an e-mail.

GETTING STARTED Students can do any of the following:

- Review personal experiences to recall the character's actions.
- Write ideas and details they might want to include in a word web that has the character's name in the center.
- Think about the character's personality and write to the person with that in mind.

DAY 4 Draft and Revise

EDITING/REVISING CHECKLIST

☑ Did I refer to the text of a story in the e-mail?

☑ Have I used subject and object pronouns correctly?

☑ Have I spelled words from other cultures correctly?

See *The Grammar and Writing Book,* pp. 140–145.

Revising Tips

Conventions

- As you read each sentence, identify its subject and predicate to be sure it is complete.
- Check that each sentence begins with a capital letter and ends with an end mark.
- In order to focus on spelling, read each sentence in the e-mail backwards.

PUBLISHING Students can read their e-mails in small groups and then ask others to tell what they would like to ask each character. Some students may wish to revise their work later.

ASSESSMENT Use the scoring rubric to evaluate students' work.

DAY 5 Connect to Unit Writing

Story	
Week 1	E-mail 411g–411h
Week 2	Journal Entry 435g–435h
Week 3	Story About an Animal 457g–457h
Week 4	Advice 483g–483h
Week 5	Describe How You Achieved a Goal 503g–503h

PREVIEW THE UNIT PROMPT

Tell a story about a character who succeeds by adapting to a new situation. Focus on an event that shows this person's resourcefulness and ingenuity. Your story may be real or imagined.

APPLY

- Refer to the text of a familiar story with a similar character to build understanding of personality traits.

Writing Trait Rubric

	4	3	2	1
Conventions	Excellent control of spelling, grammar, capitalization, and punctuation	Good control of spelling, grammar, capitalization, and punctuation	Limited control of spelling, grammar, capitalization, and punctuation	Poor control of spelling, grammar, capitalization, and punctuation
	No errors or only minor errors in e-mail	No serious errors that affect understanding in e-mail	Few distracting errors in e-mail	Many errors that affect understanding in e-mail

Spelling & Phonics **Words From Many Cultures**

OBJECTIVE

• Spell words from different cultures.

Generalization

Connect to Phonics Many words in English come from other languages and may have unexpected spellings: *khaki, ballet.* These words often do not follow the phonics rules students typically apply so other strategies must be applied for learning to spell them.

Spelling Words

1. khaki	11. macaroni
2. hula	12. polka
3. banana	13. cobra
4. ballet	14. koala
5. waltz	15. barbecue
6. tomato*	16. safari
7. vanilla	17. buffet
8. canyon	18. stampede
9. yogurt	19. karate
10. banquet	20. kiosk

Challenge Words

21. papaya	24. succotash
22. artichoke	25. tsunami
23. sauerkraut	

* Word from the selection

Spelling/Phonics Support See the ELL and Transition Handbook for spelling support.

DAY 1 Pretest and Sort

PRETEST

Use the Dictation Sentences from Day 5 to administer the pretest. Read the word, read the sentence, and then read the word again. Guide students in self-correcting their pretests and correcting any misspellings.

Monitor Progress

Spelling

If... students misspell more than 5 pretest words,	then... use words 1–10 for Strategic Intervention.
If... students misspell 1–5 pretest words,	then... use words 1–20 for On-Level practice.
If... students correctly spell all pretest words,	then... use words 1–25 for Advanced Learners.

HOMEWORK Spelling Practice Book, p. 61.

Words from Many Cultures

Generalization Many words in English come from other languages and may have unexpected spellings: **khaki, ballet.**

Word Sort Sort the list words by words you know how to spell and words that you are learning to spell. Write every word.

words I know how to spell	words I am learning to spell
1. Answers will	11. Answers will
2. vary.	12. vary.
3.	13.
4.	14.
5.	15.
6.	16.
7.	17.
8.	18.
9.	19.
10.	20.

Spelling Words
1. khaki
2. hula
3. banana
4. ballet
5. waltz
6. tomato
7. vanilla
8. canyon
9. yogurt
10. banquet
11. macaroni
12. polka
13. cobra
14. koala
15. barbecue
16. safari
17. buffet
18. stampede
19. karate
20. kiosk

Challenge Words

words I know how to spell	words I am learning to spell
21. Answers will	23. Answers will
22. vary.	24. vary.
	25.

Challenge Words
21. papaya
22. artichoke
23. sauerkraut
24. succotash
25. tsunami

School + Home **Home Activity** Your child is learning to spell words that come from other languages. Look up each word in the dictionary with your child.

▲ **Spelling Practice Book** p. 61

DAY 2 Think and Practice

TEACH

Words from different cultures may have unusual spellings for some sounds. Write *ballet* and *buffet* on the board. Underline the final *-et* in each word. Explain that this is pronounced as long *a.* Explain that in French, *et* at the end of the word is always pronounced as long *a.* Explain that *banquet* in French is pronounced like "bankay" with a long *a,* but in English it is pronounced "bankwet".

ay
ballet

FIND THE PATTERN Ask students to identify words that end in the short *a* sound. Have them group words with the short *a* sound together.

HOMEWORK Spelling Practice Book, p. 62.

Words from Many Cultures

Spelling Words

khaki	hula	banana	ballet	waltz
tomato	vanilla	canyon	yogurt	banquet
macaroni	polka	cobra	koala	barbecue
safari	buffet	stampede	karate	kiosk

Word Histories Write a list word for each description.

1. This is French for a table full of different foods.	1. buffet
2. Many students practice this Japanese form of self-defense.	2. karate
3. Native Americans introduced this fruit to the settlers.	3. tomato
4. This is a Turkish treat made from milk.	4. yogurt
5. This Polynesian dance is usually performed in a grass skirt.	5. hula
6. This is a Spanish word for a large group of running buffaloes or horses.	6. stampede
7. Although it has a French name, this dance form started in Russia.	7. ballet
8. This furry animal has kept its Australian name.	8. koala
9. Soldiers wear this greenish fabric named by the Persians and Hindus so they can't be easily seen.	9. khaki
10. This partner dance means "to turn" in German.	10. waltz
11. This is an Italian name for a well-known pasta.	11. macaroni
12. The Spanish and Portuguese used the same name for this yellow fruit.	12. banana
13. A Native American word is used to name this kind of outside cooking.	13. barbecue
14. This Polish dance is very lively.	14. polka
15. Although this word is Arabic, this type of journey is done in Africa.	15. safari
16. The Spanish named this flavorful type of bean long before there was ice cream.	16. vanilla
17. This word for a feast or a formal dinner comes from French.	17. banquet
18. This is a Spanish word for a very deep valley carved out by a river.	18. canyon
19. The name for this hooded, poisonous snake comes from the Portuguese.	19. cobra
20. This is a Turkish word for a newsstand.	20. kiosk

School + Home **Home Activity** Your child wrote words from other cultures. Go over the pronunciation of the French words. Remind your child that in French *-et* is pronounced as long *a.*

▲ **Spelling Practice Book** p. 62

DAY 3 Connect to Writing

WRITE AN E-MAIL

Ask students to write an e-mail using at least four spelling words. The e-mail can be a note to a friend or family member.

Frequently Misspelled Words

our *again*

These words may seem easy to spell, but they are often misspelled by fifth-graders. Alert students to the unique spelling of these words.

HOMEWORK Spelling Practice Book, p. 63.

Words from Many Cultures

Proofread a Poster Circle the seven spelling errors in the school poster. Write the words correctly. Write the last sentence, using correct punctuation.

Our New After-School Programs

Learn to Dance
• polka and Texas two-step
• ballet (with tutus, and toe shoes)
• waltz and other ballroom dances
• hula and dances of the Pacific

Learn Martial Arts
• karate • Judo • kung fu

Learn How to Cook
• barbecue sauces
• tomato salads
• homemade yogurt
• macaronie and cheese and other pastas
• bananna cream pie and other desserts

Sign up at the kyosk outside the office.
Bring a permission form from your parents?

1. polka   2. waltz
3. karate   4. macaroni
5. tomato   6. banana
7. kiosk
8. Bring a permission form from your parents.

Proofread Words Circle the correct spelling of the list word. Write the word.

9. The frightened cattle started to ___.
stamped   stampede   stampeed   9. stampede

10. I love the assortment of foods on the restaurant ___.
buffet   buffay   buffee   10. buffet

Spelling Words
khaki
hula
banana
ballet
waltz
tomato
vanilla
canyon
yogurt
banquet
macaroni
polka
cobra
koala
barbecue
safari
buffet
stampede
karate
kiosk

Frequently Misspelled Words
our
again

School + Home Home Activity Your child identified misspelled list words. Say a list word and spell it incorrectly. Ask your child to spell the word correctly.

▲ **Spelling Practice Book** p. 63

DAY 4 Review

REVIEW WORDS FROM OTHER CULTURES

Have partners play games of "Hangman" to review spelling words.

Spelling Strategy
Problem Parts

We all have words that are hard for us to spell.

Step 1: Ask yourself: Which part of the word gives me a problem?

Step 2: Underline the problem part.

Step 3: Picture the word. Focus on the problem part.

For example: khaki, banquet, waltz

HOMEWORK Spelling Practice Book, p. 64.

Words from Many Cultures

Spelling Words				
khaki	hula	banana	ballet	waltz
tomato	vanilla	canyon	yogurt	banquet
macaroni	polka	cobra	koala	barbecue
safari	buffet	stampede	karate	kiosk

Words in Context Write list words to complete the menu.

1. Welcome to the 5th Grade ___.   1. banquet
2. Eat all you want at the ___!   2. buffet
1st Course Appetizer
3. green salad with ___   3. tomato
4. cucumber with ___ dressing   4. yogurt
2nd Course Entrée
5. chicken served fresh from the ___ 5. barbecue
6. ___ and cheese   6. macaroni
3rd Course Dessert
7. ___ split sundae   7. banana
Your choice of
8. ___, chocolate, or strawberry ice cream 8. vanilla

Word Search Find ten list words hidden in the puzzle. Words are down, across, and diagonal. Write the words on the line.

S S C S S F S J K D A L
T T J Q K L S Y O M T K
B K A I B Q S Y A N J H
A X A M E R W R L H H A
L H S R P S A F A R I K
L N U U A E W A L T Z J
E B D I P T D K I O S K
T V H L A T E E L J U H

9. ballet
10. hula
11. khaki
12. koala
13. stampede
14. cobra
15. karate
16. kiosk
17. safari
18. waltz

School + Home Home Activity Your child has learned to read, write, and spell words from other cultures. Take turns spelling the list words.

▲ **Spelling Practice Book** p. 64

DAY 5 Posttest

DICTATION SENTENCES

1. He bought new khaki pants.
2. The hula dancers swayed.
3. A yellow banana is ripe.
4. The ballet started at three o'clock.
5. I would like to know how to waltz.
6. The tomato was delicious.
7. Add a teaspoon of vanilla.
8. The canyon was deep.
9. I like frozen yogurt.
10. Thanksgiving dinner was a banquet.
11. I love macaroni and cheese.
12. The polka is a lively dance.
13. The cobra is a hooded snake.
14. The koala lives in the trees.
15. We cooked on the barbecue pit.
16. They went on an African photo safari.
17. The buffet had many foods.
18. The cattle raced down the street in a stampede.
19. I take karate lessons.
20. I bought the newspaper at the kiosk.

CHALLENGE

21. I love the taste of papaya juice.
22. It's fun to peel and eat artichoke leaves.
23. Some like to have sauerkraut and mustard on their hotdogs.
24. Succotash is a dish of lima beans and corn.
25. The earthquake under the ocean caused a huge tsunami.

OBJECTIVES

- Formulate an inquiry question that is connected to this week's lesson focus.
- Effectively and efficiently find, evaluate, and communicate information related to an inquiry question using electronic sources.

New Literacies

Day 1	Identify Questions
Day 2	Navigate/Search
Day 3	Analyze
Day 4	Synthesize
Day 5	Communicate

NEW LITERACIES

Internet Inquiry Activity

EXPLORE CIVILIZATIONS

Use the following 5-day plan to help students conduct this week's Internet inquiry activity on civilizations. Remind students to follow classroom rules when using the Internet.

DAY 1

Identify Questions Discuss the lesson focus question: *How do people adapt to difficult situations?* Then, remind students of the civilization Wes creates for himself in *Weslandia* and why he creates it. Have students research other types of civilizations. For example, students might consider exploring the Mayan civilization or the Ancient Greek civilization.

DAY 2

Navigate/Search Explain that keywords or phrases for search engines should be as specific as possible. A keyword like *civilization* is too broad and will likely yield too many results. Suggest that they streamline their searches by using keywords such as *Mayan Civilization* or *Ancient Greece* to find Web sites that will answer their questions.

DAY 3

Analyze Have students skim and scan the Web sites they identified on Day 2 and analyze their credibility. Remind them to revise their inquiry questions as needed based on the information they find.

DAY 4

Synthesize Have students synthesize information by combining relevant ideas from different sources to develop answers to their inquiry questions. Remind students to avoid plagiarism by documenting their sources in an annotated bibliography and restating information in their own words or providing quotation marks around direct quotes. If they have to insert their own words into a direct quote, they would put them between brackets. Have students think about methods for communicating their results.

DAY 5

Communicate Have students use a word processing program to create summaries of the information they found about ancient civilizations. Encourage them to illustrate their reports with drawing tools or clip art.

Instruction Manual

TEACH

Ask students how they can find out how to bake a cake, or how to program a new cell phone. Students should mention a cookbook and an instruction manual. Make sure they understand that a cookbook is a kind of instruction manual. Explain:

- A **manual** is a book that contains instructions on how to do something.

- **Instructions** tell how to do something, usually in the form of a numbered list. Instructions also tell how to follow a **procedure**, or method of doing something.

- The instructions should be read completely before you begin.

- To follow the instructions, read the first step, do what it says, then go on to the next step. Try to visualize each step as you go.

- Manuals often contain warnings about a procedure, explaining any danger involved. These are marked with an exclamation mark, or the word WARNING or CAUTION.

Have students work in pairs, and give each partner an instruction manual. They should identify the parts that are defined above and read them carefully. Then, discuss these questions:

1. **What instructions does the manual contain?** (Possible response: How to put a table together.)

2. **What should you do after you read the instructions?** (Students should identify the first step.)

3. **What warnings might you need to know before attempting to complete the procedure?** (Students should note any warnings included in their instruction manuals.)

Fone-It M-235

Answering Machine
RECORDING AN OUTGOING MESSAGE
1. Make sure the answering machine is on.
2. Press the MENU button on the answering machine two times. You will hear "Set outgoing message." Press the SELECT button to confirm your choice.
3. Listen to the prompt. After you hear the beep, record your outgoing message. Remember to speak loudly and clearly.
4. When you have finished your message, press the SELECT button again to end the recording.

ASSESS

As students work with the manual, check that they can read and understand the instructions.

For more practice or to assess students, use Practice Book pp. 159–160.

- Review the terms *manual* and *instructions.*
- Understand how instruction manuals are organized.

▲ **Practice Book** p. 159

▲ **Practice Book** p. 160

Assessment Checkpoints *for the Week*

Selection Assessment

Use pp. 61–64 of Selection Tests to check:

 Selection Understanding

 Comprehension Skill *Draw Conclusions*

 Selection Vocabulary

blunders	fleeing
civilization	inspired
complex	rustling
envy	strategy

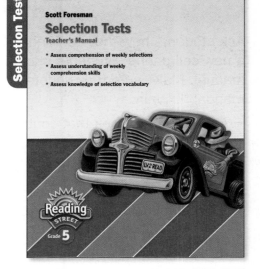

Leveled Assessment

Use pp. 91–96 of Fresh Reads for Differentiated Test Practice to check:

 Comprehension Skill *Draw Conclusions*

 REVIEW **Comprehension Skill** *Main Idea*

 Fluency *Words Correct Per Minute*

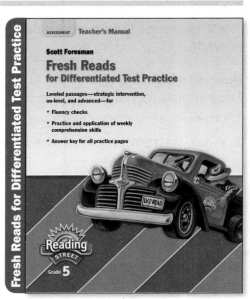

Managing Assessment

Use Assessment Handbook for:

 Observation Checklists

Record-Keeping Forms

Portfolio Assessment

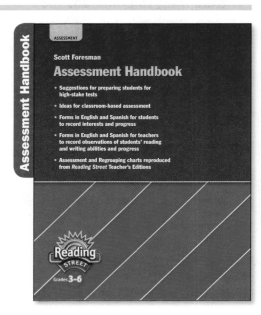

Illinois

Planning Guide for Performance Descriptors

Stretching Ourselves

Reading Street Teacher's Edition pages	**Grade 5 English Language Arts Performance Descriptors**
### Oral Language	**1B.Stage E.10.** Read age-appropriate material aloud with fluency and accuracy.
Speaking/Listening Build Concept Vocabulary: 412l, 423, 431, 435c Read Aloud: 412m	**4B.Stage E.10.** Contribute meaningfully to small and large group discussions by following accepted guidelines for verbal interaction.
### Word Work	**1A.Stage E.2.** Learn and use root words, prefixes, and suffixes to understand word meanings.
Prefixes *over-, under-, sub-, super-, out-*: 435i–435j	
### Reading	**1A.Stage E.1.** Use a combination of word analysis and vocabulary strategies (e.g., word patterns, structural analyses) within context to identify unknown words.
Comprehension Generalize: 412–413, 416–431, 434–435, 435b Predict: 412–413, 416–431, 434–435	**1B.Stage E.9.** Apply self-monitoring and self-correcting strategies continuously to clarify understanding during reading.
Vocabulary Lesson Vocabulary: 414b, 423, 431, 434 Context Clues: 414–415, 425, 435c	**1B.Stage E.10.** Read age-appropriate material aloud with fluency and accuracy. **1C.Stage E.6.** Select reading strategies for text appropriate to the reader's purpose.
Fluency Model Emotion: 412l–412m, 435a **Self-Selected Reading:** LR10–18, TR16–17	**2A.Stage E.3.** Predict how the story might be different if the author changed literary elements or techniques.
Literature Genre—Expository Nonfiction: 416 Reader Response: 432	**2A.Stage E.4.** Explain how a technique or element affects the events or characterization in a literary work. **2B.Stage E.6.** Read a wide range of nonfiction.
### Language Arts	**3A.Stage E.3.** Use a variety of sentence structures (e.g., simple, compound).
Writing Journal Entry: 435g–435h	**3C.Stage E.4.** Use available technology to design, produce, and present compositions and multimedia works.
Six-Trait Writing Focus/Ideas: 433, 435g–435h	**4B.Stage E.5.** Use appropriate grammar, word choice, and pacing.
Grammar, Usage, and Mechanics Pronouns and Antecedents: 435e–435f	**5A.Stage E.3.** Gather information based on a hypothesis: identify and use (with limited support) a variety of sources; recognize criteria for determining credible sources; determine appropriate resources.
Research/Study Technology—Telephone Directory: 435l **Technology** New Literacies: 435k	
### Unit Skills	**3A.Stage E.1.** Write paragraphs that include a variety of sentence types (i.e., declarative, interrogative, exclamatory, imperative).
Writing Story: WA2–9 **Poetry:** 504–507 **Project/Wrap-Up:** 508–509	**3C.Stage E.3.** Write creatively for a specified purpose and audience (e.g., short story, poetry, directions, song, friendly letter).

This Week's Leveled Readers

Below-Level

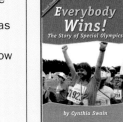

Fiction

1A.Stage E.6. Determine the meaning of a word in context when the word has multiple meanings.

2A.Stage E.4. Explain how a technique or element affects the events or characterization in a literary work.

On-Level

Nonfiction

1A.Stage E.7. Identify and interpret common idioms, similes, analogies, and metaphors.

2A.Stage E.4. Explain how a technique or element affects the events or characterization in a literary work.

Advanced

Nonfiction

1A.Stage E.8. Use additional resources (e.g., newspapers, interviews, technological resources) as applicable to clarify meanings of material.

2A.Stage E.4. Explain how a technique or element affects the events or characterization in a literary work.

Content-Area Illinois Performance Descriptors in This Lesson

Science

12A.Stage E.1. Apply scientific inquiries or technological designs to explore the patterns of change and stability at the micro- and macroscopic levels of organisms (including humans).

12A.Stage E.4. Apply scientific inquiries or technological designs to examine the nature of learned behavior or responses in all organisms (including humans).

12B.Stage E.1. Apply scientific inquiries or technological designs to categorize organisms (including humans) by their energy relationships in their environments.

Social Studies

18B.Stage E.1. Analyze how social institutions or groups meet the needs of people.

18B.Stage E.2. Explain how interactions of individuals and groups impact the local community.

Math

7B.Stage E.3. Estimate the perimeter, area, and/or volume of regular and irregular shapes and objects.

Illinois!

A FAMOUS ILLINOISAN
Walter Payton

Walter "Sweetness" Payton (1954–1999) retired from professional football in 1987 as one of the greatest running backs of all time. He got his nickname because of his personality and graceful athletic moves. Payton played for the Chicago Bears of the National Football League for thirteen years. He was inducted into the Pro Football Hall of Fame in 1993. The Walter Payton Award is given to the top college football player in Division I-AA.

Students can . . .
Create and name an academic award for excellence and write about the qualities or achievements a person would need to have to receive it.

A SPECIAL ILLINOIS PLACE
Illinois River

The Illinois River is part of a waterway system that connects the Great Lakes and the Gulf of Mexico. The Illinois River forms where the Kankakee and Des Plaines Rivers merge, about 45 miles southwest of Chicago. Peoria is a major port on the river, which flows for about 273 miles until it empties into the Mississippi River near Grafton.

Students can . . .
Look at an outline map of Illinois to trace the path of the Illinois River. Have students select a small town on the river and write a short report describing how the Illinois River has affected the town.

ILLINOIS FUN FACTS
Did You Know?

• Owen Lovejoy, who ran a station of the Underground Railroad in Princeton, was the brother of Elijah Lovejoy, a well-known abolitionist.

• *The Jungle,* Upton Sinclair's book about the Chicago meatpacking industry, was self-published, and it eventually became his most famous book.

• Completed in 1848 the ninety-seven-mile Illinois and Michigan Canal is now recognized as a National Heritage Corridor by the U.S. government.

Students can . . .
Write a report in which they describe how the Illinois and Michigan Canal affected Illinois waterways.

Unit 4
Adapting

CONCEPT QUESTION
How do people and animals adapt to different situations?

Week 1
How do people adapt to difficult situations?

Week 2
How do people adapt to living with physical limitations?

Week 3
How do animals adapt to survive?

Week 4
How do people adapt to a new school?

Week 5
Why do people try to change themselves?

Week 2

EXPAND THE CONCEPT
How do people adapt to living with physical limitations?

CONNECT THE CONCEPT

▶ **Build Background**
dedication, leg brace, polio, triumphant

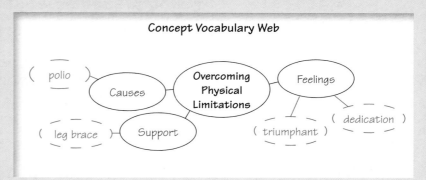

Concept Vocabulary Web

▶ **Science Content**
Animal Characteristics, Animal Survival, Food Web, Habitat

▶ **Writing**
Journal Entry

▶ **Internet Inquiry**
Adapting to Physical Limitations

Preview Your Week

How do people adapt to living with physical limitations?

BY ALDEN R. CARTER   PHOTOGRAPHS BY CAROL S. CARTER

Stretching Ourselves
Kids with *Cerebral Palsy*

Genre Expository nonfiction gives information about the real world. What special kind of information is the author giving you here?

How do Emily, Nic, and Tanner adapt to cerebral palsy?

416

Student Edition pages 416–431

Audio CD

Genre Expository Nonfiction

Vocabulary Strategy Context Clues

Comprehension Skill Generalize

Comprehension Strategy Predict

Science

Science in Reading

Paired Selection

Reading Across Texts
Think About How Helpful Technological Devices are Used

Genre
Expository Nonfiction

Text Features
Headings
Photos

Expository Nonfiction

Genre
- Some expository nonfiction explains helpful technological devices.
- The author explains how these devices work and who uses them and why.

Text Features
- Headings name the devices, and photos help explain them.
- Look over the headings and photos to see what the selection will explain.

Link to Science
Selections that deal with new technologies are important in a world like ours, with so many new inventions designed to help people. Research other helpful new technologies. Find a device that seems especially helpful and report on it to the class.

helpful tools
by Sally Hobart Alexander

Slowly, between the ages of twenty-four and twenty-six, Sally Hobart Alexander lost her sight. She went on to become an award-winning author of books for young people. In one of these books she describes tools that helped her adapt to blindness. One of these tools is Braille, a writing system that uses raised dots to stand for letters and numbers.

BRAILLE CLOTHING TAG
About the size of a fingernail, these metal tags have holes at either end for pinning or sewing onto labels. They tell me colors: "YW" for yellow, "PK" for pink, and "PP" for purple. When clothes are multicolored, I pin several tags onto the labels at once.

the exact time so often I memorized it. I'd always taken telling time for granted, and I felt lost. I developed a good sense of how long it took to do things, but my estimates could be off by ten minutes. Without a watch, I could miss a bus or an appointment. I could arrive at work late.

A Braille watch saved me. It looks like a regular wristwatch, except that the crystal pops up when you push a button, usually the winder. You can feel that the hour hand is shorter and sits below the minute hand. All the numbers have raised dots beside them. The

TALKING CLOCK
These clocks come in many varieties. The most common is pocket-sized, but I've had talking clocks inside ballpoint pens and key chains. You simply push a button, and a robot voice calls out the time.

BRAILLE WATCH
Imagine a life without clocks or watches, and you'll have an idea of my life when I first became blind. I dialed the phone number for

numbers 3, 6, and 9 have two raised dots, and the 12 has three.

BRAILLE TIMER
Usually three inches high and two inches wide, this device has raised dots by each number and works just like any other timer. I also use Braille labels on spices and cans. My microwave has a Braille pad.

Reading Across Texts
What helpful technological devices are mentioned in *Stretching Ourselves* and "Helpful Tools," and what are they used for?
Writing Across Texts Display your answers in a two-column chart.

 **Generalize** Which senses, other than sight, do these devices rely on?

434

Student Edition pages 434–435

Audio CD

Read It
ONLINE
PearsonSuccessNet.com

- Student Edition
- Leveled Readers

Leveled Readers

🎯 **Skill** Generalize

🎯 **Strategy** Predict

Lesson Vocabulary

Below-Level

On-Level

Advanced

ELL Reader

- Concept Vocabulary
- Text Support
- Language Enrichment

STRENGTH of SPIRIT

Integrate Science Standards

- **Human Body Systems**
- **Physical Limitations**
- **Disease**

✓ **Read**

Stretching Ourselves,
pp. 416–431

"Helpful Tools,"
pp. 434–435

Leveled Readers

Below-Level **On-Level** **Advanced**

- Support Concepts
- Develop Concepts
- Extend Concepts

ELL Reader

STRENGTH of SPIRIT

✓ **Build Concept Vocabulary**
Overcoming Physical
Limitations, pp. 412l–412m

✓ **Teach Science Concepts**
Polio, p. 419
Nervous System, p. 421
Assistive Technology, p. 425
The Human Eye, p. 435

✓ **Explore Science Center**
Design a Tool, p. 412k

Weekly Plan

READING

45–90 minutes

TARGET SKILLS OF THE WEEK

- **Comprehension Skill**
  Generalize
- **Comprehension Strategy**
  Predict
- **Vocabulary Strategy**
  Context Clues

LANGUAGE ARTS

30–60 minutes

Trait of the Week

Focus/Ideas

DAY 1
PAGES 412l–414b, 435a, 435e–435k

Oral Language

QUESTION OF THE WEEK *How do people adapt to living with physical limitations?*

Read Aloud: "Wilma Unlimited," 412m
Build Concepts, 412l

Comprehension/Vocabulary

Comprehension Skill/Strategy Lesson, 412–413
- Generalize **T**
- Predict

Build Background, 414a

Introduce Lesson Vocabulary, 414b
abdomen, artificial, gait, handicapped, therapist, wheelchair **T**

Read Leveled Readers

Grouping Options 412f–412g

Fluency

Model Emotion, 412l–412m, 435a

Grammar, 435e
Introduce Pronouns and Antecedents **T**

Writing Workshop, 435g
Introduce Journal Entry
Model the Trait of the Week: Focus/Ideas

Spelling, 435i
Pretest for Prefixes *over-, under-, sub-, super-, out-*

Internet Inquiry, 435k
Identify Questions

DAY 2
PAGES 414–423, 435a, 435e–435k

Oral Language

QUESTION OF THE DAY *How do specialists and others help Emily and Nic overcome their physical limitations?*

Comprehension/Vocabulary

Vocabulary Strategy Lesson, 414–415
- Context Clues **T**

Read *Stretching Ourselves,* 416–423

Grouping Options
412f–412g

- Generalize **T**
- Predict
- **REVIEW** Graphic Sources **T**

Develop Vocabulary

Fluency

Choral Reading, 435a

Grammar, 435e
Develop Pronouns and Antecedents **T**

Writing Workshop, 435g
Improve Writing with Elaboration

Spelling, 435i
Teach the Generalization

Internet Inquiry, 435k
Navigate/Search

DAILY WRITING ACTIVITIES	**Day 1** Write to Read, 412	**Day 2** Words to Write, 415 Strategy Response Log, 416, 423
DAILY SCIENCE CONNECTIONS	**Day 1** Overcoming Physical Limitations Concept Web, 412l	**Day 2** Time for Science: Nervous System, 421 Revisit the Overcoming Physical Limitations Concept Web, 423

DAILY SUCCESS PREDICTORS
for Adequate Yearly Progress

Monitor Progress and Corrective Feedback

Vocabulary — Check Vocabulary, *412l*

RESOURCES FOR THE WEEK

- Practice Book, *pp. 161–170*
- Word Study and Spelling Practice Book, *pp. 65–68*
- Grammar and Writing Practice Book, *pp. 65–68*

- Selection Test, *pp. 65–68*
- Fresh Reads for Differentiated Test Practice, *pp. 97–102*
- The Grammar and Writing Book, *pp. 146–151*

Grouping Options for Differentiated Instruction

Turn the page for the small group lesson plan.

DAY 3 — PAGES 424–433, 435a, 435e–435k

Oral Language

QUESTION OF THE DAY *How are the kids in the selection the same as and different than kids in your class?*

Comprehension/Vocabulary

Read *Stretching Ourselves,* 424–432

Grouping Options 412f–412g

- Generalize **T**
- Predict
- Context Clues **T**
- Develop Vocabulary

Reader Response
Selection Test

Fluency

Model Emotion, 435a

Grammar, 435f
Apply Pronouns and Antecedents in Writing **T**

Writing Workshop, 433, 435h
Write Now
Prewrite and Draft

Spelling, 435j
Connect Spelling to Writing

Internet Inquiry, 435k
Analyze Sources

Day 3 Strategy Response Log, 430
Look Back and Write, 432

Day 3 Time for Science: Assistive Technology, 425
Revisit the Overcoming Physical Limitations Concept Web, 431

DAY 4 — PAGES 434–435a, 435e–435k

Oral Language

QUESTION OF THE DAY *What inner traits can physically challenged people draw on to help them overcome the daily limitations confronting them?*

Comprehension/Vocabulary

Read "Helpful Tools," 434–435

Grouping Options 412f –412g

Expository Nonfiction
Reading Across Texts
Content-Area Vocabulary

Fluency

Partner Reading, 435a

Grammar, 435f
Practice Pronouns and Antecedents for Standardized Tests **T**

Writing Workshop, 435h
Draft, Revise, and Publish

Spelling, 435j
Provide a Strategy

Internet Inquiry, 435k
Synthesize Information

Day 4 Writing Across Texts, 435

Day 4 Time for Science: The Human Eye, 435

DAY 5 — PAGES 435a–435l

Oral Language

QUESTION OF THE WEEK *To wrap up the week, revisit the Day 1 question.*

Build Concept Vocabulary, 435c

Fluency

Read Leveled Readers

Grouping Options 412f–412g

Assess Reading Rate, 435a

Comprehension/Vocabulary

- Reteach Generalize, 435b **T**
- Simile, 435b
- Review Context Clues, 435c **T**

Speaking and Listening, 435d
Oral Presentation
Listen to Oral Presentations

Grammar, 435f
Cumulative Review

Writing Workshop, 435h
Connect to Unit Writing

Spelling, 435j
Posttest for Prefixes *over-, under-, sub-, super-, out-*

Internet Inquiry, 435k
Communicate Results

Research/Study Skills, 435l
Telephone Directory

Day 5 Simile, 435b

Day 5 Revisit the Overcoming Physical Limitations Concept Web, 435c

---

KEY ◉ = Target Skill **T** = Tested Skill

Comprehension Check Retelling, *432*

Fluency Check Fluency WCPM, *435a*

Vocabulary Check Vocabulary, *435c*

SUCCESS PREDICTOR

Small Group Plan *for Differentiated Instruction*

Daily Plan
AT A GLANCE

Reading
Whole Group
- Oral Language
- Comprehension/Vocabulary

Group Time
Differentiated Instruction

Meet with small groups to provide:
- Skill Support
- Reading Support
- Fluency Practice

Read

This week's lessons for daily group time can be found behind the Differentiated Instruction (DI) tab on pp. DI·12–DI·21.

Whole Group
- Fluency

Language Arts
- Grammar
- Writing
- Spelling
- Research/Inquiry
- Speaking/Listening/Viewing

Use *My Sidewalks on Reading Street* for Tier III intensive reading intervention.

DAY 1

On-Level	Strategic Intervention	Advanced
Teacher-Led *Page DI · 13*	**Teacher-Led** *Page DI · 12*	**Teacher-Led** *Page DI · 13*
• Develop Concept Vocabulary • **Read** On-Level Reader *Everybody Wins! The Story of Special Olympics*	• Reinforce Concepts • **Read** Below-Level Reader *A New Girl in Class*	• **Read** Advanced Reader *Feel, Think, Move* • Independent Extension Activity

(i) Independent Activities
While you meet with small groups, have the rest of the class...

- Visit the Reading/Library Center
- Listen to the Background Building Audio
- Finish Write to Read, p. 412
- Complete Practice Book pp. 163–164
- Visit Cross-Curricular Centers

DAY 2

On-Level	Strategic Intervention	Advanced
Teacher-Led *Pages 418–423*	**Teacher-Led** *Page DI · 14*	**Teacher-Led** *Page DI · 15*
• **Read** *Stretching Ourselves*	• Practice Lesson Vocabulary • Read Multisyllabic Words • **Read** or Listen to *Stretching Ourselves*	• Extend Vocabulary • **Read** *Stretching Ourselves*

(i) Independent Activities
While you meet with small groups, have the rest of the class...

- Visit the Reading/Library Center
- Listen to the AudioText for *Stretching Ourselves*
- Finish Words to Write, p. 415
- Complete Practice Book pp. 165–166
- Write in their Strategy Response Logs, pp. 416, 423
- Visit Cross-Curricular Centers
- Work on inquiry projects

DAY 3

On-Level	Strategic Intervention	Advanced
Teacher-Led *Pages 424–431*	**Teacher-Led** *Page DI · 16*	**Teacher-Led** *Page DI · 17*
• **Read** *Stretching Ourselves*	• Practice Generalize and Predict • **Read** or Listen to *Stretching Ourselves*	• Extend Generalize and Predict • **Read** *Stretching Ourselves*

(i) Independent Activities
While you meet with small groups, have the rest of the class...

- Visit the Reading/Library Center
- Listen to the AudioText for *Stretching Ourselves: Kids with Cerebral Palsy*
- Write in their Strategy Response Logs, p. 430
- Finish Look Back and Write, p. 432
- Complete Practice Book p. 167
- Visit Cross-Curricular Centers
- Work on inquiry projects

① Begin with whole class skill and strategy instruction.

② Meet with small groups to provide differentiated instruction.

③ Gather the whole class back together for fluency and language arts.

DAY 4

On-Level

Teacher-Led
Pages 434–435

• **Read** "Helpful Tools"

Strategic Intervention

Teacher-Led
Page DI · 18

• Practice Retelling
• **Read** or Listen to "Helpful Tools"

Advanced

Teacher-Led
Page DI · 19

• **Read** "Helpful Tools"
• Genre Study

ⓘ Independent Activities

While you meet with small groups, have the rest of the class...

• Visit the Reading/Library Center
• Listen to the AudioText for "Helpful Tools"
• Visit the Writing/Vocabulary Center
• Finish Writing Across Texts, p. 435
• Visit Cross-Curricular Centers
• Work on inquiry projects

DAY 5

On-Level

Teacher-Led
Page DI · 21

• **Reread** Leveled Reader *Everybody Wins! The Story of Special Olympics*
• Retell *Everybody Wins! The Story of Special Olympics*

Strategic Intervention

Teacher-Led
Page DI · 20

• **Reread** Leveled Reader *A New Girl in Class*
• Retell *A New Girl in Class*

Advanced

Teacher-Led
Page DI · 21

• **Reread** Leveled Reader *Feel, Think, Move*
• Share Extension Activity

ⓘ Independent Activities

While you meet with small groups, have the rest of the class...

• Visit the Reading/Library Center
• Complete Practice Book pp. 168–170
• Visit Cross-Curricular Centers
• Work on inquiry projects

Grouping Place English language learners in the groups that correspond to their reading abilities in English.

Use the appropriate Leveled Reader or other text at students' instructional level.

TiP Send home the appropriate Multilingual Summary of the main selection on Day 1.

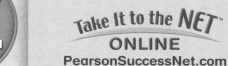

Take It to the NET™ ONLINE
PearsonSuccessNet.com

Sharon Vaughn
For research on intervention, see the article "Group Size and Time Allotted to Intervention" by Scott Foresman author S. Vaughn and S. Linan-Thompson.

TEACHER TALK

Differentiated Instruction is instruction tailored to the needs of groups of students, such as struggling students, gifted students, or English language learners.

Be sure to schedule time for students to work on the unit inquiry project "Adaptations." This week students conduct searches to find information about groups of people or animals who have adapted to different situations.

Looking Ahead

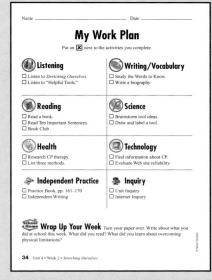

▲ **Group-Time Survival Guide**
p. 34, Weekly Contract

☑ Customize Your Plan *by Strand*

ORAL LANGUAGE

 Science

Concept Development

How do people adapt to living with physical limitations?

CONCEPT VOCABULARY

dedication   leg brace   polio   triumphant

BUILD

☐ **Question of the Week** Introduce and discuss the question of the week. This week students will read a variety of texts and work on projects related to the concept *overcoming physical limitations*. Post the question for students to refer to throughout the week. DAY 1 *412d*

☐ **Read Aloud** Read aloud "Wilma Unlimited." Then begin a web to build concepts and concept vocabulary related to this week's lesson and the unit theme, Adapting. Introduce the concept words *dedication, leg brace, polio,* and *triumphant* and have students place them on the web. Display the web for use throughout the week. DAY 1 *412l-412m*

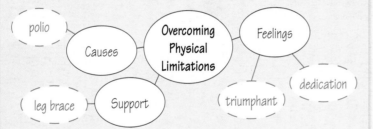

DEVELOP

☐ **Question of the Day** Use the prompts from the Weekly Plan to engage students in conversations related to this week's reading and the unit theme. **EVERY DAY** *412d-412e*

☐ **Concept Vocabulary Web** Revisit the Overcoming Physical Limitations Concept Web and encourage students to add concept words from their reading and life experiences. DAY 2 *423,* DAY 3 *431*

CONNECT

☐ **Looking Back/Moving Forward** Revisit the Overcoming Physical Limitations Concept Web and discuss how it relates to this week's lesson and the unit theme. Then make connections to next week's lesson. DAY 5 *435c*

CHECK

☐ **Concept Vocabulary Web** Use the Overcoming Physical Limitations Concept Web to check students' understanding of the concept vocabulary words *dedication, leg brace, polio,* and *triumphant.* DAY 1 *412l,* DAY 5 *435c*

VOCABULARY

STRATEGY CONTEXT CLUES
When you find a word you do not know in a text, look for clues to its meaning. You can find context clues among the words around the unfamiliar word. The situation the author is describing or the words of a character may suggest the unknown word's meaning.

LESSON VOCABULARY

abdomen	handicapped
artificial	therapist
gait	wheelchair

TEACH

☐ **Words to Know** Give students the opportunity to tell what they already know about this week's lesson vocabulary words. Then discuss word meaning. DAY 1 *414b*

☐ **Vocabulary Strategy Lesson** Use the vocabulary strategy lesson in the Student Edition to introduce and model this week's strategy, *context clues.* DAY 2 *414-415*

Vocabulary Strategy Lesson

PRACTICE/APPLY

☐ **Leveled Text** Read the lesson vocabulary in the context of leveled text. DAY 1 *LR10-LR18*

Leveled Readers

☐ **Words in Context** Read the lesson vocabulary and apply *context clues* in the context of *Stretching Ourselves.* DAY 2 *416-423,* DAY 3 *424-432*

Main Selection—Nonfiction

☐ **Writing/Vocabulary Center** Write a brief biography of a person you know or have heard of who lives with a physical challenge. **ANY DAY** *412k*

☐ **Homework** Practice Book pp. 164–165. DAY 1 *414b,* DAY 2 *415*

☐ **Word Play** Have students list words from *Stretching Ourselves* that are homophones and write sentences using both words. **ANY DAY** *435c*

ASSESS

☐ **Selection Test** Use the Selection Test to determine students' understanding of the lesson vocabulary words. DAY 3

RETEACH/REVIEW

☐ **Reteach Lesson** If necessary, use this lesson to reteach and review *context clues.* DAY 5 *435c*

❶ Use assessment data to determine your instructional focus.

❷ Preview this week's instruction by strand.

❸ Choose instructional activities that meet the needs of your classroom.

COMPREHENSION

SKILL GENERALIZE A generalization is made after thinking about a number of examples or facts and identifying what they have in common. A valid generalization can be supported by facts or details and a faulty generalization cannot.

STRATEGY PREDICT To predict means to tell what you think will happen next and why it will happen. Good readers look for clues and combine those clues with what they already know to tell what is going to happen next.

TEACH

❏ **Skill/Strategy Lesson** Use the skill/strategy lesson in the Student Edition to introduce and model *generalize* and *predict*. DAY 1 *412-413*

Skill/Strategy Lesson

❏ **Extend Skills** Teach similes. **ANY DAY** *435b*

PRACTICE/APPLY

❏ **Leveled Text** Apply *generalize* and *predict* to read leveled text. DAY 1 *LR10-LR18*

Leveled Readers

❏ **Skills and Strategies in Context** Read *Stretching Ourselves*, using the Guiding Comprehension questions to apply *generalize* and *predict*. DAY 2 *416-423*, DAY 3 *424-432*

Main Selection—Nonfiction

❏ **Skills and Strategies in Context** Read "Helpful Tools," guiding students as they apply *generalize* and *predict*. Then have students discuss and write across texts. DAY 4 *434-435*

❏ **Homework** Practice Book pp. 163, 167, 168. DAY 1 *413* DAY 3 *431*, DAY 5 *435b*

Paired Selection—Nonfiction

❏ **Fresh Reads for Differentiated Test Practice** Have students practice *generalize* with a new passage. DAY 3

ASSESS

❏ **Selection Test** Determine students' understanding of the selection and their use of *generalize*. DAY 3

❏ **Retell** Have students retell *Stretching Ourselves*. DAY 3 *432-433*

RETEACH/REVIEW

❏ **Reteach Lesson** If necessary, reteach and review *generalize*. DAY 5 *435b*

FLUENCY

SKILL EMOTION Reading with emotion means reading words as if you were the character. Changing the intonation makes the reading more expressive and lively to the listeners.

TEACH

❏ **Read Aloud** Model fluent reading by rereading "Wilma Unlimited." Focus on this week's fluency skill, emotion. DAY 1 *412l-412m, 435a*

PRACTICE/APPLY

❏ **Choral Reading** Read aloud selected paragraphs from *Stretching Ourselves*, emphasizing the intonations in your voice. Then practice as a class, doing three choral readings of the paragraphs. DAY 2 *435a*, DAY 3 *435a*

❏ **Partner Reading** Have partners practice reading with emotion and offering each other feedback. As students reread, monitor their progress toward their individual goals. DAY 4 *435a*

❏ **Listening Center** Have students follow along with the AudioText for this week's selections. **ANY DAY** *412j*

❏ **Reading/Library Center** Have students reread a selection of their choice. **ANY DAY** *412j*

❏ **Fluency Coach** Have students use Fluency Coach to listen to fluent readings or practice reading on their own. **ANY DAY**

ASSESS

❏ **Check Fluency** WCPM Do a one-minute timed reading, paying special attention to this week's skill—emotion. Provide feedback for each student. DAY 5 *412l-412m, 435a*

☑ Customize Your Plan *by Strand*

GRAMMAR

SKILL PRONOUNS AND ANTECEDENTS A pronoun takes the place of a noun or nouns. An antecedent, or referent, is the noun or nouns to which the pronoun refers. A pronoun and its antecedent must agree in number and gender.

TEACH

❑ **Grammar Transparency 17** Use Grammar Transparency 17 to teach pronouns and antecedents. DAY 1 *435e*

Grammar Transparency 17

PRACTICE/APPLY

❑ **Develop the Concept** Review the concept of pronouns and antecedents and provide guided practice. DAY 2 *435e*

❑ **Apply to Writing** Have students review something they have written and apply pronouns and antecedents. DAY 3 *435f*

❑ **Test Preparation** Examine common errors in pronouns and antecedents to prepare for standardized tests. DAY 4 *435f*

❑ **Homework** Grammar and Writing Practice Book pp. 65–67. DAY 2 *435e*, DAY 3 *435f*, DAY 4 *435f*

ASSESS

❑ **Cumulative Review** Use Grammar and Writing Practice Book p. 68. DAY 5 *435f*

RETEACH/REVIEW

❑ **Daily Fix-It** Have students find and correct errors in grammar, spelling, and punctuation. **EVERY DAY** *435e–435f*

❑ **The Grammar and Writing Book** Use pp. 146–149 of The Grammar and Writing Book to extend instruction for pronouns and antecedents. **ANY DAY**

The Grammar and Writing Book

WRITING

Trait of the Week

FOCUS/IDEAS Good writers focus on a main idea and develop this idea with strong supporting details. Having a purpose—whether it is to inform, to persuade, or to entertain—helps keep focus on the main idea.

TEACH

❑ **Writing Transparency 17A** Use the model to introduce and discuss the Trait of the Week. DAY 1 *435g*

❑ **Writing Transparency 17B** Use the transparency to show students how elaboration can improve their writing. DAY 2 *435g*

Writing Transparency 17A **Writing Transparency 17B**

PRACTICE/APPLY

❑ **Write Now** Examine the model on Student Edition p. 433. Then have students write their own journal entry. DAY 3 *435h*, DAY 4 *435h*

    Prompt Kids with special challenges are featured in *Stretching Ourselves*. Think about someone you know who has special mental or physical challenges. Now write a journal entry describing your observations and feelings about that person.

Write Now p. 433

❑ **Writing/Vocabulary Center** Write a brief biography of a person you know or have heard of who lives with a physical challenge. **ANY DAY** *412k*

ASSESS

❑ **Writing Trait Rubric** Use the rubric to evaluate students' writing. DAY 4 *435h*

RETEACH/REVIEW

❑ **The Grammar and Writing Book** Use pp. 146–151 of The Grammar and Writing Book to extend instruction for pronouns and antecedents, elaboration, and journal entry. **ANY DAY**

The Grammar and Writing Book

❶ Use assessment data to determine your instructional focus.

❷ Preview this week's instruction by strand.

❸ Choose instructional activities that meet the needs of your classroom.

SPELLING

GENERALIZATION PREFIXES *OVER-, UNDER-, SUB-, SUPER-, OUT-*
When prefixes *over-, under-, sub-, super-,* and *out-* are added to words, the base word stays the same: <u>over</u>look, <u>under</u>line, <u>sub</u>way, <u>super</u>market, <u>out</u>let. The base word is also pronounced the same as it was before the prefix was added.

TEACH

❑ **Pretest** Give the pretest for words with prefixes *over-, under-, sub-, super-, out-*. Guide students in self-correcting their pretests and correcting any misspellings. **DAY 1** *435i*

❑ **Think and Practice** Connect spelling to the phonics generalization for prefixes *over-, under-, sub-, super-, out-*. **DAY 2** *435i*

PRACTICE/APPLY

❑ **Connect to Writing** Have students use spelling words to write a journal entry. Then review frequently misspelled words: *outside, because.* **DAY 3** *435j*

❑ **Homework** Word Study and Spelling Practice Book pp. 65–68. **EVERY DAY**

RETEACH/REVIEW

❑ **Review** Review spelling words to prepare for the posttest. Then provide students with a spelling strategy—divide and conquer. **DAY 4** *435j*

ASSESS

❑ **Posttest** Use dictation sentences to give the posttest for words with prefixes *over-, under-, sub-, super-, out-*. **DAY 5** *435j*

Spelling Words

1. overlook	8. overboard	15. overcast
2. underline	9. undercurrent	16. outfield
3. subway	10. superstar	17. output
4. subset	11. overtime	18. supernatural
5. supermarket	12. supersonic	19. subdivision
6. outlet	13. submarine	20. subhead
7. underground	14. undercover	

Challenge Words

21. overwhelm	23. underestimate	25. subcommittee
22. superimpose	24. underprivileged	

*Word from the selection

RESEARCH AND INQUIRY

❑ **Internet Inquiry** Have students conduct an Internet inquiry on adapting to physical limitations. **EVERY DAY** *435k*

❑ **Telephone Directory** Review with students the features of a telephone directory and have students conduct an online search in an online telephone directory to find phone numbers of people and businesses. **DAY 5** *435l*

❑ **Unit Inquiry** Allow time for students to find information about groups of people or animals that have adapted to different situations. **ANY DAY** *391*

SPEAKING AND LISTENING

❑ **Oral Presentation.** Have students prepare an oral presentation on some of the tools and adaptive technology available to help handicapped people. **DAY 5** *435d*

❑ **Listen to Oral Presentations** Have students listen to and evaluate the oral presentations given by their classmates. **DAY 5** *435d*

Resources for
Differentiated Instruction

LEVELED READERS

▶ **Comprehension**
  - ◎ **Skill** Generalize
  - ◎ **Strategy** Predict

▶ **Lesson Vocabulary**
  - ◎ Context Clues

abdomen   artificial   handicapped   gait   therapist   wheelchair

▶ **Science Standards**
  - • **Human Body Systems**
  - • **Physical Limitations**
  - • **Disease**

Leveled Reader Database
ONLINE
PearsonSuccessNet.com

Use the Online Database of over 600 books to

- Download and print additional copies of this week's leveled readers.
- Listen to the readers being read online.
- Search for more titles focused on this week's skills, topic, and content.

On-Level

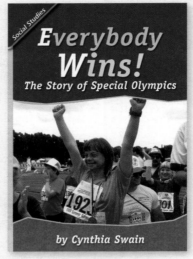

Social Studies
Everybody Wins!
The Story of Special Olympics
by Cynthia Swain

On-Level Reader

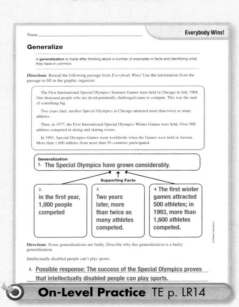

On-Level Practice TE p. LR14

On-Level Practice TE p. LR15

Strategic Intervention

Social Studies
A New Girl in Class
by Jason Lublinski
illustrated by Ron Mahoney

Below-Level Reader

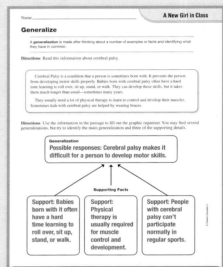

Below-Level Practice TE p. LR11

Below-Level Practice TE p. LR12

Advanced

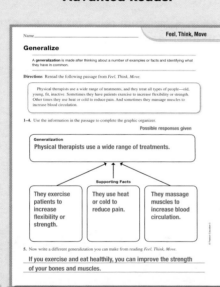

Advanced Reader

ELL Reader   **ELL Poster 17**

Teacher's Edition Notes

ELL notes throughout this lesson support instruction and reference additional resources at point of use.

Teaching Guide pp. 113–119, 244–245

- Multilingual summaries of the main selection
- Comprehension lesson
- Vocabulary strategies and word cards
- ELL Reader 5.4.2 lesson

ELL and Transition Handbook

Ten Important Sentences

- Key ideas from every selection in the Student Edition
- Activities to build sentence power

Name _____   Feel, Think, Move

Generalize

A **generalization** is made after thinking about a number of examples or facts and identifying what they have in common.

Directions Reread the following passage from *Feel, Think, Move*.

> Physical therapists use a wide range of treatments, and they treat all types of people—old, young, fit, inactive. Sometimes they have patients exercise to increase flexibility or strength. Other times they use heat or cold to reduce pain. And sometimes they massage muscles to increase blood circulation.

1–4. Use the information in the passage to complete the graphic organizer.

               Possible responses given

Generalization
Physical therapists use a wide range of treatments.

Supporting Facts

| They exercise patients to increase flexibility or strength. | They use heat or cold to reduce pain. | They massage muscles to increase blood circulation. |

5. Now write a different generalization you can make from reading *Feel, Think, Move*.

If you exercise and eat healthily, you can improve the strength

of your bones and muscles.

Advanced Practice TE p. LR17

Name _____   Feel, Think, Move

Vocabulary

Directions Write the vocabulary word that matches the definition.

Check the Words You Know

____abdomen   ____cerebral hemispheres
____coordination   ____musculoskeletal
____neurons   ____organ
____therapists

1. coordination   muscles working together smoothly for efficient movement
2. neurons   main cells of the nervous system
3. abdomen   the section of the body that holds the intestines and stomach; the belly
4. organ   an internal part of the body that performs a specific function
5. musculoskeletal   having to do with the system that includes the muscles and the skeleton
6. cerebral hemispheres   left and right halves of the brain that control the opposite sides of the body
7. therapists   specialists who provide treatment or healing of an illness or disability

Directions Write a short paragraph about how the body works to make itself move. Use at least three vocabulary words.

Paragraphs will vary.

Advanced Practice TE p. LR18

More Reading

Readers' Theater Anthology

- Fluency practice
- Five scripts to build fluency
- Poetry for oral interpretation

Leveled Trade Books

Advanced
Below-Level
On-Level

- Extended reading tied to the unit concept
- Lessons in the Trade Book Library Teaching Guide

School + Home

Homework

- Family Times Newsletter
- ELL Multilingual Selection Summaries

Take-Home Books

- Leveled Readers

Cross-Curricular Centers

 **Listening**

 Reading/Library

 Health

Listen to the Selections

MATERIALS `SINGLES`
CD player, headphones, AudioText CD, student book

LISTEN TO LITERATURE Listen to *Stretching Ourselves* and "Helpful Tools" as you follow or read along in your book. Listen for generalizations in the story.

If there is anything you don't understand, you can listen again to any section.

Read it AGAIN!

MATERIALS `SINGLES` `PAIRS` `GROUPS`
Collection of books for self-selected reading, reading logs, student book

Select a book you have already read. Record the title of the book in your reading log. You may want to read with a partner.

Choose from the following:

- **Leveled Readers**
- **ELL Readers**
- **Stories Written by Classmates**
- **Books from the Library**
- *Stretching Ourselves*

TEN IMPORTANT SENTENCES Read the Ten Important Sentences for *Stretching Ourselves*. Then locate the sentences in the student book.

BOOK CLUB What can you learn from reading about people with physical challenges? Read other stories about coping with physical challenge and discuss with the group.

Classroom Library

Find Out More

MATERIALS `SINGLES` `PAIRS`
Writing materials, Internet access, books on cerebral palsy, e-mail program

Use resources to find out more about the treatment of cerebral palsy (CP).

1. **Follow classroom rules for searching the Internet. Use a student-friendly search engine to find information about types of medical and physical therapy for people with CP.**
2. **List three methods with a brief description of each.**

EARLY FINISHERS Write an e-mail to a friend or family member to share what you learned about cerebral palsy.

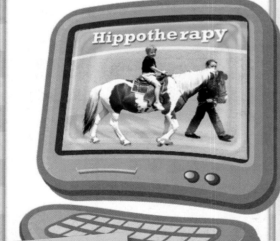

Treatment
1. Hippotherapy

Scott Foresman Reading Street Centers Survival Kit

Use the *Stretching Ourselves* materials from the Reading Street
Centers Survival Kit to organize this week's centers.

Writing/Vocabulary

Science

Technology

Write a *Biography*

MATERIALS
Writing materials, journals

`SINGLES`

Write a brief biography of a person you know or have heard of who lives with a physical challenge.

1. Make some notes about the person's life based on what you already know or by using Internet or library resources.
2. Write a journal entry describing what he or she has taught you about living with a physical challenge.

EARLY FINISHERS Write a paragraph based on your notes. Include details about how the person copes with his or her physical challenge.

> *Dear Journal,*
>   *I have a neighbor who uses a wheelchair...*

Design a TOOL

MATERIALS
Writing and art materials

`SINGLES`
`PAIRS`
`GROUPS`

Design a helpful tool that could be used by a student with physical challenges in your school.

1. Think about a physical challenge that someone might face in your school and brainstorm ideas for tools that could help him or her.
2. Draw and label the tool and its parts.
3. Then survey 3–5 classmates on the usefulness of this tool.

EARLY FINISHERS Write a caption describing the tool and explaining why it would be helpful.

Automatic Door Opener

button to open door

button to close door

Verify Sources

MATERIALS
Internet access

`SINGLES`

Identify reliable sites with information about cerebral palsy.

1. Follow classroom rules for searching the Internet for information about cerebral palsy. Use a student-friendly search engine.
2. Scan through the first five sites your search engine lists.
3. Evaluate the reliability of a site by finding out who published it, when it was published, and if it is clear, well–written, and informative.

EARLY FINISHERS Choose the site you find most reliable and explain your reasons for choosing it.

when it was published
who published it

Cerebral Palsy

by Dr. Wehmeyer
10/5/06

ALL CENTERS

Build Concepts

OBJECTIVES

- Build vocabulary by finding words related to the lesson concept.
- Listen for generalizations.

Concept Vocabulary

dedication devotion

leg brace a device used to support a leg

polio a severe, infectious, viral disease that destroys nervous tissue in the spinal cord causing paralysis and wasting away of muscles

triumphant victorious or successful

Monitor Progress

Check Vocabulary

If...	then... review the
students are unable to place words on the Web,	lesson concept. Place the words on the Web and provide additional words for practice, such as *paralyzed* and *scholarship*.

SUCCESS PREDICTOR

DAY 1 Grouping Options

Reading

Whole Group

Introduce and discuss the Question of the Week. Then use pp. 412l–414b.

Group Time

Differentiated Instruction

Read this week's Leveled Readers. See pp. 412f–412g for the small group lesson plan.

Whole Group

Use p. 435a.

Language Arts

Use pp. 435e–435k.

FLUENCY

MODEL EMOTION As you read "Wilma Unlimited," use your voice to model reading with emotion. You can speak softly and slowly when reading the introduction and first paragraph which talk about her physical limitations and with energy and building enthusiasm as you read the rest about how Wilma overcomes her limitations to become a great athletic success.

LISTENING COMPREHENSION

After reading "Wilma Unlimited," use the following questions to assess listening comprehension.

1. **What generalization can you make about Wilma Rudolph and others who overcome physical limitations?** *(Possible response: People who overcome physical limitations are courageous and determined.)* **Generalize**

2. **What caused Wilma Rudolph to switch from basketball to track?** *(A college coach liked the way she ran when she played basketball and helped her get a track-and-field scholarship.)* **Cause and Effect**

BUILD CONCEPT VOCABULARY

Start a web to build concepts and vocabulary related to this week's lesson and the unit theme.

- Draw the Overcoming Physical Limitations Concept Web.
- Read the sentence with the word *polio* again. Ask students to pronounce *polio* and discuss its meaning.
- Place *polio* in an oval attached to *Causes.* Explain that *polio* is related to this concept. Read the sentences in which *leg brace, dedication* and *triumphant* appear. Have students pronounce the words, place them on the web, and provide reasons.
- Brainstorm additional words and categories for the web. Keep the web on display and add words throughout the week.

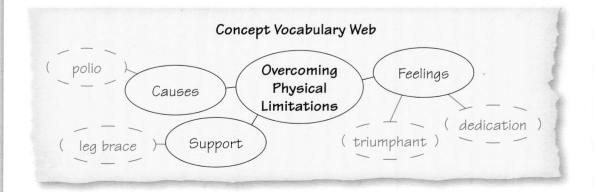

Concept Vocabulary Web

Wilma Unlimited

by Kathleen Krull

Olympic runner Wilma Rudolph contracted polio as a child, resulting in a paralyzed left leg. She survived, but it was assumed that she would never walk without the aid of a leg brace, much less run. In this passage, Wilma overcomes her physical limitation with hard work and dedication.

Whispers rippled throughout the gathering. Wilma Rudolph was walking. Row by row, heads turned toward her as she walked alone down the aisle. Her large family, all her family's friends, everyone from school—each person stared wide-eyed. The singing never stopped; it seemed to burst right through the walls and into the trees. Finally, Wilma reached a seat in the front and began singing too, her smile triumphant.

Wilma practiced walking as often as she could after that, and when she was twelve years old, she was able to take off the brace for good. She and her mother realized she could get along without it, so one memorable day they wrapped the hated brace in a box and mailed it back to the hospital.

As soon as Wilma sent that box away, she knew her life was beginning all over again.

After years of sitting on the sidelines, Wilma couldn't wait to throw herself into basketball, the game she most liked to watch. She was skinny, but no longer tiny. Her long, long legs would propel her across the court and through the air, and she knew all the rules and all the moves.

In high school, she led her basketball team to one victory after another. Eventually, she took the team all the way to the Tennessee state championships. There, to everyone's astonishment, her team lost.

Wilma had become accustomed to winning. Now she slumped on the bench, all the liveliness knocked out of her.

But at the game that day was a college coach. He admired Wilma's basketball playing but was especially impressed by the way she ran. He wanted her for his track-and-field team.

With his help, Wilma won a full athletic scholarship to Tennessee State University. She was the first member of her family to go to college.

Eight years after she mailed her brace away, Wilma's long legs and years of hard work carried her thousands of miles from Clarksville, Tennessee. The summer of 1960 she arrived in Rome, Italy, to represent the United Stated at the Olympic Games—as a runner.

Activate Prior Knowledge

Before students listen to the Read Aloud, ask them what they know about physical limitations and how they affect people.

Set Purpose

Read aloud the title and have students predict what the selection will be about.

Read the introduction aloud. Have students listen for generalizations and details that can be used to prove or disprove their validity.

Creative Response

Have students work in groups to reenact the scene in which Wilma first walks in front of her family and friends. Remind students to use facial expressions to convey emotions. *Drama*

Access Content Before reading, share this summary: As a child, Wilma had polio. Her left leg was paralyzed and she wore a brace. She worked hard to walk again. She returned her brace to the hospital and began to play basketball. She won an athletic scholarship to college and later represented the U.S. at the Olympics as a sprinter.

School + Home **Homework** Send home this week's Family Times newsletter.

SKILLS ⟷ STRATEGIES IN CONTEXT

Generalize Predict

OBJECTIVES

- Identify and make generalizations.
- Use generalizations to predict.

Skills Trace
Generalize

Introduce/Teach	TE: 5.4 412–413, 458–459; 5.5 604–605
Practice	Practice Book: 163, 167, 168, 183, 187, 188, 243, 247, 248
Reteach/Review	TE: 5.4 435b, 483b, 493, DI-53, DI-55; 5.5 625b, DI-56
Test	Selection Test: 65–68, 73–76, 97–100; Benchmark Test: Unit 4

INTRODUCE

Read or write the following on the board: *Many students in our school have disabilities. Several students wear glasses that help them see better. Some have hearing aids that help them to hear. Still others have wheelchairs that help them get around the building and their classrooms.* Ask students to identify the generalization. *(Many students in our school have disabilities.)*

Have students read the information on p. 412. Explain the following:

- Some authors use broad statements, or generalizations, in their writing.

- Not all generalizations are valid. So, before accepting the validity of a generalization, be sure to look for details that support it.

- Recognizing generalizations can help you predict other points the author will make.

Use Skill Transparency 17 to teach generalizing and predicting.

Comprehension

Skill
Generalize

Strategy
Predict

Generalize

- An author may write similar details about different things or people. You can use these similar details to make a general statement that covers all the things or people. This statement is called a generalization.

- A valid generalization can be supported by facts or details. A faulty generalization cannot.

- Sometimes an author makes a generalization and uses a clue word such as *all, many,* or *in general* to signal it.

General Statement—Clue word?

Detail	Detail	Detail

Strategy: Predict

Active readers try to predict what will happen next. When you read a generalization, be on the lookout for similar details that fit it. You can also use a generalization to predict other details that fit it.

Write to Read

1. Read *CP*. Using a graphic organizer like the one above, write the generalization that the author makes about cerebral palsy.

2. Write a generalization of your own about people you know. Give three details that support your generalization.

412

Strategic Intervention

Generalize Remind students that generalizations are broad statements that often include clue words such as *in general, many,* or *all.* Ask students to identify other words that may signal generalizations. *(always, never, most)* Reread the sentence, *Many students in our school have handicaps.* Then have students identify the clue word *(many)* that helps them know the statement is a generalization.

ELL

Access Content

Beginning/Intermediate For a Picture It! lesson on generalize, see ELL Teaching Guide, pp. 113–114.

Advanced Before students read "CP," have them read the first sentence in the third paragraph. Ask them to identify the key word that signals that the author is making a generalization. Then ask them to look for the facts that support the generalization.

CP

You might see a person in a wheelchair and think, "That person must have hurt his legs." But that is not always the case. He may have cerebral palsy (CP).

CP is a disorder that happens when the brain is damaged before or during birth. It might also happen when a child is very young. This brain damage leads to problems with moving, and sometimes with speaking, seeing, hearing, or learning.

1 **Skill** Look for clue words in this next paragraph that signal the author is making a generalization.

In general, people with CP do not have full control of their muscles. In some cases, muscles may move when the person does not want them to. Some people with CP have quick, jerky body movements. Others have smaller, slower movements of the face, neck, arms, and legs. In some cases, muscles may not move at all. That's why some people with CP must use wheelchairs.

2 **Strategy** What kinds of details do you predict you will read about next?

3 **Strategy** What other problems can you predict for people without full control of their muscles?

We don't have a cure for cerebral palsy. However, there are treatments that can help. Many children and adults with this disorder live full, complete, and happy lives.

4 **Skill** In the final paragraph, what generalization does the author make about people with CP?

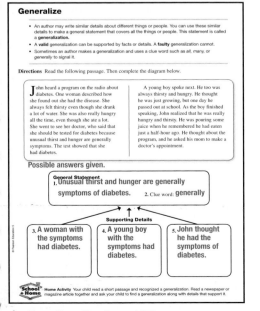

413

Available as **Skill Transparency** 17

▲ **Practice Book** p. 163

TEACH

1 **SKILL** Use paragraph 3 to model how to use clue words to identify a generalization.

Think Aloud **MODEL** The third paragraph begins with the words "In general." I know that these words often signal a generalization. As I keep reading, I find that the words *in general* precede a broad statement that applies to many people: "People with CP do not have full control of their muscles." This is a generalization.

2 **STRATEGY** Use a generalization to predict.

Think Aloud **MODEL** Since the first sentence in the paragraph expresses a generalization about the muscles of people with CP, I predict that the author will provide details to support the generalization. I think the following sentences will tell how CP affects a person's muscles.

PRACTICE AND ASSESS

3 **STRATEGY** Answers will vary but may include issues related to learning or sports.

4 **SKILL** Generalization: Many children and adults with CP live full, complete, and happy lives.

WRITE Have students complete steps 1 and 2 of the Write to Read activity. You might consider using this as a whole-class activity.

Monitor Progress	
🎯 Generalize	
If... students are unable to complete **Write to Read** on p. 412,	**then...** use Practice Book p. 163 to provide additional practice.

Tech Files
ONLINE

Students can use a student-friendly search engine and the key words *nervous system disorders* or *muscular diseases* to look for more information about other diseases that affect muscle coordination and use. Be sure to follow classroom guidelines for Internet use.

Build Background Use ELL Poster 17 to build background and vocabulary for the lesson concept of overcoming physical limitations.

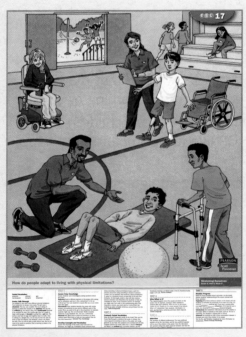

▲ **ELL Poster** 17

Build Background

ACTIVATE PRIOR KNOWLEDGE

BEGIN A KWL CHART about cerebral palsy.

- Give students two to three minutes to write as many things as they know about cerebral palsy. Prompt them with categories from the Concept Web from p. 412l. Record what students know in the first column of the KWL chart.

- Give students two minutes to write three questions they would like to ask about cerebral palsy. Record questions in the second column of the KWL chart. Add a question of your own.

- Tell students that, as they read, they should look for the answers to their questions and note any new information to add to the chart.

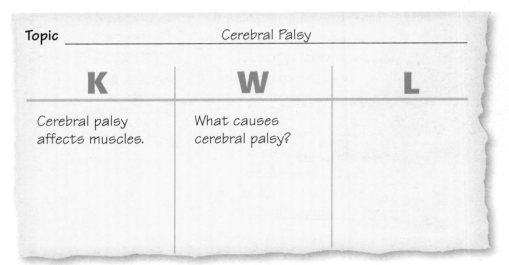

Topic	Cerebral Palsy	
K	**W**	**L**
Cerebral palsy affects muscles.	What causes cerebral palsy?	

▲ **Graphic Organizer** 4

BACKGROUND BUILDING AUDIO This week's audio explores the challenges of cerebral palsy. After students listen, discuss what they found most surprising about the disease.

Background Building Audio

Introduce Vocabulary

DEFINITION CARDS

Write each of the Words to Know on an index card. On separate cards, write the definition of each word. Read each word aloud to the students and then read the definitions. Have students think about where they may have seen or heard some of these words. ***Activate Prior Knowledge***

Distribute the definition and word cards to the students. Have one student hold up and read a definition card. The student with the correct word match stands up and says the word. Repeat with reading the word first and then the matching definition.

Point out that one of this week's words is a homophone *(gait)* and another is a multiple-meaning word *(stroke)*. Make students aware that they may learn new definitions for these words. (For additional practice with multiple meaning words, see p. 435c.) ***Homophones • Multiple-Meaning Words***

Also, have students use these steps for reading multisyllabic words. (See the Multisyllabic Word Routine on p. DI·1.)

1. **Look for Meaningful Word Parts** (base words, endings, prefixes, suffixes, roots) Think about the meaning of each part. Use the parts to read the word. Model: I see the suffix *-ist* at the end of *therapist*. The word *therapist* comes from the root word *therapy* which means "treatment of diseases, injuries, or disorders," and *-ist* means "an expert in a particular field." Therefore, *therapist* means "a person who specializes in the treatment of diseases, injuries, or disorders."

2. **Chunk Words with No Recognizable Parts** Say each chunk slowly. Then say the chunks fast to make a word. Model: *ar, ti, fi, cial—artificial.*

Lesson Vocabulary

WORDS TO KNOW

T abdomen the part of the body containing the stomach, intestines, and other important organs

T artificial made by human skill or labor; not natural

T gait a manner of walking or running

T handicapped having a physical or mental disability

T therapist a person who specializes in treatment of diseases, injuries, or disorders

T wheelchair a chair on wheels, used by people who are sick or who are unable to walk

MORE WORDS TO KNOW

blender an electric kitchen appliance for grinding, mixing, or beating

cerebral palsy paralysis caused by damage to the brain before or at birth

stroke a sudden attack of illness, especially one caused by a blood clot or bleeding in the brain

T = Tested Word

Vocabulary

Directions Choose the word from the box that best matches each definition. Write the word on the line.

artificial — 1. made by human skill or labor; not natural

gait — 2. manner of walking or running

handicapped — 3. having a physical or mental disability

abdomen — 4. the part of the body containing the stomach, the intestines, and other important organs

therapist — 5. person who specializes in the treatment of diseases, or injuries

Check the Words You Know
___abdomen
___artificial
___gait
___handicapped
___therapist
___wheelchair

Directions Complete each sentence with the correct word from the box. Write the word on the line shown to the left.

wheelchair — 6. Malik used a _____ because the muscles in his legs were not strong.

therapist — 7. Every week, he went to an appointment with his physical _____, who helped him do exercises to strengthen his legs.

gait — 8. He could walk on his own, but his _____ was still awkward.

abdomen — 9. They also worked on the muscles in his _____ and chest so he would not get a sore back.

handicapped — 10. Malik never thought of himself as _____ because he worked so hard and could tell he was making progress.

Write a Newspaper Article
On a separate sheet of paper, write a newspaper article about a person who has a disability or chronic illness. Write about the difficulties this person deals with every day. Use as many vocabulary words as you can.
Newspaper articles should include words from the vocabulary list and details about a disability or chronic illness.

Home Activity Your child identified and used vocabulary words from *Stretching Ourselves*. Read a story or nonfiction article with your child about someone who has a disability or a chronic illness. Discuss any unfamiliar terms that appear in the article.

▲ **Practice Book** p. 164

Vocabulary Strategy

INTRODUCE

Discuss the strategy for context clues using the steps on p. 414 .

TEACH

- Have students read "Physical Therapists," paying attention to how vocabulary is used.
- Model using context clues to determine the meaning of *handicapped*.

 Think Aloud **MODEL** As I read the first paragraph, it talks about therapists who work with people who are hurt or have trouble moving. *Handicapped* must mean "having a physical disability."

Words to Know

therapist

handicapped

gait

artificial

wheelchair

abdomen

Remember

Try the strategy. Then, if you need more help, use your glossary or dictionary.

Vocabulary Strategy
for Unfamiliar Words

Context Clues When you find a word you do not know in a text, look for clues to its meaning. The situation the author is describing or the words of a character may suggest the unknown word's meaning.

1. Read the words around the unknown word. Do they suggest a meaning for this word?

2. If not, then read the sentences around the word. Look for examples, comparisons, or contrasts that suggest the meaning of the word.

3. Think of a meaning and test it. Does this meaning make sense?

4. If you cannot find the meaning quickly, look it up in a dictionary or talk with a friend about it.

As you read "Physical Therapists," look for clues to the meaning of each unknown word in the words and sentences around it.

414

DAY 2 Grouping Options

Reading
Whole Group Discuss the Question of the Day. Then use pp. 414–417.

Group Time Differentiated Instruction
Read *Stretching Ourselves.* See pp. 412f–412g for the small group lesson plan.

Whole Group Use p. 435a.

Language Arts
Use pp. 435e–435k.

Strategic Intervention

 Context Clues Have students work with partners to determine the meaning of *gait* by following the steps on p. 414.

ELL

Access Content Use ELL Poster 17 to preteach vocabulary. Choose from the following to meet language proficiency levels.

Beginning Point out clues on p. 415, paragraph 3, that show what a *therapist* does.

Intermediate Before reading, have students choose a vocabulary word and use it to complete a vocabulary frame. After reading, have students verify the definition.

Advanced Teach the lesson on pp. 414–415. Have students determine whether any of the tested words have cognates in their home languages.

Resources for home-language words may include parents, bilingual staff members, bilingual dictionaries, or online translation sources.

Physical Therapists

The work of a physical therapist can be very rewarding. This person works with people who are hurt or have problems moving because of a physical condition. Sports players with hurt muscles or bones may visit a therapist. People who suffer from diseases that make it hard to move also see a therapist regularly. They may be handicapped by sickness, but exercise and training can help them move more easily.

A person who has had a broken leg needs to use it as it heals. The body learns how to move again after resting a long time. The muscles have become shorter. They need to be stretched and trained. This can mean the difference between walking with a limp or with a smooth gait.

Watch a therapist at work. You may see him or her helping a person with an artificial leg learn how to walk again. It is a very different job from walking on two whole legs. The therapist may be massaging and stretching the muscles of someone who must use a wheelchair. A person who cannot move much needs to work the muscles of arms, legs, abdomen, and back. Otherwise, they become very weak and small. Everyone wants to be able to move well!

Words to Write

Write a journal entry telling what you think it would be like to have a disorder such as cerebral palsy. Use as many words from the Words to Know list as you can.

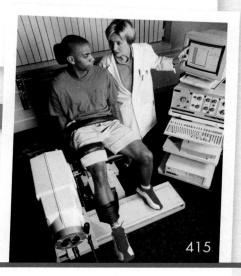

415

PRACTICE AND ASSESS

- Have students determine the meanings of the remaining words and explain the context clues they used.
- Point out that context clues aren't always available. Students may have to use the glossary or a dictionary to find the exact meaning of some words.
- If you made definition cards on p. 414, have students review the word meanings.
- Have students complete Practice Book p. 165.

WRITE Writing should include lesson vocabulary words that describe what it is like to have a disability.

Monitor Progress

Context Clues

If... students need more practice with the lesson vocabulary,	**then...** use Tested Vocabulary Cards.

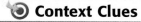

Vocabulary · Context Clues

- When you find a word you do not know in a text, look for clues to its meaning.
- You can find **context clues** among the words around the unfamiliar word.

Directions Read the following passage about disabilities. Then answer the questions below.

Anita's friend Jessica asked her a hard question. "Anita, how come some people at school say you are handicapped? You walk like everyone else and don't have to use a wheelchair."

Anita thought carefully about how she would answer. "My disability is hard for people to see. I am autistic. It is hard for me to understand what other people are telling me or if they are happy or sad. Sometimes my voice sounds artificial like a robot's."

Jessica said, "You do have your ways, but you and I talk just fine."

"You are used to me," said Anita. "I also go to a speech therapist every week to help me learn how to talk with other people."

Possible answers given.

1. What does *wheelchair* mean? What context clues helped you to determine the meaning?
   A *wheelchair* is used by people who can't walk. Because Anita can walk, she doesn't have to use a wheelchair.

2. What does *disability* mean? What context clues helped you to determine the meaning?
   a handicap; Jessica asks why people think Anita is handicapped.

3. What does *artificial* mean? What clues help you to determine the meaning?
   not natural; Anita says her voice is like a robot's.

4. How would using context clues help you determine the meaning of *speech therapist*?
   A *speech therapist* helps people learn how to speak. Anita says the speech therapist helps her learn to talk.

5. What context clues helped you understand what *autistic* means?
   disability; hard to understand other people; voice sounds artificial

School + Home **Home Activity** Your child identified and used context clues to understand new words of a passage. Have a discussion with your child in which you use context clues to give clues to the meaning of new words.

▲ **Practice Book** p. 165

Prereading Strategies

GENRE STUDY

Expository Nonfiction

Stretching Ourselves is expository nonfiction. Explain that expository nonfiction contains factual materials and communicates information about the real world.

PREVIEW AND PREDICT

Have students preview the selection title and illustration and identify the topic of this selection. Students should use lesson vocabulary words as they talk about what they expect to learn.

Strategy Response Log

Ask Questions Have students ask two questions about the ways children with cerebral palsy adapt to their condition. Students will answer their questions in the Strategy Response Log activity on p. 423.

416

Genre

Expository nonfiction gives information about the real world. What special kind of information is the author giving you here?

ELL

Access Content Use the pictures and quotations to help students preview the selection. Point to each child and provide students with language to talk about his or her physical limitations.

Consider having students read the selection summary in English or in students' home languages. See the Multilingual Summaries in the ELL Teaching Guide, pp. 117–119.

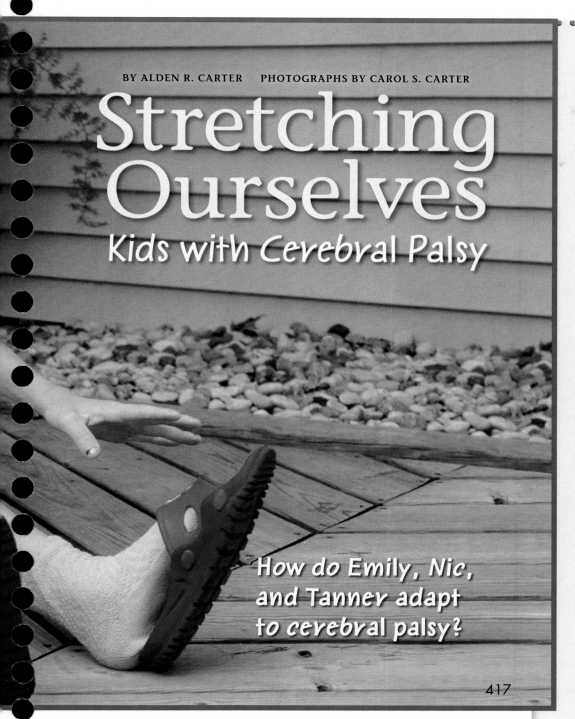

BY ALDEN R. CARTER   PHOTOGRAPHS BY CAROL S. CARTER

Stretching Ourselves
Kids with Cerebral Palsy

How do Emily, Nic, and Tanner adapt to cerebral palsy?

417

SET PURPOSE

Read the first page of the selection aloud to students. Have them consider their preview discussion and tell what they hope to find out as they read.

Remind students to look for details to make generalizations as they read.

STRATEGY RECALL

Students have now used these before-reading strategies:

- preview the selection to be aware of its genre, features, and possible content;
- activate prior knowledge about that content and what to expect of that genre;
- make predictions;
- set a purpose for reading.

Remind students that, as they read, they should monitor their own comprehension. If they realize something does not make sense, they can regain their comprehension by using fix-up strategies they have learned, such as:

- use phonics and word structure to decode new words;
- use context clues or a dictionary to figure out meanings of new words;
- adjust their reading rate—slow down for difficult text, speed up for easy or familiar text, or skim and scan just for specific information;
- reread parts of the text;
- read on (continue to read for clarification);
- use text features such as headings, subheadings, charts, illustrations, and so on as visual aids to comprehension;
- make a graphic organizer or a semantic organizer to aid comprehension;
- use reference sources, such as an encyclopedia, dictionary, thesaurus, or synonym finder;
- use another person, such as a teacher, a peer, a librarian, or an outside expert, as a resource.

After reading, students will use these strategies:

- summarize or retell the text;
- answer questions they or others pose;
- reflect to make new information become part of their prior knowledge.

AudioText

Guiding Comprehension

1 ⟳ Generalize • Inferential

Find the generalization about people with cerebral palsy on p. 418, paragraph 4. Is it valid? Why?

The generalization is that most people with cerebral palsy have tight muscles and tendons. It is a valid generalization because the rest of the information in the paragraph supports it.

Monitor Progress

⟳ Generalize

If... students are unable to recognize the generalization,	**then...** use the skill and strategy instruction on p. 419.

---

2 Cause and Effect • Literal

What caused Emily's cerebral palsy?

Her brain did not receive enough oxygen while she was in her mother's womb.

Tech Files
ONLINE

Students can learn more about cerebral palsy on the Internet by typing the keywords *cerebral palsy* into a student-friendly search engine. Be sure to follow classroom rules for Internet use.

Bedtime always comes too soon at Emily's house. After snack and medicine, her dad helps her stretch her arms, hands, and legs.

"Sassafras!" she growls. "Rhubarb!"

"You okay, Emmers?" he asks.

"Yep," Emily says, because even if stretching hurts, it helps her to move better.

1 Emily has cerebral palsy (CP). Most people with CP have tight muscles and tendons. Tendons are the thin, stretchy cords that connect muscles to bones. Our bodies move when muscles contract and relax, pulling or releasing tendons that move the bones of our arms, legs, hands, or spines. Stretching helps the muscles and tendons to work more freely.

2 Emily has CP because her brain did not receive enough oxygen while she was in her mother's womb. The brain

418

⟲ SKILLS ⟷ STRATEGIES IN CONTEXT

Generalize

TEACH

- Tell students that generalizations are broad statements that apply to many examples. Some generalizations use clue words such as *always, most, all* or *usually.*

- Generalizations are valid if they can be supported by the text.

- Model recognizing and determining the validity of generalizations on p. 418.

Think Aloud **MODEL** I read the sentence "Most people with CP have tight muscles and tendons" and noticed the word *most.* This is a clue that the sentence probably is a generalization. The generalization is valid because I can find details to support it in the rest of the paragraph.

PRACTICE AND ASSESS

Ask if the sentence "Bedtime always comes too soon at Emily's house" states a generalization and if so, why. *(Yes, it is a generalization. "Always" is a clue word and the sentence is a broad statement.)*

Time for SOCIAL STUDIES

Polio

Polio is another illness that affects people's muscles and their ability to walk. One very famous American who was struck with polio was Franklin Delano Roosevelt, or FDR, the 32nd President of the United States. FDR was struck with poliomyelitis in the summer of 1921. He suffered great pain and became partially paralyzed, forcing him to use a wheelchair. With hard work, Roosevelt was able to stand and walk using leg braces. Roosevelt went on to be elected president in 1932, and was re-elected three times.

EXTEND SKILLS

Photo Essay

Point out that this selection is a photo essay. Photo essays are a collection of photographs and text around a specific topic that are written to entertain or inform. The photos are meant to make the information more real. In this case, the photo essay was written to inform readers about living with cerebral palsy.

Guiding Comprehension

3 **Graphic Sources • Inferential**

Question the Author **Why do you think the author chose to use photographs to illustrate this selection?**

Possible response: He wanted to make the subject more real and understandable.

Monitor Progress

REVIEW **Graphic Sources**

If... students have difficulty interpreting graphic resources,	**then...** use the skill and strategy instruction on p. 421.

---

4 **Draw Conclusions • Critical**

Text To Self **Does Emily remind you of someone you know or have heard of who lives with a disability? Explain.**

Possible response: Yes, she reminds me of an aunt I have who is blind. She can read Braille and has a seeing-eye dog to help her get around.

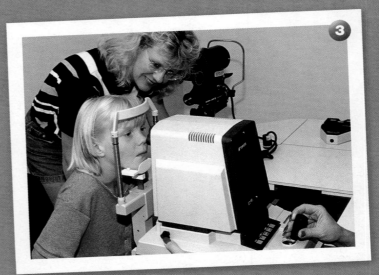

"I'm not 'sweetie,' I'm souvy," Emily says, but she has to grin.

420

ELL

Extend Language Write the word *affect* on the board. Tell students that *affect* means to make something happen. Write *effect* on the board. Explain that an *effect* is a result. Use each word in a sentence. Then challenge pairs of students to make a sentence with each word.

controls how we move, speak, see, smell, hear, and learn. People with CP can have trouble with any or all of these things. There is no cure for CP, and they must work hard to learn things that come easily to others. Emily practiced a whole summer with her mom and her brother Andrew, learning how to skate.

Because the muscles and tendons in her legs are tight, Emily's movements are stiff, and she walks slightly bent forward. Twice a week, Emily's mom takes her to see a physical therapist.

"I'm real bossy with my legs," she tells the therapist.

"That's good!" Ms. Park says. "But this morning, just relax. We're going to do a gait test to see how your legs are working with each other. Then we'll know the best exercises for you."

Emily's had operations on the muscles of her feet, bladder, and eyes. They've helped, but she's impatient. "Radishes!" she mutters, when she has to have another test to see how well her eyes are working together.

Emily's mom says, "Try again, sweetie."

"I'm not 'sweetie,' I'm *soury*," Emily says, but she has to grin.

Having CP is tough. Emily used to get upset a lot. But she practices staying calm by mothering her dolls and caring for her dogs. Bole and Zuko don't always do what she wants, but she's learned to talk firmly instead of yelling.

4

Cerebral palsy can affect how much and how fast a person can learn. Tasks that are simple for most people can be big challenges for people with CP. At school, Emily attends a special class for kids who need extra help. Today Mrs. Bauer

421

Nervous System

TIME FOR Science

The human nervous system consists of the central nervous system (the brain and the spinal cord) and the nerves. The nervous system carries signals through the nerves to the spinal cord and on to the brain. The brain processes that information and sends messages to the muscles, which in turn respond and enable us to walk, talk, feel, taste, smell, and so on. Cerebral palsy and multiple sclerosis are two conditions that affect the nervous system's ability to function properly.

Graphic Sources REVIEW

TEACH

- Explain to students that photographs are one form of graphic sources, but others include charts, graphs, maps, or other illustrations.
- Tell students that authors use graphic sources to enhance the text.
- Model why the author chose photographs for graphic sources in this selection.

Think Aloud **MODEL** When I look at the photographs in this selection I see pictures of real people, like Emily, who live with cerebral palsy. I think the author used photographs on purpose to make cerebral palsy seem more real.

PRACTICE AND ASSESS

- Have students look at the bottom photograph on p. 420 and tell what it says about Emily. *(It shows that even though she has a disability, she is just like other kids who like to play with their dogs.)*
- To assess, use Practice Book 166.

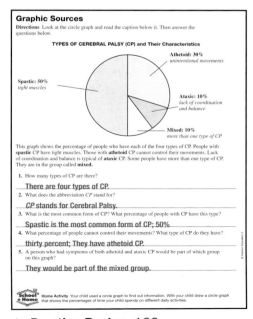

▲ **Practice Book** p. 166

Stretching Ourselves **421**

Guiding Comprehension

5 **Figurative Language • Inferential**

What does Emily mean when she says she is "like flowers and a rainbow"?

She is covered with all different colors of paint.

6 **Compare and Contrast • Inferential**

How does Nic's case of CP compare to Emily's?

Nic has a more severe case of CP—he spends most of his time in a wheelchair and can only speak a few words. Emily has greater mobility and can speak well.

7 **Draw Conclusions • Inferential**

How would you describe Nic?

Possible answers: brave, hard-working, positive, funny.

---

is teaching them how to take better care of their hair, teeth, and skin. Emily grumbles about a snarl in Lizzy's hair.

"Celery!" Lizzy yelps.

"No vegetables!" Mrs. Bauer says. "Just keep at it. And, Emily be gentle."

Emily also gets extra help for reading and math and then goes to regular classes for art, social studies, and music. She's especially good at art, and never minds getting paint all over **5** herself. "I'm like flowers and a rainbow!" she says.

Emily and Nic are friends at Grant School. Nic has CP because his brain was badly damaged during birth. He spends **6** most of his time in a wheelchair and can speak only a few words. But no one likes playing ball, making jokes, or teasing the teachers more than Nic.

Every day Nic practices simple words with Ms. Larson, a speech therapist. She also helps him learn the buttons on his computer, which has an artificial voice. Nic's favorite button is "Give me a big bear hug!"

A lot of the other kids think his computer is pretty cool. At recess, Nic shows them how to use it. He makes it say "Let's play ball" and "Let's swing."

At the end of the school day, Nic rides the handicapped bus home. When Gale, his bus driver, starts the elevator, Nic likes **7** to make crashing sounds. "Oh, my gosh, you're breaking the elevator again!" Gale yells.

While his mom gets supper ready, Nic reads books with his cousin Shylo. Turning the pages is pretty good practice for his hands. He particularly likes books about bulldozers, farms, and football.

422

Access Content Nic likes books about bulldozers. Tell students that a *bulldozer* is a powerful tractor used for clearing land by moving earth and rocks. Ask students if they have ever seen a bulldozer at a construction site.

RESEARCH/STUDY SKILLS
Telephone Directory

TEACH

Ask students where they can look to find the phone number for a classmate or for a local pet store. Lead them to suggest using telephone directories. Show a print telephone directory to point out the following features, but emphasize that all of the same information is available in online directories.

- A **telephone directory** lists names, phone numbers, and addresses for people and businesses.

- The **white pages** list phone numbers for people and businesses in alphabetical order. When searching online you need to provide a city and state for the search.

- The **yellow pages** list phone numbers and ads for businesses. Entries are grouped alphabetically by type of business. When searching online you need to provide a city and state for the search.

Have students work in groups to use computers to search an online telephone directory. If computers are not available, have students look at a sample picture of an online directory search page. Then, discuss these questions.

1. **When searching an online directory, what information do you need to find someone's telephone number?** *(A person's last name. For better results, last name, first name, city, and state.)*

2. **Will you get good search results if you only know someone's first name and the city where he or she lives? Explain.** *(No; there could be many people in the city with the same first name.)*

ASSESS

As students become familiar with online directories, be sure they can identify the information necessary for a successful search and are able to distinguish between searching the white pages and searching the yellow pages. If computers are available, you may provide students with time to conduct at least one search.

For more practice or to assess students, use Practice Book pp. 169–170.

▲ **Practice Book** p. 169

▲ **Practice Book** p. 170

Assessment Checkpoints *for the Week*

Selection Assessment

Use pp. 65–68 of Selection Tests to check:

 Selection Understanding

 Comprehension Skill *Generalize*

 Selection Vocabulary
abdomen
artificial
gait
handicapped
therapist
wheelchair

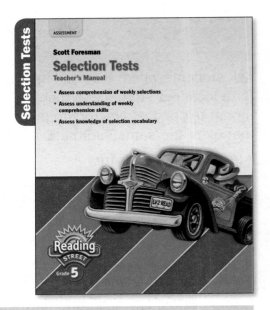

ASSESSMENT

Scott Foresman
Selection Tests
Teacher's Manual
• Assess comprehension of weekly selections
• Assess understanding of weekly comprehension skills
• Assess knowledge of selection vocabulary

Selection Tests

Reading STREET Grade 5

Leveled Assessment

On-Level
Strategic Intervention
Advanced

Use pp. 97–102 of Fresh Reads for Differentiated Test Practice to check:

 Comprehension Skill *Generalize*

 REVIEW Comprehension Skill
Graphic Sources

 Fluency *Words Correct Per Minute*

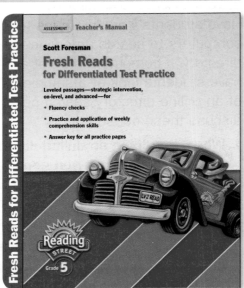

ASSESSMENT Teacher's Manual

Scott Foresman
Fresh Reads
for Differentiated Test Practice
Leveled passages—strategic intervention, on-level, and advanced—for
• Fluency checks
• Practice and application of weekly comprehension skills
• Answer key for all practice pages

Fresh Reads for Differentiated Test Practice

Reading STREET Grade 5

Managing Assessment

Use Assessment Handbook for:

 Observation Checklists

 Record-Keeping Forms

 Portfolio Assessment

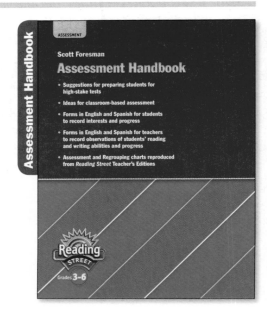

ASSESSMENT

Scott Foresman
Assessment Handbook
• Suggestions for preparing students for high-stake tests
• Ideas for classroom-based assessment
• Forms in English and Spanish for students to record interests and progress
• Forms in English and Spanish for teachers to record observations of students' reading and writing abilities and progress
• Assessment and Regrouping charts reproduced from *Reading Street Teacher's Editions*

Assessment Handbook

Reading STREET Grades 3–6

Illinois

Planning Guide for Performance Descriptors

Exploding Ants

Reading Street Teacher's Edition pages	Grade 5 English Language Arts Performance Descriptors
Oral Language **Speaking/Listening** Build Concept Vocabulary: 436l, 447, 451, 457c Read Aloud: 436m	**1B.Stage E.10.** Read age-appropriate material aloud with fluency and accuracy. **4B.Stage E.10.** Contribute meaningfully to small and large group discussions by following accepted guidelines for verbal interaction.
Word Work Homophones: 457i–457j	**1A.Stage E.1.** Use a combination of word analysis and vocabulary strategies (e.g., word patterns, structural analyses) within context to identify unknown words.
Reading **Comprehension** Graphic Sources: 436–437, 440–451, 454–457, 457b Monitor and Fix Up: 436–437, 440–451, 454–457 **Vocabulary** Lesson Vocabulary: 438b, 447, 451, 454 Context Clues: 438–439, 447, 457c **Fluency** Model Tempo and Rate: 436l–436m, 457a **Self-Selected Reading:** LR19–27, TR16–17 **Literature** Genre—Expository Nonfiction: 440 Reader Response: 452	**1A.Stage E.1.** Use a combination of word analysis and vocabulary strategies (e.g., word patterns, structural analyses) within context to identify unknown words. **1B.Stage E.7.** Identify structure (e.g., description, compare, cause/effect, sequence) of nonfiction text to improve comprehension. **1B.Stage E.9.** Apply self-monitoring and self-correcting strategies continuously to clarify understanding during reading. **1B.Stage E.10.** Read age-appropriate material aloud with fluency and accuracy. **1C.Stage E.6.** Select reading strategies for text appropriate to the reader's purpose. **2A.Stage E.7.** Use comprehension strategies (e.g., association, categorization, graphic organizers) to enhance understanding.
Language Arts **Writing** Tell a Story About an Animal: 457g–457h **Six-Trait Writing** Word Choice: 453, 457g–457h **Grammar, Usage, and Mechanics** Possessive Pronouns: 457e–457f **Research/Study** Magazine/Periodical: 457l **Technology** New Literacies: 457k	**1A.Stage E.8.** Use additional resources as applicable to clarify meanings of material. **3C.Stage E.3.** Write creatively for a specified purpose and audience. **4B.Stage E.5.** Use appropriate grammar, word choice, and pacing. **5A.Stage E.3.** Gather information based on a hypothesis: identify and use (with limited support) a variety of sources; recognize criteria for determining credible sources; determine appropriate resources.
Unit Skills **Writing** Story: WA2–9 **Poetry:** 504–507 **Project/Wrap-Up:** 508–509	**3A.Stage E.1.** Write paragraphs that include a variety of sentence types. **3C.Stage E.3.** Write creatively for a specified purpose and audience.

This Week's Leveled Readers

Below-Level

2A.Stage E.7. Use comprehension strategies (e.g., association, categorization, graphic organizers) to enhance understanding.

2B.Stage E.6. Read a wide range of nonfiction (e.g., books, newspapers, magazines, textbooks, visual media).

Nonfiction

On-Level

2A.Stage E.7. Use comprehension strategies (e.g., association, categorization, graphic organizers) to enhance understanding.

2A.Stage E.8. Identify ways in which fiction and nonfiction works are organized differently.

Nonfiction

Advanced

2A.Stage E.7. Use comprehension strategies (e.g., association, categorization, graphic organizers) to enhance understanding.

2B.Stage E.1. Create an extension to a literary text (e.g., alternate ending, additional dialog for a character).

Nonfiction

Content-Area Illinois Performance Descriptors in This Lesson

Science

11A.Stage E.5. Analyze data to produce reasonable explanations: comparing and summarizing data from multiple trials; interpreting trends; evaluating conflicting data; determining sources of error.

12B.Stage E.1. Apply scientific inquiries or technological designs to categorize organisms (including humans) by their energy relationships in their environments.

12B.Stage E.2. Apply scientific inquiries or technological designs to explain competitive, adaptive and survival potential of species in different local or global ecosystems.

Social Studies

16A.Stage E.2. Describe trends during a time period using political, economic, environmental, and social data from appropriate graphs or charts.

16E.Stage E.12. Describe how various people around the globe used animals to cultivate crops in early world history.

Math

6A.Stage E.2. Show equivalent representations of a number by changing from one form to another form (e.g., standard form to expanded form, fraction to decimal, decimal to percent, improper fraction to mixed number).

Illinois!

NATIVE AMERICANS OF ILLINOIS
The Illiniwek Confederacy

The Illiniwek Confederacy was originally made up of about twelve different groups of Native Americans. The Illini controlled much of what is now Illinois until the mid-1600s, when other Native American groups moved in. The Illini were known for their body tattoos. Warriors often shaved their heads except for a scalp lock and areas around their ears.

Students can . . .
Research the Illiniwek Confederacy. Have students make a poster showing the different groups that formed the confederation.

A SPECIAL ILLINOIS PLACE
Galesburg

Galesburg is the county seat of Knox County, in west-central Illinois. It was settled in 1836. The following year, the Knox Manual Labor College opened. The school's name was shortened to Knox College in 1857. The college's campus was the site of the fifth Lincoln-Douglas debate in 1858. Poet Carl Sandburg was born and raised in Galesburg. His childhood home is now a historic site.

Students can . . .
Write a poem about their community. Encourage students to share or read the poems with their classmates.

ILLINOIS FUN FACTS
Did You Know?

- Belleville is home to the second oldest U.S. symphony orchestra, which was formed in the 1860s.

- Workers dug the six-foot-deep, ninety-six-mile-long Illinois and Michigan Canal using only picks and shovels.

- With only 175 soldiers under his command, George Rogers Clark captured Kaskaskia and Cahokia from the British during the American Revolution.

Students can . . .
Find out the names of some communities in the Illinois region during the American Revolution. Have students use an outline map of Illinois to mark the locations of communities that still exist today, including Kaskaskia and Cahokia.

Unit 4
Adapting

CONCEPT QUESTION
How do people and animals adapt to different situations?

Week 1
How do people adapt to difficult situations?

Week 2
How do people adapt to living with physical limitations?

Week 3
How do animals adapt to survive?

Week 4
How do people adapt to a new school?

Week 5
Why do people try to change themselves?

EXPAND THE CONCEPT
How do animals adapt to survive?

CONNECT THE CONCEPT

▶ **Build Background**
African black mambas, constrictors, reptiles

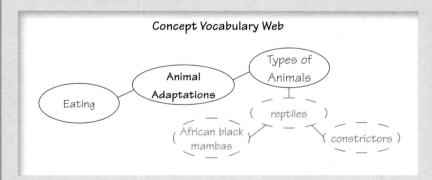

Concept Vocabulary Web

▶ **Science Content**
Biomes, Human Adaptations, Animal Experiments

▶ **Writing**
Story About an Animal

▶ **Internet Inquiry**
Animal Adaptations

Preview Your Week

How do animals adapt to survive?

exploding ants

by Joanne Settel, Ph.D.

Amazing **Facts** About How Animals Adapt

How do insects adapt to find food, shelter, and safety?

Genre **Expository nonfiction** explains what certain things are and how they came to be or behave. As you read, notice how the author explains insect behavior.

440

Student Edition pages 440–451

Audio CD

Genre Expository Nonfiction
Vocabulary Strategy Context Clues
Comprehension Skill Graphic Sources
Comprehension Strategy Monitor and Fix Up

Paired Selection

Reading Across Texts
Make a List About a Creature

Genre
Experiment

Text Features
Purpose
Materials
Step-by-Step Instructions

Science in Reading

Experiment
Genre
- Experiments tell how to perform a trial or test to find out about something.
- Most experiments deal with some kind of science.

Text Features
- The author begins by stating the purpose of the experiment and the materials needed to perform it. Then come step-by-step instructions, from start to finish.
- Scan the steps to get an idea of what the experiment is about.

Link to Science
Experiments are at the heart of science. Scientists use them to discover and test new ideas. Perform the experiment yourself and share your results with the class.

THE CREATURE FROM THE
Adapting Lagoon
from www.nasa.gov

This science experiment is from the National Aeronautics and Space Administration (NASA). It's intended for fifth-grade students in a science class, but anyone can do it. All you need is thought and imagination.

PURPOSE
To design an animal with adaptations to a specific environment

MATERIALS

pencil, colored pencils, or markers

construction or drawing paper

science journal

PROCEDURE
1. Read over the criteria and background information.
2. Brainstorm possible creature designs that would meet the criteria listed. Check off the criteria that can be incorporated into the design.
3. Select the design that best meets the criteria.
4. Illustrate your creature in the science journal and describe each appendage and how it is used.

Graphic Sources How do the illustrations help you imagine the experiment?

454

Student Edition pages 454–457

Audio CD

Read It
ONLINE
PearsonSuccessNet.com
- Student Edition
- Leveled Readers

TIME FOR Science

Integrate Science Standards
- **Animals**
- **Environments/Biomes**
- **Adaptations**

Leveled Readers

⊙ **Skill** Graphic Sources

⊙ **Strategy** Monitor and Fix Up

Lesson Vocabulary

Below-Level

On-Level

Advanced

ELL Reader
- Concept Vocabulary
- Text Support
- Language Enrichment

✔ **Read**

Exploding Ants,
pp. 440–451

"The Creature from the Adapting Lagoon,"
pp. 454–457

Leveled Readers

Below-Level — **On-Level** — **Advanced**

- Support Concepts • Develop Concepts • Extend Concepts

ELL Reader

✔ **Build Concept Vocabulary**
Animal Adaptations,
pp. 436l–436m

✔ **Teach Science Concepts**
Biomes, p. 445
Human Adaptations, p. 449
Animal Experiments, p. 455

✔ **Explore Science Center**
Explore Animals, p. 436k

Weekly Plan

READING

45–90 minutes

TARGET SKILLS OF THE WEEK

Comprehension Skill
Graphic Sources

Comprehension Strategy
Monitor and Fix Up

Vocabulary Strategy
Context Clues

DAY 1 — PAGES 436l–438b, 457a, 457e–457k

Oral Language

QUESTION OF THE WEEK *How do animals adapt to survive?*

Read Aloud: "Snake Scientist," 436m
Build Concepts, 436l

Comprehension/Vocabulary

Comprehension Skill/Strategy Lesson, 436–437
  Graphic Sources **T**
  Monitor and Fix Up
Build Background, 438a
Introduce Lesson Vocabulary, 438b
critical, enables, mucus, scarce, specialize, sterile **T**

Read Leveled Readers

Grouping Options 436f–436g

Fluency

Model Tempo and Rate, 436l–436m, 457a

DAY 2 — PAGES 438–447, 457a, 457e–457k

Oral Language

QUESTION OF THE DAY *What animal ways of eating and finding shelter seem especially gross?*

Comprehension/Vocabulary

Vocabulary Strategy Lesson, 438–439
  Context Clues **T**

Read *Exploding Ants*, 440–447

Grouping Options 436f–436g

  Graphic Sources **T**
  Context Clues
  REVIEW Author's Purpose **T**
  Develop Vocabulary

Fluency

Echo Reading, 457a

LANGUAGE ARTS

30–60 minutes

Trait of the Week

Word Choice

Grammar, 457e
Introduce Possessive Pronouns **T**

Writing Workshop, 457g
Introduce Telling a Story About an Animal
Model the Trait of the Week: Word Choice

Spelling, 457i
Pretest for Homophones

Internet Inquiry, 457k
Identify Questions

Grammar, 457e
Develop Possessive Pronouns **T**

Writing Workshop, 457g
Improve Writing with Mood

Spelling, 457i
Teach the Generalization

Internet Inquiry, 457k
Navigate/Search

DAILY WRITING ACTIVITIES

Day 1 Write to Read, 436

Day 2 Words to Write, 439
Strategy Response Log, 440, 447

DAILY SCIENCE CONNECTIONS

Day 1 Animal Adaptations Concept Web, 436l

Day 2 Time for Science: Biomes, 445
Revisit the Animal Adaptations Concept Web, 447

DAILY SUCCESS PREDICTORS

for Adequate Yearly Progress

Monitor Progress and Corrective Feedback

Vocabulary Check Vocabulary, *436l*

RESOURCES FOR THE WEEK

- Practice Book, *pp. 171–180*
- Word Study and Spelling Practice Book, *pp. 69–72*
- Grammar and Writing Practice Book, *pp. 69–72*

- Selection Test, *pp. 69–72*
- Fresh Reads for Differentiated Test Practice, *pp. 103–108*
- The Grammar and Writing Book, *pp. 152–157*

Grouping Options for Differentiated Instruction

Turn the page for the small group lesson plan.

DAY 3   PAGES 448–453, 457a, 457e–457k

Oral Language

QUESTION OF THE DAY *How does the ability of a snake to gulp down prey larger than itself help it survive?*

Comprehension/Vocabulary

Read *Exploding Ants*, 448–452

Grouping Options 436f–436g

- Graphic Sources **T**
- Monitor and Fix Up
- Develop Vocabulary

Reader Response

Selection Test

Fluency

Model Tempo and Rate, 457a

Grammar, 457f
Apply Possessive Pronouns in Writing **T**

Writing Workshop, 453, 457h
Write Now
Prewrite and Draft

Spelling, 457j
Connect Spelling to Writing

Internet Inquiry, 457k
Analyze Sources

Day 3   Strategy Response Log, 450
Look Back and Write, 452

Day 3   Time for Science: Human Adaptations, 449
Revisit the Animal Adaptations Concept Web, 451

DAY 4   PAGES 454–457a, 457e–457k

Oral Language

QUESTION OF THE DAY *What adaptations do you think humans would have to undergo if they lived like fish in an underwater environment?*

Comprehension/Vocabulary

Read "The Creature from the Adapting Lagoon," 454–457

Grouping Options 436f –436g

Experiment
Reading Across Texts
Content-Area Vocabulary

Fluency

Partner Reading, 457a

Grammar, 457f
Practice Possessive Pronouns for Standardized Tests **T**

Writing Workshop, 457h
Draft, Revise, and Publish

Spelling, 457j
Provide a Strategy

Internet Inquiry, 457k
Synthesize Information

Day 4   Writing Across Texts, 457

Day 4   Time for Science: Animal Experiments, 455

DAY 5   PAGES 457a–457l

Oral Language

QUESTION OF THE WEEK *To wrap up the week, revisit the Day 1 question.*

Build Concept Vocabulary, 457c

Fluency

Read Leveled Readers

Grouping Options 436f–436g

Assess Reading Rate, 457a

Comprehension/Vocabulary

- Reteach Graphic Sources, 457b **T**
Metaphor, 457b
- Review Context Clues, 457c **T**

Speaking and Listening, 457d
Description
Listen to Poetry

Grammar, 457f
Cumulative Review

Writing Workshop, 457h
Connect to Unit Writing

Spelling, 457j
Posttest for Homophones

Internet Inquiry, 457k
Communicate Results

Research/Study Skills, 457l
Magazine/Periodical

Day 5   Metaphor, 457b

Day 5   Revisit the Animal Adaptations Concept Web, 457c

KEY ◉ = Target Skill   **T** = Tested Skill

Comprehension   Check Retelling, *452*

Fluency   Check Fluency WCPM, *457a*

Vocabulary   Check Vocabulary, *457c*

SUCCESS PREDICTOR

Small Group Plan *for Differentiated Instruction*

Daily Plan
AT A GLANCE

Reading
Whole Group
- Oral Language
- Comprehension/Vocabulary

Group Time
Differentiated Instruction

Meet with small groups to provide:
- Skill Support
- Reading Support
- Fluency Practice

Read

This week's lessons for daily group time can be found behind the Differentiated Instruction (DI) tab on pp. DI·22–DI·31.

Whole Group
- Fluency

Language Arts
- Grammar
- Writing
- Spelling
- Research/Inquiry
- Speaking/Listening/Viewing

Use *My Sidewalks on Reading Street* for Tier III intensive reading intervention.

DAY 1

On-Level	Strategic Intervention	Advanced
Teacher-Led *Page DI·23*	**Teacher-Led** *Page DI·22*	**Teacher-Led** *Page DI·23*
• Develop Concept Vocabulary • **Read** On-Level Reader *Changing to Survive: Bird Adaptations*	• Reinforce Concepts • **Read** Below-Level Reader *Surviving the Weather: Animals in Their Environments*	• **Read** Advanced Reader *A Home for Humans in Outer Space: Is It Possible?* • Independent Extension Activity

(i) Independent Activities
While you meet with small groups, have the rest of the class...

- Visit the Reading/Library Center
- Listen to the Background Building Audio
- Finish Write to Read, p. 436
- Complete Practice Book pp. 173–174
- Visit Cross-Curricular Centers

DAY 2

On-Level	Strategic Intervention	Advanced
Teacher-Led *Pages 442–447*	**Teacher-Led** *Page DI·24*	**Teacher-Led** *Page DI·25*
• **Read** *Exploding Ants*	• Practice Lesson Vocabulary • Read Multisyllabic Words • **Read** or Listen to *Exploding Ants*	• Extend Vocabulary • **Read** *Exploding Ants*

(i) Independent Activities
While you meet with small groups, have the rest of the class...

- Visit the Reading/Library Center
- Listen to the AudioText for *Exploding Ants*
- Finish Words to Write, p. 439
- Complete Practice Book pp. 175–176
- Write in their Strategy Response Logs, pp. 440, 447
- Visit Cross-Curricular Centers
- Work on inquiry projects

DAY 3

On-Level	Strategic Intervention	Advanced
Teacher-Led *Pages 448–451*	**Teacher-Led** *Page DI·26*	**Teacher-Led** *Page DI·27*
• **Read** *Exploding Ants*	• Practice Graphic Sources and Monitor and Fix Up • **Read** or Listen to *Exploding Ants*	• Extend Graphic Sources and Monitor and Fix Up • **Read** *Exploding Ants*

(i) Independent Activities
While you meet with small groups, have the rest of the class...

- Visit the Reading/Library Center
- Listen to the AudioText for *Exploding Ants*
- Write in their Strategy Response Logs, p. 450
- Finish Look Back and Write, p. 452
- Complete Practice Book p. 177
- Visit Cross-Curricular Centers
- Work on inquiry projects

① Begin with whole class skill and strategy instruction.

② Meet with small groups to provide differentiated instruction.

③ Gather the whole class back together for fluency and language arts.

DAY 4

On-Level
Teacher-Led
Pages 454–457
- **Read** "The Creature from the Adapting Lagoon"

Strategic Intervention
Teacher-Led
Page DI · 28
- Practice Retelling
- **Read** or Listen to "The Creature from the Adapting Lagoon"

Advanced
Teacher-Led
Page DI · 29
- **Read** "The Creature from the Adapting Lagoon"
- Genre Study

ⓘ Independent Activities

While you meet with small groups, have the rest of the class...

- Visit the Reading/Library Center
- Listen to the AudioText for "The Creature from the Adapting Lagoon"
- Visit the Writing/Vocabulary Center
- Finish Writing Across Texts, p. 457
- Visit Cross-Curricular Centers
- Work on inquiry projects

DAY 5

On-Level
Teacher-Led
Page DI · 31
- **Reread** Leveled Reader *Changing to Survive: Bird Adaptations*
- Retell *Changing to Survive: Bird Adaptations*

Strategic Intervention
Teacher-Led
Page DI · 30
- **Reread** Leveled Reader *Surviving the Weather: Animals in Their Environments*
- Retell *Surviving the Weather: Animals in Their Environments*

Advanced
Teacher-Led
Page DI · 31
- **Reread** Leveled Reader *A Home for Humans in Outer Space: Is It Possible?*
- Share Extension Activity

ⓘ Independent Activities

While you meet with small groups, have the rest of the class...

- Visit the Reading/Library Center
- Complete Practice Book pp. 178–180
- Visit Cross-Curricular Centers
- Work on inquiry projects

 Grouping Place English language learners in the groups that correspond to their reading abilities in English.

Use the appropriate Leveled Reader or other text at students' instructional level.

TiP Send home the appropriate Multilingual Summary of the main selection on Day 1.

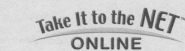 **Take It to the NET** ONLINE
PearsonSuccessNet.com

P. David Pearson
For ideas on teaching comprehension strategies, see the article "Developing Expertise in Reading Comprehension" by Scott Foresman author P. David Pearson and others.

TEACHER TALK

Fix-up strategies are strategies readers use when they realize they do not understand something. Adjusting reading rate, rereading, and using a reference source are a few fix-up strategies.

Looking Ahead
Be sure to schedule time for students to work on the unit inquiry project "Adaptations." This week students analyze information they have gathered about groups of people or animals who have adapted to different situations.

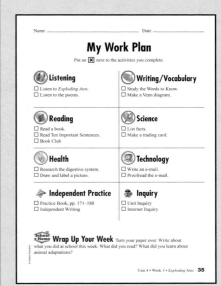

▲ **Group-Time Survival Guide** p. 35, Weekly Contract

Exploding Ants

Customize Your Plan *by Strand*

ORAL LANGUAGE

 *Science*

Concept Development

How do animals adapt to survive?

CONCEPT VOCABULARY

African black mambas   *constrictors*   *reptiles*

BUILD

❏ **Question of the Week** Introduce and discuss the question of the week. This week students will read a variety of texts and work on projects related to the concept *animal adaptations*. Post the question for students to refer to throughout the week. **DAY 1** *436d*

❏ **Read Aloud** Read aloud "Snake Scientist." Then begin a web to build concepts and concept vocabulary related to this week's lesson and the unit theme, Adapting. Introduce the concept words *African black mambas, constrictors,* and *reptiles* and have students place them on the web. Display the web for use throughout the week. **DAY 1** *436l–436m*

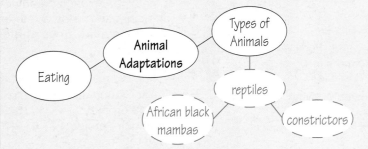

DEVELOP

❏ **Question of the Day** Use the prompts from the Weekly Plan to engage students in conversations related to this week's reading and the unit theme. **EVERY DAY** *436d–436e*

❏ **Concept Vocabulary Web** Revisit the Animal Adaptations Concept Web and encourage students to add concept words from their reading and life experiences. **DAY 2** *447,* **DAY 3** *451*

CONNECT

❏ **Looking Back/Moving Forward** Revisit the Animal Adaptations Concept Web and discuss how it relates to this week's lesson and the unit theme. Then make connections to next week's lesson. **DAY 5** *457c*

CHECK

❏ **Concept Vocabulary Web** Use the Animal Adaptions Concept Web to check students' understanding of the concept vocabulary words *African black mambas, constrictors,* and *reptiles.* **DAY 1** *436l,* **DAY 5** *457c*

VOCABULARY

◉ STRATEGY CONTEXT CLUES
When you are reading, you may come across a difficult or unfamiliar word. Sometimes an author writes a synonym, a different word that almost means the same thing, to help you understand the difficult or unfamiliar word.

LESSON VOCABULARY	
critical	scarce
enables	specialize
mucus	sterile

TEACH

❏ **Words to Know** Give students the opportunity to tell what they already know about this week's lesson vocabulary words. Then discuss word meaning. **DAY 1** *438b*

❏ **Vocabulary Strategy Lesson** Use the vocabulary strategy lesson in the Student Edition to introduce and model this week's strategy, *context clues.* **DAY 2** *438-439*

Vocabulary Strategy Lesson

PRACTICE/APPLY

❏ **Leveled Text** Read the lesson vocabulary in the context of leveled text. **DAY 1** *LR19-LR27*

❏ **Words in Context** Read the lesson vocabulary and apply *context clues* in the context of *Exploding Ants.* **DAY 2** *440-447,* **DAY 3** *448-452*

Leveled Readers

❏ **Writing/Vocabulary Center** Use a Venn diagram to show similarities and differences in the ways that owls and snakes digest their food. **ANY DAY** *436k*

Main Selection—Nonfiction

❏ **Homework** Practice Book pp. 174–175. **DAY 1** *438b,* **DAY 2** *439*

❏ **Word Play** Have students find related words from the following verbs and identify their parts of speech: *adapt, survive,* and *defend.* **ANY DAY** *457c*

ASSESS

❏ **Selection Test** Use the Selection Test to determine students' understanding of the lesson vocabulary words. **DAY 3**

RETEACH/REVIEW

❏ **Reteach Lesson** If necessary, use this lesson to reteach and review *context clues.* **DAY 5** *457c*

❶ Use assessment data to determine your instructional focus.

❷ Preview this week's instruction by strand.

❸ Choose instructional activities that meet the needs of your classroom.

COMPREHENSION

SKILL GRAPHIC SOURCES Graphic sources are graphs, maps, pictures, photographs, and diagrams that organize information and help strengthen understanding of the text.

STRATEGY MONITOR AND FIX UP To monitor means to stop reading occasionally and check to be sure you understand what you are reading. Fix up means to do something to regain understanding when you do not understand or are confused.

TEACH

❑ **Skill/Strategy Lesson** Use the skill/strategy lesson in the Student Edition to introduce and model *graphic sources* and *monitor and fix up.* DAY 1 436-437

Skill/Strategy Lesson

❑ **Extend Skills** Teach metaphors. **ANY DAY** 457b

PRACTICE/APPLY

❑ **Leveled Text** Apply *graphic sources* and *monitor and fix up* to read leveled text. DAY 1 LR19-LR27

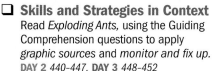

Leveled Readers

❑ **Skills and Strategies in Context** Read *Exploding Ants,* using the Guiding Comprehension questions to apply *graphic sources* and *monitor and fix up.* DAY 2 440-447, DAY 3 448-452

Main Selection—Nonfiction

❑ **Skills and Strategies in Context** Read "The Creature from the Adapting Lagoon," guiding students as they apply *graphic sources* and *monitor and fix up.* Then have students discuss and write across texts. DAY 4 454-457

❑ **Homework** Practice Book pp. 173, 177, 178 DAY 1 437, DAY 3 451, DAY 5 457b

Paired Selection—Nonfiction

❑ **Fresh Reads for Differentiated Test Practice** Have students practice *graphic resources* with a new passage. DAY 3

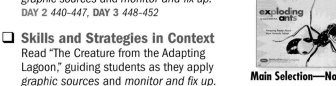

ASSESS

❑ **Selection Test** Determine students' understanding of the selection and their use of *graphic sources.* DAY 3

❑ **Retell** Have students retell *Exploding Ants.* DAY 3 452-453

RETEACH/REVIEW

❑ **Reteach Lesson** If necessary, reteach and review *graphic sources.* DAY 5 457b

FLUENCY

SKILL TEMPO AND RATE. Reading with appropriate tempo means that you take breaths at appropriate times and pause at punctuation. Reading with an appropriate rate means that you do not read too fast or too slow.

TEACH

❑ **Read Aloud** Model fluent reading by rereading "Snake Scientist." Focus on this week's fluency skill, tempo and rate. DAY 1 436l-436m, 457a

PRACTICE/APPLY

❑ **Echo Reading** Read aloud selected paragraphs from *Exploding Ants,* modeling appropriate reading rate and tempo. Have students practice, doing three echo readings of the selected paragraphs. DAY 2 457a, DAY 3 457a

❑ **Partner Reading** Have partners practice reading aloud, reading with appropriate rate and tempo and offering each other feedback. As students reread, monitor their progress toward their individual fluency goals. DAY 4 457a

❑ **Listening Center** Have students follow along with the AudioText for this week's selections. **ANY DAY** 436j

❑ **Reading/Library Center** Have students reread a selection of their choice. **ANY DAY** 436j

❑ **Fluency Coach** Have students use Fluency Coach to listen to fluent readings or practice reading on their own. **ANY DAY**

ASSESS

❑ **Check Fluency** WCPM Do a one-minute timed reading, paying special attention to this week's skill—tempo and rate. Provide feedback for each student. DAY 5 457a

☑ Customize Your Plan *by Strand*

GRAMMAR

SKILL POSSESSIVE PRONOUNS Possessive pronouns show who or what owns something. Some examples of possessive pronouns are *my, your, mine, her, hers, his, its,* and *ours.* Possessive pronouns do not use an apostrophe.

TEACH

❑ **Grammar Transparency 18** Use Grammar Transparency 18 to teach possessive pronouns. **DAY 1** *457e*

Grammar Transparency 18

PRACTICE/APPLY

❑ **Develop the Concept** Review the concept of possessive pronouns and provide guided practice. **DAY 2** *457e*

❑ **Apply to Writing** Have students review something they have written and apply possessive pronouns. **DAY 3** *457f*

❑ **Test Preparation** Examine common errors in possessive pronouns to prepare for standardized tests. **DAY 4** *457f*

❑ **Homework** Grammar and Writing Practice Book pp. 69–71. **DAY 2** *457e,* **DAY 3** *457f,* **DAY 4** *457f*

ASSESS

❑ **Cumulative Review** Use Grammar and Writing Practice Book p. 72. **DAY 5** *457f*

RETEACH/REVIEW

❑ **Daily Fix-It** Have students find and correct errors in grammar, spelling, and punctuation. **EVERY DAY** *457e–457f*

❑ **The Grammar and Writing Book** Use pp. 152–155 of The Grammar and Writing Book to extend instruction for possessive pronouns. **ANY DAY**

The Grammar and Writing Book

WRITING

Trait of the Week

WORD CHOICE Good writers choose their words carefully. Strong verbs, specific nouns, and vivid adjectives help writers elaborate on their ideas. Well-chosen words make writing clear and lively.

TEACH

❑ **Writing Transparency 18A** Use the model to introduce and discuss the Trait of the Week. **DAY 1** *457g*

❑ **Writing Transparency 18B** Use the transparency to show students how mood can improve their writing. **DAY 2** *457g*

Writing Transparency 18A **Writing Transparency 18B**

PRACTICE/APPLY

❑ **Write Now** Examine the model on Student Edition p. 453. Then have students write their own story about an animal. **DAY 3** *453, 457h,* **DAY 4** *457h*

  Prompt The author of *Exploding Ants* describes unusual or unexpected animal behaviors. Think about your own experiences observing animals. Now write a story about an animal whose behavior surprised you.

Write Now p. 453

❑ **Writing/Vocabulary Center** Use a Venn diagram to show similarities and differences in the ways that owls and snakes digest their food. **ANY DAY** *436k*

ASSESS

❑ **Writing Trait Rubric** Use the rubric to evaluate students' writing. **DAY 4** *457h*

RETEACH/REVIEW

❑ **The Grammar and Writing Book** Use pp. 152–157 of The Grammar and Writing Book to extend instruction for possessive pronouns, mood, and animal stories. **ANY DAY**

The Grammar and Writing Book

SPELLING

GENERALIZATION **HOMOPHONES** A homophone is a word that sounds exactly like another word but has a different spelling and meaning: *cent, sent*. Homophones occur because many letters and letter combinations make more than one sound.

TEACH

❏ **Pretest** Give the pretest for homophones. Guide students in self-correcting their pretests and correcting any misspellings. **DAY 1** *457i*

❏ **Think and Practice** Connect spelling to the phonics generalization for homophones. **DAY 2** *457i*

PRACTICE/APPLY

❏ **Connect to Writing** Have students use spelling words to write a description. Then review frequently misspelled words: *when, then, went.* **DAY 3** *457j*

❏ **Homework** Word Study and Spelling Practice Book pp. 69–72. **EVERY DAY**

RETEACH/REVIEW

❏ **Review** Review spelling words to prepare for the posttest. Then provide students with a spelling strategy—rhyming helpers. **DAY 4** *457j*

ASSESS

❏ **Posttest** Use dictation sentences to give the posttest for words with homophones. **DAY 5** *457j*

Spelling Words

1. cent	8. their*	15. pale
2. sent	9. there*	16. pail
3. scent	10. they're*	17. aloud
4. threw	11. chili	18. allowed
5. through*	12. chilly	19. course
6. weather	13. tide	20. coarse
7. whether	14. tied	

Challenge Words

21. counsel	23. bizarre	25. patients
22. council	24. bazaar	26. patience

*Word from the selection

RESEARCH AND INQUIRY

❏ **Internet Inquiry** Have students conduct an Internet inquiry on animal adaptations. **EVERY DAY** *457k*

❏ **Magazine/Periodical** Review and analyze the features and format of a magazine article and then discuss how students can use these resources to find information. **DAY 5** *457l*

❏ **Unit Inquiry** Allow time for students to analyze information they have gathered about groups of people or animals who have adapted to different situations. **ANY DAY** *391*

SPEAKING AND LISTENING

❏ **Description** Have students brainstorm a list of descriptive words to describe animals and then use some of those words to present a description of an animal and its features. **DAY 5** *457d*

❏ **Listen to Poetry** Have students listen to a poem about an animal and answer questions. **DAY 5** *457d*

Resources for
Differentiated Instruction

LEVELED READERS

▶ **Comprehension**
- ◎ **Skill** Graphic Sources
- ◎ **Strategy** Monitor and Fix Up

▶ **Lesson Vocabulary**
- ◎ **Context Clues**

critical
enables
mucus
scarce
sterile
specialize

▶ **Science Standards**
- Animals
- Environments/Biomes
- Adaptations

Leveled Reader Database ONLINE

PearsonSuccessNet.com

Use the Online Database of over 600 books to
- Download and print additional copies of this week's leveled readers.
- Listen to the readers being read online.
- Search for more titles focused on this week's skills, topic, and content.

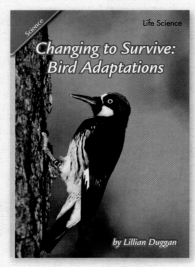

On-Level Reader

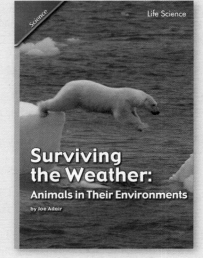

Below-Level Reader

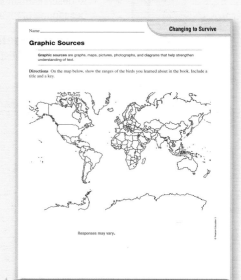

◎ **On-Level Practice** TE p. LR23

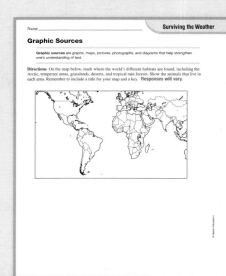

◎ **Below-Level Practice** TE p. LR20

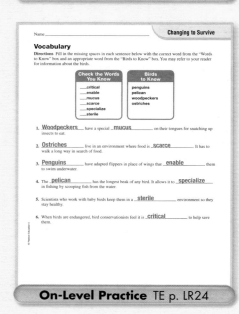

◎ **On-Level Practice** TE p. LR24

◎ **Below-Level Practice** TE p. LR21

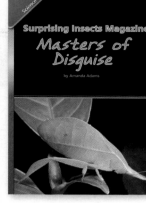 

Advanced

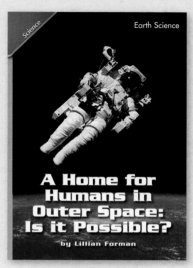

Advanced Reader
A Home for Humans in Outer Space: Is it Possible?
by Lillian Forman

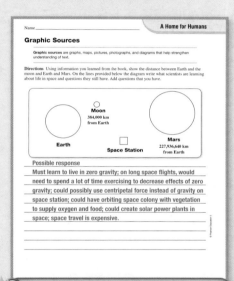

Advanced Practice TE p. LR26

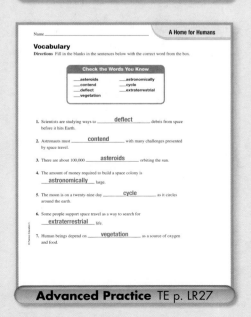

Advanced Practice TE p. LR27

ELL Reader
Surprising Insects Magazine — Masters of Disguise by Amanda Adams

ELL Poster 18

Teacher's Edition Notes

ELL notes throughout this lesson support instruction and reference additional resources at point of use.

Teaching Guide pp. 120–126, 246–247
- Multilingual summaries of the main selection
- Comprehension lesson
- Vocabulary strategies and word cards
- ELL Reader 5.4.3 lesson

ELL and Transition Handbook

Ten Important Sentences
- Key ideas from every selection in the Student Edition
- Activities to build sentence power

More Reading

Readers' Theater Anthology
- Fluency practice
- Five scripts to build fluency
- Poetry for oral interpretation

Leveled Trade Books

Below-Level
Advanced
On-Level

- Extended reading tied to the unit concept
- Lessons in the Trade Book Library Teaching Guide

School + Home

Homework
- Family Times Newsletter
- ELL Multilingual Selection Summaries

Take-Home Books
- Leveled Readers

Family Times

Cross-Curricular Centers

Listening

Listen to the Selections

MATERIALS `SINGLES`
CD player, headphones, AudioText CD, student book

LISTEN TO LITERATURE Listen to *Exploding Ants* and "The Creature from the Adapting Lagoon" as you follow or read along in your book.

If there is anything you don't understand, you can listen again to any section.

Reading/ Library

Read It Again!

MATERIALS `SINGLES` `PAIRS` `GROUPS`
Collection of books for self-selected reading, reading logs, student book

Select a book you have already read. Record the title of the book in your reading log. You may want to read with a partner.

Choose from the following:

- **Leveled Readers**
- **ELL Readers**
- **Stories Written by Classmates**
- **Books from the Library**
- *Exploding Ants*

TEN IMPORTANT SENTENCES Read the Ten Important Sentences for *Exploding Ants*. Then locate the sentences in the student book.

BOOK CLUB Gather as a group to discuss the illustrations in *Exploding Ants*. How do the illustrations help you better understand the information in the story? Find other nonfiction books with interesting illustrations and share your favorites with the group.

Health

Understand Digestion

MATERIALS `SINGLES`
Writing and art materials, reference sources

Animals have different ways of digesting and using food. Research information on the human digestive system.

1. **Locate information about the human digestive system.**
2. **Draw a picture of the digestive system.**
3. **Label its parts.**

EARLY FINISHERS Make a list describing the important steps in the human digestive process.

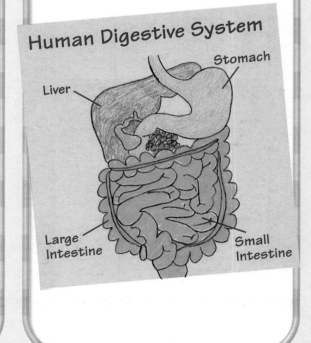

Human Digestive System

Liver — Stomach — Large Intestine — Small Intestine

Scott Foresman Reading Street Centers Survival Kit

Use the *Exploding Ants* materials from the Reading Street Centers Survival Kit to organize this week's centers.

Writing/Vocabulary

Compare *Digestion*

MATERIALS `SINGLES`
Writing materials, Venn diagram

Use a Venn diagram to show similarities and differences in the ways that owls and snakes digest their food.

1. List the eating habits of owls in the left circle.
2. List the eating habits of snakes in the right circle.
3. List the eating habits that are similar to both animals in the middle circle.

EARLY FINISHERS Write a short paragraph summarizing your findings.

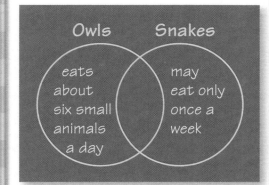

Science

Explore Animals

MATERIALS `SINGLES`
Writing and art materials, student book

Explore the ways that animals are adapted to their environments.

1. Choose an animal from *Exploding Ants.*
2. Find and list 2 to 3 interesting facts about that animal.
3. Make a trading card with a picture of the animal on the front and the facts you found on the back.

EARLY FINISHERS Design an information poster about your animal. Illustrate it with pictures. Display your poster in your classroom.

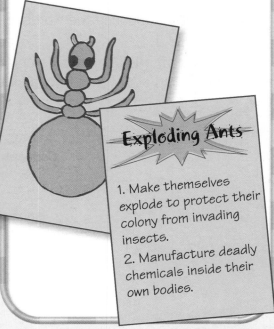

Exploding Ants

1. Make themselves explode to protect their colony from invading insects.
2. Manufacture deadly chemicals inside their own bodies.

Technology

Compose an *E-mail*

MATERIALS `SINGLES` `PAIRS`
E-mail program

Share some fun animal facts with a friend or family member.

1. Follow classroom rules for composing and sending an e-mail to someone you know.
2. Write a list of the five strangest animal facts you learned and send it to a friend or family member who you think would find it interesting.
3. Include a subject line and proofread your message before sending it.

EARLY FINISHERS Add a fact to your list that you make up and challenge a friend to guess which fact is false.

To: Dad
From: John
Subject: Animal Facts

Dear Dad,
Did you know?
1. Ants regurgitate honey to feed other ants.

ALL CENTERS

OBJECTIVES

- Build vocabulary by finding words related to the lesson concept.
- Listen to identify author's purpose.

Concept Vocabulary

African black mambas poisonous snakes from Africa that are related to cobras

constrictors snakes that kill prey by crushing it in their coils

reptiles cold-blooded animals with backbones and lungs, usually covered with horny plates or scales

Monitor Progress

Check Vocabulary

If...	then... review the
students are unable to place words on the Web,	lesson concept. Place the words on the Web and provide additional words for practice, such as *dinosaurs* and *prey*.

SUCCESS PREDICTOR

DAY 1 Grouping Options

Reading

Whole Group
Introduce and discuss the Question of the Week. Then use pp. 436l–438b.

Group Time
Differentiated Instruction
Read this week's Leveled Readers. See pp. 436f–436g for the small group lesson plan.

Whole Group
Use p. 457a.

Language Arts
Use pp. 457e–457k.

Build Concepts

FLUENCY

MODEL TEMPO AND RATE As you read "Snake Scientist," keep your pace slow and steady. Be sure to enunciate words that convey scientific information, such as *extinct, scale-covered,* and *cold-blooded.*

LISTENING COMPREHENSION

After reading "Snake Scientist," use the following questions to assess listening comprehension.

1. **What is the author's purpose for writing "Snake Scientist"? Explain your answer.** *(He is writing to inform readers about snakes.)* **Author's Purpose**

2. **How are snakes like and unlike dinosaurs?** *(They are both reptiles; dinosaurs are extinct but snakes are not.)* **Compare and Contrast**

BUILD CONCEPT VOCABULARY

Start a web to build concepts and vocabulary related to this week's lesson and the unit theme.

- Draw the Animal Adaptations Concept Web.

- Read the sentence with the word *reptiles* again. Ask students to pronounce *reptiles* and discuss its meaning.

- Place *reptiles* in an oval attached to *Types of Animals.* Explain that students can list different kinds of reptiles in ovals attached to this category. Read the sentences in which *African black mambas* and *constrictors* appear. Have students pronounce the words, place them on the web, and provide reasons.

- Brainstorm additional words and categories for the web. Keep the web on display and add words throughout the week.

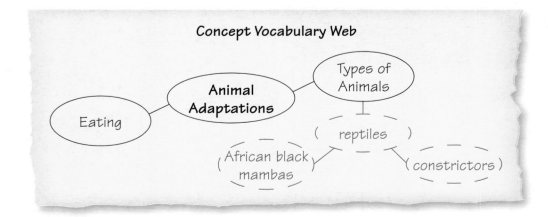

Concept Vocabulary Web

SNAKE SCIENTIST

by Sy Montgomery

Many people are afraid of snakes. But don't be afraid! You'll miss out on some amazing and mysterious animals. Some people claim snakes are more interesting than dinosaurs—and they aren't extinct.

Both snakes and dinosaurs are reptiles—scale-covered, cold-blooded animals. Lizards, crocodiles, and turtles are reptiles, too. But snakes are perhaps the most unusual and fascinating members of the family: long, thin tubes without legs, eye-lids, or ears. And yet snakes are the superheroes of the reptile world, with abilities that other reptiles don't have.

Snakes are agile and quick. African black mambas can slither five miles per hour. Snakes flow across land, climb high into trees, burrow deep into the ground, and swim across marshes, lakes, and even oceans. Some kinds, like the sea snakes that have paddle-shaped tails, swim so well they never come out on land at all. And the so-called flying snakes of Southeast Asia and the East Indies hurl themselves from treetops and glide through the air.

Though snakes have no ears, they sense vibrations with the bones of their jaws that we, with our ears, perceive as sound. With forked tongues, they "taste" odors, picking up chemical information that leads them along an invisible trail to a frog or a rat or another snake. When a snake flicks its tongue in and out, it is collecting chemical particles and transferring them to a special organ in the roof of their mouth called the Jacobson's organ. If one tip of the forked tongue picks up more particles than the other, the snake knows which direction to follow.

Snakes abilities seem almost magical. They can swallow prey bigger than their own heads by the incredible feat of unhinging their jaws from their skulls. Some snakes, such as vipers, have evolved poisonous saliva— venom—to kill their prey; other constrictors like boas and anacondas, literally hug their food to death. Snakes can go for weeks or months without a meal. They can "see" heat with special heat receptors in their heads called pit organs.

And snakes can shed their skin—even the "skin" over their eyeballs. Shedding begins at the lips, and as the snake crawls out of the old skin it turns inside out, sort of like a person peeling off a sweater. If you find a shed skin, the tail points in the direction in which the snake was moving.

No wonder people around the world regard snakes with amazement.

SKILLS ↔ STRATEGIES IN CONTEXT

Graphic Sources
Monitor/Fix Up

OBJECTIVES

◉ Use graphic sources to aid comprehension.

◉ Monitor comprehension by using graphic sources.

Skills Trace

◉ **Graphic Sources**

Introduce/Teach	TE: 5.3 364–365; 5.4 436–437; 5.5 536–537
Practice	Practice Book: 143, 147, 148, 166, 173, 177, 178, 213, 217, 218, 226, 246
Reteach/Review	TE: 5.3 383b, DI·56; 5.4 421, 457b, DI·54; 5.5 559b, 569, 613, DI·53
Test	Selection Test: 57–60, 69–72, 85–88; Benchmark Test: Unit 5

INTRODUCE

Show students a map of the United States. Ask them what information this graphic source gives. Discuss what written information the graphic source could clarify. *(Possible responses: The map shows the geographic features of North Carolina. It could clarify information about where cities grew up.)*

Have students read the information on p. 436. Explain the following:

• Graphic sources can help you understand information in a text.

• You can use graphic sources and other references to monitor and fix up problems in understanding what you read.

Use Skill Transparency 18 to teach graphic sources and monitor and fix up.

exploding ants

Comprehension

Skill
Graphic Sources

Strategy
Monitor and Fix Up

Graphic Sources

• A graphic source, such as a picture, diagram, or chart, organizes information and makes it easy to see.

• Preview the graphic sources in a selection to help you predict what you will be reading about.

• As you read, compare the information in the text with the graphic source.

Strategy: Monitor and Fix Up

Good readers make sure they understand what they read. If a graphic source is part of a text, you can use it to help you understand. You can also use other references to help you. If you do not understand a word, you can look it up in a dictionary. If you need more information about a subject, you can check an encyclopedia.

Write to Read

1. Read "Ant Facts." Use both the text and the diagram to write a paragraph about an ant's antennae. Tell what they look like and what they are for. Include how to pronounce the word.

2. Use the diagram to write a description of the legs of an ant.

436

◉ **Graphic Sources** Explain that there are many kinds of graphic sources. In "Ant Facts," there is a diagram. To help students use the diagram, have them examine it before they begin reading. Have students point to these parts of the ant as you say them aloud: *head, abdomen, hind leg, foreleg, thorax, antennae, middle leg,* and *mandible.*

ELL

Access Content

Beginning/Intermediate For a Picture It! lesson on graphic sources, see ELL Teaching Guide, pp. 120–121.

Advanced Before students read "Ant Facts," have them look at the diagram and talk about the parts of an ant. Discuss the number of legs, antennae, body sections, and mandibles ants have.

Ant Facts.

Have you ever observed an ant crawling across a sidewalk lugging food back to its colony? To you, the food is the tiniest scrap. But to the ant, its size and weight are tremendous. Ants can carry objects that weigh several times more than they do. That is only one of the amazing facts about ants.

There are thousands of different species of ants. Some harvest their own food. Some wage war. Some take slaves. Yet all ants share certain characteristics.

An ant's body is divided into three sections: the head, the thorax, and the abdomen. An ant's head is large with two antennae, which are used for smelling and feeling. Its mouth has two sets of mandibles. One set is for carrying. The other is for chewing. The thorax is the middle part of the ant. It's connected to the abdomen by a small, waistlike section. The abdomen is large and oval-shaped.

1 **Skill** Preview the title and the diagram. What do you think you will be reading about ants?

2 **Strategy** What are antennae? If you don't know, look at the diagram. If you want to find out how to pronounce the word *antennae*, in which reference source would you look?

3 **Strategy** What is a mandible? If you don't know, where could you look to find out?

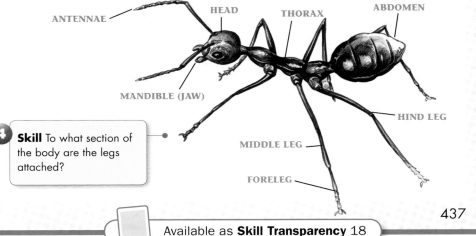

ANTENNAE   HEAD   THORAX   ABDOMEN

MANDIBLE (JAW)

HIND LEG

MIDDLE LEG

FORELEG

4 **Skill** To what section of the body are the legs attached?

437

Available as **Skill Transparency** 18

Graphic Sources

- A **graphic source**, such as a picture, diagram, or chart, organizes information visually.
- Preview the graphic sources to help you predict what you will be reading about.

Directions Study the following diagram. Then answer the questions below.

GRASSHOPPER (diagram labels: antennae, head, thorax, abdomen, compound eyes, jaws, wings, walking legs, jumping legs)

1. What is the purpose of this diagram?
   Possible answer: The diagram shows the different parts of a grasshopper's body.
2. What are the three parts of the grasshopper's body?
   The three parts are the abdomen, thorax, and head.
3. What do grasshoppers use to hop, walk, and fly?
   Grasshoppers use their jumping legs for hopping, walking legs for walking, and wings for flying.
4. How many legs does the grasshopper have? How does the diagram show you this?
   six; The diagram uses arrows and labels to show the legs.
5. What is the location of the grasshopper's two front legs? What other job might the front legs perform in addition to walking?
   close to the grasshopper's jaws; Possible answer: Grasshoppers might use the front legs to hold food while they eat.

School + Home **Home Activity** Your child used a graphic source to answer questions. Together, read a newspaper or magazine article that includes a graphic source. Ask your child to answer questions about the article based on the information shown in the graphic source.

▲ **Practice Book** p. 173

TEACH

1 **SKILL** Preview the article.

Think Aloud **MODEL** The title of the article tells me that it's about ants. The diagram gives me more specific information. It suggests that I'll be reading about the different parts of an ant's body.

2 **STRATEGY** Use graphic sources and other references to help understand the text.

Think Aloud **MODEL** From the text I know that an ant uses its antennae for smelling and feeling. However, I'm not sure what antennae are, so I will look at the diagram. Now I know what antennae are. I also know that I could look in a dictionary to find out how to pronounce the word.

PRACTICE AND ASSESS

3 **STRATEGY** A *mandible* is a jaw. I could look at the diagram or in a dictionary to find out what a *mandible* is.

4 **SKILL** thorax

WRITE Have students complete steps 1 and 2 of the Write to Read activity. Call on volunteers to read aloud their paragraphs and descriptions. Discuss how students used the diagram to help them.

Monitor Progress
Graphic Sources

If... students are unable to complete **Write to Read** on p. 436,	**then...** use Practice Book p. 173 to provide additional practice.

Prereading Strategies

OBJECTIVES

- Use graphic sources to improve understanding of text.
- Monitor comprehension by using graphic sources.

GENRE STUDY

Expository Nonfiction

Exploding Ants is expository nonfiction, which gives information about the real world.

PREVIEW AND PREDICT

Have students preview the graphic sources and discuss the topics they think this selection will cover. Students should use lesson vocabulary words as they talk about what they expect to learn.

Strategy Response Log

Activate Prior Knowledge Have students record at least three things they know about animal adaptation. Students will check and, if needed, fix up their understanding in the Strategy Response Log activity on p. 447.

exploding ants

by Joanne Settel, Ph.D.

Amazing **Facts** About How Animals Adapt

 Genre **Expository nonfiction** explains what certain things are and how they came to be or behave. As you read, notice how the author explains insect behavior.

440

 ELL

Access Content Read aloud the subheads in the selection. (The words in leaves are also subheads.) Point to the pictures and help students name the animals and insects.

Consider having students read the selection summary in English or in students' home languages. See the Multilingual Summaries in the ELL Teaching Guide, pp. 124–126.

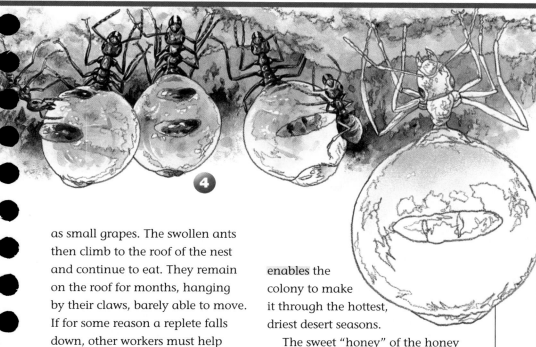

as small grapes. The swollen ants then climb to the roof of the nest and continue to eat. They remain on the roof for months, hanging by their claws, barely able to move. If for some reason a replete falls down, other workers must help drag its large, balloonlike body back up to the ceiling.

When food supplies outside the nest run low, the repletes become the feeders. Hungry nest mates now gather round for food. They touch the repletes' antennae with their own. The repletes then regurgitate big drops of golden honey.

The extra food provided by the repletes is important to the colony survival. Honey ants live in large colonies in dry desert regions of North America, Africa, and Australia, where food is often scarce. Storing food in their living honey jars

enables the colony to make it through the hottest, driest desert seasons.

The sweet "honey" of the honey ant repletes is not only food for other ants, but also for some people. The aborigines in Australia consider the swollen honey ants to be sweet treats and pop them into their mouths like candy.

445

Biomes

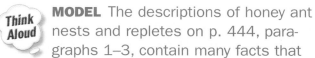

A *biome* is an ecological system with its own kind of climate, plants, animals, and other living things. There are two types of aquatic biomes, freshwater and marine. The forest biome is tremendously important to humans, but is constantly threatened by pollution and deforestation. The desert biome covers areas of the Earth's surface that get less than 50 cm of precipitation per year. The grasslands biome is characterized by grasses as opposed to large shrubs or trees. Tundra, the coldest biome, consists of treeless plains in the arctic regions of the world.

Author's Purpose REVIEW

TEACH

- Remind students that authors write for one or more reasons.
- Explain that an author's purpose can affect the way you read and comprehend text.

Think Aloud **MODEL** The descriptions of honey ant nests and repletes on p. 444, paragraphs 1–3, contain many facts that I need to read carefully to understand. This tells me that the author is writing to inform.

PRACTICE AND ASSESS

- Have students identify text features that indicate that the author is writing to inform. *(Possible response: The selection has a lot of pictures. They work with the words to give information about animal adaptations.)*
- To assess, use Practice Book p. 176.

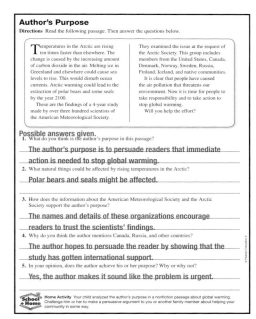

Author's Purpose

Directions Read the following passage. Then answer the questions below.

Temperatures in the Arctic are rising ten times faster than elsewhere. The change is caused by the increasing amount of carbon dioxide in the air. Melting ice in Greenland and elsewhere could cause sea levels to rise. This would disturb ocean currents. Arctic warming could lead to the extinction of polar bears and some seals by the year 2100.

These are the findings of a 4-year study made by over three hundred scientists of the American Meteorological Society.

They examined the issue at the request of the Arctic Society. This group includes members from the United States, Canada, Denmark, Norway, Sweden, Russia, Finland, Iceland, and native communities.

It is clear that people have caused the air pollution that threatens our environment. Now it is time for people to take responsibility and to take action to stop global warming.

Will you help the effort?

Possible answers given.

1. What do you think is the author's purpose in this passage?

   The author's purpose is to persuade readers that immediate action is needed to stop global warming.

2. What natural things could be affected by rising temperatures in the Arctic?

   Polar bears and seals might be affected.

3. How does the information about the American Meteorological Society and the Arctic Society support the author's purpose?

   The names and details of these organizations encourage readers to trust the scientists' findings.

4. Why do you think the author mentions Canada, Russia, and other countries?

   The author hopes to persuade the reader by showing that the study has gotten international support.

5. In your opinion, does the author achieve his or her purpose? Why or why not?

   Yes, the author makes it sound like the problem is urgent.

School + Home **Home Activity** Your child analyzed the author's purpose in a nonfiction passage about global warming. Challenge him or her to make a persuasive argument to you or another family member about helping your community in some way.

▲ **Practice Book** p. 176

Guiding Comprehension

5 🔄 **Vocabulary • Context Clues**

What is a synonym for the word *mandibles* on p. 446? How do you know?

Jaws. The clue word *or* signals another meaning for *mandibles*.

6 **Compare and Contrast • Inferential**

What do *Camponotus* ants and *Globitermes sulfureus* termites have in common?

When threatened, both animals burst open and spray a harmful liquid on their opponents.

7 **Draw Conclusions • Inferential**

Text to World **Explain why adaptation is important for all animal species, not just insects.**

Possible response: Adaptation is important to all animals' survival. Specialized features help animals avoid predators, find food, and build shelters.

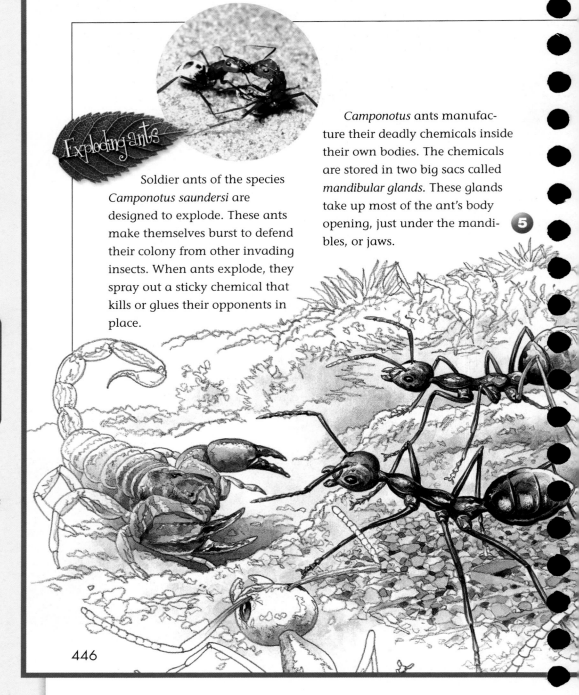

Exploding ants

Soldier ants of the species *Camponotus saundersi* are designed to explode. These ants make themselves burst to defend their colony from other invading insects. When ants explode, they spray out a sticky chemical that kills or glues their opponents in place.

Camponotus ants manufacture their deadly chemicals inside their own bodies. The chemicals are stored in two big sacs called *mandibular glands.* These glands take up most of the ant's body opening, just under the mandibles, or jaws.

5

446

E L L

Access Content Tell students that an *intruder* is a person or animal that forces its way into a place where it was not invited.

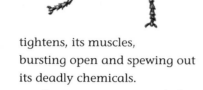

MANDIBULAR GLANDS

EXPLODING ABDOMEN

When an intruder approaches, the *Camponotus* ant will release small amounts of its special chemical to warn away the invader. If the intruder actually attacks, however, the *Camponotus* ant takes the next step. It violently contracts, or tightens, its muscles, bursting open and spewing out its deadly chemicals.

Camponotus ants aren't the only insect with this unusual behavior. It turns out that soldiers of the termite species *Globitermes sulfureus* are also exploders, bursting open when threatened and spraying a sticky yellow liquid all over their opponents.

6
7

447

Context Clues

TEACH

Model finding a synonym for the word *mandibles* on p. 446.

Think Aloud **MODEL** Some sentences contain a synonym near a difficult word to help readers understand that word. Within the same sentence that *mandibles* appears, I see the clue word *or* which tells me that *jaws* is a synonym for *mandibles*, or another word that means the same. Sometimes the context gives an example of the unknown word or an action of the unknown word, which helps me figure out its meaning.

PRACTICE AND ASSESS

Have students find a synonym for *intruder* on p. 447, paragraph 1. *(invader)* Then have students find an example of the context giving an example that defines the word. *(exploders)*

Strategy Response Log

Monitor Comprehension Have students check the three things they wrote about animal adaptation. (See p. 440.) Then have students record two new pieces of information about ants in their semantic webs as they complete the selection.

Develop Vocabulary

PRACTICE LESSON VOCABULARY

Students orally respond to each question.

1. **Can *mucus* be found in the antennae or the mouth?** *(mouth)*
2. **Is a *sterile* bandage clean or filthy?** *(clean)*
3. **Are water and food *critical* to adaptation or to survival?** *(survival)*

BUILD CONCEPT VOCABULARY

Review previous concept words with students. Ask if students have come across any words today in their reading or elsewhere that they would like to add to the Animal Adaptations Concept Web, such as *spewing* and *threatened*.

If you want to teach this selection in two sessions,

Guiding Comprehension

If you are teaching this selection in two days, discuss the graphic sources so far and review the vocabulary.

8 🎯 **Graphic Sources • Critical**

What do the illustrations on p. 448 show you about owls that the text does not?

They show how an owl looks, its habitat, and its young.

Monitor Progress

🎯 **Graphic Sources**

If... students have difficulty using graphic sources to improve their understanding,	**then...** use the skill and strategy instruction on p. 449.

---

9 **Cause and Effect • Literal**

What causes owls to spit up pellets?

The owl swallows its prey whole. It digests the soft, nutritious parts and it spits up the rest as waste, in the form of pellets.

DAY 3 Grouping Options

Reading
Whole Group Discuss the Question of the Day.

Group Time Differentiated Instruction
Read *Exploding Ants.* See pp. 436f–436g for the small group lesson plan.

Whole Group Discuss the Reader Response questions on p. 452. Then use p. 457a.

Language Arts
Use pp. 457e–457k.

Getting it down

A ball of bones

8

Every evening before it goes off to hunt, an owl spits up a few balls of fur and bones. The balls, or pellets, are what's left of the owl's last meal. An owl preys on small animals, such as mice, moles, shrews, birds, and insects. When the feathered predator captures its prey, it doesn't take the time to kill its victim and then pick out the fleshy, nutritious parts. It simply swallows the animal whole. Then the owl digests all the soft stuff, the muscles and organs. The

rest, the fur, feathers, teeth, and bones, are wastes. The owl gets rid of these by regurgitating a pellet.

9

Owls normally spit up two pellets a day. Over time the pellets pile up and form large heaps under the owl's roosting, or resting, site. By examining these

448

ELL

Extend Language Explain that *prey* is an animal that is hunted by another animal for food. "To prey" means to hunt for food.

pellets, scientists can learn all about an owl's diet. A pellet of a barn owl, for example, usually contains entire skeletons of two or three mammals, lots of fur, and insect parts. That means that a barn owl gulps down around six small mammals a day.

Six small mammals at two to six ounces each seems like a lot of meat for a bird that weighs less than one pound. The twelve-ounce owl, however, doesn't get fat on this feast. Most of its food is just the fur and bones that get chucked up as round pellets.

OWL PELLETS

449

Graphic Sources Monitor/Fix Up

TEACH

Have students use the illustrations on p. 448 to go beyond the text to improve their understanding about owls.

 Think Aloud **MODEL** The text mostly talks about how owls hunt and digest their prey. The illustrations add to my understanding by showing what young owls look like and where they live. At first, I a pictured a pellet as a small smooth ball but the picture shows that they are, like the author says, hunks of fur and bones.

PRACTICE AND ASSESS

Have students work in pairs to analyze the illustration on p. 449 and discuss what it shows. (what owl pellets look like)

Human Adaptations

TIME FOR Science

The human body adapts to a wide range of environmental conditions. This enables us to survive in most regions of the world, despite climate and humidity. When in high altitudes, our bodies adapt so that we are able to receive the oxygen we need. The human body has also developed behaviors to help us survive in extreme temperatures such as staying in motion to ward off cold, and sweating to survive in extreme heat.

EXTEND SKILLS

Jargon

Remind students that jargon is the language of a special group. Scientists have their own unique jargon. For example, *repletes* is a scientific term that refers to honey ants. Have students find examples of other scientific jargon in *Exploding Ants*.

Guiding Comprehension

10 **Author's Purpose • Inferential**

The author's main purpose with this selection is to inform. What additional purpose does she have? Explain.

Possible response: To entertain. You can tell from the informal tone she sometimes uses, like "Gulping down a whole pig or chicken... [is] no big deal."

11 **Cause and Effect • Inferential**

Why can a snake eat large prey whole?

A snake's jaw can open very wide.

12 **Compare and Contrast • Inferential**

Text to World **What animal adaptations have you observed or heard about in the world around you?**

Possible response: I've noticed birds using bits of paper or cloth in their nests. I think birds adapted to living in cities by using materials that were available to them.

Strategy Response Log

Summarize When students finish reading the selection, provide this prompt: What kinds of amazing facts are discussed in *Exploding Ants*? Write your response as a brief summary of the selection.

Big, big gulps

10 Gulping down a whole pig or chicken may sound like an impossible task for a snake. But it's no big deal for a twenty-foot python. In fact, many snakes often swallow food much bigger than their own heads. Even very small snakes may feast on mice, rats, birds, frogs, and whole eggs.

The snake's ability to swallow big prey results from the special design of its jaw. The bones of its mouth are loosely joined to its skull. A stretchy strip of tissue called a *ligament* holds together the two halves of the lower jaw. When the snake swallows its dinner, its mouth can stretch wide **11** open. The lower jaw-bones spread apart and each bone moves separately to pull the prey into the mouth.

Snakes generally try to gulp down their food headfirst. This causes the prey's legs to fold back as the snake swallows. In addition, the snake's sharp teeth are curved

450

ELL

Understanding Idioms Explain that the phrase *grab a meal* means "to have something to eat." Ask students how often most snakes "grab a meal." *(once a week)*

backward, preventing the squirming prey from wiggling back out. As the snake works its food down its throat, it pushes its windpipe out of its mouth. This means that it doesn't have to stop breathing as it swallows.

Because snakes eat such big meals, they don't need to eat every day. Most snakes only have to grab a meal once a week, and some only eat once every month. Large pythons hold the record, however. After feasting on a pig or chicken, these huge snakes can go for more than a year without any other food! **12**

Develop Vocabulary

PRACTICE LESSON VOCABULARY

Have students orally respond *yes* or *no* to each question and provide a reason for each answer.

1. Is water *scarce* in the desert? *(Yes; water is hard to find.)*

2. Does an animal *specialize* in order to digest its food? *(No; an animal will specialize in order to survive in its environment.)*

3. Is a frog's slimy skin the main thing that *enables* it to catch insects? *(No; a frog's long, sticky tongue helps him catch insects.)*

BUILD CONCEPT VOCABULARY

Review previous concept words with students. Ask if students have come across any words today in their reading or elsewhere that they would like to add to the Animal Adaptations concept web, such as *prey* and *design*.

Monitor and Fix-Up

Have students review the graphic sources to clarify any questions or misunderstandings they may have about the selection. Use Practice Book p. 177.

SELF-CHECK

Students can ask themselves these questions to assess their ability to use the skill and strategy.

- Did I use the illustrations to help me understand the text as I read?
- Did I make sure I understood the selection as I read it?
- Did I use the illustrations to help me clarify any questions or misunderstandings?

Monitor Progress

Graphic Sources

If... students have difficulty using graphic sources to monitor and fix-up comprehension,	**then...** use the Reteach Lesson on p. 457b.

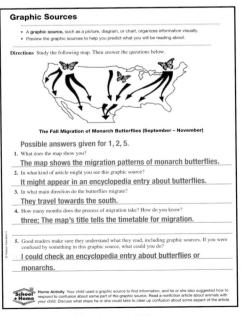

▲ **Practice Book** p. 177

Reader Response

Open for Discussion Personal Response

MODEL I'd call it gross, but I'm not a scientist. A scientist may have a different opinion than I do.

Comprehension Check Critical Response

1. Possible response: I might organize it by showing a picture of each animal with a caption describing what it is doing.
Author's Purpose

2. Possible response: The illustrations show animal adaptations, such as the "living honey jars." **Graphic Sources**

3. Barn owls eat so much because most of their food is indigestible fur and bones.
 Monitor and Fix Up

4. Possible response: If animals did not *specialize* and all ate the same things, then food would become very *scarce*. **Vocabulary**

 Look Back and Write For test practice, assign a 10–15 minute time limit. For assessment, see the Scoring Rubric at the right.

Retell

Have students retell *Exploding Ants*.

Monitor Progress

Check Retelling Rubric 4 3 2 1

If... students have difficulty retelling the selection,	then... use the Retelling Cards and the Scoring Rubric for Retelling on p. 453 to assist fluent retelling.

SUCCESS PREDICTOR

 ELL

Check Retelling Have students use the selection illustrations to guide their retellings. For more ideas on assessing students' retellings, see the ELL and Transition Handbook.

Reader Response

Open for Discussion This selection may not be appropriate for dinner table conversation. But would a true scientist call it gross? What is your opinion?

1. *Exploding Ants* begins with a general idea: "Why animals do gross things." Then the author gives specific examples that show why. Is this the way you would organize a selection like this, or do you have other ideas? Think Like an Author

2. The title includes the words "Amazing Facts About How Animals Adapt." Look at the illustrations and discuss how they help explain the title. Graphic Sources

3. Why do barn owls eat about six small mammals a day, and how can they accomplish this amazing feat? Reread pages 448–449 and discuss the details. Monitor and Fix Up

4. The author states that animals *specialize* in what they eat. How does this specialization help them? What would happen if they did not specialize? Use words from the Words to Know list to answer these questions. Vocabulary

 Look Back and Write Exactly how do soldier ants operate? Review the facts on pages 446–447. Then write a task list for a loyal soldier ant.

Meet author **Joanne Settel on page 767.**

452

Scoring Rubric Look Back and Write

Top-Score Response A top-score response will use details from pp. 446–447 of the selection to list steps a soldier ant takes to defend the colony from invaders.

Example of a Top-Score Response (1) Watch closely for intruders. (2) Release chemicals as a warning to stay away. (3) If attacked, tighten muscles to explode abdomen and spray attacker.

For additional rubrics, see p. WA10.

Write Now

Animal Story

Prompt

The author of *Exploding Ants* describes unusual or unexpected animal behaviors. Think about your own experiences observing animals.

Now write a story about an animal whose behavior surprised you.

Writing Trait

Effective **word choice** means using exact nouns, strong verbs, and vivid adjectives for your story.

Student Model

Strong, precise nouns, verbs, and adjectives show effective word choice.

Events are told in order shown with time-order phrases.

Conclusion reveals surprise asked for in prompt.

One summer, we had a family of barred owls living in the leafy tops of the maple trees in our yard. We watched the drama unfold as Mama Owl taught her young owlets to fly and hunt.

Over time, the hungry hunters picked our neighborhood clean of mice, snakes, and other small animals. Now the alley cats were lean and hungry.

One day, an owl spied a tasty treat in the grass—a long, slithery snake. The owl swooped down, gripped the snake in its talons, and flew off in triumph. Imagine its disappointment when the owl discovered that its prize was, in fact, a piece of garden hose!

Use the model to help you write your own animal story.

453

Write Now

Look at the Prompt Explain that each sentence in the prompt has a purpose.

- Sentence 1 presents a topic.
- Sentence 2 suggests students think about the topic.
- Sentence 3 tells what to write—a story.

Strategies to Develop Word Choice

Have students

- draw a picture of or visualize their animal and list details.
- use vivid words to describe the animal and its actions.

NO: funny skin
YES: wrinkled, grey hide
NO: got the snake.
YES: swooped down on the snake.

For additional suggestions and rubric, see pp. 457g–457h.

Writer's Checklist

☑ **Focus** Do all sentences help develop the story?

☑ **Organization** Are events told in logical sequence?

☑ **Support** Do details help readers visualize things?

☑ **Conventions** Are verb tenses consistent?

Scoring Rubric — Expository Retelling

Rubric 4 3 2 1	4	3	2	1
Connections	Makes connections and generalizes beyond the text	Makes connections to other events, texts, or experiences	Makes a limited connection to another event, text, or experience	Makes no connection to another event, text, or experience
Author's Purpose	Elaborates on author's purpose	Tells author's purpose with some clarity	Makes some connection to author's purpose	Makes no connection to author's purpose
Topic	Describes the main topic	Identifies the main topic with some details early in retelling	Identifies the main topic	Retelling has no sense of topic
Important Ideas	Gives accurate information about events, steps, and ideas using details and key vocabulary	Gives accurate information about events, steps, and ideas with some detail and key vocabulary	Gives limited or inaccurate information about events, steps, and ideas	Gives no information about events, steps, and ideas
Conclusions	Draws conclusions and makes inferences to generalize beyond the text	Draws conclusions about the text	Is able to draw few conclusions about the text	Is unable to draw conclusions or make inferences about the text

Retelling Plan

☑ **Week 1** Assess Strategic Intervention students.

☑ **Week 2** Assess Advanced students.

☑ **This week assess Strategic Intervention students.**

☐ **Week 4** Assess On-Level students.

☐ **Week 5** Assess any students you have not yet checked during this unit.

Use the Retelling Chart on p. TR17 to record retelling.

Selection Test To assess with *Exploding Ants*, use Selection Tests, pp. 69–72.

Fresh Reads for Differentiated Test Practice For weekly leveled practice, use pp. 103–108.

Retelling

SUCCESS PREDICTOR

Science in Reading

DAY 4

OBJECTIVES

- Examine features of experiments.
- Practice a test-taking strategy.
- Compare and contrast across texts.

PREVIEW/USE TEXT FEATURES

As students preview "The Creature from the Adapting Lagoon," have them look at the introduction, subheads, and illustrations. After they preview ask:

- **How can you tell that this is a serious scientific experiment?** *(Possible response: It was created by NASA for use in fifth-grade science classes.)*

- **How do the step-by-step instructions help you understand the experiment?** *(Possible response: The steps break the procedure into parts, which makes it easier to understand.)*

Link to Science

Set out the needed materials. Then read the purpose aloud and make sure students understand the task before they begin.

DAY 4 Grouping Options

Reading
Whole Group Discuss the Question of the Day.

Group Time Differentiated Instruction
Read "The Creature from the Adapting Lagoon." See pp. 436f–436g for the small group lesson plan.

Whole Group Use p. 457a.

Language Arts
Use pp. 457e–457k.

Science in Reading

Experiment

Genre

- An experiment is a trial or test used to find out about something.

- Most experiments deal with some kind of science.

Text Features

- The author states the purpose of the experiment and the materials needed. Then come step-by-step instructions.

- Scan the steps to get an idea of what the experiment is about.

Link to Science

Experiments are at the heart of science. Scientists use them to discover and test new ideas. Perform the experiment yourself and share your results with the class.

454

THE CREATURE FROM THE
Adapting Lagoon

from www.nasa.gov

This science experiment is from the National Aeronautics and Space Administration (NASA). It's intended for fifth-grade students in a science class, but anyone can do it. All you need is thought and imagination.

Content-Area Vocabulary	Science
adaptations	changes in structure, form, or habits to suit conditions Adaptations may be inherited within a species to increase rates of reproduction and survival.
criteria	rules or standards for making a judgment
predators	animals that live by killing and eating other animals

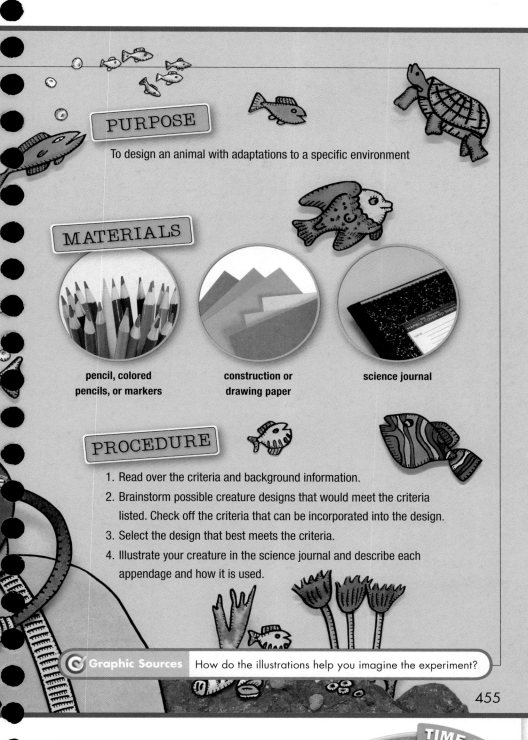

PURPOSE

To design an animal with adaptations to a specific environment

MATERIALS

pencil, colored pencils, or markers

construction or drawing paper

science journal

PROCEDURE

1. Read over the criteria and background information.
2. Brainstorm possible creature designs that would meet the criteria listed. Check off the criteria that can be incorporated into the design.
3. Select the design that best meets the criteria.
4. Illustrate your creature in the science journal and describe each appendage and how it is used.

Graphic Sources How do the illustrations help you imagine the experiment?

455

EXPERIMENT

Use the sidebar on p. 454 to guide discussion.

- Explain to students that an experiment gives step-by-step instructions for performing a test or investigation.

- Point out that the steps are usually numbered, but they could be presented with clue words such as *first*, *next*, *then*, and *finally*.

- Discuss with students the importance of following the steps in order and adjusting reading rate when trying to solve problems or as in doing experiments.

 **AudioText**

Graphic Sources

Possible response: The illustrations show some of the criteria that the design should meet.

Animal Experiments

 TIME FOR Science

By experimenting with animals, scientists have gained data that show how humans will react to traveling and living in space. In 1948, in White Sands, New Mexico, a rhesus macaque monkey named Albert was launched into space in a V2 rocket. At that time, no one knew whether humans could survive space travel. Experimenting with animals helped scientists find the answer. Today, scientists take animals into space to find answers to questions concerning diverse topics such as genetics and microgravity.

ELL

Access Content Preview the selection by reading aloud the title and the Introduction. Point out that students will be reading a science experiment. Have them take turns reading the subheads aloud. Identify the meanings of *procedure* ("way of doing something") and *criteria* ("rules for making a judgment"). Ask students to use the pictures to help them predict what the experiment will be about.

TEST PRACTICE

Strategies for Nonfiction

USE SUBHEADS Explain to students that a subhead lets the reader know what information he or she will be reading. When a selection has subheads, such as the boxed subheads in "The Creature from the Adapting Lagoon," we can use them to locate information to answer test questions. Provide the following strategy.

Use the Strategy

1. Read the test question and locate a keyword or phrase.
2. Scan the subheads in the experiment, looking for matches to your keyword or phrase.
3. When you find a match, read the information to find an answer to the test question.

GUIDED PRACTICE Have students discuss how they would use the strategy to answer the following question.

What is the goal of "The Creature from the Adapting Lagoon" experiment?

INDEPENDENT PRACTICE After students answer the following test question, discuss the process they used to find information.

Which criteria will you focus on when designing your animal's eating adaptation?

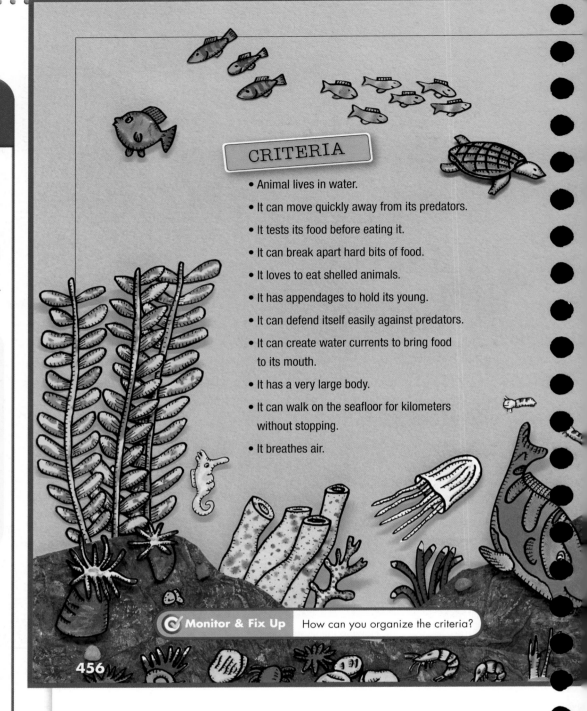

CRITERIA

- Animal lives in water.
- It can move quickly away from its predators.
- It tests its food before eating it.
- It can break apart hard bits of food.
- It loves to eat shelled animals.
- It has appendages to hold its young.
- It can defend itself easily against predators.
- It can create water currents to bring food to its mouth.
- It has a very large body.
- It can walk on the seafloor for kilometers without stopping.
- It breathes air.

 Monitor & Fix Up How can you organize the criteria?

456

E L L

Test Practice Write the Independent Practice test question on the board. Work with students to identify a keyword *(criteria)* that they could use for their answer search. Have students scan the subheads, looking for the keyword. Ask students to answer the test question in a complete sentence.

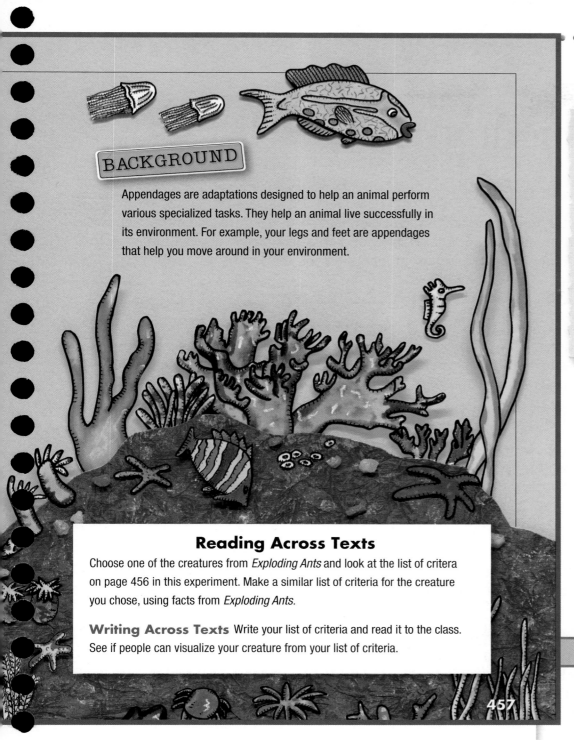

BACKGROUND

Appendages are adaptations designed to help an animal perform various specialized tasks. They help an animal live successfully in its environment. For example, your legs and feet are appendages that help you move around in your environment.

Reading Across Texts

Choose one of the creatures from *Exploding Ants* and look at the list of criteria on page 456 in this experiment. Make a similar list of criteria for the creature you chose, using facts from *Exploding Ants*.

Writing Across Texts Write your list of criteria and read it to the class. See if people can visualize your creature from your list of criteria.

457

CONNECT TEXT TO TEXT

Reading Across Texts

Read the criteria list on p. 456 aloud. Discuss with students the focus of each criterion *(animal's habitat, defense mechanism, eating habits, mobility)*. Have students use this information to help them develop criteria lists for their creatures from *Exploding Ants*.

Writing Across Texts Have students take turns reading aloud their criteria lists. Encourage students to listen to the complete list before trying to guess the creature.

◎ **Monitor and Fix Up**

Possible response: I would definitely reread the criteria before I begin the experiment. I would organize the criteria by categories such as physical needs or special skills.

Fluency Assessment Plan

☑ **Week 1** Assess Advanced students.

☑ **Week 2** Assess Strategic Intervention students.

☑ **This week assess On-Level students.**

☐ **Week 4** Assess Strategic Intervention students.

☐ **Week 5** Assess any students you have not yet checked during this unit.

Set individual goals for students to enable them to reach the year-end goal.

• Current Goal: 120–128 wcpm

• Year-End Goal: 140 wcpm

English language learners may be able to decode some English words but still not know the meanings. Help students recognize that they will understand sentences better and read more fluently as they learn more English words.

To develop fluent readers, use Fluency Coach.

DAY 5   Grouping Options

Reading
Whole Group
Revisit the Question of the Week.

Group Time
Differentiated Instruction
Reread this week's Leveled Readers. See pp. 436f–436g for the small group lesson plan.

Whole Group
Use p. 457b–457c.

Language Arts
Use pp. 457d–457l.

TEMPO AND RATE
Fluency

DAY 1

Model Reread aloud "Snake Scientist" on p. 436m. Explain that you will read the nonfiction article slowly and carefully, paying special attention to scientific words. Model for students as you read.

DAY 2

Echo Reading Read aloud paragraphs 2 and 3 on p. 444. Have students notice how you adjust your rate for scientific words, such as *repletes* and *regurgitated.* Then lead students in three echo readings of paragraphs 2 and 3, p. 444.

DAY 3

Model Read aloud p. 446. Have students notice how you enunciate the words *mandibular glands* and *mandibles* that convey scientific information. Have students practice as a class by leading them in three echo readings.

DAY 4

Partner Reading Partners practice reading aloud p. 446 three times. Students should read slowly and confidently and offer each other feedback.

Monitor Progress   Check Fluency WCPM

As students reread, monitor their progress toward their individual fluency goals. Current Goal: 120–128 words correct per minute. End-of-Year Goal: 140 words correct per minute.

If... students cannot read fluently at a rate of 120–128 words correct per minute,

then... make sure students practice with text at their independent level. Provide additional fluency practice, pairing nonfluent readers with fluent readers.

If... students already read at 140 words correct per minute,

then... they do not need to reread three to four times.

SUCCESS PREDICTOR

DAY 5

Assessment
Individual Reading Rate Use the Fluency Assessment Plan and do a one-minute timed reading of either selection from this week to assess students in Week 3. Pay special attention to this week's skill, tempo and rate. Provide corrective feedback for each student.

RETEACH

🎯 Graphic Sources

TEACH

Review the definition of *graphic sources* on p. 436. Students can complete Practice Book p. 178 on their own, or you can complete it as a class. Tell them to read the diagram showing the stages of a butterfly's life counterclockwise, following the numbered pictures in order, from 1–4.

ASSESS

Have partners discuss what the illustration at the top of p. 451 shows and find the text that it supports. *(Possible response: The picture shows a snake swallowing its prey whole. It supports the text on pp. 450–451).*

For additional instruction on graphic sources, see DI · 54.

EXTEND SKILLS

Metaphor

TEACH

A metaphor is a comparison between two unlike things that are alike in at least one way.

- In a metaphor, the similarity is implied—not stated using words of comparison.
- A metaphor calls attention to certain qualities of one or both things being compared.

Have students reread pp. 444–445. Discuss the metaphor comparing repletes to "living honey jars".

ASSESS

Working in small groups, have students write their own metaphors comparing an animal in the selection to something else. *(Possible response: The Camponotus ant is a bomb.)*

OBJECTIVES

- 🎯 Recognize and use graphic sources visually to gain information quickly.
- ● Write a metaphor.

Skills Trace	
🎯 **Graphic Sources**	
Introduce/Teach	TE: 5.3 364–365; 5.4 436–437; 5.5 536–537
Practice	Practice Book: 143, 147, 148, 166, 173, 177, 178, 213, 217, 218, 226, 246
Reteach/Review	**TE: 5.3 383b, DI•56; 5.4 421, 457b, DI•54; 5.5 559b, 569, 613, DI•53**
Test	Selection Test: 57–60, 69–72, 85–88; Benchmark Test: Unit 5

ELL

Access Content Reteach the skill by reviewing the Picture It! lesson on graphic sources in the ELL Teaching Guide, pp. 121–122.

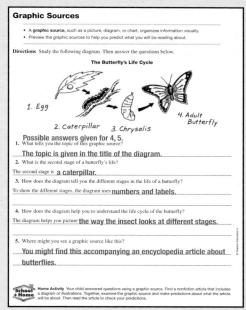

▲ **Practice Book** p. 178

Vocabulary and Word Study

VOCABULARY STRATEGY

🎯 Context Clues

UNFAMILIAR WORDS Remind students to use context clues to determine the meanings of unfamiliar words. Have each student choose an unfamiliar word from *Exploding Ants* and complete a word frame for it. Students should base their predicted definitions on context clues from the selection and write sentences using the word in similar contexts. They should use a dictionary for the verified definitions and write other sentences using the exact definitions.

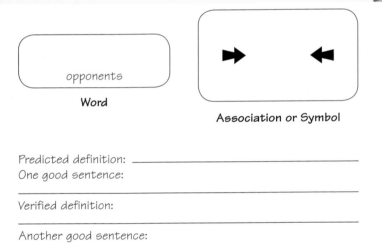

Word: opponents

Association or Symbol: ➡➡ ⬅

Predicted definition: _____

One good sentence: _____

_____

Verified definition: _____

_____

Another good sentence: _____

_____

Related Words

From the verb *specialize* you can find other related parts of speech such as *special* (adjective) or *specialty* (noun). Have students find related words from these verbs and identify their parts of speech.

Verb	Related Words
adapt	adaptation (n.); adaptable (adj.)
survive	
defend	

BUILD CONCEPT VOCABULARY

Animal Adaptations

LOOKING BACK Remind students of the question of the week: *How do animals adapt to survive?* Discuss how this week's Concept Web of vocabulary words relates to the theme of adaptation. Ask students if they have any words or categories to add. Discuss whether the words and categories are appropriately related to the concept.

MOVING FORWARD Preview the title of the next selection, *The Stormi Giovanni Club*. Ask students which Concept Web words might apply to the new selection based on the title alone.

Put a star next to these words on the web.

Display the Concept Web and revisit the vocabulary words as you read the next selection to check predictions.

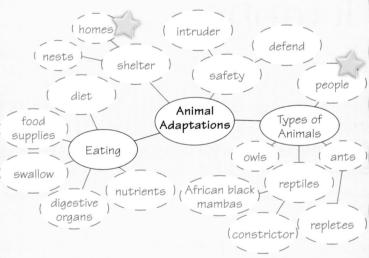

Monitor Progress

Check Vocabulary

If... students suggest words or categories that are not related to the concept,	**then...** review the words and categories on the Concept Web and discuss how they relate to the lesson concept.

SUCCESS PREDICTOR

Speaking and Listening

SPEAKING

Description

SET-UP Have students give a description of the animal they wrote about in Writing Workshop. They may choose to describe another animal instead.

PLANNING Students should begin by brainstorming a list of descriptive words to describe their animals. Suggest that they focus on sensory words, such as words that describe what the animal looks like, what it sounds like, and what it feels like. Encourage them to study photos of their animals as they brainstorm. In addition to their animals' basic physical features, students may want to describe other aspects, such as interesting habits or adaptive features.

VISUAL AIDS Encourage students to include visual aids in their presentations to show their animals and their animals' interesting features. Students can bring in photos from books or the Internet.

Organization Tips
- First tell what the animal is and where it is found. Then tell what you're going to describe about it.
- Describe everything about one feature, such as your animals' claws, before going on to another feature, such as its nest or diet.
- Keep in mind the time line for completion of your report.

LISTENING

Listen to Poetry

Have students listen to a poem about an animal. If available, you can play a recording of a poem, or read one aloud. After students listen, have them discuss these questions as a class.

1. **How does the speaker feel about the animal described in the poem? Use details from the poem to support your answer.** *(Guide students to note the speaker's tone and language.)*

2. **What is the purpose of the poem? How do you know?**

3. **How is the poem different from an informational article about animals?**

Support Vocabulary Use the following to review and extend vocabulary and to explore lesson concepts further:
- ELL Poster 18, Days 3–5 instruction
- Vocabulary Activities and Word Cards in ELL Teaching Guide, pp. 122–123

Assessment For information on assessing students' speaking and listening, see the ELL and Transition Handbook.

Vocabulary

SUCCESS PREDICTOR

Grammar   **Possessive Pronouns**

OBJECTIVES

- Define and identify possessive pronouns.
- Use possessive pronouns in writing.
- Become familiar with possessive pronoun assessment on high-stakes tests.

Monitor Progress

Grammar

If... students have difficulty identifying possessive pronouns,	then... provide additional instruction and practice in The Grammar and Writing Book pp. 152–155.

DAILY FIX-IT

This week use Daily Fix-It Transparency 18.

Spiral REVIEW

Support Grammar See the Grammar Transition lessons in the ELL and Transition Handbook.

▲ **The Grammar and Writing Book**
For more instruction and practice, use pp. 152–155.

DAY 1   Teach and Model

DAILY FIX-IT

1. A skunk sprays a bad-smelling sent to keep enemys away. *(scent; enemies)*

2. That serves as there protection? *(their protection.)*

READING-GRAMMAR CONNECTION

Write this sentence on the board:

Animals often put their body parts to good use.

Explain that *their* is a possessive pronoun. It is used in the place of the possessive noun, *animals',* to show that the animals own, or possess, the body parts.

Display Grammar Transparency 18. Read aloud the definitions and sample sentences. Work through the items.

Possessive Pronouns

Possessive pronouns show who or what owns, or possesses, something. *My, mine, your, yours, her, hers, his, its, our, ours, their,* and *theirs* are possessive pronouns.
- Use *my, your, her, our,* and *their* before nouns.
  This is *my* cat. It was *her* dog. They fed *their* fish.
- Use *mine, yours, hers, ours,* and *theirs* alone.
  The cat is *mine.* The dog was *hers.* The fish are *theirs.*
- *His* and *its* can be used both: before nouns and alone.
  He found *his* dog. The dog is *his.*
  The dog hurt *its* paw. The paw is *its.*
- Do not use an apostrophe with a possessive pronoun.

Directions Underline the pronoun that correctly completes each sentence.

1. Ants use (theirs, *their*) antennae for touch and smell.
2. That nest under the tree is (their, *theirs*).
3. An ant has two stomachs in (*its*, our) abdomen.
4. One stomach stores food for other ants to share, and another stomach holds (it's, *its*) own food.
5. The queen is larger than the other ants, and (*her*, hers) body is an egg factory.
6. All the worker ants are sterile, so the egg-laying task is all (her, *hers*).
7. A male ant lives apart from the colony and plays (*his*, theirs) part by mating with the queen.
8. I sometimes get ants in (*my*, hers) house.
9. The house with purple trim is (my, *mine*).
10. Don't have (*your*, theirs) picnic next to an ant colony!

Directions Write the possessive pronoun that can replace the underlined word or words.

11. Steven brought <u>Steven's</u> ant farm to class.
    his
12. The class and I spent <u>the class's and my</u> time watching them work.
    our
13. Ms. Pearce told us about <u>Ms. Pearce's</u> trip to South America.
    her
14. She saw army ants marching to and from <u>the army ants'</u> colony.
    their

Unit 4 Exploding Ants   Grammar **18**

▲ **Grammar Transparency** 18

DAY 2   Develop the Concept

DAILY FIX-IT

3. Because clear scales cover the eyes of a snake. It's eyes are always open. *(snake, Its)*

4. Snakes raises their body temperature by laying in the sun. *(raise; lying)*

GUIDED PRACTICE

Review the concept of possessive pronouns.

- **Possessive pronouns** show who or what owns something.
- *My, your, her, our,* and *their* are used before nouns.
- *Mine, yours, hers, ours,* and *theirs* are used alone.
- *His* and *its* can be used both before nouns and alone.
- No possessive pronoun uses an apostrophe.

HOMEWORK Grammar and Writing Practice Book p. 69.

Possessive Pronouns

Possessive pronouns show who or what owns, or possesses, something. *My, mine, your, yours, her, hers, his, its, our, ours, their,* and *theirs* are possessive pronouns.
- Use *my, your, her, our,* and *their* before nouns.
  Is that *your* cat? It was *her* gerbil. They pet *our* dog.
- Use *mine, yours, hers, ours,* and *theirs* alone.
  The cat is *yours.* That gerbil is *hers.* The dog is *ours.*
- *His* and *its* can be used both before nouns and alone.
  He lost *his* ferret. The ferret is *his.*
  The dog lost *its* collar. The collar is *its.*
- Do not use an apostrophe with a possessive pronoun.

Directions Replace the underlined words or phrases with possessive pronouns. Rewrite the sentences.

1. An ant colony relies on <u>the ant colony's</u> queen.
   An ant colony relies on its queen.
2. Both males and females have wings on the <u>males' and females'</u> bodies.
   Both males and females have wings on their bodies.
3. The queen ant flies to a new location to start a colony, then sheds <u>the queen's</u> wings.
   The queen ant flies to a new location to start a colony, then sheds her wings.
4. Ants are very strong for <u>ants'</u> size and can carry 25 times <u>ants'</u> weight.
   Ants are very strong for their size and can carry 25 times their weight.
5. Most of us think that ants are pests to be swept out of <u>most of us's</u> way.
   Most of us think that ants are pests to be swept out of our way.

Home Activity Your child learned about possessive pronouns. Ask your child to make up sentences about objects at home that belong to him or her, to the family, and to others. Have your child identify the possessive pronouns he or she uses.

▲ **Grammar and Writing Practice Book** p. 69

DAY 3 Apply to Writing

DAILY FIX-IT

5. They're are a snake under that chair! *(There is)*

6. That is mine snake named sue. *(my; Sue)*

WATCH FOR ITS AND IT'S

Explain that the contraction *it's* stands for the words *it is* and is never used to show possession. No possessive pronoun uses an apostrophe.

No: Its a shame that owl broke it's wing.

Yes: It's a shame that owl broke its wing.

- Have students review something they have written to see if they can improve it by correcting mistakes in their use of possessive pronouns.

HOMEWORK Grammar and Writing Practice Book p. 70.

Possessive Pronouns

Directions Underline the error in each sentence. Write the correct possessive pronoun in the space above the error.

its
(1) Each animal is adapted to it's environment. (2) For example, snakes have temperature
their   **their**
sensing organs on they're heads. (3) They can use these organs to locate there prey in the dark.
her
(4) My corn snake Lolamae can take a whole mouse or egg in hers mouth. (5) She can unhinge
her   **hers**
her's bottom jaw to fit in a big meal. (6) The aquarium in the corner is her. (7) Lolamae will be
your   **my**
happy to slither up yours arm. (8) It took mine mom a long time to get used to Lolamae too.

Directions Write a paragraph about pets you and your friends have owned. Describe some unique features of the pets. Use at least five possessive pronouns. Underline the possessive pronouns in your paragraph.

Possible answer: My family and I have ordinary pets.
Tigger is my orange cat, and Wolfus is a hound
that belongs to our family. However, my friend
Van is another matter! Most people have fish
in their aquariums. Van has tarantulas in his.
He says spiders make great pets. That is one
person's opinion. What is yours?

Home Activity Your child learned how to use possessive pronouns in writing. Have your child write interview questions to ask you about a prized possession and then write your answers below the questions.

▲ **Grammar and Writing Practice Book** p. 70

DAY 4 Test Preparation

DAILY FIX-IT

7. On saturday morning you can bring you dog for training. *(Saturday; your)*

8. Dogs are allways aloud in the pet store. *(always allowed)*

STANDARDIZED TEST PREP

Test Tip

Although possessive nouns use an apostrophe *(Jean's dog)*, possessive pronouns never do *(her dog)*.

No: A dog loves it's owner.

Yes: A dog loves its owner.

No: That dog is her's.

Yes: That dog is hers.

HOMEWORK Grammar and Writing Practice Book p. 71.

Possessive Pronouns

Directions Write the letter of the possessive pronoun that correctly completes each sentence in the paragraph.

(1) Last night I heard a haunting sound outside _____ window. (2) My brother and I ran into _____ yard to find out what it was. (3) He shined _____ flashlight up into a tree. (4) We saw two big eyes, and _____ unblinking stare unnerved me. (5) It was only a screech owl, but _____ hoot sounded eerie. (6) Since that night, owls have become a hobby of _____. (7) Mom loaned me some of _____ biology books. (8) Did you know that owls can turn _____ heads almost completely around? (9) This is an adaptation of _____ that allows them to turn their heads to follow a moving object. (10) Now Mom and I spend _____ free time on weekends bird watching.

1. A mine
   Ⓑ my
   C theirs
   D hers

2. A her
   B hers
   Ⓒ our
   D theirs

3. A mine
   Ⓑ his
   C its
   D their

4. A your
   B its
   Ⓒ their
   D theirs

5. A theirs
   Ⓑ its
   C hers
   D her

6. Ⓐ mine
   B our
   C their
   D it's

7. A hers
   Ⓑ her
   C their
   D theirs

8. A our
   B her
   Ⓒ their
   D my

9. A hers
   B his
   Ⓒ their
   Ⓓ theirs

10. A mine
    B my
    Ⓒ ours
    Ⓓ our

Home Activity Your child prepared for taking tests on possessive pronouns. Have your child choose a magazine article and find possessive pronouns in it. Ask him or her to name the person or thing each possessive pronoun stands for.

▲ **Grammar and Writing Practice Book** p. 71

DAY 5 Cumulative Review

DAILY FIX-IT

9. That fish is pail so it will blend in with the sandy ocean botem. *(pale; bottom)*

10. Animals bodies and behaviors are adapted to its environments. *(Animals'; their)*

ADDITIONAL PRACTICE

Assign pp. 152–155 in The Grammar and Writing Book.

EXTRA PRACTICE Grammar and Writing Practice Book p. 139.

TEST PREPARATION Grammar and Writing Practice Book pp. 155–156.

ASSESSMENT

CUMULATIVE REVIEW Grammar and Writing Practice Book p. 72.

Possessive Pronouns

Directions Write the letter of the possessive pronoun that can replace the underlined word or words in each phrase.

B 1. Aaron's and Mike's question   A her
E 2. Mr. Shaefer's lesson   B their
D 3. the book's index   C our
C 4. Sam's and my interest   D its
A 5. Mom's degree   E his

Directions Underline the pronoun that correctly completes each sentence.

6. We will catch fireflies in (theirs, our) hands.

7. Which of these jars is (your, yours)?

8. Be sure to punch air holes in (it's, its) top.

9. Dusk is (their, theirs) time to glow and flash.

10. I have ten fireflies in (my, mine) jar.

11. The light flashes from (their, it's) abdomen.

12. We let the fireflies go. Our friends released (their, theirs) later.

Directions Write the possessive pronoun that can replace the underlined word or words.

13. A snake sheds a snake's skin when it outgrows it.
    its

14. This bleached-out turtle shell is the one belonging to me.
    mine

15. Zara and Ted explained that the rat was Zara's and the hamster was Ted's.
    hers; his

Home Activity Your child reviewed possessive pronouns. Ask your child to list the possessive pronouns on this page, use each one in an example sentence, and tell you what possessive noun the possessive pronoun replaces.

▲ **Grammar and Writing Practice Book** p. 72

Writing Workshop Tell a Story About an Animal

ELL

Word Choice Work with students to use vivid words that appeal to readers' senses. A bilingual dictionary, picture dictionary, or thesaurus, as well as other home-language speakers, may help provide words that create pictures for readers.

Writing Traits

FOCUS/IDEAS The details build and develop the plot.

ORGANIZATION/PARAGRAPHS The story flows from beginning to middle to end with logical paragraph breaks.

VOICE The writing conveys personality and feeling.

WORD CHOICE Lively verbs, precise nouns, and vivid modifiers engage readers.

SENTENCES The dialogue sounds natural. Sentences are varied and interesting.

CONVENTIONS There is excellent control and accuracy. Quotation marks are used accurately with commas and end marks.

DAY 1 Model the Trait

READING-WRITING CONNECTION

- *Exploding Ants* gives facts about remarkable animal adaptations.
- Vivid and specific concrete language helps readers to picture animals in action and creates admiration for them.
- Students will write a **story about an animal** using lively and vivid language to create a mood.

MODEL WORD CHOICE Discuss Writing Transparency 18A. Then discuss the model and the writing trait of word choice.

 I see that the writer uses the word *saunter,* rather than walk, to more specifically describe the cat's relaxed, unconcerned attitude, despite the fact that its owners have been frantically calling for it. The writer also uses specific describing words such as *yawning blissfully* to help readers visualize the scene.

Story About an Animal

A **story** tells about an event or how characters solve a problem. It has a beginning, middle, and end. Dialogue, style, and tone are tools that a writer uses to give a story a certain feeling, or mood. For example, the mood might be humorous or suspenseful.

The Missing Cat

"I can't find Bear!" cried June. Bear was June's half-grown kitten. His name came from his habit of disappearing into boxes and bags and under beds. He would sleep peacefully in the dark while the whole family called and searched. Finally, he would saunter out, yawning blissfully. June decided that the cat was in fact hibernating. These hidey holes were as close to a cave as he could get.

Descriptive details create a humorous picture.

Mom asked, "Have you looked in his favorite caves?"

"Of course, Mom!" June groaned. "Where can he be?"

Dialogue sounds natural.

They sat at the kitchen table and thought. Then they heard a tiny scratching sound. It was coming from one of the drawers! Somehow, Bear had squeezed his way into a kitchen drawer. Now he was happily wedged into the tiniest cave yet.

Finally, June and Mom got Bear unstuck. He walked away, tail in the air, as if he'd just checked out of a deluxe hotel!

Ending creates a memorable, humorous image.

Unit 4 Exploding Ants — Writing Model **18A**

▲ **Writing Transparency** 18A

DAY 2 Improve Writing

WRITER'S CRAFT
Mood

Display Writing Transparency 18B. Read the directions and work together to identify the mood of each paragraph.

ESTABLISH A MOOD

 Tomorrow we will write stories about animals that surprised us. What details could be used to capture a mood of surprise? I could say, "The bug suddenly soared about ten feet backwards, all the while facing me." This describes a surprising action exactly. I could say, "I stopped dead in my tracks and rubbed my eyes." This statement has a tone of astonishment.

GUIDED WRITING Some students may need more help identifying mood. Have them read parts of different stories aloud and talk about the feelings these words elicit.

Mood

The **mood** of a story is the overall feeling it creates for the reader. For example, the mood may be humorous, serious, or suspenseful. Descriptive details, the things characters say, and the tone with which they speak are some things that help create the mood.

Directions Match each passage with the mood it creates.

    suspenseful   admiring

1. I had to give that housefly credit. I had swatted at it dozens of times. It neatly avoided my swatter every time. How did it always manage to take off just before the swatter hit? It could see in any direction, I knew, with its compound eyes. It could fly in any direction instantly, without runway or fuel. It could land on the ceiling, out of reach, because its legs were fitted with barbs for hanging on.

   admiring

2. I held my breath. "All right," I said to myself, "The bear has seen you. Now what?" Should I run for it? Would it attack? What did it want? I stood frozen to the ground. It was like one of those awful dreams where you can't move. The bear snuffled noisily at the air and stood on its hind legs, eyeing me carefully. I could only hope it would go for the food in my tent. I began mentally measuring the distance from the bear to me and from me to the car. If it turned toward the tent, I just might be able to make it to the car.

   suspenseful

Directions On a separate sheet of paper, write a passage about an animal in which you build a specific mood. Write the mood you hope to create on the first line. Then write your passage.

Possible answer: Mood: frightened. The spider sat right in front of my nose. I had run under the tree to hide from my brother and came within two inches of the biggest, blackest spider I had ever seen! Its long pointed legs raised one by one, reminding me of daggers. My whole body began to quake, and chills ran up my spine. "Please," I prayed, "don't let it be a jumping spider!"

Unit 4 Exploding Ants — Writer's Craft **18B**

▲ **Writing Transparency** 18B

DAY 3 Prewrite and Draft

READ THE WRITING PROMPT
on page 453 in the Student Edition.

The author of Exploding Ants *describes unusual and unexpected animal behaviors.*

Think about your own experiences observing animals.

Now write a story about an animal whose behavior surprised you.

Writing Test Tips

- State the problem or event you will describe. What events make up the beginning, middle, and end?
- Choose a mood and list words that go with that mood.
- Write dialogue that sounds like natural speech.

GETTING STARTED Students can do any of the following:

- Make a story plan listing the animal, any characters, and plot events.
- Brainstorm vivid verbs, precise nouns, and describing words to create an image of the animal.
- Experiment with dialogue: what characters will say and how they will say it.

DAY 4 Draft and Revise

EDITING/REVISING CHECKLIST

☑ Did I create a mood with my choice of details?

☑ Have I used possessive pronouns correctly?

☑ Did I use the correct homophone for the context?

See *The Grammar and Writing Book,* pp. 152-157.

Revising Tips

Word Choice

- Choose words that communicate a specific mood or tone.
- Refer to dictionaries and thesauruses for word choice and correct spelling.
- Avoid wording that sounds stiff and unnatural.
- Use a precise noun or verb to convey your meaning.

PUBLISHING Suggest that students illustrate their stories with animal pictures that enhance the mood. Some students may wish to revise their work later.

ASSESSMENT Use the scoring rubric to evaluate students' work.

DAY 5 Connect to Unit Writing

Story	
Week 1	E-mail 411g–411h
Week 2	Journal Entry 435g–435h
Week 3	Story About an Animal 457g–457h
Week 4	Advice 483g–483h
Week 5	Describe How You Achieved a Goal 503g–503h

PREVIEW THE UNIT PROMPT

Tell a story about a character who succeeds by adapting to a new situation. Focus on an event that shows this person's resourcefulness. Your story may be real or imagined.

APPLY

- A story has a beginning, middle, and end and focuses on one incident or event.
- Use words, details, style, and tone to create mood in a story.

Writing Trait Rubric

	4	3	2	1
Word Choice	Vivid style created by use of exact nouns, strong verbs, exciting adjectives, and clear figurative language	Some style created by strong and precise words	Little style created by strong, precise words; some lack of clarity	Word choice vague or incorrect
	Uses strong, specific words that make story clear, lively, and energetic	Uses some specific words that make story clear and vivid at times	Needs more precise word choice to create style and clarity in story	Story made dull or unclear by vague, repetitive, and limited word choice

Spelling & Phonics Homophones

OBJECTIVE

● Spell homophones.

Generalization

Connect to Phonics A homophone is a word that sounds exactly like another word but has a different spelling and meaning: *cent, sent.* Homophones occur because many letters and letter combinations make more than one sound.

Spelling Words

1. cent	11. chili
2. sent	12. chilly
3. scent	13. tide
4. threw	14. tied
5. through*	15. pale
6. weather	16. pail
7. whether	17. aloud
8. their*	18. allowed
9. there*	19. course
10. they're*	20. coarse

Challenge Words

21. counsel	24. bazaar
22. council	25. patients
23. bizarre	26. patience

* Words from the selection

ELL

Spelling/Phonics Support See the ELL and Transition Handbook for spelling support.

DAY 1 Pretest and Sort

PRETEST

Use the Dictation Sentences from Day 5 to administer the pretest. Read the word, read the sentence, and then read the word again. Guide students in self-correcting their pretests and correcting any misspellings.

Monitor Progress

Spelling

If... students misspell more than 5 pretest words,	**then**... use words 1–10 for Strategic Intervention.
If... students misspell 1–5 pretest words,	**then**... use words 1–20 for On-Level practice.
If... students correctly spell all pretest words,	**then**... use words 1–26 for Advanced Learners.

HOMEWORK Spelling Practice Book, p. 69.

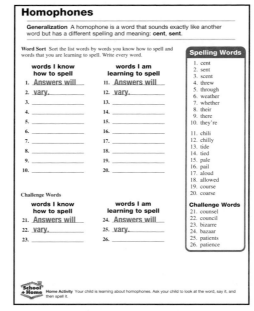

▲ **Spelling Practice Book** p. 69

DAY 2 Think and Practice

TEACH

Explain that homonyms are words with the same sound but different spelling and meaning. Write *threw* and *through* on the board. Point and say each word. Underline the /oo/ sound in each word and say it aloud. Cross out and write *oo*. Then point to each word and use it in a sentence. Repeat with other homonyms.

oo	oo
through	threw

FIND THE PATTERN Ask students to circle the word parts in each homophone pair or group that are spelled differently.

HOMEWORK Spelling Practice Book, p. 70.

Homophones

Spelling Words				
cent	sent	scent	threw	through
weather	whether	their	there	they're
chili	chilly	tide	tied	pale
pail	aloud	allowed	course	coarse

Words in Context Write homophones to complete each sentence.

On a (1)____ day, hot, spicy (2)____ with cheese really tastes good.

1. chilly   2. chili

We made sure the boats were (3)____ down securely against the rising (4)____.

3. tied   4. tide

The (5)____ will determine (6)____ or not we play the game.

5. weather   6. whether

I (7)____ away for that special one (8)____ offer for my favorite perfume (9)____.

7. sent   8. cent   9. scent

Speaking (10)____ is not (11)____ in the library.

10. aloud   11. allowed

You (12)____ the ball so far that it went (13)____ the window!

12. threw   13. through

(14)____ starting (15)____ lemonade business over (16)____ near the bakery.

14. They're   15. their   16. there

The golf (17)____ is designed to be challenging. It has sand, water traps, woods, and smooth and (18)____ grass.

17. course   18. coarse

The (19)____ child carried the (20)____ onto the beach.

19. pale   20. pail

▲ **Spelling Practice Book** p. 70

DAY 3 Connect to Writing

WRITE A DESCRIPTION

Have students write a description of a favorite pet, game, sport, or trip. Have students use at least four list words in their description.

Frequently Misspelled Words

when   *then*
went

These words may seem easy to spell, but they are often misspelled by fifth-graders because they are easy to confuse with other words. Alert students to these frequently misspelled words.

HOMEWORK Spelling Practice Book, p. 71.

Homophones

Proofread an Ad Circle six spelling errors. Write the words correctly. Find one capitalization error. Write the sentence correctly.

On a chilly day, shout (allowed) for our delicious (chilly!)
It will warm you through and (threw!) Ask about our
99¢ (sent) special. If the (whether) is bad, call us. We (Deliver)
for free! Of course, (their) is no finer taste treat!

1. **aloud**	2. **chili**
3. **through**	4. **cent**
5. **weather**	6. **there**

7. **We deliver for free!**

Spelling Words
cent
sent
scent
threw
through
weather
whether
their
there
they're
chili
chilly
tide
tied
pale
pail
aloud
allowed
course
coarse

Proofread Words Circle the correct spelling of the list words. Write the word.

8. Burlap is a ____ fabric.
   corse   coarse   (coarse)   8. **coarse**
9. I think ____ going on a class trip tomorrow.
   (they're)   their   they'ar   9. **they're**
10. Sky blue is a ____ color.
   pail   (pale)   paile   10. **pale**
11. Your perfume has a lovely ____.
   (scent)   cent   sent   11. **scent**
12. I am not sure ____ I can go.
   weather   (whether)   weather   12. **whether**
13. The sailor ____ down the ship's hatch.
   tide   teid   (tied)   13. **tied**
14. The candy cost one ____.
   scent   (cent)   sent   14. **cent**
15. The score was even and the game was ____.
   tide   teid   (tied)   15. **tied**

Frequently Misspelled Words
their
there
they're

School + Home Home Activity Your child identified misspelled and misused homophones. Say a homophone in a sentence and have your child spell it.

▲ **Spelling Practice Book** p. 71

DAY 4 Review

REVIEW HOMOPHONES

Have partners write each list word on small index cards. Cards are shuffled and each player gets three cards. Players ask each other if they have a matching homophone for a card they have in their hand. If the partner has a card, it is handed over, if not, the player picks a card. Homophone pairs and groups are placed on the table. Play continues until all of the cards are paired/grouped.

Spelling Strategy
Rhyming Helpers

It is sometimes hard to remember which homophone spelling to use. Rhymes can help. For example:

pail/hail
I used a pail to catch the hail.

coarse/hoarse
My voice was coarse because I was hoarse.

HOMEWORK Spelling Practice Book, p. 72.

Homophones

Spelling Words				
cent	sent	scent	threw	through
weather	whether	their	there	they're
chili	chilly	tide	tied	pale
pail	aloud	allowed	course	coarse

Word Search Circle eight list words that are hidden in the puzzle. Write each word you find.

	1. **aloud**
	2. **chilly**
	3. **course**
	4. **pail**
	5. **their**
	6. **through**
	7. **tied**
	8. **whether**

Words in Context Write a list word to complete each sentence.

9. Ninety-nine plus one ____ more equals one dollar.   9. **cent**
10. The pitcher ____ the ball over the plate.   10. **threw**
11. We had ____ with our hot dog.   11. **chili**
12. The ____ was perfect for the beach.   12. **weather**
13. The boy needs sunscreen on his ____ skin.   13. **pale**
14. Swimming is not ____ when the lifeguard is off-duty.   14. **allowed**
15. She ____ her classmate a party invitation.   15. **sent**
16. The rose had a wonderful ____.   16. **scent**
17. We looked for seashells when the ____ was out.   17. **tide**
18. The ____ fabric was itchy.   18. **coarse**

School + Home Home Activity Your child has learned to read, write, and spell homophones. Say a homophone and spell it. Ask your child to say and spell the other homophone.

▲ **Spelling Practice Book** p. 72

DAY 5 Posttest

DICTATION SENTENCES

1. A penny is one cent.

2. I sent a letter to my pen pal.

3. The flower had a sweet scent.

4. The pitcher threw a curve ball.

5. I cut through the fabric.

6. I hope the weather is nice today.

7. Did you decide whether to have carrots or corn?

8. Their cage door was open.

9. The popcorn stand is over there.

10. They're coming home tomorrow.

11. Chili peppers are hot and spicy.

12. It's damp and chilly outside today.

13. At low tide, the beach is wide.

14. I tied my laces three times.

15. Lilac is a pale purple color.

16. The farmer carried a pail of milk.

17. I like to read poetry aloud.

18. Pets are not allowed in the zoo.

19. I took a pottery course.

20. The sandpaper feels coarse.

CHALLENGE

21. A lawyer offers legal counsel.

22. The city council voted to install a stop light.

23. Some things are meant to be strange and bizarre.

24. The open-air bazaar had food, clothing, and crafts for sale.

25. The patients read magazines in the doctor's waiting room.

26. I don't have enough patience to solve that puzzle.

- Formulate an inquiry question that is connected to this week's lesson focus.
- Effectively and efficiently find, evaluate, and communicate information related to an inquiry question using electronic sources.

New Literacies	
Day 1	**Identify Questions**
Day 2	**Navigate/Search**
Day 3	**Analyze**
Day 4	**Synthesize**
Day 5	**Communicate**

NEW LITERACIES

Internet Inquiry Activity

EXPLORE ANIMAL ADAPTATIONS

Use the following 5-day plan to help students conduct this week's Internet inquiry activity on animal adaptations. Remind students to follow classroom rules when using the Internet.

DAY 1

Identify Questions Discuss the lesson focus question: *How do animals adapt to survive?* Brainstorm ideas for specific inquiry questions about animal adaptations and survival. For example, students might want to learn about chameleons and how they adapt by changing color. Have students work individually, in pairs, or in small groups to write inquiry questions they want to answer. Students should formulate hypotheses to guide their inquiries.

DAY 2

Navigate/Search Have students write a brief description of the adaptations they want to find. Have them choose keywords and enter them into a student-friendly search engine. Students should scan the descriptions from the search before proceeding to the sites.

DAY 3

Analyze Have students skim and scan the Web sites they identified on Day 2. Circulate around the classroom to verify that the Web sites they've found answer their basic questions, and suggest that they narrow their searches or revise their inquiry questions if necessary.

DAY 4

Synthesize Have students synthesize information from Day 3 by combining the most important pieces of information from each Web site they used. Remind them to document their sources and avoid plagiarism by restating information in their own words. Encourage them to think about adding some form of visual element to their final products.

DAY 5

Communicate Have students share their inquiry results in the form of oral reports with posters featuring drawings, clip art, or some form of graphic organizers.

RESEARCH/STUDY SKILLS
Magazine/Periodical

TEACH

Ask students to name reference sources where they might locate new research about animals. Students may need prompting before they mention science or nature magazines. Explain these features of a magazine article.

- A **periodical** is a **magazine** that contains current information in the form of articles, opinion columns, letters, reports, advertisements, and reviews.
- The **headline** or **title** expresses the topic of the article.
- Most magazines include a **Table of Contents** which tells the reader what information is in the magazine and where to find it.
- Most magazines follow the **5 Ws and How** format. The article will tell you *Who? What? When? Where? Why?* and *How?*

Give students photocopies of an article from a children's science or nature magazine. Have students read the article. Then, discuss these questions as a class:

1. **Identify the 5 Ws and How the article answers.** *(Responses will vary. Call on volunteers to read aloud the relevant text.)*

2. **What does the title tell you about the article? Based on the title, did the article cover what you expected?** *(Responses will vary but may suggest the title tells the article's main idea.)*

ASSESS

Make sure students can identify the 5 Ws and How and understand the function of the article's title.

For more practice or to assess students, use Practice Book pp. 179–180.

- Understand features of a magazine article.
- Analyze the format and features of a magazine article.

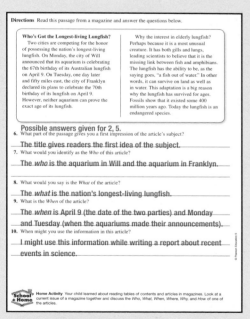

▲ **Practice Book** p. 179

▲ **Practice Book** p. 180

Assessment Checkpoints *for the Week*

Selection Assessment

Use pp. 69–72 of Selection Tests to check:

 Selection Understanding

  Comprehension Skill *Graphic Sources*

Selection Vocabulary
critical
enables
mucus
scarce
specialize
sterile

Leveled Assessment

- On-Level
- Strategic Intervention
- Advanced

Use pp. 103–108 of Fresh Reads for Differentiated Test Practice to check:

  Comprehension Skill *Graphic Sources*

 REVIEW Comprehension Skill *Author's Purpose*

Fluency *Words Correct Per Minute*

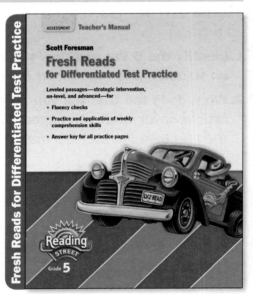

Managing Assessment

Use Assessment Handbook for:

 Observation Checklists

 Record-Keeping Forms

 Portfolio Assessment

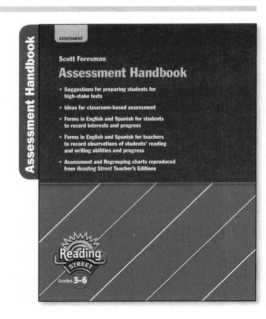

Illinois

Planning Guide for Performance Descriptors

The Stormi Giovanni Club

Reading Street Teacher's Edition pages   **Grade 5 English Language Arts Performance Descriptors**

Oral Language

Speaking/Listening Build Concept Vocabulary: 458l, 469, 477, 483c
Read Aloud: 458m

1B.Stage E.10. Read age-appropriate material aloud with fluency and accuracy.

4B.Stage E.10. Contribute meaningfully to small and large group discussions by following accepted guidelines for verbal interaction.

Word Work

Suffixes *-ible, -able:* 483i–483j

1A.Stage E.2. Learn and use root words, prefixes, and suffixes to understand word meanings.

Reading

Comprehension Generalize: 458–459, 462–477, 480–483, 483b
Story Structure: 458–459, 462–477, 480–483
Vocabulary Lesson Vocabulary: 460b, 469, 477, 480
Context Clues: 460–461, 473, 483c
Fluency Model Tone of Voice: 458l–458m, 483a
Self-Selected Reading: LR28–36, TR16–17
Literature Genre—Play: 462
Reader Response: 478

1A.Stage E.1. Use a combination of word analysis and vocabulary strategies (e.g., word patterns, structural analyses) within context to identify unknown words.

1B.Stage E.9. Apply self-monitoring and self-correcting strategies continuously to clarify understanding during reading.

1C.Stage E.4. Compare the content and organization (e.g., themes, topics, text structure, story elements) of various selections.

1C.Stage E.6. Select reading strategies for text appropriate to the reader's purpose.

2A.Stage E.2. Identify literary elements and techniques in literary genres and tell how they affect the story.

2A.Stage E.4. Explain how a technique or element affects the events or characterization in a literary work.

Language Arts

Writing Letter of Advice: 483g–483h
Six-Trait Writing Voice: 479, 483g–483h
Grammar, Usage, and Mechanics Indefinite and Reflexive Pronouns: 483e–483f
Research/Study Thesaurus: 483l
Technology New Literacies: 483k

1A.Stage E.8. Use additional resources (e.g., newspapers, interviews, technological resources) as applicable to clarify meanings of material.

4B.Stage E.5. Use appropriate grammar, word choice, and pacing.

5C.Stage E.1. Select an appropriate format to accommodate characteristics of audiences (e.g., age, background, interest level, group size) and purposes of the presentation (e.g., inform, persuade, entertain).

Unit Skills

Writing Story: WA2–9
Poetry: 504–507
Project/Wrap-Up: 508–509

3A.Stage E.1. Write paragraphs that include a variety of sentence types (i.e., declarative, interrogative, exclamatory, imperative).

3C.Stage E.3. Write creatively for a specified purpose and audience (e.g., short story, poetry, directions, song, friendly letter).

This Week's Leveled Readers

Below-Level

1B.Stage E.1. Set a purpose for reading and adjust as necessary before and during reading.

2A.Stage E.4. Explain how a technique or element affects the events or characterization in a literary work.

Fiction

On-Level

1B.Stage E.5. Distinguish between significant and minor details.

2A.Stage E.4. Explain how a technique or element affects the events or characterization in a literary work.

Nonfiction

Advanced

1C.Stage E.5. Recognize similarities/differences of varying styles or points of view.

2A.Stage E.4. Explain how a technique or element affects the events or characterization in a literary work.

Fiction

Content-Area Illinois Performance Descriptors in This Lesson

Social Studies

14A.Stage E.1. Give examples of civic and personal responsibilities of students and adults.

14D.Stage E.2. Produce a plan to increase student and/or parent involvement in school activities.

16D.Stage E.6. Discuss how the roles of men, women, and children in past cultures have changed over time.

17C.Stage E.2. Map the location of students in your school by coloring the different areas (cafeteria, classrooms, gym, etc.) to show different population densities at a given time of day.

18B.Stage E.1. Analyze how social institutions or groups meet the needs of people.

Science

12A.Stage E.4. Apply scientific inquiries or technological designs to examine the nature of learned behavior or responses in all organisms.

13B.Stage E.3. Investigate the interactions of societal decisions in science and technology innovations and discoveries.

Math

6A.Stage E.2. Show equivalent representations of a number by changing from one form to another form (e.g., standard form to expanded form, fraction to decimal, decimal to percent, improper fraction to mixed number).

Illinois!

A FAMOUS ILLINOISAN
Ernest Hemingway

Ernest Hemingway (1899–1961) was born and raised in Oak Park, a suburb of Chicago. He spent considerable time with his family in upper Michigan, where he learned to hunt and fish—activities that would appear in his writing throughout his career. Hemingway won the 1953 Pulitzer Prize in fiction for his novel *The Old Man and the Sea,* the story of an elderly Cuban fisherman.

Students can . . .
Find out more about the Pulitzer Prize. Have students make a list of the Pulitzer Prize categories and then make up a new category and create an award for it.

A SPECIAL ILLINOIS PLACE
Ravinia

In 1905 the A.C. Frost Company created Ravinia in northern Illinois as an amusement park. The Martin Theatre is the only building that remains from the original site. In 1910 the first version of Ravinia Park came to an end, and a group of private citizens founded the Ravinia Company. Today Ravinia is a musical venue that hosts the oldest summer musical festival in North America.

Students can . . .
Find out the names of some artists who have performed at Ravinia. Have students choose one name and write a brief biography of that person.

ILLINOIS FUN FACTS
Did You Know?

• East St. Louis, directly across the Mississippi from St. Louis, Missouri, was originally called Illinoistown.

• The blue stripes on Chicago's flag represent the Chicago River and its two branches.

• When the Harold Washington Center of the Chicago Public Library system opened in 1991, it was listed in the Guinness Book of Records as the largest public library building in the world.

Students can . . .
Write an essay explaining the importance of libraries. Have students share their essays with the class.

Unit 4
Adapting

Week 4

EXPAND THE CONCEPT
How do people adapt to a new school?

Time for SOCIAL STUDIES

CONCEPT QUESTION
How do people and animals adapt to different situations?

CONNECT THE CONCEPT

▶ **Build Background**
count on, settle in

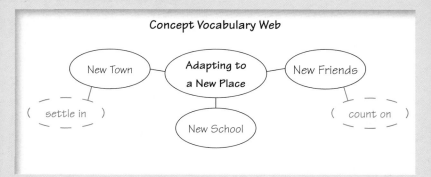

Concept Vocabulary Web

New Town — Adapting to a New Place — New Friends

(settle in)   New School   (count on)

Week 1

How do people adapt to difficult situations?

Week 2

How do people adapt to living with physical limitations?

Week 3

How do animals adapt to survive?

Week 4

How do people adapt to a new school?

Week 5

Why do people try to change themselves?

▶ **Social Studies Content**
Moving, E-mail, Friendship

▶ **Writing**
Advice

▶ **Internet Inquiry**
E-mail

Preview Your Week

How do people adapt to a new school?

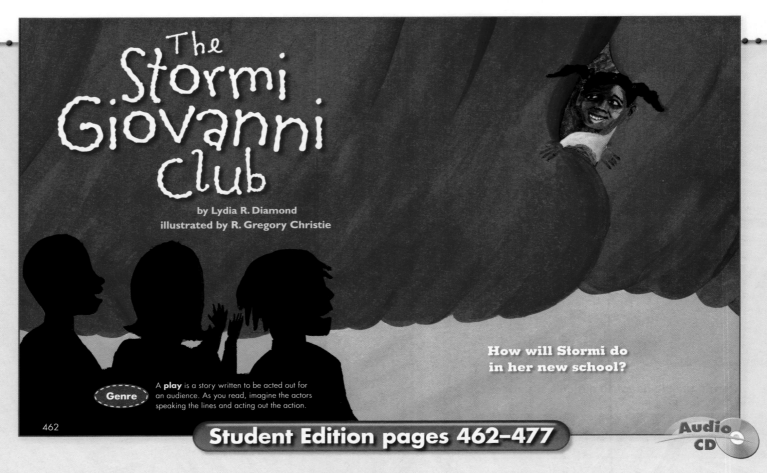

The Stormi Giovanni Club

by Lydia R. Diamond
illustrated by R. Gregory Christie

How will Stormi do in her new school?

Genre A **play** is a story written to be acted out for an audience. As you read, imagine the actors speaking the lines and acting out the action.

462

Student Edition pages 462–477

Audio CD

Genre	Play
Vocabulary Strategy	Context Clues
Comprehension Skill	Generalize
Comprehension Strategy	Story Structure

Paired Selection

SOCIAL STUDIES

Reading Across Texts
Make a List of Problems Students Face at School

Genre
Newspaper Article

Text Features
Headlines, Datelines, and Illustrations

Social Studies in Reading

Newspaper Article

Genre
- A newspaper article tells readers about current events, issues, people, and places of interest.
- News articles should report facts—actual events and quotations.

Text Features
- A news article begins with a headline that gives readers an idea of what the article is about.
- A dateline, which gives the day the article appeared, often follows the headline.
- Before reading, scan the headline and illustrations to see what the article is about.

Link to Social Studies
Find out about dress codes in your school and other schools in your area. Are there differences? Why?

480

50¢ City & Suburbs; 75¢ Elsewhere

FASHION

TUESDAY APRIL 15, 2003

Think DRESS codes are a drag?

by Emilie Ostrander
Special to the Tribune

While shopping for new clothes, Elyse B., 13, of Mt. Prospect, Illinois, also is scouting for hot trends. Dressed in a bright pink tank top and denim capris, Elyse says she's found an outfit she likes. The catch? Her school dress code bans tank tops—and the penalty is anything but stylish. "If they catch you, you have to change into your gym uniform," she says.

For Elyse, shopping for new clothes is all about looking good without getting in trouble. "We

Savvy Shoppers Can Still Look Cool for School

can't wear spaghetti straps, halter tops, or tube tops," she explains. "Tank top straps must be the width of two fingers, and shorts and skirts have to be longer than 5 inches above the knee."

As we get into spring, many kids are ready to take their warm-weather clothes to school. But some school districts say certain styles are banned from the classroom, and there are consequences for kids who disobey.

Author's Purpose What is the author's purpose or purposes?

Student Edition pages 480–483

Audio CD

Read It
ONLINE
PearsonSuccessNet.com

- Student Edition
- Leveled Readers

Leveled Readers

◉ **Skill** Generalize
◉ **Strategy** Story Structure
Lesson Vocabulary

Moving
by Vera Douglas

Below-Level

The New Kid at School
by Elena Orum

On-Level

Nathaniel Comes to Town
by Johanna Riviero

Advanced

ELL Reader

· Concept Vocabulary
· Text Support
· Language Enrichment

In This New Place
Poems
by Linda Marino
Illustrated by Rosario Valderrama

Time for
SOCIAL STUDIES

Integrate Social Studies Standards

- **Individual Development**
- **Interactions**
- **Groups**
- **Communication**

✓ **Read**

The Stormi Giovanni Club,
pp. 462–477

"Think Dress Codes Are a Drag?"
pp. 480–483

Leveled Readers

Below-Level · On-Level · Advanced
· Support Concepts · Develop Concepts · Extend Concepts

ELL Reader

✓ **Build Concept Vocabulary**
Adapting to a New Place,
pp. 458l–458m

✓ **Teach Social Studies Concepts**
Moving, p. 467
E-Mail, p. 471
Friendship, p. 473

✓ **Explore Social Studies Center**
Share Helpful Hints, p. 458k

The Stormi Giovanni Club **458c**

Weekly Plan

READING

45–90 minutes

TARGET SKILLS OF THE WEEK

Comprehension Skill
Generalize

Comprehension Strategy
Story Structure

Vocabulary Strategy
Context Clues

LANGUAGE ARTS

30–60 minutes

Trait of the Week

Voice

DAY 1 — PAGES 458l–460b, 483a, 483e–483k

Oral Language

QUESTION OF THE WEEK *How do people adapt to a new school?*

Read Aloud: "Only Fiona," 458m
Build Concepts, 458l

Comprehension/Vocabulary

Comprehension Skill/Strategy Lesson, 458–459
Generalize **T**
Story Structure
Build Background, 460a

Introduce Lesson Vocabulary, 460b
cavities, combination, demonstrates, episode, profile, strict **T**

Read Leveled Readers

Grouping Options 458f–458g

Fluency

Model Tone of Voice, 458l–458m, 483a

Grammar, 483e
Introduce Indefinite and Reflexive Pronouns **T**

Writing Workshop, 483g
Introduce Letter of Advice
Model the Trait of the Week: Voice

Spelling, 483i
Pretest for Suffixes *-ible, -able*

Internet Inquiry, 483k
Identify Questions

DAY 2 — PAGES 460–469, 483a, 483e–483k

Oral Language

QUESTION OF THE DAY *What challenges does Stormi face as a new student?*

Comprehension/Vocabulary

Vocabulary Strategy Lesson, 460
Context Clues **T**

Read *The Stormi Giovanni Club,* 462–469

Grouping Options 458f–458g

Generalize **T**
Story Structure
REVIEW Draw Conclusions **T**
Develop Vocabulary

Fluency

Choral Reading, 483a

Grammar, 483e
Develop Indefinite and Reflexive Pronouns **T**

Writing Workshop, 483g
Improve Writing with Good Conclusions

Spelling, 483i
Teach the Generalization

Internet Inquiry, 483k
Navigate/Search

DAILY WRITING ACTIVITIES

Day 1 Write to Read, 458

Day 2 Words to Write, 461
Strategy Response Log, 462, 469

DAILY SOCIAL STUDIES CONNECTIONS

Day 1 Adapting to a New Place Concept Web, 458l

Day 2 Time for Social Studies: Moving, 467
Revisit the Adapting to a New Place Concept Web, 469

DAILY SUCCESS PREDICTORS
for Adequate Yearly Progress

Monitor Progress and Corrective Feedback

Vocabulary — Check Vocabulary, *458l*

RESOURCES FOR THE WEEK

- Practice Book, *pp. 181–190*
- Word Study and Spelling Practice Book, *pp. 73–76*
- Grammar and Writing Practice Book, *pp. 73–76*
- Selection Test, *pp. 73–76*
- Fresh Reads for Differentiated Test Practice, *pp. 109–114*
- The Grammar and Writing Book, *pp. 158–163*

Grouping Options for Differentiated Instruction

Turn the page for the small group lesson plan.

DAY 3 — PAGES 470–479, 483a, 483e–483k

Oral Language

QUESTION OF THE DAY *What do Stormi's experiences teach her about making friends?*

Comprehension/Vocabulary

Read *The Stormi Giovanni Club,* 470–478

Grouping Options 458f–458g

- 🔘 Generalize **T**
- 🔘 Story Structure
- 🔘 Context Clues **T**
- Develop Vocabulary

Reader Response

Selection Test

Fluency

Model Tone of Voice, 483a

Grammar, 483f
Apply Indefinite and Reflexive Pronouns in Writing **T**

Writing Workshop, 479, 483h
Write Now
Prewrite and Draft

Spelling, 483j
Connect Spelling to Writing

Internet Inquiry, 483k
Analyze Sources

Day 3 Strategy Response Log, 476
Look Back and Write, 478

Day 3 Time for Social Studies: E-mail, 471
Friendship, 473; Revisit the Adapting to a
New Place Concept Web, 477

DAY 4 — PAGES 480–483a, 483e–483k

Oral Language

QUESTION OF THE DAY *What do you think is the significance of having a school dress code?*

Comprehension/Vocabulary

Read *"Think Dress Codes Are a Drag?"*
480–483

Grouping Options 458f –458g

Newspaper Article
Reading Across Texts
Content-Area Vocabulary

Fluency

Partner Reading, 483a

Grammar, 483f
Practice Indefinite and Reflexive Pronouns for
Standardized Tests **T**

Writing Workshop, 483h
Draft, Revise, and Publish

Spelling, 483j
Provide a Strategy

Internet Inquiry, 483k
Synthesize Information

Day 4 Writing Across Texts, 483

Day 4 Social Studies Center: Share Helpful
Hints, 458k

DAY 5 — PAGES 483a–483l

Oral Language

QUESTION OF THE WEEK *To wrap up the week, revisit the Day 1 question.*
Build Concept Vocabulary, 483c

Fluency

Read Leveled Readers

Grouping Options 458f–458g

Assess Reading Rate, 483a

Comprehension/Vocabulary

- 🔘 Reteach Generalize, 483b **T**
- Mood, 483b
- 🔘 Review Context Clues, 483c **T**

Speaking and Listening, 483d
Advice
Listen to Advice

Grammar, 483f
Cumulative Review

Writing Workshop, 483h
Connect to Unit Writing

Spelling, 483j
Posttest for Suffixes *-ible, -able*

Internet Inquiry, 483k
Communicate Results

Research/Study Skills, 483l
Thesaurus

Day 5 Mood, 483b

Day 5 Revisit the Adapting to a New Place Concept
Web, 483c

KEY 🔘 = Target Skill **T** = Tested Skill

Comprehension — Check Retelling, *478*

Fluency — Check Fluency WCPM, *483a*

Vocabulary — Check Vocabulary, *483c*

SUCCESS PREDICTOR

Small Group Plan *for Differentiated Instruction*

Daily Plan
AT A GLANCE

Reading
Whole Group
- Oral Language
- Comprehension/Vocabulary

Group Time
Differentiated Instruction

Meet with small groups to provide:
- Skill Support
- Reading Support
- Fluency Practice

Read

This week's lessons for daily group time can be found behind the Differentiated Instruction (DI) tab on pp. DI·32–DI·41.

Whole Group
- Fluency

Language Arts
- Grammar
- Writing
- Spelling
- Research/Inquiry
- Speaking/Listening/Viewing

Use *My Sidewalks on Reading Street* for Tier III intensive reading intervention.

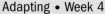

DAY 1

On-Level	Strategic Intervention	Advanced
Teacher-Led *Page DI·33*	**Teacher-Led** *Page DI·32*	**Teacher-Led** *Page DI·33*
• Develop Concept Vocabulary • **Read** On-Level Reader *The New Kid at School*	• **Reinforce** Concepts • **Read** Below-Level Reader *Moving*	• **Read** Advanced Reader *Nathaniel Comes to Town* • Independent Extension Activity

ⓘ Independent Activities

While you meet with small groups, have the rest of the class...

- Visit the Reading/Library Center
- Listen to the Background Building Audio
- Finish Write to Read, p. 458
- Complete Practice Book pp. 183–184
- Visit Cross-Curricular Centers

DAY 2

On-Level	Strategic Intervention	Advanced
Teacher-Led *Pages 464–469*	**Teacher-Led** *Page DI·34*	**Teacher-Led** *Page DI·35*
• **Read** *The Stormi Giovanni Club*	• Practice Lesson Vocabulary • Read Multisyllabic Words • **Read** or Listen to *The Stormi Giovanni Club*	• Extend Vocabulary • **Read** *The Stormi Giovanni Club*

ⓘ Independent Activities

While you meet with small groups, have the rest of the class...

- Visit the Reading/Library Center
- Listen to the AudioText for *The Stormi Giovanni Club*
- Finish Words to Write, p. 461
- Complete Practice Book pp. 185–186
- Write in their Strategy Response Logs, pp. 462, 469
- Visit Cross-Curricular Centers
- Work on inquiry projects

DAY 3

On-Level	Strategic Intervention	Advanced
Teacher-Led *Pages 470–477*	**Teacher-Led** *Page DI·36*	**Teacher-Led** *Page DI·37*
• **Read** *The Stormi Giovanni Club*	• Practice Generalize and Story Structure • **Read** or Listen to *The Stormi Giovanni Club*	• Extend Generalize and Story Structure • **Read** *The Stormi Giovanni Club*

ⓘ Independent Activities

While you meet with small groups, have the rest of the class...

- Visit the Reading/Library Center
- Listen to the AudioText for *The Stormi Giovanni Club*
- Write in their Strategy Response Logs, p. 476
- Finish Look Back and Write, p. 478
- Complete Practice Book p. 187
- Visit Cross-Curricular Centers
- Work on inquiry projects

① Begin with whole class skill and strategy instruction.

② Meet with small groups to provide differentiated instruction.

③ Gather the whole class back together for fluency and language arts.

DAY 4

On-Level
Teacher-Led
Pages 480–483

- **Read** "Think Dress Codes Are a Drag?"

Strategic Intervention
Teacher-Led
Page DI • 38

- Practice Retelling
- **Read** or Listen to "Think Dress Codes Are a Drag?"

Advanced
Teacher-Led
Page DI • 39

- **Read** "Think Dress Codes Are a Drag?"
- Genre Study

ⓘ Independent Activities

While you meet with small groups, have the rest of the class...

- Visit the Reading/Library Center
- Listen to the AudioText for "Think Dress Codes Are a Drag?"
- Visit the Writing/Vocabulary Center

- Finish Writing Across Texts, p. 483
- Visit Cross-Curricular Centers
- Work on inquiry projects

DAY 5

On-Level
Teacher-Led
Page DI • 41

- **Reread** Leveled Reader *The New Kid at School*
- Retell *The New Kid at School*

Strategic Intervention
Teacher-Led
Page DI • 40

- **Reread** Leveled Reader *Moving*
- Retell *Moving*

Advanced
Teacher-Led
Page DI • 41

- **Reread** Leveled Reader *Nathaniel Comes to Town*
- Share Extension Activity

ⓘ Independent Activities

While you meet with small groups, have the rest of the class...

- Visit the Reading/Library Center
- Complete Practice Book pp. 188–190

- Visit Cross-Curricular Centers
- Work on inquiry projects

ELL

Grouping Place English language learners in the groups that correspond to their reading abilities in English.

Use the appropriate Leveled Reader or other text at students' instructional level.

TiP Send home the appropriate Multilingual Summary of the main selection on Day 1.

Take It to the NET™ ONLINE
PearsonSuccessNet.com

Peter Afflerbach
For ideas on assessing engagement, see the article "Engaged Assessment of Engaged Readers" by Scott Foresman author Peter Afflerbach.

TEACHER TALK

Curriculum compacting
is a technique for content acceleration. Students skip work they already have mastered and complete more challenging content.

Looking Ahead

Be sure to schedule time for students to work on the unit inquiry project "Adaptations." This week students synthesize information about groups of people or animals who have adapted to different situations.

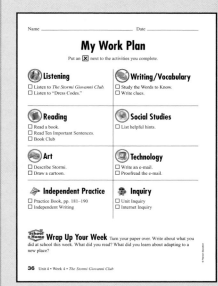

My Work Plan
Put an ☒ next to the activities you complete.

Listening
☐ Listen to *The Stormi Giovanni Club*.
☐ Listen to "Dress Codes."

Writing/Vocabulary
☐ Study the Words to Know.
☐ Write clues.

Reading
☐ Read a book.
☐ Read Ten Important Sentences.
☐ Book Club

Social Studies
☐ List helpful hints.

Art
☐ Describe Stormi.
☐ Draw a cartoon.

Technology
☐ Write an e-mail.
☐ Proofread the e-mail.

Independent Practice
☐ Practice Book, pp. 181–190
☐ Independent Writing

Inquiry
☐ Unit Inquiry
☐ Internet Inquiry

Wrap Up Your Week Turn your paper over. Write about what you did at school this week. What did you read? What did you learn about adapting to a new place?

36 Unit 4 • Week 4 • *The Stormi Giovanni Club*

▲ **Group-Time Survival Guide**
p. 36, Weekly Contract

☑ Customize Your Plan *by Strand*

ORAL LANGUAGE

SOCIAL STUDIES

Concept Development

How do people adapt to a new school?

CONCEPT VOCABULARY
count on   *settle in*

BUILD

❑ **Question of the Week** Introduce and discuss the question of the week. This week students will read a variety of texts and work on projects related to the concept *adapting to a new place*. Post the question for students to refer to throughout the week. DAY 1 *458d*

❑ **Read Aloud** Read aloud "Only Fiona." Then begin a web to build concepts and concept vocabulary related to this week's lesson and the unit theme, Adapting. Introduce the concept words *count on* and *settle in* and have students place them on the web. Display the web for use throughout the week. DAY 1 *458l–458m*

DEVELOP

❑ **Question of the Day** Use the prompts from the Weekly Plan to engage students in conversations related to this week's reading and the unit theme. **EVERY DAY** *458d–458e*

❑ **Concept Vocabulary Web** Revisit the Adapting to a New Place Concept Web and encourage students to add concept words from their reading and life experiences. DAY 2 *469*, DAY 3 *477*

CONNECT

❑ **Looking Back/Moving Forward** Revisit the Adapting to a New Place Concept Web and discuss how it relates to this week's lesson and the unit theme. Then make connections to next week's lesson. DAY 5 *483c*

CHECK

❑ **Concept Vocabulary Web** Use the Adapting to a New Place Concept Web to check students' understanding of the concept vocabulary words *count on* and *settle in*. DAY 1 *458l*, DAY 5 *483c*

VOCABULARY

⟳ STRATEGY CONTEXT CLUES
Sometimes when you are reading, you come across a word you do not know. You can use the context, the words and sentences around the word, to find clues to help figure out the meaning.

LESSON VOCABULARY
cavities   episode
combination   profile
demonstrates strict

TEACH

❑ **Words to Know** Give students the opportunity to tell what they already know about this week's lesson vocabulary words. Then discuss word meaning. DAY 1 *460b*

❑ **Vocabulary Strategy Lesson** Use the vocabulary strategy lesson in the Student Edition to introduce and model this week's strategy, *context clues*. DAY 2 *460-461*

Vocabulary Strategy Lesson

PRACTICE/APPLY

❑ **Leveled Text** Read the lesson vocabulary in the context of leveled text. DAY 1 *LR28-LR36*

❑ **Words in Context** Read the lesson vocabulary and apply *context clues* in the context of *The Stormi Giovanni Club*. DAY 2 *462-469*, DAY 3 *470-478*

Leveled Readers

❑ **Writing/Vocabulary Center** Use the Words to Know to write clues for a crossword puzzle. **ANY DAY** *458k*

❑ **Homework** Practice Book pp. 184–185. DAY 1 *460b*, DAY 2 *461*

Main Selection—Drama

❑ **Word Play** Have small groups of students brainstorm a list of city nicknames they have heard of or make up some of their own. Have groups quiz each other to see if they can identify cities by their nicknames. **ANY DAY** *483c*

ASSESS

❑ **Selection Test** Use the Selection Test to determine students' understanding of the lesson vocabulary words. DAY 3

RETEACH/REVIEW

❑ **Reteach Lesson** If necessary, use this lesson to reteach and review *context clues*. DAY 5 *483c*

① Use assessment data to determine your instructional focus.

② Preview this week's instruction by strand.

③ Choose instructional activities that meet the needs of your classroom.

COMPREHENSION

⊙ SKILL GENERALIZE To generalize is to make a broad statement or rule that applies to several examples.

⊙ STRATEGY STORY STRUCTURE Story structure is how a fictional story or article is put together. The structure of a story includes how the story begins (the problem), how it builds through the middle (rising action and climax), and how it ends (resolution).

TEACH

☐ **Skill/Strategy Lesson** Use the skill/strategy lesson in the Student Edition to introduce and model *generalize* and *story structure*. DAY 1 *458-459*

☐ **Extend Skills** Teach mood. ANY DAY *483b*

Skill/Strategy Lesson

PRACTICE/APPLY

☐ **Leveled Text** Apply *generalize* and *story structure* to read leveled text. DAY 1 *LR28-LR36*

☐ **Skills and Strategies in Context** Read *The Stormi Giovanni Club*, using the Guiding Comprehension questions to apply *generalize* and *story structure*. DAY 2 *462-469*, DAY 3 *470-478*

Leveled Readers

☐ **Skills and Strategies in Context** Read "Think Dress Codes Are a Drag?," guiding students as they apply *generalize* and *story structure*. Then have students discuss and write across texts. DAY 4 *480-483*

Main Selection—Drama

☐ **Homework** Practice Book pp. 183, 187, 188. DAY 1 *459*, DAY 3 *477*, DAY 5 *483b*

☐ **Fresh Reads for Differentiated Test Practice** Have students practice *generalize* with a new passage. DAY 3

Paired Selection—Nonfiction

ASSESS

☐ **Selection Test** Determine students' understanding of the selection and their use of *generalize* DAY 3

☐ **Retell** Have students retell *The Stormi Giovanni Club*. DAY 3 *478-479*

RETEACH/REVIEW

☐ **Reteach Lesson** If necessary, reteach and review *generalize*. DAY 5 *483b*

FLUENCY

SKILL TONE OF VOICE Adjusting your tone of voice allows you to show different emotions as you read. Thinking about what is happening or how a character feels can help you know how to use your voice while reading. Emotions such as desperation or suspense are easily conveyed through a changing tone of voice.

TEACH

☐ **Read Aloud** Model fluent reading by rereading "Only Fiona." Focus on this week's fluency skill, tone of voice. DAY 1 *458l-458m, 483a*

PRACTICE/APPLY

☐ **Choral Reading** Read aloud selected paragraphs from *The Stormi Giovanni Club*, emphasizing the changing inflections in your voice. Then practice as a class, doing three choral readings of the selected paragraphs. DAY 2 *483a*, DAY 3 *483a*

☐ **Partner Reading** Have partners practice reading aloud, reading with changing inflections to reflect different characters' emotions, and offering each other feedback. As students reread, monitor their progress toward their individual fluency goals. DAY 4 *483a*

☐ **Listening Center** Have students follow along with the AudioText for this week's selections. ANY DAY *458j*

☐ **Reading/Library Center** Have students reread a selection of their choice. ANY DAY *458j*

☐ **Fluency Coach** Have students use Fluency Coach to listen to fluent readings or practice reading on their own. ANY DAY

ASSESS

☐ **Check Fluency** WCPM Do a one-minute timed reading, paying special attention to this week's skill— tone of voice. Provide feedback for each student. DAY 5 *483a*

☑ Customize Your Plan *by Strand*

GRAMMAR

SKILL INDEFINITE AND REFLEXIVE PRONOUNS *Indefinite pronouns* such as *somebody* or *no one,* may not refer to specific words. They do not always have definite antecedents. *Reflexive pronouns* reflect the action of the verb back on the subject. Reflexive pronouns end in *-self* or *-selves.*

TEACH

❑ **Grammar Transparency 19** Use Grammar Transparency 19 to teach indefinite and reflexive pronouns. DAY 1 *483e*

Grammar Transparency 19

PRACTICE/APPLY

❑ **Develop the Concept** Review the concept of indefinite and reflexive pronouns and provide guided practice. DAY 2 *483e*

❑ **Apply to Writing** Have students review something they have written and apply indefinite and reflexive pronouns. DAY 3 *483f*

❑ **Test Preparation** Examine common errors in indefinite and reflexive pronouns to prepare for standardized tests. DAY 4 *483f*

❑ **Homework** Grammar and Writing Practice Book pp. 73–75. DAY 2 *483e*, DAY 3 *483f*, DAY 4 *483f*

ASSESS

❑ **Cumulative Review** Use Grammar and Writing Practice Book p. 76. DAY 5 *483f*

RETEACH/REVIEW

❑ **Daily Fix-It** Have students find and correct errors in grammar, spelling, and punctuation. **EVERY DAY** *483e–483f*

❑ **The Grammar and Writing Book** Use pp. 158–161 of The Grammar and Writing Book to extend instruction for indefinite and reflexive pronouns. **ANY DAY**

The Grammar and Writing Book

WRITING

Trait of the Week

VOICE Good writers have a strong voice—a personality that comes through in the tone and style of their writing. Voice shows that a writer knows and cares about a topic. A strong voice speaks directly to readers and keeps their attention.

TEACH

❑ **Writing Transparency 19A** Use the model to introduce and discuss the Trait of the Week. DAY 1 *483g*

❑ **Writing Transparency 19B** Use the transparency to show students how good conclusions can improve their writing. DAY 2 *483g*

Writing Transparency 19A   **Writing Transparency 19B**

PRACTICE/APPLY

❑ **Write Now** Examine the model on Student Edition p. 479. Then have students write their own letter of advice. DAY 3 *479, 483h*, DAY 4 *483h*

> **Prompt** In *The Stormi Giovanni Club*, other people help Stormi adjust to a new school. Think about a situation in which you could offer help or advice. Now write a letter of advice to someone in that situation.

Write Now p. 479

❑ **Writing/Vocabulary Center** Use the Words to Know to write clues for a crossword puzzle. **ANY DAY** *458k*

ASSESS

❑ **Writing Trait Rubric** Use the rubric to evaluate students' writing. DAY 4 *483h*

RETEACH/REVIEW

❑ **The Grammar and Writing Book** Use pp. 158–163 of The Grammar and Writing Book to extend instruction for indefinite and reflexive pronouns, good conclusions, and letters of advice. **ANY DAY**

The Grammar and Writing Book

1 Use assessment data to determine your instructional focus.

2 Preview this week's instruction by strand.

3 Choose instructional activities that meet the needs of your classroom.

SPELLING

GENERALIZATION SUFFIXES -IBLE, -ABLE   When adding the suffix *-ible* or *-able*, there are no sound clues to help you decide which form to use: *agreeable, flexible*. The vowel sound spelled by the letters *ib* and *ab* is the /ə/ and can be spelled many different ways.

TEACH

❑ **Pretest** Give the pretest for words with suffixes *-ible, -able*. Guide students in self-correcting their pretests and correcting any misspellings. **DAY 1** *483i*

❑ **Think and Practice** Connect spelling to the phonics generalization for suffixes *-ible, -able*. **DAY 2** *483i*

PRACTICE/APPLY

❑ **Connect to Writing** Have students use spelling words to make a poster. Then review frequently misspelled words: *when, then, went*. **DAY 3** *483j*

❑ **Homework** Word Study and Spelling Practice Book pp. 73–76. **EVERY DAY**

RETEACH/REVIEW

❑ **Review** Review spelling words to prepare for the posttest. Then provide students with a spelling strategy—divide and conquer. **DAY 4** *483j*

ASSESS

❑ **Posttest** Use dictation sentences to give the posttest for words with suffixes *-ible, -able*. **DAY 5** *483j*

Spelling Words

1. sensible	8. reasonable	15. allowable
2. washable	9. favorable	16. divisible
3. available	10. breakable	17. hospitable*
4. agreeable	11. convertible	18. reversible
5. fashionable	12. forgettable	19. responsible
6. valuable	13. laughable	20. tolerable
7. flexible	14. sociable	

Challenge Words

21. noticeable	23. disposable	25. collapsible
22. conceivable	24. biodegradable	

*Word from the selection

RESEARCH AND INQUIRY

❑ **Internet Inquiry** Have students conduct an Internet inquiry on e-mail. **EVERY DAY** *483k*

❑ **Thesaurus** Review the features associated with a thesaurus and discuss how students can use a thesaurus to locate synonyms. **DAY 5** *483l*

❑ **Unit Inquiry** Allow time for students to synthesize the information they gathered about groups of people or animals who have adapted to different situations. **ANY DAY** *391*

SPEAKING AND LISTENING

❑ **Advice** Have students write and present a speech on giving advice to a group of new students adapting to their new school. **DAY 5** *483d*

❑ **Listen to Advice** Have students reflect on the advice they were given by classmates and answer questions. **DAY 5** *483d*

Resources for Differentiated Instruction

LEVELED READERS

▶ **Comprehension**

◎ **Skill** Generalize

◎ **Strategy** Story Structure

▶ **Lesson Vocabulary**

◎ **Context Clues**

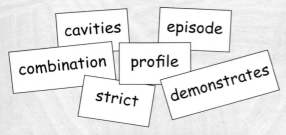

cavities episode combination profile strict demonstrates

▶ **Social Studies Standards**

- **Individual Development**
- **Interactions**
- **Groups**
- **Communication**

Leveled Reader Database ONLINE

PearsonSuccessNet.com

Use the Online Database of over 600 books to

- Download and print additional copies of this week's leveled readers.
- Listen to the readers being read online.
- Search for more titles focused on this week's skills, topic, and content.

On-Level

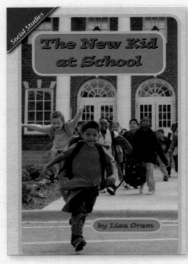

On-Level Reader

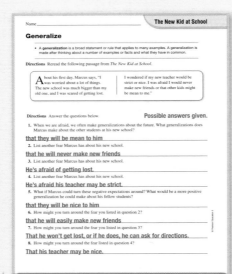

On-Level Practice TE p. LR32

On-Level Practice TE p. LR33

Strategic Intervention

Below-Level Reader

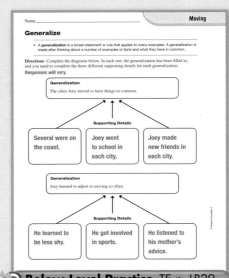

Below-Level Practice TE p. LR29

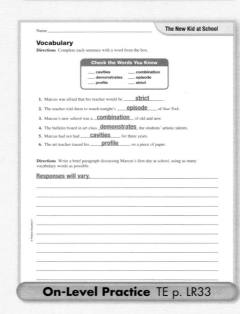

Below-Level Practice TE p. LR30

Advanced

Advanced Reader
Nathaniel Comes to Town
by Johanna Biviano

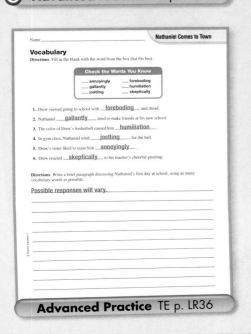

Name _____ **Nathaniel Comes to Town**

Generalize

- A **generalization** is a broad statement or rule that applies to many examples. A generalization is made after thinking about a number of examples or facts and what they have in common.

Directions What are some of the difficulties faced by Nathaniel as a new student? What can you generalize about the difficulties that all new students face?

1-5.
Nathaniel needs to make new friends, needs to find his way in his
new class, and he needs to make Drew be his best friend.
In general, all new students have to make new friends at a new
school and fit in with the other students.

Directions Based on Drew's experiences, what can you generalize about how difficult it is to help a new student find his way?

6-10.
Drew has trouble because Nathaniel is younger than him and he's
afraid that other students will make fun of him for having a younger
friend. He gets jealous when Nathaniel sits down with one of his
friends for lunch, and later that day he snaps at him.
In general, it's very hard to fit a new person into an existing group of
friends at school. But many of Drew's problems were overcome by
the end of the story.

Advanced Practice TE p. LR35

Name _____ **Nathaniel Comes to Town**

Vocabulary
Directions Fill in the blank with the word from the box that fits best.

Check the Words You Know
- annoyingly
- gallantly
- jostling
- foreboding
- humiliation
- skeptically

1. Drew viewed going to school with __foreboding__ and dread.
2. Nathaniel __gallantly__ tried to make friends at his new school.
3. The color of Drew's basketball caused him __humiliation__.
4. In gym class, Nathaniel tried __jostling__ for the ball.
5. Drew's sister liked to tease him __annoyingly__.
6. Drew reacted __skeptically__ to his teacher's cheerful greeting.

Directions Write a brief paragraph discussing Nathaniel's first day at school, using as many vocabulary words as possible.

Possible responses will vary.
_____
_____
_____
_____

Advanced Practice TE p. LR36

ELL Reader

ELL Poster 19

Teacher's Edition Notes

ELL notes throughout this lesson support instruction and reference additional resources at point of use.

Teaching Guide pp. 127–133, 248–249
- Multilingual summaries of the main selection
- Comprehension lesson
- Vocabulary strategies and word cards
- ELL Reader 5.4.4 lesson

ELL and Transition Handbook

Ten Important Sentences
- Key ideas from every selection in the Student Edition
- Activities to build sentence power

More Reading

Readers' Theater Anthology
- Fluency practice
- Five scripts to build fluency
- Poetry for oral interpretation

Leveled Trade Books

Advanced
Below-Level
On-Level

- Extended reading tied to the unit concept
- Lessons in the Trade Book Library Teaching Guide

School + Home

Homework
- Family Times Newsletter
- ELL Multilingual Selection Summaries

Take-Home Books
- Leveled Readers

The Stormi Giovanni Club

SKILLS ⟷ STRATEGIES IN CONTEXT

Generalize
Story Structure

Skills Trace
⟲ Generalize

Introduce/Teach	TE: 5.4 412–413, 458–459; 5.5 604–605
Practice	Practice Book: 163, 167, 168, 183, 187, 188, 196, 243, 247, 248
Reteach/Review	TE: 5.4 435b, 483b, 493, DI-53, DI-55; 5.5 625b, DI-56
Test	Selection Test: 65–68, 73–76, 97–100; Benchmark Test: Unit 4

INTRODUCE

Write a sentence starter on the board: *Most of the students in the class are....* Have volunteers look around the room and use what they see to complete the sentences. *(For example: Most of the students in the class are ready for lunch.)* Point out that the completed sentences are generalizations about the students in the class.

Have students read the information on p. 458. Explain the following:

- A generalization is a statement about what several people or things have in common.

- Knowing how stories are generally structured can help you identify, understand, and remember key ideas.

Use Skill Transparency 19 to teach generalize and story structure.

Comprehension

Skill
Generalize

Strategy
Story Structure

⟲ Generalize

- To generalize is to make a broad statement or rule that applies to several examples.

- Active readers pay close attention to what authors tell them about story characters and make generalizations about those characters as they read.

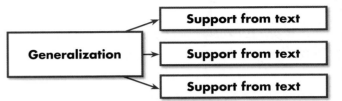

```
                              → Support from text
Generalization  →  Support from text
                              → Support from text
```

⟲ Strategy: Story Structure

Active readers notice story structure. They note the problem characters must deal with and the rising action, climax, and outcome. Generally, authors identify the problem at the start. They work through the problem as the action rises in the middle, and then solve it with the climax and outcome.

Write to Read

1. Read "Thirty Pounds of Trouble." Make a graphic organizer similar to the one above about the story's main character, Tag.

2. Use your graphic organizer to decide whether you would like a dog like Tag and tell why.

458

Strategic Intervention

⟲ **Generalize** To help students understand how to generalize, work with them to create a three-column chart. In the first column, list names of popular TV shows. In the second column, list main characters in each show. In the third column, help students create generalizations about the characters using the following sentence starter: *Most of the characters in this show are....* Later, discuss students' generalizations.

ELL

Access Content

Beginning/Intermediate For a Picture It! lesson on generalize, see ELL Teaching Guide, pp. 127–128.

Advanced Before students read "Thirty Pounds of Trouble," have a volunteer read the first sentence aloud. This statement is a generalization. Students can make up two or three statements that support this generalization.

Thirty Pounds of Trouble

A new canine member in the family can bring joy. It can also bring trouble. Tag was our new dog, a mutt with the silliest grin. He weighed thirty pounds—thirty pounds of genuine trouble.

Tag commenced to wailing like a wolf whenever the moon came up, which kept us up all night. When he was inside, he whined to be let outside. When he was outside, he whimpered to get back in. He would crouch behind the couch and come hurtling out at Mother, and when Father was on the phone, Tag would seize the cord and yank the receiver away.

Finally, Mother and Father had absolutely no patience left. "Tag has got to go," they said.

"No," I cried. I adored that canine rascal, even if he did make munchies of my homework and conceal my socks in the rose bushes. I just had to find a way to keep Tag!

I know it sounds incredible, but six weeks later Tag graduated Obedience School at the head of his class. I think Tag was as surprised as we were. Now he is quiet and polite pretty much all the time. He still has that silly grin though, and he still hides my socks in the rose bushes.

1 **Strategy** Generally, the story's problem is told at the start. What is the problem here?

2 **Skill** Which generalization can you make?
a) Tag likes people.
b) Tag upsets people.
c) Tag is expensive.

3 **Strategy** Generally, the action rises in the middle. What is the high point of the story so far?

4 **Skill** What generalization can you make about the narrator's feelings for Tag? How does the text support it?

459

Available as **Skill Transparency** 19

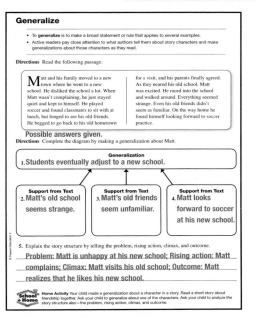

▲ **Practice Book** p. 183

TEACH

1 **STRATEGY** Model locating a problem in a story.

Think Aloud **MODEL** I know that the problem usually appears at the beginning of a story. The first paragraph tells me that the family got a new dog that is "thirty pounds of trouble." This gives me a clue about the problem. In the second paragraph, I find out that the dog is a little out of control. Now I know that the dog's behavior is the problem.

2 **SKILL** Model how to make a generalization.

Think Aloud **MODEL** I know that a generalization tells what several people or things have in common. From paragraph 2, I know that Tag's bad behavior is bothering several people in the house. Therefore, the correct generalization is *b*.

PRACTICE AND ASSESS

3 **STRATEGY** Possible response: The high point occurs when the parents say, "Tag has got to go."

4 **SKILL** Possible response: Generalization: The narrator is generally pleased with how Tag has improved. Support: Tag graduated Obedience School at the head of his class. Now he is quiet and polite most of the time.

WRITE Have students complete steps 1 and 2 of the Write to Read activity. You might consider using this as a whole-class activity.

Monitor Progress
 **Generalize**

If... students are unable to complete **Write to Read** on p. 458,	**then...** use Practice Book p. 183 to provide additional practice.

ONLINE

Students can find out more about making new friends by using the keywords *making friends* or *going back to school* on a student-friendly search engine. Be sure to follow classroom rules for Internet use.

ELL

Build Background Use ELL Poster 19 to build background and vocabulary for the lesson concept of adapting to a new school.

▲ **ELL Poster** 19

Build Background

ACTIVATE PRIOR KNOWLEDGE

MAKE A CONCEPT WEB about making new friends.

- Give students two to three minutes to brainstorm ideas about making new friends.
- Have them use a concept web to record their ideas.
- Tell students that, as they read, they should look for more ideas to add to their concept web.

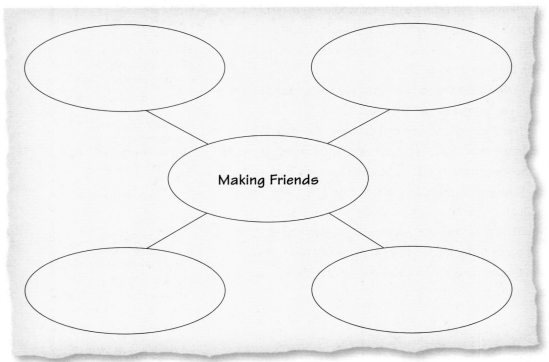

▲ **Graphic Organizer** 15

BACKGROUND BUILDING AUDIO This week's audio explores adapting to a new school. After students listen, discuss what they found out and what surprised them most about going to a new school.

Background Building Audio

Introduce Vocabulary

WORD RATING CHART

Create word rating charts using the categories *Know, Have Seen,* and *Don't Know.*

Word Rating Chart

Word	Know	Have Seen	Don't Know
cavities	✓		
combination		✓	
demonstrates		✓	
episode			✓
profile			✓
strict	✓		

▲ **Graphic Organizer** 5

Read each word to students and have them check one of the three columns: *Know* (know and can use); *Have Seen* (have seen or heard the word; don't know meaning); *Don't Know* (don't know the word). ***Activate Prior Knowledge***

Have students share where they may have seen some of these words. Point out that some of this week's words have multiple meanings *(profile)* and students may learn new definitions for these words. ***Multiple-Meaning Words***

Check charts with students at the end of the week and have them make changes to their ratings.

Use the Multisyllabic Word Routine on p. DI·1 to help students read multisyllabic words.

Lesson Vocabulary

WORDS TO KNOW

T cavities hollow places; holes in teeth caused by decay

T combination a series of numbers or letters dialed in opening a certain kind of lock

T demonstrates shows how a thing is done

T episode one part of a story that is published or broadcast in several parts, one at a time

T profile *low profile,* moderate attitude or position, deliberately chosen in order to avoid notice

T strict very careful in following a rule or making others follow it

MORE WORDS TO KNOW

audacious rudely bold

digressed turned aside from the main subject in talking or writing

scintillating sparkling; flashing

T = Tested Word

Vocabulary

Directions Choose the word from the box that best matches each definition below. Write the word on the line.

cavities	**1.** hollow places in teeth caused by decay
demonstrates	**2.** shows how a thing is done
strict	**3.** very careful in following a rule or making others follow it
episode	**4.** one part of a story that is published or broadcast in several parts
profile	**5.** attitude or position

Check the Words You Know
___cavities
___combination
___demonstrates
___episode
___profile
___strict

Directions Choose the word from the box that best matches each clue below. Write the word on the line.

episode	**6.** This is one in a series.
combination	**7.** This opens some locks.
strict	**8.** Some teachers act this way.
profile	**9.** A movie star would have a high one of these.
cavities	**10.** If you don't brush your teeth, you might get these.

Write a Friendly Letter
On a separate sheet of paper, write a friendly letter that you might send to a relative telling about the beginning of a new school year. Use as many vocabulary words as you can.
Letters should include words from the vocabulary list as well as information typical to a new school year.

Home Activity Your child identified and used vocabulary words from *The Stormi Giovanni Club.* Read a story or nonfiction article with your child. Have him or her point out unfamiliar words. Together try to figure out the meaning of each word by using the words that appear near it.

▲ **Practice Book** p. 184

Vocabulary Strategy

⊙ Use context clues to determine word meaning.

INTRODUCE

Discuss the strategy for context clues using the steps on p. 460 .

TEACH

- Have students read "Trouble in TV Land," paying attention to any unknown words as they read.

- Model using context clues to determine the meaning of *cavities*.

Think Aloud **MODEL** As I read the sentences around *cavities* I understand that they are talking about taking care of teeth and preventing tooth decay. I think *cavities* must mean "holes in your teeth caused by decay."

DAY 2 Grouping Options

Reading

Whole Group Discuss the Question of the Day. Then use pp. 460–463.

Group Time Differentiated Instruction
Read *The Stormi Giovanni Club.* See pp. 458f–458g for the small group lesson plan.

Whole Group Use p. 483a.

Language Arts
Use pp. 483e–483k.

Words to Know

episode

demonstrates

profile

cavities

strict

combination

Remember

Try the strategy. Then, if you need more help, use your glossary or dictionary.

Vocabulary Strategy
for Unfamiliar Words

Context Clues Sometimes when you are reading, you come across a word you do not know. You can use the context—the words and sentences around the word—to find clues to its meaning.

1. Reread the sentence in which the unknown word appears. Does the author give you a clue, such as a synonym?

2. If not, read the sentences around the sentence with the unknown word. Does the author give you clues, such as examples or explanations?

3. Put the clues together and decide what you think the word means.

4. Try the meaning in the sentence. Does it make sense?

As you read "Trouble in TV Land," look for context clues that help you figure out the meanings of the vocabulary words.

460

Strategic Intervention

⊙ **Context Clues** Have students work with partners to follow the steps on p. 460 for other Words to Know.

ELL

Access Content Use ELL Poster 19 to preteach vocabulary. Choose from the following to meet language proficiency levels.

Beginning/Intermediate Ask students to share what they know about the words *profile*, *strict*, and *combination* in their home languages. For example, the Spanish cognates are: *perfil*, *estricto*, and *combinación*.

Advanced Teach the lesson on pp. 460–461. Have students return to the word rating chart and make appropriate changes to their ratings.

Resources for home-language words may include parents, bilingual staff members, bilingual dictionaries, or online translation sources.

TROUBLE IN TV LAND

Can a TV show teach you how to win friends in the real world? Most sitcoms solve problems in thirty minutes flat, minus about eight minutes of commercials. They present an extremely simple and reassuring view of the world. A single episode demonstrates how to teach a bully the value of kindness or how to overcome your worst fears. Nice-looking young people have a high profile in these shows, and they almost always solve their problems by the end. Plus, the commercials tell you things like how to prevent cavities and whiten your teeth. These commercial messages claim they can save you from tooth decay and so much more. If you will only buy the right clothes and choose the right cell phone, everyone will love you and you will be happy.

In the real world, problems aren't so easily solved. Things you don't enjoy, like having a strict teacher or parent, may actually be good for you. Everyone has problems. Some are as simple as forgetting a locker combination, but others are tough. You can't just make a wish and watch a failing grade go away, for example. To solve problems in the real world, you must be honest and willing to try hard, sometimes for a long time.

Words to Write

Write a letter to your favorite fictional TV character about the way he or she solves problems. Are that character's shows realistic? State your opinion and give reasons to support it. Use words in the Words to Know list if you can.

461

PRACTICE AND ASSESS

- Have students define the remaining Words to Know and explain the context clues they used.
- Review how to use the glossary or dictionary for words that students can't define in context.
- If you began a word rating chart on p. 460b, have students reassess their ratings.
- Have students complete Practice Book p. 185.

WRITE Have students follow the form of a friendly letter and use two or more Words to Know to help them express their opinions.

Monitor Progress

Context Clues

If... students need more practice with the lesson vocabulary,	**then...** use Tested Vocabulary Cards.

Vocabulary · Context Clues

- Sometimes when you are reading, you see an unfamiliar word. Use the **context**, or words around the unfamiliar word, to find clues to its meaning.
- Context clues include synonyms, examples, and explanations.

Directions Read the following passage. Then answer the questions below.

In class, Meg's teacher demonstrated, or showed, how to open the new lockers. "Dial the combination and then pull the handle," she said. Instead of paying attention, however, Meg talked to her friend about an episode of her favorite TV show, the last one of the series. "Meg, you are not supposed to talk while I am talking. I am very strict about following this rule. Please stay in class during recess," her teacher said sternly. Meg was very embarrassed, but she was glad she didn't have to stay after school. She had to go to the dentist to have her cavities filled after school.

1. What does *demonstrated* mean? What clue helps you to determine the meaning?
   Demonstrated means "showed." The clue is the synonym *showed.*

2. What does *combination* mean? How does the context help you to determine the meaning?
   Combination means "a series of numbers used in opening a lock." The clue is the word *dial.*

3. What is an *episode*? What clue helps you to determine this?
   Episode means "a story that is one in a series." The phrase "last one in the series" helps to define *episode.*

4. How do context clues help you determine the meaning of *strict*?
   Strict means "careful in following the rules." The phrases "following this rule" and "sternly" are context clues.

5. What does *cavities* mean? How can you use context clues to determine the meaning?
   Cavities means "holes or hollow places." The word "filled" is a context clue.

Home Activity Your child read a short passage and used context clues to understand new words. Work with your child to identify unfamiliar words in an article. Ask your child to find context clues to help with the understanding of the new words. Confirm the meanings with your child.

▲ **Practice Book** p. 185

Prereading Strategies

OBJECTIVES

- Generalize about text to improve comprehension.
- Use story structure to help support generalizations.

GENRE STUDY

Play

The Stormi Giovanni Club is a play. Explain that a play is a story written to be performed by actors for an audience. It is written in the form of a script.

PREVIEW AND PREDICT

Have students preview the selection title and illustrations and predict what they think the title means. Students should use lesson vocabulary words during the discussion.

Strategy Response Log

Predict Have students write their predictions in their Strategy Response Logs. Students will check their predictions in the Strategy Response Log activity on p. 469.

The Stormi Giovanni Club

by Lydia R. Diamond
illustrated by R. Gregory Christie

Genre A **play** is a story written to be acted out for an audience. As you read, imagine the actors speaking the lines and acting out the action.

462

ELL

Activate Prior Knowledge ELL students may share the experiences of being new in a school or country. Encourage students to talk about why it is important to make new friends.

Consider having students read the selection summary in English or in students' home languages. See the Multilingual Summaries in the ELL Teaching Guide, pp. 131–133.

How will Stormi do in her new school?

463

SET PURPOSE

Read the first page of the selection aloud to students. Have them consider their preview discussion and tell what they hope to understand as they read the selection.

Remind students to make generalizations about Stormi as they read.

STRATEGY RECALL

Students have now used these before-reading strategies:

- preview the selection to be aware of its genre, features, and possible content;
- activate prior knowledge about that content and what to expect of that genre;
- make predictions;
- set a purpose for reading.

Remind students that, as they read, they should monitor their own comprehension. If they realize something does not make sense, they can regain their comprehension by using fix-up strategies they have learned, such as:

- use phonics and word structure to decode new words;
- use context clues or a dictionary to figure out meanings of new words;
- adjust their reading rate—slow down for difficult text, speed up for easy or familiar text, or skim and scan just for specific information;
- reread parts of the text;
- read on (continue to read for clarification);
- use text features such as headings, subheadings, charts, illustrations, and so on as visual aids to comprehension;
- make a graphic organizer or a semantic organizer to aid comprehension;
- use reference sources, such as an encyclopedia, dictionary, thesaurus, or synonym finder;
- use another person, such as a teacher, a peer, a librarian, or an outside expert, as a resource.

After reading, students will use these strategies:

- summarize or retell the text;
- answer questions they or others pose;
- reflect to make new information become part of their prior knowledge.

Audio CD AudioText

Guiding Comprehension

1 Characters • Inferential

What have you learned so far about Stormi?

Possible response: She's going to a new school. She's not looking forward to it. She has a sense of humor.

2 🎯 Generalize • Inferential

What generalization can you make about how Stormi feels about starting a new school?

Possible response: She's not happy about having to start yet another new school.

Monitor Progress
🎯 Generalize

If... students are unable to make a generalization,	**then...** use the skill and strategy instruction on p. 465.

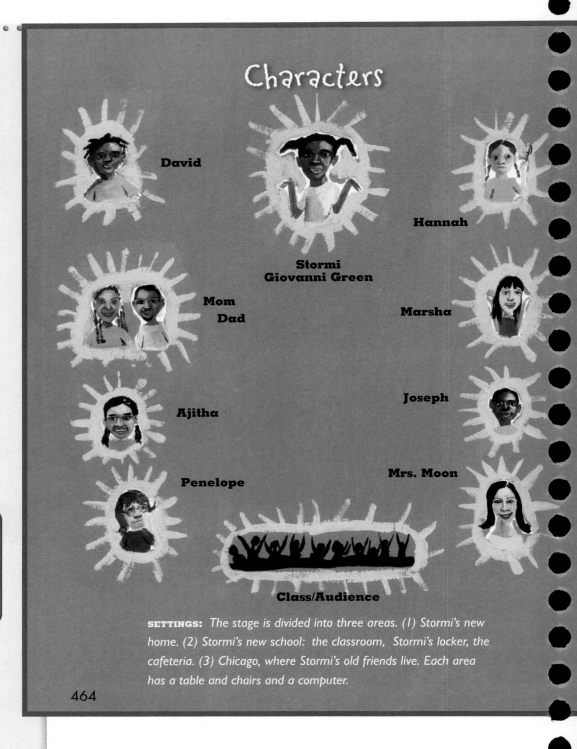

Characters

David

Stormi Giovanni Green

Hannah

Mom Dad

Marsha

Ajitha

Joseph

Penelope

Mrs. Moon

Class/Audience

SETTINGS: *The stage is divided into three areas. (1) Stormi's new home. (2) Stormi's new school: the classroom, Stormi's locker, the cafeteria. (3) Chicago, where Stormi's old friends live. Each area has a table and chairs and a computer.*

464

Access Content Point to the list of characters on p. 464. Explain that the audience is a group of people gathered to see or hear a performance. Tell students that throughout this play, Stormi speaks to the audience, or the class.

SCENE I

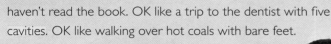

SETTING: *Stormi's new home. There are unpacked boxes everywhere.* MOM *holds Stormi's backpack.*

MOM: Stormi, hurry up.

STORMI *(off stage):* Coming, Mom.

MOM: You don't want to be late on your first day.

STORMI *(entering):* No. Wouldn't want that. *(to* AUDIENCE*)* I would rather not go at all.

MOM: Honey, don't frown. You've started at a new school before. It'll be OK.

STORMI: Yeah. *(to* AUDIENCE*)* OK like a book report due and you haven't read the book. OK like a trip to the dentist with five cavities. OK like walking over hot coals with bare feet.

*(*MOM *hands* STORMI *her backpack and exits.)*

465

SKILLS ↔ STRATEGIES IN CONTEXT

Generalize

TEACH

- Tell students that a generalization is a broad statement or rule that applies to many examples.
- Authors sometimes make generalizations in the text, and readers sometimes make generalizations based on what they have read.

Think Aloud **MODEL** In the first scene between Stormi and her mother I can tell that Stormi is unhappy about starting at a new school. She says going to a new school is like going to the dentist with five cavities.

PRACTICE AND ASSESS

To assess students, ask which statement below is a generalization. *(Choice b)*

a) Stormi and her family have moved before.

b) Moving to a new place is usually difficult for people.

c) Stormi has a backpack.

Guiding Comprehension

3 **Draw Conclusions • Inferential**

What conclusion can you draw about the relationship between Stormi and her friends in Chicago?

They were close friends.

Monitor Progress

REVIEW Draw Conclusions

If... students have difficulty drawing conclusions,	then... use the skill and strategy instruction on p. 467.

4 **Author's Purpose • Critical**

Question the Author **In Scene II, why do you think the author includes the scenes with Stormi's friends in Chicago?**

To show Stormi's close friends and how they feel about her moving away.

5 **Predict • Critical**

Do you think Stormi will like her new school and make new friends? Why?

Possible response: Eventually she will, but at first it will be hard.

ONLINE

Students can learn more about the life and work of the famous poet Stormi is named after by typing *Nikki Giovanni* into a student-friendly search engine. Be sure to follow classroom guidelines for Internet use.

SCENE II

SETTINGS: *In Stormi's new school,* STORMI *is in the classroom.* MOM *stands near her. In Chicago,* DAVID, PENELOPE, *and* MARSHA *stand around table.*

STORMI *(to* AUDIENCE*):* Hi. I'm Stormi Giovanni Green. I'm named after Nikki Giovanni, the famous poet. I am not a happy camper! See, Mom and Dad move around a lot with their jobs, and since I'm the kid, I go too. They're college professors. Dad teaches philosophy. Philosophers try to figure out how you know what's true and what's not true, and why some things are right and some things are wrong. I only kind of understand. Mom teaches teachers how to teach. Oops, lost my train of thought. Mom says I'm distressed. . . .

MOM: No, Stormi, you've **digressed.**

*(*MOM *exits.)*

STORMI: **Digressed,** right. Got off the topic. OK. I just moved here from Chicago where I had great friends, played basketball, and was on the speech team. Moving is for the birds. So this time, no new friends. In fact, no anything that I'll just have to say goodbye to. From now on it's the Stormi Giovanni Club, and I'm the only member. When I told Marsha and Penelope I was moving they said:

MARSHA & PENELOPE: NOOO!!!!

STORMI: And I said, "Yes." And they said:

MARSHA & PENELOPE: NOOO!!!!

STORMI: And I said, "Yes." And they said:

MARSHA & PENELOPE: NOOO!!!

STORMI: And David said:

466

Understanding Idioms Explain that "for the birds" is an idiom that means worthless or ridiculous. So, Stormi thinks moving is ridiculous.

DAVID: Stop! Don't say "no" again. It'll be OK.

MARSHA: Sure, we can e-mail.

PENELOPE: And telephone.

DAVID: And send letters.

PENELOPE: But it won't be the same! **3**

STORMI *(to AUDIENCE):* That didn't make me feel better.

(In Chicago, DAVID and MARSHA exit. In classroom, MRS. MOON enters.) **4**

STORMI: So, here I am, in homeroom, on the first day of school, keeping a low profile.

MRS. MOON: Welcome, Stormi. Please tell us about yourself.

STORMI *(to CLASS):* I'm Stormi Giovanni. From Chicago.

MRS. MOON: Please tell us about Chicago.

STORMI: It's called the Windy City *(pause)* because it's windy.

MRS. MOON: All right. Let's welcome Stormi Giovanni, class. On the count of three. One, two, three . . .

(MRS. MOON gestures for the class to speak.)

CLASS: WELCOME, STORMI GIOVANNI! **5**

(MRS. MOON exits classroom. STORMI sits at classroom computer.)

467

Moving

The United States is a mobile society. A recent U.S. Bureau of the Census report showed that between March 2003, and March 2004, 39 million, or 14% of the population, moved within the United States. Students in military families move three times more often than children from civilian families.

SKILLS ⟷ STRATEGIES IN CONTEXT

Draw Conclusions REVIEW

TEACH

- Remind students that drawing conclusions means forming reasonable opinions after thinking about the facts and details of what they have read.

- Model drawing a conclusion about Stormi's relationship with her Chicago friends.

Think Aloud **MODEL** The dialogue between Stormi and her friends shows that they didn't want her to move away and promised to keep in touch. I can draw the conclusion that Stormi and her friends were very close and that they will miss each other a lot.

PRACTICE AND ASSESS

- Have students draw a conclusion about how Stormi feels when she's introduced to the class.

- To assess, use Practice Book p. 186.

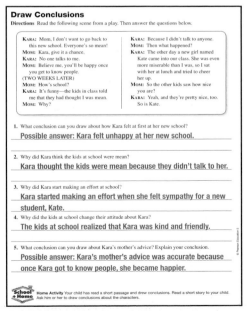

▲ **Practice Book** p. 186

Guiding Comprehension

6 **Cause and Effect • Inferential**

What happens when Hannah tries to find out more about Stormi? Why does Stormi respond that way?

Stormi is rude to her and tells her she doesn't want to talk. She does this because she doesn't want to make new friends.

7 **Characters • Inferential**

Describe Hannah based on what you learn about her on pp. 468–469.

Possible answer: She's friendly and outgoing. She's trying to get to know Stormi.

8 **Compare and Contrast • Critical**

Text to Text **Think about the main character and her problem. Does this play remind you of any other stories you've read?**

Answers will vary, but students should tell about another story they've read about someone who was uncomfortable in a new situation.

STORMI: Well, I lived through homeroom. Things were OK until study hall, when I went online to check my e-mail.

(In Chicago, PENELOPE sits at computer and types.)

PENELOPE: Dear Stormi, I miss you so much. Fifth grade is definitely better than fourth. Everyone says hi. Write to me about your new friends. Love, Penelope.

(In Chicago, PENELOPE exits. In classroom, HANNAH enters and stands behind STORMI. Pens stick out of Hannah's hair, from behind her ears, and hang on a string around her neck.)

STORMI *(typing):* Dear Penelope, FYI, I won't be making friends. Love, Stormi G.

HANNAH *(tapping STORMI on the shoulder):* Do you have a pen? Maybe a roller ball or a ballpoint? Black or blue is best. I don't really go in for the funky colors, you know, the greens and pinks.

STORMI: Oh, I'll look.

(STORMI searches through her backpack.)

468

Access Content Tell students that *FYI* is an abbreviation for "for your information." Explain that it is an expression people use when they want to call attention to something, especially in business.

HANNAH: We aren't allowed to use school computers for e-mail. Mr. Morgan is very strict about that. *(pause)* A mechanical pencil might be all right.

STORMI: I have a yellow #2 pencil.

HANNAH *(examining Stormi's pencil and frowning):* No, thanks. *(handing pencil back)* So, you're the new girl?

STORMI: I guess so.

HANNAH: What brings you here?

STORMI: I don't want to talk about it.

HANNAH: OK. *(pause)* My friends Ajitha and Joseph and I sit together at lunch. If you want, tomorrow you can— 6

STORMI: I always bring a book.

HANNAH: Oh. Don't let Mr. Morgan see you on e-mail— it's a guaranteed detention. 7

STORMI: Thanks. Gotta go. 8

SCENE III

SETTINGS: STORMI *is in her new home. In Chicago,* MARSHA *is at the computer with* DAVID *looking over her shoulder.*

STORMI *(to audience):* Well, I made it through my first day. There's never much homework on the first day so I read a story in my creative writing class and made book covers. Marsha taught me this really cool way to make covers out of the funny papers. I finished and decided to check e-mail. I can go online for an hour after homework as long as Mom checks it first.

469

⊙ STRATEGY SELF-CHECK

Story Structure

Remind students that story structure is how a story, or play, is organized. Most stories include four parts: conflict, rising action, climax, and resolution. Explain that at this point in the play they have not reached the climax or resolution.

SELF-CHECK

Students can ask themselves these questions to assess their ability to use the skill and strategy.

- Was I able to identify the conflict and rising action in the play so far?
- Was I able to make generalizations about the play based on the conflict?

Monitor Progress
⊙ **Generalize**

If… students have difficulty using story structure to make a generalization,	**then…** revisit the skill lesson on p. 458.

Strategy Response Log

Confirm Predictions Were the predictions you made accurate? (See p. 462.) Revise your old predictions. Then make new ones about the rest of the selection.

Develop Vocabulary

PRACTICE LESSON VOCABULARY

Students orally respond *yes* or *no* to each question and provide a reason for each answer.

1. Are *cavities* found in your mouth? *(Yes; cavities are holes in teeth.)*

2. If a teacher *demonstrates* an experiment, is it assigned? *(No; it's clearly shown how it works.)*

3. Is Mr. Morgan *strict* about writing e-mail messages in school? *(Yes; He is firm about the rules.)*

BUILD CONCEPT VOCABULARY

Review previous concept words with students. Ask if students have met any words today in their reading or elsewhere that they would like to add to the Adapting to a New School concept web, such as *distressed.*

If you want to teach this play in two sessions, stop here.

Guiding Comprehension

If you are teaching the play in two days, discuss any generalizations and review the vocabulary.

9 Summarize • Inferential

Summarize what happened to Stormi since she started her new school.

Mrs. Moon welcomed her to the class, she met Hannah, she e-mailed David and Marsha, and her dad asked her to try to make friends.

10 Generalize • Inferential

What generalization can you make about Stormi's friends from their e-mails?

They are thinking about her and miss her.

Monitor Progress
Generalize

If... students have difficulty identifying generalizations,	**then...** use the skill and strategy instruction on p. 471.

DAY 3 Grouping Options

Reading
Whole Group Discuss the Question of the Day.

Group Time Differentiated Instruction
Read *The Stormi Giovanni Club.* See pp. 458f–458g for the small group lesson plan.

Whole Group Discuss the Reader Response questions on p. 478. Then use p. 483a.

Language Arts
Use pp. 483e–483k.

9

MARSHA *(typing):* Dear Stormi, Lunch was a drag without you. But David told us a stupid joke and before we knew it we were laughing anyway. Oh, wait, David wants to say hi.

DAVID *(typing):* Hey, what do you call a cross between a television and a pizza? A really bad idea. You can do it with any two things. Funny, huh? Get it? *(MARSHA pokes DAVID's shoulder.)*

MARSHA *(typing):* Me again. Isn't that the silliest thing? I bet you're making lots of new friends. OK. Later, Alligator.

(MARSHA and DAVID exit.)

STORMI *(typing):* Hey guys. I miss you. School is OK. *(to AUDIENCE)* OK like you forget your permission slip and miss the field trip. OK like your Dad's playoff game's on TV the same night as the "to be continued" episode of your favorite show. OK like vegetarian meatloaf. *(typing)* Not much to write about. Bye.

(STORMI shuts off computer and sits on the floor, legs crossed, looking sad and lonely.)

STORMI: In my old house there was this little room under the stairs. Probably a closet, but it sloped down so there really wasn't enough room in it for anything. I hung a flashlight in there, and put a rug on the floor and made some pillows. I would go there anytime I was sad, or even just needed to think. Here I just have my room.

(DAD enters.)

DAD: How was school?

STORMI: OK I guess, Dad. *(to AUDIENCE)* OK like . . . never mind . . . you get it. It was not OK.

470

Understanding Idioms Restate the sentence "Lunch was a drag without you." Explain that *a drag* means "boring."

DAD: Make any new friends?

STORMI: No.

DAD: Could you try to make just one new friend? For me?

STORMI: You should make your own friends, Dad.

DAD (laughs): Could you try to make just one friend for *you*, then?

STORMI: I make no promises. Could you try to raise my allowance?

DAD: I make no promises, Pumpkin.

(DAD starts to leave.)

DAD: Take a look at the bay window in the living room. I thought we could hang a curtain from the ceiling and let that be your own private space.

STORMI: Thanks, Dad. I'll look at it.

(DAD exits.)

471

E-mail

Time for **SOCIAL STUDIES**

Stormi and her friends depend on e-mail to stay in touch. The first e-mail was sent in 1971. In the beginning, it was mainly used by scientists and researchers as a way to share information. It could only be sent to computers that were all connected to the same host computer. In recent years, e-mail has become the most popular application.

SKILLS ⟷ STRATEGIES IN CONTEXT

Generalize Story Structure

TEACH

- Remind students that when they make a generalization they need details from the text to support it.

- Model using story structure to support a generalization about Stormi's friends.

Think Aloud **MODEL** On p. 470, I can generalize that Stormi's friends miss her because Marsha's e-mail says, "Lunch was a drag without you."

PRACTICE AND ASSESS

Ask students to make a generalization about Stormi's dad and support it with details from the story. *(He is supportive and wishes she would make friends. He asks her to try for his sake.)*

EXTEND SKILLS

Slang

Authors often use slang, or informal language, to make characters seem authentic. For example, Marsha writes "Later, Alligator" at the end of her e-mail, which is an expression friends might say to each other. Find other examples of slang in this play.

The Stormi Giovanni Club 471

Guiding Comprehension

11 **Cause and Effect • Inferential**

What caused Stormi to say her second day at school was worse than the first?

She lost the paper with her locker number on it. Then she had to find the other paper with the combination on it.

12 **Vocabulary • Context Clues**

Use context clues to determine the meaning of *passion* on p. 473.

Clues: Hannah collects pens; something cool. Meaning: very strong liking for something

---

Monitor Progress

Context Clues

If... students have difficulty using context clues to determine the meaning of *passion*,	**then...** use the vocabulary strategy instruction on p. 473.

SCENE IV

SETTINGS: *STORMI's locker in the hallway of her new school. Later, the school cafeteria.*

STORMI *(to AUDIENCE while removing things from her backpack):* The second day was worse than the first. I lost the little piece of paper that had my locker number on it, and I had to go to the office to get a new one. Then I had to dump everything out of my backpack to find the other little piece of paper that had the combination on it.

11 Then I had to figure out how to make the combination lock work.

(HANNAH, JOSEPH, and AJITHA enter.)

HANNAH: Do you always talk to yourself?

472

ELL

Access Content Explain that *unicorns* are imaginary animals that look like horses, but have one long horn in the middle of their foreheads.

STORMI: I wasn't. I was just—

HANNAH: Whatever. I wanted you to meet Joseph. He talks to himself too.

STORMI: Hi.

JOSEPH: Hi. This is Ajitha. Ajitha, Stormi Giovanni.

AJITHA: After the poet?

STORMI (surprised): Yeah.

AJITHA: Are you having a hard time with your locker?

STORMI: We didn't have locks at my old school.

AJITHA: You don't have to lock it. I put tape on the side of mine to keep it open. Like this.

(AJITHA shows STORMI.)

STORMI: Cool. Hannah, did you find a pen?

HANNAH: I got a couple of interesting ones.

JOSEPH: Hannah collects pens.

HANNAH: I'm looking for the perfect pen.

STORMI: Why?

HANNAH: When I was little my grandpa gave me this old silver fountain pen. I wasn't supposed to take it out of the house, but I did, and I lost it. I keep thinking I'll find something almost as cool. It's my passion.

STORMI: That's cool. I have a friend who collects unicorns.

JOSEPH: Next period is lunch if you want. . . .

STORMI: I have a book.

(STORMI exits.)

473

DURING READING

⟳ VOCABULARY STRATEGY

Context Clues

TEACH

Model using context clues to figure out the meaning of *passion* on p. 473.

Think Aloud **MODEL** On p. 473 Hannah is talking about collecting pens and looking for the perfect one. From this I can tell she really likes pens, so *passion* must mean to have a strong liking for something.

PRACTICE AND ASSESS

Have students use context clues to determine the meaning of *period* on p. 473. *(Clues: lunch. Meaning: one of the parts of a school day)*

Friendship

Friendships are very important for physical and emotional health. Research shows that making and having a circle of friends helps with learning and intellectual development in children. Other studies have shown that friendships can help strengthen the immune system. People who have friendships have a longer life expectancy.

Time for **SOCIAL STUDIES**

Guiding Comprehension

13 🔵 **Vocabulary • Context Clues**

Use context clues to determine the meaning of *hospitable* on p. 474.

Clues: no reason to be rude; just trying to be nice. Meaning: giving friendly treatment to friends or strangers.

14 **Characters • Critical**

Why do you think Hannah continues to be friendly to Stormi even after Stormi is rude to her and her friends?

Possible response: Hannah likes Stormi and understands that she is having a hard time being new in school.

15 🔵 **Generalize • Inferential**

Make a generalization about Hannah and her friends. Support it with details from the play.

Hannah and her friends are friendly and understanding because they keep trying to be nice to Stormi. They invite her to sit with them at lunch.

Monitor Progress	
🔵 **Generalize**	
If... students have difficulty generalizing,	**then...** use the skill and strategy instruction on p. 475.

AJITHA: That was audacious. *(pause)* Rude and bold.

HANNAH: She's OK.

JOSEPH: It would be hard to start a new school.

13 **AJITHA:** That's no reason to be rude. We were only trying to be hospitable and gregarious.

JOSEPH: I was just trying to be nice.

(They sit at a table in the school cafeteria and begin eating lunch. STORMI enters.)

STORMI *(to AUDIENCE):* Lunch at a new school is the worst. There's this awful time when you have your tray and you have to figure out where to sit. A book can really help. I sit alone and act like I'm reading. I have to act because it's hard to read in all of that noise. But today my plan didn't work. The cafeteria was packed.

AJITHA: Stormi, you can sit with us.

474

ELL

Activate Prior Knowledge Discuss the reasons why Stormi might have behaved rudely to Hannah and her friends. *(She was feeling insecure, nervous and didn't want them to know that.)*

JOSEPH: What are you reading?

STORMI: *A Wrinkle in Time.*

AJITHA: That book is quite scintillating.

HANNAH: Don't mind her. She likes to use big words. She's not trying to make you feel stupid.

STORMI *(to AJITHA):* Do you write stories?

(AJITHA pulls out a dictionary.)

AJITHA: I try to learn a new word every day. *(reading from dictionary)* Scintillate: to sparkle, gleam.

JOSEPH: *A Wrinkle in Time* is sparkly?

HANNAH: You can sit here and read if you want to.

(STORMI sits.)

JOSEPH: I thought I would try out for the play.

HANNAH: If you do, I will too.

(STORMI tries to look like she's reading but is drawn into the conversation.)

HANNAH: It's *The Wizard of Oz,* right?

STORMI: We did that at my old school. I wanted to be the Lion so badly, but I was too small for the suit. I ended up designing the set.

AJITHA: I could enjoy that.

JOSEPH: I want to be the scarecrow. **15**

(JOSEPH does a funny scarecrow imitation, with limp knees and wobbly head movements.)

475

Generalize

TEACH

- Remind students that a generalization is a broad statement that applies to many examples.
- Model making a generalization about Hannah and her friends on p. 474.

Think Aloud **MODEL** First, I know that Hannah and her friends have tried to talk to Stormi and have invited her to sit with them at lunch, but she said no to their invitation. When Stormi can't find a place to sit in the cafeteria, they invite her to sit with them again, even though she was rude the first time. This tells me that Hannah and her friends are friendly and understanding towards Stormi.

PRACTICE AND ASSESS

- Have students state a generalization about Stormi's feelings towards Hannah and her friends at the end of p. 475. *(She begins to take an interest in them.)*
- Remind them to back up their generalization with details. *(Stormi begins talking to them and the stage directions say Stormi is "drawn into the conversation.")*

Guiding Comprehension

16 **Compare and Contrast • Critical**

Compare and contrast Stormi's friends in Chicago with her new friends.

Possible responses: Compare: David and Joseph both have a funny sense of humor. Hannah and Penelope both like to collect things. They like to sit together at lunch. Contrast: Joseph acts in plays. Hannah collects pens, but Penelope collects unicorns.

17 **Main Idea • Critical**

Text to Self **Describe an experience you had with being the new person in a group. How did it feel? What did you do?**

Answers will vary but should include descriptions of personal experiences where students had to adapt to new groups of people.

Strategy Response Log

Summarize When students finish reading the selection, provide this prompt: In four or five sentences, explain the most important things that happen in *The Stormi Giovanni Club*.

STORMI (*to* AUDIENCE): Lunch was almost as much fun as listening to David's lame jokes would have been. So, I've been thinking. You know how it is when you hurt your finger? Like maybe the pointing finger on the hand you write with. (*STORMI holds up finger and demonstrates.*) All of a sudden you notice all of these things you do with that finger. It hurts to put on a glove. It hurts to sharpen your pencil. It hurts to tie your shoe. And you think, I sure will be happy when this finger is better. Then one day you notice that it's better. You almost can't remember when it stopped hurting. You just didn't notice. It's the same with moving. You can't know when you will stop missing the last place so much it hurts, but you can't stop tying your shoes either. Hey, that sounds a little philosophical. My father would be proud.

(*HANNAH steps forward.*)

HANNAH: Look at this.

STORMI (*pointing to* AUDIENCE): I'm talking.

(*HANNAH notices* AUDIENCE *for the first time.*)

HANNAH: Oh. Hi.

AUDIENCE: Hi.

HANNAH: Look. (*She holds up a pen.*) A limited edition, 2001 four color, ball point gel ink pen, a rare and beautiful thing. . . .

(*STORMI sits at the school computer.*)

476

ELL

Extend Language Tell students that a person who is *stuck up* has too high an opinion of himself or herself or of what he or she can do.

STORMI *(typing):* Hey, guys. I'm sorry I haven't had much to tell you. It's silly, but I thought I would feel better if I didn't make friends. I felt worse and I think people thought I was mean. Anyway, I've met some pretty interesting people. David, you'd like Joseph. He has this funny sense of humor and likes to act in plays. There's this really odd girl who I think is my favorite. She collects pens. Like your unicorns, Penelope.... And Ajitha uses all of these big words, but she isn't stuck up or anything. *(to AUDIENCE)* So, I've decided to let other members into the Stormi Giovanni Club. Really, it's better that way I think. **17**

The End

477

Develop Vocabulary

PRACTICE LESSON VOCABULARY

Students orally respond *true* or *false* to each statement and provide a reason if the answer is *false*.

1. A *combination* helps you find your locker. *(False; a combination helps you open the locker door.)*

2. A television *episode* is one show from a season. *(True)*

3. Keeping a low *profile* means you want people to notice you. *(False; a low profile means you don't want people to notice you.)*

BUILD CONCEPT VOCABULARY

Review previous concept words with students. Ask if students have come across any words that they would like to add to the Adapting to a New School Concept Web, such as *missing* and *hurting*.

Story Structure

Have students complete a story sequence chart. *(Conflict: Stormi moves to a new school; Rising Action: She resists making friends; Climax: Stormi sits with Hannah and the others at lunch and begins to like them; Resolution: Stormi decides to be friends.)* Ask students to make a new generalization about Stormi based on how she solves her problem. *(She is willing to change her mind about her new school.)*

SELF-CHECK

Students can ask themselves these questions to assess their ability to use the skill and strategy.

- Was I able to identify main elements of the story structure?
- Was I able to make generalizations?
- Did understanding the story structure help me better understand the play?

Monitor Progress	
Generalize	
If... students have trouble generalizing,	**then...** use the Reteach lesson on p. 483b.

Generalize

- To **generalize** is to make a broad statement or rule that applies to several examples.
- Active readers pay close attention to what authors tell them about story characters and make generalizations about those characters as they read.

Directions Read the following scene from a play. Then answer the questions below.

> **PRINCIPAL:** We're welcoming a student who's new to Harper School. Everyone, meet Dylan. Dylan, do you have any questions for the other students?
> **DYLAN:** What do I need to know?
> **KAMALI:** Most kids wear jeans.
> **KIM:** And T-shirts. But if you have bad words on your T-shirt, you'll be in the principal's office.
> **DAVID:** Also, there's lunch.
> **DYLAN** (sounding stressed): I guess every school is different...
> **KAMALI:** You have to get your tray a
>
> certain way.
> **KIM:** And only teachers sit by the door.
> **DAVID:** And there are Harper terms. The "field" is the blacktop, and "breakfast club" is detention.
> **DYLAN:** Wait, wait! I'm getting the feeling it's hard to fit in here.
> **DAVID:** Don't worry, we'll take you through it.
> **KIM:** Yes, we'll show you the ropes. You'll like it here.
> **DYLAN:** Thanks a lot!

1. What is the purpose of the meeting with the new student?
   The purpose is to help Dylan adjust to Harper School.
2. What generalization can you make about the attitude of Harper students at the meeting?
   The Harper students are trying to be helpful.
3. How can you generalize about the kind of advice the students give?
   The students give practical information about the school.
4. How does the advice make Dylan feel at first? How do you think Dylan's feelings change?
   He seems worried; He seems happy for the help.
5. Explain the structure of this scene. How does a problem grow during the rising action and come to a climax? What is the outcome?
   Problem: Dylan is a new student; Rising action: Harper students give advice and Dylan gets worried; Climax: students reassure Dylan; Outcome: Dylan feels better

School + Home Home Activity Your child read a short passage and made generalization about the characters. Read a story about school with your child. Work together to make generalizations about the main character.

▲ **Practice Book** p. 187

Reader Response

Open for Discussion Personal Response

MODEL I would think about how Stormi felt about being new in school and how the kids tried to be friendly to her. I would think how the cast would say their lines to express their feelings.

Comprehension Check Critical Response

1. Responses will vary, but should include specific references to the character and dialogue. **Author's Purpose**

2. Possible response: Newcomers often feel lonely. Stormi misses her school and friends in Chicago, so much that she says she won't make new friends again. ◉ **Generalize**

3. Possible response: She eventually makes friends. It makes her feel worse, not better, to keep to herself. ◉ **Story Structure**

4. Possible response: "OK like five cavities"; "OK like a strict diet of prunes." ◉ **Vocabulary**

Look Back and Write For test practice, assign a 10–15 minute time limit. For assessment, see the Scoring Rubric at the right.

Retell

Have students retell *The Stormi Giovanni Club.*

Monitor Progress

Check Retelling Rubric 4 3 2 1

If... students have difficulty retelling the play,	then... use the Retelling Cards and the Scoring Rubric for Retelling on p. 479 to assist fluent retelling.

SUCCESS PREDICTOR

Check Retelling Before students do their retellings, go through the illustrations with them, verifying that they know the characters' names. For more ideas on assessing students' retellings, see the ELL and Transition Handbook.

Reader Response

Open for Discussion What is this play saying about being a newcomer and about helping one? How will you perform this play so that the audience gets the message?

1. Choose a scene and imagine yourself playing a character. Decide whether the playwright's dialogue makes it easy for you to "become" the character you're playing. **Think Like an Author**

2. Make a generalization about newcomers suggested by the play. Then look for details in the text that support this generalization. **Generalize**

3. Stormi acts differently at the start of the play than at the end. Discuss how she changes along the way and why. **Story Structure**

4. Stormi tells the audience humorous examples of what she really means when she or her mom says that school is "OK." Write one of these examples. Then write one of your own. Use words from the Words to Know list. **Vocabulary**

Look Back and Write In this play, each character is a true individual. Take Hannah, for instance. What is her passion and why? Look back at page 473 and then write your answer.

Meet author **Lydia R. Diamond** on page 771 and illustrator **R. Gregory Christie** on page 772.

478

Scoring Rubric Look Back and Write

Top-Score Response A top-score response will use details from p. 473 to explain that Hannah's passion for pens makes her unique.

Example of a Top-Score Response Hannah is a unique individual because her passion is to find the perfect pen in order to replace a silver fountain pen of her grandfather's that she lost. This information shows that Hannah is a character who values family possessions. It also reveals that she wants to make up for her irresponsible act and that she has determination.

For additional rubrics, see p. WA10.

Write Now

Letter of Advice

Prompt

In *The Stormi Giovanni Club*, other people help Stormi adjust to a new school. Think about a situation in which you could offer help or advice. Now write a letter of advice to someone in that situation.

Writing Trait

Voice reveals a writer's attitude and feelings toward the subject and audience.

Student Model

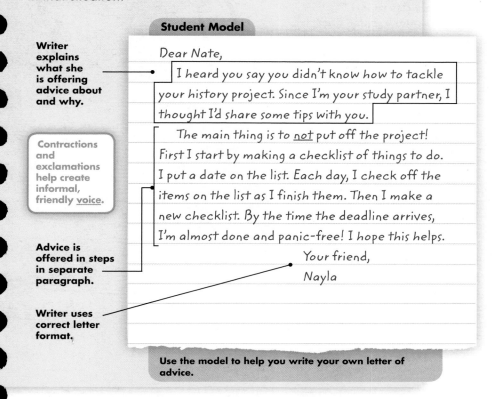

Writer explains what she is offering advice about and why.

Dear Nate,

I heard you say you didn't know how to tackle your history project. Since I'm your study partner, I thought I'd share some tips with you.

Contractions and exclamations help create informal, friendly voice.

The main thing is to <u>not</u> put off the project! First I start by making a checklist of things to do. I put a date on the list. Each day, I check off the items on the list as I finish them. Then I make a new checklist. By the time the deadline arrives, I'm almost done and panic-free! I hope this helps.

Advice is offered in steps in separate paragraph.

Your friend,
Nayla

Writer uses correct letter format.

Use the model to help you write your own letter of advice.

479

Write Now

Look at the Prompt Have students identify and discuss key words and phrases in the prompt. *(situation in which you could offer help or advice, letter of advice)*

Strategies to Develop Voice

Have students

- identify their audience and purpose and decide on a voice that matches both.
- use language that conveys honesty and sincerity to the reader.

NO: Listen to me because I'm an expert on the subject.

YES: I'd like to help you because I've been in your place and I know what you're feeling.

- use language that sets an appropriate tone for their audience.

For additional suggestions and rubric, see pp. 483g–483h.

Hints for Better Writing

- Carefully read the prompt.
- Support your ideas with information and details.
- Use words that help readers understand.
- Proofread and edit your work.

Scoring Rubric — Narrative Retelling

Rubric 4 3 2 1	4	3	2	1
Connections	Makes connections and generalizes beyond the text	Makes connections to other events, stories, or experiences	Makes a limited connection to another event, story, or experience	Makes no connection to another event, story, or experience
Author's Purpose	Elaborates on author's purpose	Tells author's purpose with some clarity	Makes some connection to author's purpose	Makes no connection to author's purpose
Characters	Describes the main character(s) and any character development	Identifies the main character(s) and gives some information about them	Inaccurately identifies some characters or gives little information about them	Inaccurately identifies the characters or gives no information about them
Setting	Describes the time and location	Identifies the time and location	Omits details of time or location	Is unable to identify time or location
Plot	Describes the problem, goal, events, and ending using rich detail	Tells the problem, goal, events, and ending with some errors that do not affect meaning	Tells parts of the problem, goal, events, and ending with gaps that affect meaning	Retelling has no sense of story

Retelling Plan

☑ **Week 1** Assess Strategic Intervention students.

☑ **Week 2** Assess Advanced students.

☑ **Week 3** Assess Strategic Intervention students.

☑ **This week assess On-Level students.**

☐ **Week 5** Assess any students you have not yet checked during this unit.

Use the Retelling Chart on p. TR16 to record retelling.

Selection Test To assess with The *Stormi Giovanni Club*, use Selection Tests, pp. 73–76.

Fresh Reads for Differentiated Test Practice For weekly leveled practice, use pp. 109–114.

Retelling

SUCCESS PREDICTOR

Social Studies in Reading

PREVIEW/USE TEXT FEATURES

As students preview "Think Dress Codes Are a Drag?" have them look at the article's headline and illustrations. After they preview ask:

- **What can you learn about the article from the headline?** *(The article is about a dress code or set of rules.)*

- **What can you learn about the article from the illustrations?** *(The article is about clothes to wear to school. Since the illustrations are amusing, perhaps the article itself will be light in tone.)*

Link to Social Studies

Have students brainstorm to identify ways to find out about dress codes in other schools. Write students' ideas on the board.

DAY 4 Grouping Options

Reading
Whole Group Discuss the Question of the Day.

Group Time **Differentiated Instruction**
Read "Think Dress Codes Are a Drag?" See pp. 458f–458g for the small group lesson plan.

Whole Group Use p. 483a.

Language Arts
Use pp. 483e–483k.

Social Studies in Reading

50¢ City & Suburbs: 75¢ Elsewhere

Newspaper Article

Genre

- A newspaper article tells readers about current events, issues, people, and places of interest.

- News articles report facts—actual events—and people's opinions.

Text Features

- A headline gives readers an idea of what the article is about.

- News articles often start with a brief story that sets the scene for the discussion that follows.

- The writer includes quotations that show differing opinions.

Link to Social Studies
Find out about dress codes in your school and other schools in your area. Are there differences? Why?

480

Content-Area Vocabulary — Social Studies

bans	forbids; prohibits
codes	sets of rules
penalty	punishment

Access Content Lead a picture walk to reinforce vocabulary, such as *capris, spaghetti straps* (p. 481), *midriff* (p. 482), and *sagging* (p. 483). Ask students to talk about the kinds of clothes they like to wear.

TUESDAY
APRIL 15, 2003

Think Dress Codes are a drag?

by Emilie Ostrander
Special to the *Tribune*

While shopping for new clothes, Elyse B., 13, of Mt. Prospect, Illinois, also is scouting for hot trends. Dressed in a bright pink tank top and denim capris, Elyse says she's found an outfit she likes. The catch? Her school dress code bans tank tops—and the penalty is anything but stylish. "If they catch you, you have to change into your gym uniform," she says.

For Elyse, shopping for new clothes is all about looking good without getting in trouble. "We

Savvy Shoppers Can Still Look Cool for School

can't wear spaghetti straps, halter tops, or tube tops," she explains. "Tank top straps must be the width of two fingers, and shorts and skirts have to be longer than 5 inches above the knee."

As we get into spring, many kids are ready to take their warm-weather clothes to school. But some school districts say certain styles are banned from the classroom, and there are consequences for kids who disobey.

Author's Purpose What is the author's purpose or purposes?

481

NEWSPAPER ARTICLE

Use the sidebar on p. 480 to guide discussion.

- Point out that a newspaper article is a source of information. It contains facts, not opinions.
- Explain to students that a news article usually includes a dateline, headline, byline, lead paragraph, and body.
- Have students identify the lead in "Think Dress Codes Are a Drag?" Discuss with students what purpose or purposes the lead serves.

 **AudioText**

Author's Purpose

The author is writing mainly to inform.

Strategies for Nonfiction

USE LEADS Explain that a lead paragraph in a newspaper article contains the most important information. It answers the questions *Who? What? When? Where? Why?* and *How?* Students can use the lead to help answer test questions. Provide the following strategy.

Use the Strategy

1. Read the test question.
2. If the question is asking *Who? What? When? Where?* or *Why?* look for the information in the lead paragraph.

GUIDED PRACTICE Have students discuss how they would use the strategy to answer the following question.

What is Elyse B. doing?

INDEPENDENT PRACTICE After students answer the following test question, discuss the process they used to find information.

Why can't Elyse B. purchase whatever she likes?

APRIL 15, 2003

Paula J. Hlavacek is the principal of Elm Middle School in Elmwood Park. At her school, parents are contacted the first time a student breaks the code. A second offense means a trip to detention.

It may not seem like a lot of fun, but Hlavacek says the dress code is there for good reason. "When you come to school, you must be dressed for a work day in school," she says. "Clothes that are cut very short or expose the midriff are beachwear. School is a very different place."

While dress codes may seem unfair, Hlavacek says students can expect the same restrictions for their teachers. "Whatever rules we hold for them, we hold for ourselves," she says. So while students can't wear tank tops in scorching weather, neither can their teachers.

Ryan M., 16, of Lincolnwood says he doesn't dress like his dean [principal of a private school]. "I like to wear my pants low," he says, something his dean can't

stand. Once, Ryan's dean had him take off his belt so he could fix it. "He told me that I wouldn't have an excuse for walking around with my pants 'sagging' anymore," Ryan says.

While Ryan and Elyse wish their school dress codes were less

Generalize How is a rule a kind of generalization?

482

Independent Practice Before students do the Independent Practice test question, verify that they understand what *dress code* means. Explain that Elyse would dress differently were it not for the dress code. Point out the unacceptable tank top in the illustration on p. 480.

strict, Kyah K., 8, of Aurora says she thinks dress codes are a good idea. "Sometimes everyone wants to be cool, so they wear really tacky clothes," she says. "I think they should obey the rules and wear those clothes at home."

Being creative is key to still being in style and not breaking the school dress code, says Gregg Andrews, fashion director for [a department store]. "It's about creating personal style," he says.

Kyah says she has an eye for style, and thinks clothes can say a lot about a person. "My clothes say that I'm a creative person," she says. "I try to put on some mismatchy things or things that will go together very well."

Reading Across Texts

Look back at *The Stormi Giovanni Club* and this newspaper article. Make a list of problems that the students in these selections face during a typical day at school.

Writing Across Texts Write some advice on how to successfully deal with each of these problems. Combine your results with classmates' advice. Assemble a book of advice on how to get along in school.

483

CONNECT TEXT TO TEXT

Reading Across Texts

Have students list the problems on the left side of a T-chart.

Writing Across Texts Students can record their advice for each problem on the right side of the T-chart. When students are finished, work with them to create one master chart. Then have students work in small groups to assemble the book of advice, each group having responsibility for one task, such as book cover, table of contents, illustrations, and text.

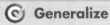 **Generalize**

Possible response: Like a generalization, a rule can be applied to many examples.

Writing Workshop Letter of Advice

OBJECTIVES

- Identify the characteristics of a letter of advice.
- Write advice to a student at a new school.
- Focus on voice.
- Use a rubric.

Genre Letter of Advice
Writer's Craft Good Conclusions
Writing Trait Voice

Voice Encourage English learners to use a bilingual dictionary if available to find powerful verbs to express feelings. For example, *delighted* or *cheerful* could express happiness. See more writing support in the ELL and Transition Handbook.

Writing Traits

FOCUS/IDEAS The letter is focused on suggestions to help a new student fit in.

ORGANIZATION/PARAGRAPHS The letter has a greeting, body, closing, and signature. The body is divided into logical paragraphs.

VOICE The writer is caring and sincere and speaks to the individual.

WORD CHOICE Words are specific and accurate (*meets after school on Tuesdays*), and they sound natural.

SENTENCES Sentences are well constructed and varied.

CONVENTIONS There is excellent control and accuracy.

DAY 1 Model the Trait

READING-WRITING CONNECTION

- *The Stormi Giovanni Club* explores a girl's difficulties adjusting to a new school; each character has a unique voice.

- The story addresses the trauma of starting over with honesty and humor; the main character draws realistic conclusions.

- Students will write a **letter of advice,** drawing good conclusions in a sincere voice.

MODEL VOICE Discuss Writing Transparency 19A. Then discuss the model and the writing trait of voice.

 Think Aloud The writer establishes a friendly and welcoming voice by beginning with the exclamation, "Welcome to Wilshire Elementary School!" She sounds sincerely happy that Terry has come to Wilshire. Her explanations about the people and opportunities at school are clear and helpful.

Advice

You may be asked to give **advice**, or specific suggestions for solving a problem. Advice columnists give advice every day as they respond to people's letters. They use logic and what they know about a situation to draw conclusions and suggest a plan of action. Use similar strategies when you give advice.

Advice from Alison

Dear Terry,

Welcome to Wilshire Elementary School! You say in your letter that you are interested in plants and computers. Wilshire has an active Plant Club that meets after school on Tuesdays in the greenhouse. Kids in this club learn about growing and caring for plants. Twice a year, they take plants they have grown to nursing homes around town.

It is logical to conclude that Plant Club will interest someone who is interested in plants.

Details give a new student information about Plant Club.

As a fifth grader, you'll have six weeks of computer class in the spring. You'll learn about software and the Internet. Ms. Punti tells some funny jokes too!

As for making friends, kids at Wilshire are friendly. Just be sure you wear a smile to school. Also, ask people for help in learning new routines. Once you start talking, you'll soon find friends who fit you like a glove!

Suggestions give specific actions to help make friends.

Good luck!

Alison

Unit 4 The Stormi Giovanni Club   Writing Model **19A**

▲ **Writing Transparency** 19A

DAY 2 Improve Writing

WRITER'S CRAFT
Good Conclusions

Display Writing Transparency 19B. Read the directions and work together to draw logical conclusions based on given information.

Think Aloud **DRAW GOOD CONCLUSIONS** Tomorrow we will write letters of advice. That will require drawing conclusions about how to solve a problem. Suppose a friend wants permission to go to an overnight party. I could conclude that she should give her parents lots of information about how safe the situation will be. I will need to draw conclusions based on my experiences with sleepovers and the facts about this party.

GUIDED WRITING Some students may need more help drawing conclusions. Work with them as they offer conclusions about the selection and explain why their conclusions are logical.

Good Conclusions

To draw **good conclusions**, think about the facts and details you have learned from reading. Also, think about what you already know. Make a general statement based on these clues.

Directions Choose the best conclusion for the paragraph. Write the letter on the line. Then write a sentence telling why your choice is best.

Fifth graders have many heavy textbooks. I can't even fit all my books into my backpack, and it is a big one! We also have to move to different classrooms several times a day. Sometimes we have to go upstairs or downstairs carrying that heavy load. I know several kids who have sore backs because of this. My best friend even had to see a doctor about muscle pain.

D

A Fifth graders should not have textbooks!
B Fifth graders should be given weight training for stronger muscles.
C Fifth graders should study only one subject for two weeks.
D Fifth graders should have lockers to store textbooks they aren't using.

Possible answer: D. Lockers will solve the problem. No other conclusion is logical or reasonable for an elementary school.

Directions Write a good conclusion for the paragraph below.

When kids get to fifth grade, they often begin middle school. This means they attend school at a new building. For the first time, they have a whole team of teachers. This means kids travel to different classrooms for reading, math, science, and so on. The time allowed to pass between classes is four minutes. A sticky locker can make a kid late for class.

Possible answer: These are only a few of the stresses that fifth graders must cope with in their new environment.

Unit 4 The Stormi Giovanni Club   Writer's Craft **19B**

▲ **Writing Transparency** 19B

DAY 3 Prewrite and Draft

READ THE WRITING PROMPT

on page 479 in the Student Edition.

In The Stormi Giovanni Club, *other people help Stormi adjust to a new school.*

Think about a situation in which you could offer help or advice.

Now write a letter of advice to someone in that situation.

Writing Test Tips

- Include specific information about the situation and the advice you can offer.
- Draw conclusions based on facts about the situation and what you know from personal experience.
- Include all the parts of a friendly letter.

GETTING STARTED Students can do any of the following.

- Summarize the facts or knowledge they have gained about this kind of situation.
- List suggestions for solving the problem that make sense based on the facts.
- Brainstorm supporting details for the advice to be given.

DAY 4 Draft and Revise

EDITING/REVISING CHECKLIST

☑ Are the conclusions in my letter logical?

☑ Have I used indefinite and reflexive pronouns correctly?

☑ Did I spell words that end with *-ible* and *-able* correctly?

See *The Grammar and Writing Book,* pp. 158–163.

Revising Tips

Voice

- Write sentences that sound like natural speech.
- Deal honestly but sincerely with the writer's problem.
- Let your feelings show in your choice of words.

PUBLISHING Students can use their letters to create an advice column on a bulletin board. Some students may wish to revise their work later.

ASSESSMENT Use the scoring rubric to evaluate students' work.

DAY 5 Connect to Unit Writing

Story	
Week 1	E-mail 411g–411h
Week 2	Journal Entry 435g–435h
Week 3	Story About an Animal 457g–457h
Week 4	Advice 483g–483h
Week 5	Describe How You Achieved a Goal 503g–503h

PREVIEW THE UNIT PROMPT

Tell a story about a character who succeeds by adapting to a new situation. Focus on an event that shows this person's resourcefulness. Your story may be real or imagined.

APPLY

- A story has a beginning, middle, and end and focuses on one incident or event.
- The end of a story should be a logical conclusion to the action.

Writing Trait Rubric

	4	3	2	1
Voice	Excellent sense of writer's attitude toward topic; strongly engages audience and speaks directly to them	Clear sense of how writer feels and thinks; engages audience	Some sense of how writer feels and thinks; weak attempt to engage audience	No sense of how writer feels and thinks about topic; no attempt to engage audience
	Uses well-chosen words in letter to clearly show feelings toward topic	Uses words in letter that show some feelings about topic	Needs to use more words in letter that show feelings about topic	Uses no words in letter that show feelings about topic

Spelling & Phonics Suffixes *-ible, -able*

OBJECTIVE

● Identify and spell suffixes *-ible* and *-able.*

Generalization

Connect to Phonics When adding the suffix *-ible* or *-able,* there are no sound clues to help you decide which form to use: *agreeable, flexible.* The vowel sound spelled by the letters *ib* and *ab* is the /ə/ and can be spelled many different ways.

Spelling Words

1. sensible	11. convertible
2. washable	12. forgettable
3. available	13. laughable
4. agreeable	14. sociable
5. fashionable	15. allowable
6. valuable	16. divisible
7. flexible	17. hospitable*
8. reasonable	18. reversible
9. favorable	19. responsible
10. breakable	20. tolerable

Challenge Words

21. noticeable	24. biodegradable
22. conceivable	25. collapsible
23. disposable	

* Word from the selection

ELL

Spelling/Phonics Support See the ELL and Transition Handbook for spelling support.

DAY 1 Pretest and Sort

PRETEST

Use the Dictation Sentences from Day 5 to administer the pretest. Read the word, read the sentence, and then read the word again. Guide students in self-correcting their pretests and correcting any misspellings.

Monitor Progress

Spelling

If… students misspell more than 5 pretest words,	**then…** use words 1–10 for Strategic Intervention.
If… students misspell 1–5 pretest words,	**then…** use words 1–20 for On-Level practice.
If… students correctly spell all pretest words,	**then…** use words 1–25 for Advanced Learners.

HOMEWORK Spelling Practice Book, p. 73.

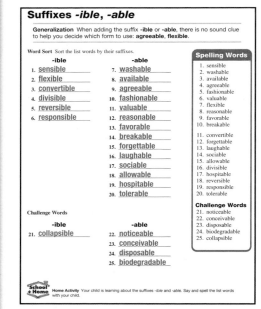

▲ **Spelling Practice Book** p. 73

DAY 2 Think and Practice

TEACH

Draw columns on the board. Label the left column *-able,* and the right column *-ible.* Say a list word and ask students in which column the word should be written. Do not correct. Do this with all the list words. Then have students compare the words on the board to their word lists. Have volunteers come to the board and write the words in the correct column where applicable.

> *reversible*

FIND THE PATTERN Ask students to draw a line between the word and the suffix. Have them identify which words have changed when a suffix has been added and which have not.

HOMEWORK Spelling Practice Book, p. 74.

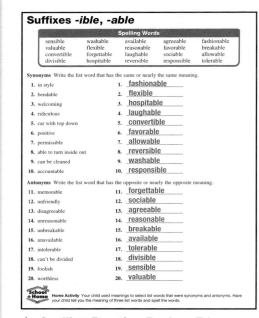

▲ **Spelling Practice Book** p. 74

DAY 3 — Connect to Writing

MAKE A POSTER

Have students make a poster that advertises an item, event, movie, book, or similar item. Encourage them to use as many list words as they can in the poster to grab attention and provide information.

Frequently Misspelled Words

when   then   went

These words may seem easy to spell, but they are often misspelled by fifth-graders. Alert students to these frequently misspelled words.

HOMEWORK Spelling Practice Book, p. 75.

Suffixes -ible, -able

Proofread an Article Find five spelling errors and one capitalization error in the article. Circle the errors and write the corrections on the line.

Spelling Words
sensible
washable
available
agreeable
fashionable
valuable
flexible
reasonable
favorable
breakable
convertible
forgettable
laughable
sociable
allowable
divisible
hospitable
reversible
responsible
tolerable

Fashion Sense

Store buyers are responsible for ordering (fashionible) clothing customers will like. Last year, (m)rs. Clark, the store buyer, ordered dozens of reversible sweaters. The sweaters were (washible.) (availible) in a variety of colors, and at (a reasonible) price. When the sweaters sold out quickly, the buyer knew she had made a (sensable) choice.

1. fashionable   2. washable
3. available   4. reasonable
5. sensible   6. Mrs.

Proofread Words Circle the correct spelling of the list word.

7. The gymnast is as ___ as a rubber band.
   flexable   flexibel   (flexible)
8. Porcelain china is delicate and ___.
   (breakable)   brakeable   breakible
9. Be ___ to your guests when they visit.
   hospital   (hospitable)   hospitible
10. I'd love to have a car with a ___ top.
   (convertible)   convertable   convertibel
11. Sixty-three is ___ by seven.
   dividable   divisable   (divisible)
12. Eat three ___ and balanced meals every day.
   (sensible)   sensable   senseble

Frequently Misspelled Words
when
then
went

School + Home Home Activity Your child identified misspelled list words. Ask your child to spell three list words that end in -ible and three list words that end in -able.

▲ **Spelling Practice Book** p. 75

DAY 4 — Review

REVIEW SUFFIXES

Have partners take turns saying the base word of each list word to a partner. The partner responds by adding the suffix and then spelling the word. Partners should say and spell each of the list words.

Spelling Strategy
Divide and Conquer

It's easier to remember how to spell words if you break them into parts first. Draw a line between the word and its suffix. Study the word one part at a time.

HOMEWORK Spelling Practice Book, p. 76.

Suffixes -ible, -able

Spelling Words			
sensible	washable	available	agreeable	fashionable
valuable	flexible	reasonable	favorable	breakable
convertible	forgettable	laughable	sociable	allowable
divisible	hospitable	reversible	responsible	tolerable

Crossword Puzzle Use clues to find the list words. Write each letter in a box.

Across
6. friendly
7. levelheaded
8. silly
9. welcoming
10. positive

Down
1. stylish
2. bearable
3. unmemorable
4. precious
5. bendable

Definitions Write the list word that fits the definition.
11. anything that can be cleaned with soap and water
12. separable into equal parts
13. able to obtain
14. fragile and delicate

11. washable
12. divisible
13. available
14. breakable

School + Home Home Activity Your child has learned to read, write, and spell with suffixes. Have your child pick out the five hardest words to review with you.

▲ **Spelling Practice Book** p. 76

DAY 5 — Posttest

DICTATION SENTENCES

1. Those are sensible shoes.
2. Cotton fabrics are washable.
3. Good seats were still available.
4. The terms were agreeable.
5. People like fashionable clothing.
6. Gold is valuable.
7. The flexible straw bent slightly.
8. That store has reasonable prices.
9. The play got a favorable review.
10. The plates are breakable.
11. The convertible sofa can be used as a bed for guests.
12. That boring movie is forgettable.
13. The silly dog was laughable.
14. Bees are sociable animals.
15. Staying up late is allowable on Friday.
16. One hundred is divisible by ten.
17. The host has been hospitable to all the guests.
18. My coat is reversible.
19. A lifeguard is responsible for all the swimmers.
20. Heat is tolerable with air conditioning.

CHALLENGE

21. The new paint made a noticeable difference in the room.
22. It was conceivable that the reporter misheard the information.
23. Let's use disposable dishes at the party.
24. Grass clippings are biodegradable.
25. The collapsible table was stored in the closet for later use.

OBJECTIVES

- Formulate an inquiry question that is connected to this week's lesson focus.

- Effectively and efficiently find, evaluate, and communicate information related to an inquiry question using electronic sources.

New Literacies	
Day 1	**Identify Questions**
Day 2	**Navigate/Search**
Day 3	**Analyze**
Day 4	**Synthesize**
Day 5	**Communicate**

NEW LITERACIES

Internet Inquiry Activity

EXPLORE E-MAIL

Use the following 5-day plan to help students conduct this week's Internet inquiry activity about e-mail. Remind students to follow classroom rules when using the Internet.

DAY 1

Identify Questions Discuss the lesson focus question: *How do people adapt to a new school?* Then have students recall how Stormi relies on e-mail to communicate with her friends back home and how her teacher won't allow them to use school computers for e-mail. Brainstorm ideas for specific inquiry questions about using e-mail. For example, students might want to learn about rules for e-mail etiquette. Have students work individually, in pairs, or in small groups to write inquiry questions they want to answer.

DAY 2

Navigate/Search Explain the keyword *e-mail* will likely yield thousands of sites, so the choice of keyword should be specific, such as *e-mail etiquette.* Point out that keywords will appear as bold type in Web site descriptions. Students should use the words around the bold keywords as context clues to determine if a site contains relevant information.

DAY 3

Analyze Have students skim and scan the Web sites they identified on Day 2. Ask them to read each site for information that relates to their inquiry questions, taking notes as they go. Students should analyze information for credibility, reliability, and usefulness by looking at who the author is, what his or her background is on the topic, and when it was published.

DAY 4

Synthesize Have students synthesize information from Day 3 to answer their inquiry questions. Ask them to think about the best methods for sharing the information with the rest of the class.

DAY 5

Communicate Have students decide how they want to share their inquiry results. Students might want to write and print e-mails to the class that summarize the results of their inquiries.

RESEARCH/STUDY SKILLS

Thesaurus

TEACH

Ask students where they should look if they want to find a synonym for the word *digress.* Students may need prompting before they mention a thesaurus. Show a thesaurus to students and explain how to use it.

- A **thesaurus** is a book of synonyms, words that mean the same or almost the same as another word.
- Not all synonyms mean exactly the same. It is important to check in a dictionary the meaning of a synonym you find in a thesaurus to make sure that the synonym has the meaning you want.
- Most print thesauruses have an index in the back. You look up the word in the index for which you want synonyms.
- With electronic thesauruses, you type a word into a search box.
- With a word processor thesaurus, you highlight the word and use the thesaurus under TOOLS to find synonyms.

Have students work in groups to practice using a thesaurus—print, electronic, or word processing—and a dictionary. Each group should find the best synonym for a lesson vocabulary word from *The Stormi Giovanni Club*. Then, discuss these questions:

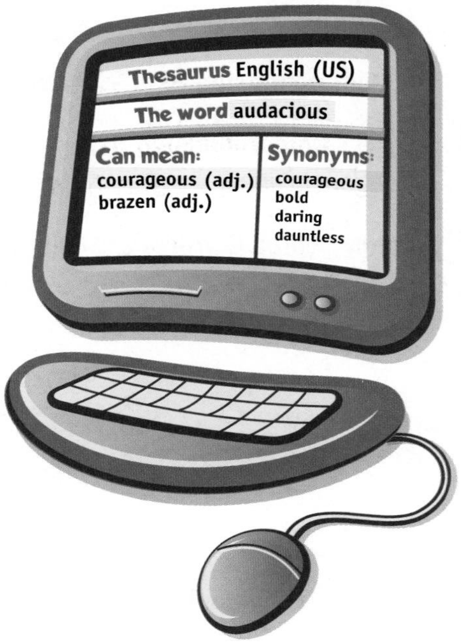

1. How might you need to change the form of *cavities* to find a synonym? *(From the plural to the singular, cavity)*

2. Suppose you find these synonyms for *scintillating: witty, good, smart, piquant, clever.* How do you choose the best one? *(You look up the synonyms whose meanings you do not know in a dictionary.)*

ASSESS

As students work with the thesaurus, check that they are able to locate synonyms for words, either using the index in a print thesaurus or using the appropriate method in an electronic thesaurus. Be sure they use a dictionary to check the meanings of synonyms.

For more practice or to assess students, use Practice Book pp. 189–190.

OBJECTIVES

- Review terms associated with a thesaurus.
- Use a thesaurus to locate synonyms.

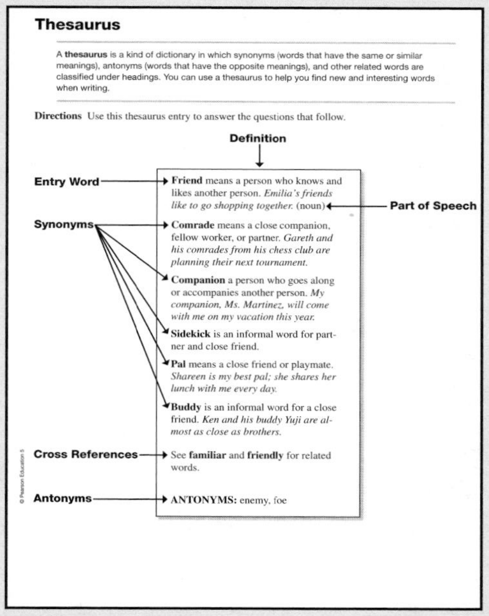

Thesaurus

A **thesaurus** is a kind of dictionary in which synonyms (words that have the same or similar meanings), antonyms (words that have the opposite meanings), and other related words are classified under headings. You can use a thesaurus to help you find new and interesting words when writing.

Directions Use this thesaurus entry to answer the questions that follow.

▲ **Practice Book** p. 189

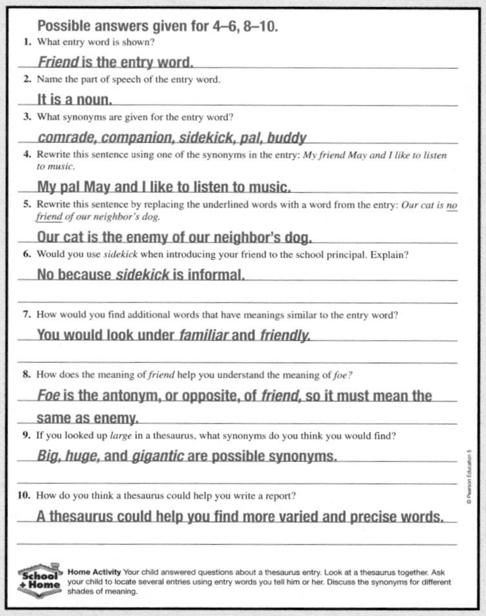

Possible answers given for 4–6, 8–10.

1. What entry word is shown?
   Friend is the entry word.
2. Name the part of speech of the entry word.
   It is a noun.
3. What synonyms are given for the entry word?
   comrade, companion, sidekick, pal, buddy
4. Rewrite this sentence using one of the synonyms in the entry: *My friend May and I like to listen to music.*
   My pal May and I like to listen to music.
5. Rewrite this sentence by replacing the underlined words with a word from the entry: *Our cat is no friend of our neighbor's dog.*
   Our cat is the enemy of our neighbor's dog.
6. Would you use *sidekick* when introducing your friend to the school principal. Explain?
   No because *sidekick* is informal.
7. How would you find additional words that have meanings similar to the entry word?
   You would look under *familiar* and *friendly.*
8. How does the meaning of *friend* help you understand the meaning of *foe?*
   Foe is the antonym, or opposite, of *friend,* so it must mean the same as enemy.
9. If you looked up *large* in a thesaurus, what synonyms do you think you would find?
   Big, huge, and *gigantic* are possible synonyms.
10. How do you think a thesaurus could help you write a report?
    A thesaurus could help you find more varied and precise words.

School + Home **Home Activity** Your child answered questions about a thesaurus entry. Look at a thesaurus together. Ask your child to locate several entries using entry words you tell him or her. Discuss the synonyms for different shades of meaning.

▲ **Practice Book** p. 190

Assessment Checkpoints *for the Week*

Selection Assessment

Use pp. 73–76 of Selection Tests to check:

- ☑ **Selection Understanding**
- ☑ **Comprehension Skill** *Generalize*
- ☑ **Selection Vocabulary**
  cavities
  combination
  demonstrates
  episode
  profile
  strict

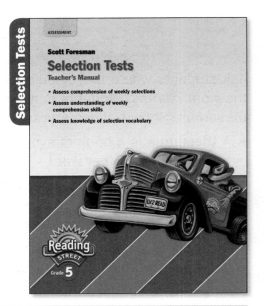

ASSESSMENT

Scott Foresman
Selection Tests
Teacher's Manual
- Assess comprehension of weekly selections
- Assess understanding of weekly comprehension skills
- Assess knowledge of selection vocabulary

Reading STREET
Grade 5

Leveled Assessment

On-Level
Strategic Intervention
Advanced

Use pp. 109–114 of Fresh Reads for Differentiated Test Practice to check:

- ☑ **Comprehension Skill** *Generalize*
- ☑ **REVIEW** **Comprehension Skill**
  Draw Conclusions
- ☑ **Fluency** *Words Correct Per Minute*

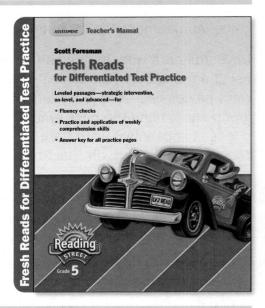

ASSESSMENT   Teacher's Manual

Scott Foresman
Fresh Reads
for Differentiated Test Practice

Leveled passages—strategic intervention, on-level, and advanced—for
- Fluency checks
- Practice and application of weekly comprehension skills
- Answer key for all practice pages

Reading STREET
Grade 5

Managing Assessment

Use Assessment Handbook for:

- ☑ **Observation Checklists**
- ☑ **Record-Keeping Forms**
- ☑ **Portfolio Assessment**

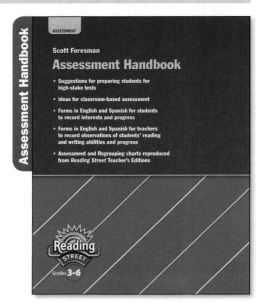

ASSESSMENT

Scott Foresman
Assessment Handbook
- Suggestions for preparing students for high-stake tests
- Ideas for classroom-based assessment
- Forms in English and Spanish for students to record interests and progress
- Forms in English and Spanish for teachers to record observations of students' reading and writing abilities and progress
- Assessment and Regrouping charts reproduced from *Reading Street* Teacher's Editions

Reading STREET
Grades 3–6

① Begin with whole class skill and strategy instruction.

② Meet with small groups to provide differentiated instruction.

③ Gather the whole class back together for fluency and language arts.

DAY 4

On-Level	Strategic Intervention	Advanced
Teacher-Led *Pages 500–503*	**Teacher-Led** *Page DI · 48*	**Teacher-Led** *Page DI · 49*
• **Read** "All About Gymnastics"	• Practice Retelling • **Read** or Listen to "All About Gymnastics"	• **Read** "All About Gymnastics" • Genre Study

ⓘ Independent Activities

While you meet with small groups, have the rest of the class...

• Visit the Reading/Library Center
• Listen to the AudioText for "All About Gymnastics"
• Visit the Writing/Vocabulary Center

• Finish Writing Across Texts, p. 503
• Visit Cross-Curricular Centers
• Work on inquiry projects

DAY 5

On-Level	Strategic Intervention	Advanced
Teacher-Led *Page DI · 51*	**Teacher-Led** *Page DI · 50*	**Teacher-Led** *Page DI · 51*
• **Reread** Leveled Reader *Strange Sports with Weird Gear* • Retell *Strange Sports with Weird Gear*	• **Reread** Leveled Reader *Let the Games Begin: History of the Olympics* • Retell *Let the Games Begin: History of the Olympics*	• **Reread** Leveled Reader *What Makes Great Athletes* • Share Extension Activity

ⓘ Independent Activities

While you meet with small groups, have the rest of the class...

• Visit the Reading/Library Center
• Complete Practice Book pp. 198–200

• Visit Cross-Curricular Centers
• Work on inquiry projects

Grouping Place English language learners in the groups that correspond to their reading abilities in English.

Use the appropriate Leveled Reader or other text at students' instructional level.

TiP Send home the appropriate Multilingual Summary of the main selection on Day 1.

Take It to the NET ONLINE
PearsonSuccessNet.com

Deborah Simmons and Edward Kame'enui
For research on word recognition and diverse learners, see the article "Understanding the Primary Role of Word Recognition..." by Scott Foresman authors Deborah Simmons and Ed Kame'enui, and D. Chard.

TEACHER TALK

Structural analysis is the process of using knowledge of base words, endings, and affixes to decode words.

Be sure to schedule time for students to work on the unit inquiry project "Adaptations." This week students present graphic organizers with information about the ways people or animals adapt.

Looking Ahead

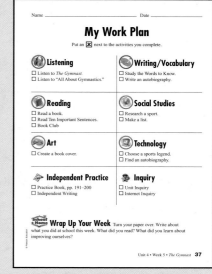

Name _____ Date _____

My Work Plan

Put an ☒ next to the activities you complete.

Listening
☐ Listen to *The Gymnast*.
☐ Listen to "All About Gymnastics."

Writing/Vocabulary
☐ Study the Words to Know.
☐ Write an autobiography.

Reading
☐ Read a book.
☐ Read Ten Important Sentences.
☐ Book Club

Social Studies
☐ Research a sport.
☐ Make a list.

Art
☐ Create a book cover.

Technology
☐ Choose a sports legend.
☐ Find an autobiography.

Independent Practice
☐ Practice Book, pp. 191–200
☐ Independent Writing

Inquiry
☐ Unit Inquiry
☐ Internet Inquiry

Wrap Up Your Week Turn your paper over. Write about what you did at school this week. What did you read? What did you learn about improving ourselves?

Unit 4 • Week 5 • *The Gymnast* **37**

▲ **Group-Time Survival Guide** p. 37, Weekly Contract

The Gymnast **484g**

☑ Customize Your Plan *by Strand*

ORAL LANGUAGE

Concept Development

Why do people try to change themselves?

CONCEPT VOCABULARY

champion   competitive   develop   perfected

BUILD

☐ **Question of the Week** Introduce and discuss the question of the week. This week students will read a variety of texts and work on projects related to the concept *improving ourselves*. Post the question for students to refer to throughout the week. **DAY 1** *484d*

☐ **Read Aloud** Read aloud "The Winning Stroke." Then begin a web to build concepts and concept vocabulary related to this week's lesson and the unit theme, Adapting. Introduce the concept words *champion, competitive, develop,* and *perfected* and have students place them on the web. Display the web for use throughout the week. **DAY 1** *484l–484m*

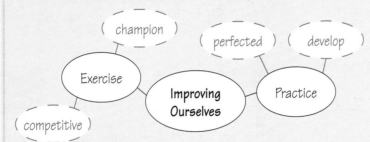

DEVELOP

☐ **Question of the Day** Use the prompts from the Weekly Plan to engage students in conversations related to this week's reading and the unit theme. **EVERY DAY** *484d–484e*

☐ **Concept Vocabulary Web** Revisit the Improving Ourselves Concept Web and encourage students to add concept words from their reading and life experiences. **DAY 2** *493,* **DAY 3** *497*

CONNECT

☐ **Looking Back** Revisit the Improving Ourselves Concept Web and discuss how it relates to this week's lesson and the unit theme. **DAY 5** *503c*

CHECK

☐ **Concept Vocabulary Web** Use the Improving Ourselves Concept Web to check students' understanding of the concept vocabulary words *champion, competitive, develop,* and *perfected.* **DAY 1** *484l,* **DAY 5** *503c*

VOCABULARY

STRATEGY WORD STRUCTURE Recognizing a suffix can help you figure out the meaning of an unknown word. A suffix is a syllable added to the end of a base word that changes the base word's meaning.

LESSON VOCABULARY

bluish   skidded
cartwheels   somersault
gymnastics   throbbing
hesitation   wincing
limelight

TEACH

☐ **Words to Know** Give students the opportunity to tell what they already know about this week's lesson vocabulary words. Then discuss word meaning. **DAY 1** *486b*

☐ **Vocabulary Strategy Lesson** Use the vocabulary strategy lesson in the Student Edition to introduce and model this week's strategy, *word structure.* **DAY 2** *486–487*

Vocabulary Strategy Lesson

PRACTICE/APPLY

☐ **Leveled Text** Read the lesson vocabulary in the context of leveled text. **DAY 1** *LR37–LR45*

☐ **Words in Context** Read the lesson vocabulary and apply *word structure* in the context of *The Gymnast.* **DAY 2** *488–493,* **DAY 3** *494–498*

Leveled Readers

☐ **Writing/Vocabulary Center** Think of a memorable event in your own life and create an autobiographical story outline for it. **ANY DAY** *484k*

Main Selection—Nonfiction

☐ **Homework** Practice Book pp. 194–195. **DAY 1** *486b,* **DAY 2** *487*

☐ **Word Play** Using the words *gymnastics* and *philosophy* invite teams of students to come up with related words. **ANY DAY** *503c*

ASSESS

☐ **Selection Test** Use the Selection Test to determine students' understanding of the lesson vocabulary words. **DAY 3**

RETEACH/REVIEW

☐ **Reteach Lesson** If necessary, use this lesson to reteach and review *word structure.* **DAY 5** *503c*

COMPREHENSION

SKILL DRAW CONCLUSIONS A conclusion is a sensible decision you make after you think about facts or details that you read. Drawing conclusions may also be known as making inferences. Often prior knowledge can help you draw, or make, a conclusion.

STRATEGY VISUALIZE Visualizing, or creating pictures of the story in your mind, can help you understand what is happening in what you are reading. It can also help you draw conclusions about what is happening and why.

TEACH

❑ **Skill/Strategy Lesson** Use the skill/strategy lesson in the Student Edition to introduce and model *draw conclusions* and *visualize*. DAY 1 484-485

❑ **Extend Skills** Teach similes. ANY DAY 503b

Skill/Strategy Lesson

PRACTICE/APPLY

❑ **Leveled Text** Apply *draw conclusions* and *visualize* to read leveled text. DAY 1 LR37-LR45

❑ **Skills and Strategies in Context** Read "The Gymnast," using the Guiding Comprehension questions to apply *draw conclusions* and *visualize*. DAY 2 488-493, DAY 3 494-498

Leveled Readers

❑ **Skills and Strategies in Context** Read "All About Gymnastics," guiding students as they apply *draw conclusions* and *visualize*. Then have students discuss and write across texts. DAY 4 500-503

Main Selection—Nonfiction

❑ **Homework** Practice Book pp. 193, 197, 198. DAY 1 485, DAY 3 497, DAY 5 503b

Paired Selection—Nonfiction

❑ **Fresh Reads for Differentiated Test Practice** Have students practice *draw conclusions* with a new passage. DAY 3

ASSESS

❑ **Selection Test** Determine students' understanding of the selection and their use of *draw conclusions*. DAY 3

❑ **Retell** Have students retell "The Gymnast." DAY 3 498-499

RETEACH/REVIEW

❑ **Reteach Lesson** If necessary, reteach and review *draw conclusions*. DAY 5 503b

FLUENCY

SKILL PUNCTUATION CLUES Punctuation within text guides readers. Punctuation shows a reader where to pause (periods or commas), change inflection (question marks), and express emotion (exclamation marks).

TEACH

❑ **Read Aloud** Model fluent reading by rereading "The Winning Stroke." Focus on this week's fluency skill, punctuation clues. DAY 1 484l-484m, 503a

PRACTICE/APPLY

❑ **Echo Reading** Read aloud selected paragraphs from "The Gymnast," modeling changing inflections, expressions, and pauses. Then practice as a class, doing three echo readings of the selected paragraphs. DAY 2 503a, DAY 3 503a

❑ **Partner Reading** Have partners practice reading aloud, following punctuation clues and offering each other feedback. As students reread, monitor their progress toward their individual fluency goals. DAY 4 503a

❑ **Listening Center** Have students follow along with the AudioText for this week's selections. ANY DAY 484j

❑ **Reading/Library Center** Have students reread a selection of their choice. ANY DAY 484j

❑ **Fluency Coach** Have students use Fluency Coach to listen to fluent readings or practice reading on their own. ANY DAY

ASSESS

❑ **Check Fluency** WCPM Do a one-minute timed reading, paying special attention to this week's skill— punctuation clues. Provide feedback for each student. DAY 5 503a

☑ Customize Your Plan *by Strand*

GRAMMAR

SKILL USING *WHO* AND *WHOM* The pronoun *who* is used as a subject in a sentence or clause. The pronoun *whom* is used as an object (object of a preposition or direct object).

TEACH

❑ **Grammar Transparency 20** Use Grammar Transparency 20 to teach using *who* and *whom*. **DAY 1** *503e*

Grammar Transparency 20

PRACTICE/APPLY

❑ **Develop the Concept** Review the concept of using *who* and *whom* and provide guided practice. **DAY 2** *503e*

❑ **Apply to Writing** Have students review something they have written and apply using *who* and *whom*. **DAY 3** *503f*

❑ **Test Preparation** Examine common errors in using *who* and *whom* to prepare for standardized tests. **DAY 4** *503f*

❑ **Homework** Grammar and Writing Practice Book pp. 77–79. **DAY 2** *503e*, **DAY 3** *503f*, **DAY 4** *503f*

ASSESS

❑ **Cumulative Review** Use Grammar and Writing Practice Book p. 80. **DAY 5** *503f*

RETEACH/REVIEW

❑ **Daily Fix-It** Have students find and correct errors in grammar, spelling, and punctuation. **EVERY DAY** *503e–503f*

❑ **The Grammar and Writing Book** Use pp. 164–167 of The Grammar and Writing Book to extend instruction for using *who* and *whom*. **ANY DAY**

The Grammar and Writing Book

WRITING

Trait of the Week

WORD CHOICE Good writers choose their words carefully. Strong verbs, specific nouns, and vivid adjectives help writers elaborate on their ideas. Well-chosen and exact words make writing clear and lively.

TEACH

❑ **Writing Transparency 20A** Use the model to introduce and discuss the Trait of the Week. **DAY 1** *503g*

❑ **Writing Transparency 20B** Use the transparency to show students how sensory details can improve their writing. **DAY 2** *503g*

Writing Transparency 20A **Writing Transparency 20B**

PRACTICE/APPLY

❑ **Write Now** Examine the model on Student Edition p. 499. Then have students write their own description. **DAY 3** *499, 503h*, **DAY 4** *503h*

> **Prompt** In "The Gymnast," a boy learns that he can't be anybody but himself. Think about an important lesson you have learned. Now write a description of the lesson and how you learned it.

Write Now p. 499

❑ **Writing/Vocabulary Center** Think of a memorable event in your own life and create an autobiographical story outline for it. **ANY DAY** *484k*

ASSESS

❑ **Writing Trait Rubric** Use the rubric to evaluate students' writing. **DAY 4** *503h*

RETEACH/REVIEW

❑ **The Grammar and Writing Book** Use pp. 164–169 of The Grammar and Writing Book to extend instruction for using *who* and *whom*, sensory details, and descriptions. **ANY DAY**

The Grammar and Writing Book

❶ Use assessment data to determine your instructional focus.

❷ Preview this week's instruction by strand.

❸ Choose instructional activities that meet the needs of your classroom.

SPELLING

GENERALIZATION NEGATIVE PREFIXES When adding prefixes *il-*, *in-*, *im-*, and *ir-*, make no change in the base word: *il*legal, *in*visible, *im*possible, *ir*regular. All of the prefixes mean "not." Vowels before double consonants usually have a short sound.

TEACH

❑ **Pretest** Give the pretest for words with negative prefixes. Guide students in self-correcting their pretests and correcting any misspellings. DAY 1 *503i*

❑ **Think and Practice** Connect spelling to the phonics generalization for negative prefixes. DAY 2 *503i*

PRACTICE/APPLY

❑ **Connect to Writing** Have students use spelling words to write a description. Then review frequently misspelled words: *through*, *always*. DAY 3 *503j*

❑ **Homework** Word Study and Spelling Practice Book pp. 77–80. **EVERY DAY**

RETEACH/REVIEW

❑ **Review** Review spelling words to prepare for the posttest. Then provide students with a spelling strategy—divide and conquer. DAY 4 *503j*

ASSESS

❑ **Posttest** Use dictation sentences to give the posttest for words with negative prefixes. DAY 5 *503j*

Spelling Words

1. invisible	8. impatient	15. illogical
2. illiterate	9. independent	16. indefinite
3. irregular	10. incorrect	17. inappropriate
4. irresistible	11. inactive	18. immobile
5. impossible	12. imperfect	19. irresponsible
6. informal	13. impolite	20. inexpensive
7. illegal	14. immature	

Challenge Words

21. irrelevant	23. intolerant	25. impersonal
22. irreparable	24. indisputable	

*Word from the selection

RESEARCH AND INQUIRY

❑ **Internet Inquiry** Have students conduct an Internet inquiry on gymnastics. **EVERY DAY** *503k*

❑ **Graphs** Review the terms and features associated with different types of graphs, and discuss how students can use graphs to gather and display information. DAY 5 *503l*

❑ **Unit Inquiry** Allow time for students to present the information they gathered about the ways people or animals adapt to different situations. **ANY DAY** *391*

SPEAKING AND VIEWING

❑ **Informational Speech** Have students write and deliver an informational speech about a gymnast or gymnastics. DAY 5 *503d*

❑ **Analyze a Video** Have students view a video that focuses on gymnastics and answer questions. DAY 5 *503d*

Resources for Differentiated Instruction

LEVELED READERS

▶ **Comprehension**
- ◎ **Skill** Draw Conclusions
- ◎ **Strategy** Visualize

▶ **Lesson Vocabulary**
- ◎ Word Structure

bluish · skidded · hesitation · wincing · limelight · somersault · gymnastics · cartwheels · throbbing

▶ **Social Studies Standards**
- **Individual Development and Identity**
- **Sports**

Leveled Reader Database ONLINE
PearsonSuccessNet.com

Use the Online Database of over 600 books to
- Download and print additional copies of this week's leveled readers.
- Listen to the readers being read online.
- Search for more titles focused on this week's skills, topic, and content.

On-Level

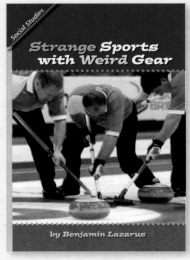

Social Studies
Strange Sports with Weird Gear
by Benjamin Lazarus

On-Level Reader

Name _____ Strange Sports

Draw Conclusions

A **conclusion** is a sensible decision reached after thinking about details or facts in what is read.

Directions Based on the equipment used in each sport, answer the following questions.
Possible responses given

1. Does curling take a lot of strength?
   Yes, because the equipment is heavy and difficult to move.

2. Are rhythmic gymnasts hurt easily?
   No, because they don't need to wear protective gear.

3. Can jai alai be dangerous?
   Yes, because the players wear protective head and hand gear.

4. Why are the ropes used by rhythmic gymnasts often made to look like snakes?
   to make their routine more exciting

5. Which of the three sports would you like to try? Why?
   rhythmic gymnastics because I like to dance

◎ **On-Level Practice** TE p. LR41

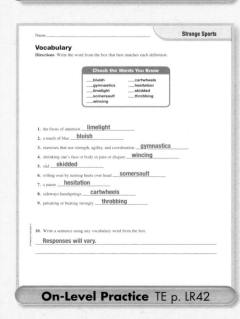

Name _____ Strange Sports

Vocabulary
Directions Write the word from the box that best matches each definition.

Check the Words You Know
- bluish
- gymnastics
- limelight
- somersault
- wincing
- cartwheels
- hesitation
- skidded
- throbbing

1. the focus of attention **limelight**
2. a touch of blue **bluish**
3. exercises that use strength, agility, and coordination **gymnastics**
4. shrinking one's face or body in pain or disgust **wincing**
5. slid **skidded**
6. rolling over by turning heels over head **somersault**
7. a pause **hesitation**
8. sideways handsprings **cartwheels**
9. pulsating or beating strongly **throbbing**

10. Write a sentence using any vocabulary word from the box.
   Responses will vary.

◎ **On-Level Practice** TE p. LR42

Strategic Intervention

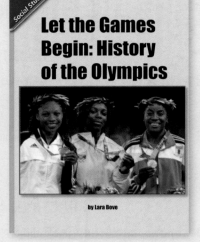

Social Studies
Let the Games Begin: History of the Olympics
by Lara Bove

Below-Level Reader

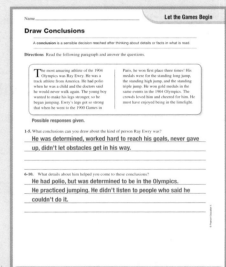

Name _____ Let the Games Begin

Draw Conclusions

A **conclusion** is a sensible decision reached after thinking about details or facts in what is read.

Directions Read the following paragraph and answer the questions.

The most amazing athlete of the 1904 Olympics was Ray Ewry. He was a track athlete from America. He had polio when he was a child and the doctors said he would never walk again. The young boy wanted to make his legs stronger, so he began jumping. Ewry's legs got so strong that when he went to the 1900 Games in Paris, he won first place three times! His medals were for the standing long jump, the standing high jump, and the standing triple jump. He won gold medals in the same events in the 1904 Olympics. The crowds loved him and cheered for him. He must have enjoyed being in the limelight.

Possible responses given.

1-5. What conclusions can you draw about the kind of person Ray Ewry was?
   He was determined, worked hard to reach his goals, never gave up, didn't let obstacles get in his way.

6-10. What details about him helped you come to these conclusions?
   He had polio, but was determined to be in the Olympics.
   He practiced jumping. He didn't listen to people who said he couldn't do it.

◎ **Below-Level Practice** TE p. LR38

Name _____ Let the Games Begin

Vocabulary
Directions Write the word from the box that best matches each definition.

Check the Words You Know
- bluish
- gymnastics
- limelight
- somersault
- wincing
- cartwheels
- hesitation
- skidded
- throbbing

1. the focus of attention **limelight**
2. having a blue tint **bluish**
3. exercises that use strength, agility, and coordination **gymnastics**
4. shrinking one's face or body in pain or disgust **wincing**
5. slid **skidded**
6. rolling over by turning heels over head **somersault**
7. a pause **hesitation**
8. sideways handsprings **cartwheels**
9. pulsating or beating strongly **throbbing**

10. Write a sentence using any vocabulary word from the box.
   Responses will vary.

◎ **Below-Level Practice** TE p. LR39

Advanced

Advanced Reader

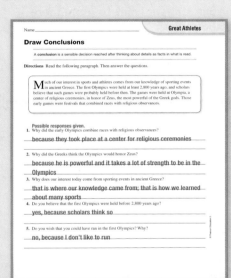

Draw Conclusions

Advanced Practice TE p. LR44

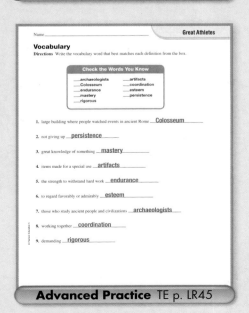

Vocabulary

Advanced Practice TE p. LR45

ELL

ELL Reader

ELL Poster 20

Teacher's Edition Notes

ELL notes throughout this lesson support instruction and reference additional resources at point of use.

Teaching Guide pp. 134–140, 250–251

- Multilingual summaries of the main selection
- Comprehension lesson
- Vocabulary strategies and word cards
- ELL Reader 5.4.5 lesson

ELL and Transition Handbook

Ten Important Sentences

- Key ideas from every selection in the Student Edition
- Activities to build sentence power

More Reading

Readers' Theater Anthology

- Fluency practice
- Five scripts to build fluency
- Poetry for oral interpretation

Leveled Trade Books

Advanced

Below-Level

On-Level

- Extended reading tied to the unit concept
- Lessons in the Trade Book Library Teaching Guide

Homework

- Family Times Newsletter
- ELL Multilingual Selection Summaries

Take-Home Books

- Leveled Readers

Cross-Curricular Centers

 **Listening**

 Reading/Library

 **Art**

Listen to the Selections

MATERIALS [SINGLES]
CD player, headphones, AudioText CD, student book

LISTEN TO LITERATURE Listen to "The Gymnast" and "All About Gymnastics" as you follow or read along in your book. Listen to draw conclusions about the characters and events in "The Gymnast".

If there is anything you don't understand, you can listen again to any section.

Read It Again!

MATERIALS [SINGLES] [PAIRS] [GROUPS]
Collection of books for self-selected reading, reading logs, student book

Select a book you have already read. Record the title of the book in your reading log. You may want to read with a partner.

Choose from the following:

- **Leveled Readers**
- **ELL Readers**
- **Stories Written by Classmates**
- **Books from the Library**
- **"The Gymnast"**

TEN IMPORTANT SENTENCES Read the Ten Important Sentences for "The Gymnast". Then locate the sentences in the student book.

BOOK CLUB Look at "Meet Authors" on p. 763 of the student book to help you set up an author study of Gary Soto. What can you tell about the author based on this story? Read other books by Soto and get together with a group to share your favorites.

Design a Book Cover

MATERIALS [SINGLES]
Writing and art materials

Design a book cover for your autobiography.

1. **Think about an image that will make your readers want to learn more about you.**
2. **Design and draw the cover for your book. Don't forget to add the title and author!**

EARLY FINISHERS Write a paragraph for the back of the book jacket summarizing the subject of the book.

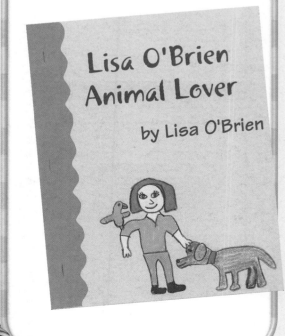

Scott Foresman Reading Street Centers Survival Kit
Use *The Gymnast* materials from the Reading Street
Centers Survival Kit to organize this week's centers.

Writing/ Vocabulary

Social Studies

Technology

Write About *Your Life*

MATERIALS `SINGLES`
Writing materials, outline form

In "The Gymnast", the narrator describes a single event in his childhood. Think of a memorable event in your own life and create an autobiographical story outline for it.

1. Use an outline to organize the major topics of your autobiography.
2. Below each main heading list the subtopics you will cover.
3. Below the main headings, list details you want to include.
4. Add a title.

EARLY FINISHERS Use the outline to write the first paragraph of your autobiography.

Title: Moving Day
A. Leaving our Old House
  1. A huge blue moving van came to pick up our things.
  2. Said a sad goodbye to my friends in the neighborhood.

Explore a New Interest

MATERIALS `SINGLES`
Writing materials, library and Internet access

Find out more about a sport or hobby that interests you.

1. Think of a sport or hobby that you've always wanted to learn more about.
2. Follow classroom rules for using library or Internet resources to learn more about it.
3. Make a list of things you learned about the sport or hobby.

EARLY FINISHERS Find someone you know who already plays the sport or hobby. List 2 or 3 facts about this person.

Lacrosse

1. Lacrosse is the oldest team sport in North America.
2. Lacrosse was first played by Native Americans.

Search For Information

MATERIALS `SINGLES` `PAIRS` `GROUPS`
Internet access

Choose a favorite sports legend. Search for an autobiography of his or her life.

1. Follow classroom rules for using the Internet to search for information. Use a student-friendly search engine.
2. For keywords, type the person's name followed by *autobiography*. You can search a library database the same way to see if you can locate a book.
3. If you are unable to find any sources, repeat the process for another sports legend.

EARLY FINISHERS Read to find out when, how, and why this person became involved in his or her sport.

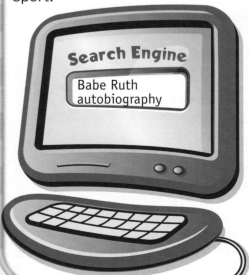

Search Engine

Babe Ruth autobiography

ALL CENTERS

OBJECTIVES

- Build vocabulary by finding words related to the lesson concept.
- Listen to draw conclusions.

Concept Vocabulary

champion person that wins first place in a game or contest

competitive involving trying to win something

develop to work to have something

perfected removed all faults from

Monitor Progress

Check Vocabulary

If...	then... review the
students are unable to place words on the Web,	lesson concept. Place the words on the Web and provide additional words for practice, such as *mastered, churning,* and *wake*.

SUCCESS PREDICTOR

DAY 1 Grouping Options

Reading
Whole Group
Introduce and discuss the Question of the Week. Then use pp. 484l–486b.

Group Time
Differentiated Instruction
Read this week's Leveled Readers. See pp. 484f–484g for the small group lesson plan.

Whole Group
Use p. 503a.

Language Arts
Use pp. 503e–503k.

Build Concepts

FLUENCY

MODEL PUNCTUATION CLUES As you read "The Winning Stroke," make a point of pausing after commas and periods. Change your intonation to indicate a question or exclamation—for example, "Just watch this takeoff!"

LISTENING COMPREHENSION

After reading "The Winning Stroke," use the following questions to assess listening comprehension.

1. **Do you think Jerry will turn out to be a champion swimmer? Why?** *(Possible response: He will be a champion because he is enthusiastic and determined.)* **Draw Conclusions**

2. **Make a generalization about the sport of competitive swimming.** *(Possible response: It is very hard work and it requires a lot of practice.)* **Generalize**

BUILD CONCEPT VOCABULARY

Start a web to build concepts and vocabulary related to this week's lesson and the unit theme.

- Draw the Improving Ourselves Concept Web.

- Read the sentence with the word *competitive* again. Ask students to pronounce *competitive* and discuss its meaning.

- Place *competitive* in an oval attached to *Exercise*. Explain that *competitive* is related to this concept. Read the sentences in which *champion, develop,* and *perfected* appear. Have students pronounce the words, place them on the web, and provide reasons.

- Brainstorm additional words and categories for the web. Keep the web on display and add words throughout the week.

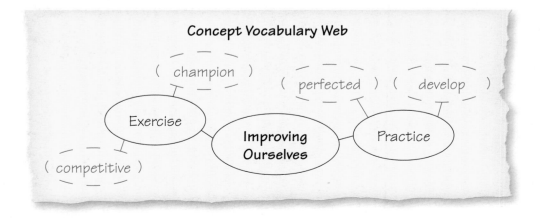

Concept Vocabulary Web

The Winning Stroke

by Matt Christopher

Jerry Grayson is new to the sport of competitive swimming, and to the Boston Blues swim team. He isn't sure he has what it takes to be a champion swimmer, but he is willing to try his hardest.

When Tony arrived at the shallow end, Coach Fulton described the way he wanted Jerry to practice his turns.

"You two guys start out with Jerry about ten feet away. Swim toward the edge, and then all three of you do your turns at the same time. I want you to develop a rhythm to it that's solid and dependable, Jerry. And when you have it down, you can practice on your own. Tanya, you're not doing anything right now," he called to her. "Come over and keep an eye on their turns. I'll be back in fifteen minutes."

The next quarter of an hour went like a breeze. Jerry could hardly believe how natural the turn had become after he got it right. How could he even have thought of racing until he knew stuff like this?

During the next week, Jerry managed to work in some extra coaching from Mr. Fulton, Tony, or Tanya—and even from some of the other members of the team once in a while.

After he perfected his flip turn, he learned how to dive perfectly.

"A long shallow dive can cut seconds from your time," Tanya explained. "The farther out you go, the less distance you have to swim. And if you don't have to come up from below, you can start swimming sooner. The same is true for the backstroke takeoff. Push yourself as far as possible from the wall."

And with each session, he got more and more comfortable. By the end of the week, he couldn't resist showing Tanya how well he had mastered one of his big problems.

"Just watch this takeoff!" he shouted. Then he demonstrated how well he had learned to start off in a backstroke race. As he pushed himself off from the side of the pool, Tanya jumped in on one side and Tony, who appeared out of nowhere, jumped in on the other. The two of them started backstroking furiously next to him, churning up a tidal wave of water in their combined wake.

But Jerry wasn't ruffled. He kept his head and continued to do exactly what he had learned. When he touched the opposite edge of the pool, Wayne Cabot shouted down to the three of them.

"The winner by a good palm and a half, Jerry Grayson!"

The winner—Jerry Grayson! It sounded great. Deep down, he knew that he would love to hear those words in a real race.

SKILLS ←→ STRATEGIES IN CONTEXT

Draw Conclusions Visualize

OBJECTIVES

- Draw conclusions using information in the text and prior knowledge.
- Visualize to draw conclusions.

Skills Trace

Draw Conclusions

Introduce/Teach	TE: 5.4 392–393, 484–485; 5.6 634–635
Practice	Practice Book: 153, 157, 158, 186, 193, 197, 198, 253, 257, 258, 276, 296
Reteach/Review	TE: 5.4 411b, 467, 503b, DI·52, DI·56; 5.6 653b, 683, 687, 735, 745, DI·52
Test	Selection Test: 61–64, 77–80, 101–104; Benchmark Test: Units 4,6

INTRODUCE

Read the following aloud: *Students are lined up early at the bus stop. They are all wearing new shoes and carrying new backpacks. A clean and shiny bus can be seen heading in their direction.* Then ask, "Do you think this scene takes place at the beginning of the school year or the end?" *(the beginning)* "How do you know?" *(Everything is clean and new.)*

Have students read the information on p. 484. Explain the following:

- To draw conclusions you need to evaluate the information in the text while thinking about your own knowledge and experiences.
- Visualizing enables you to become involved with the text and draw conclusions about what is happening and why.

Use Skill Transparency 20 to teach draw conclusions and visualize.

The Gymnast

Comprehension

Skill
Draw Conclusions

Strategy
Visualize

Draw Conclusions

- A conclusion is a sensible decision you make after you think about facts or details that you read.
- Drawing conclusions may also be called making inferences.
- Use your prior knowledge to help you draw conclusions.

Strategy: Visualize

Active readers visualize as they read. They make pictures in their mind. Visualizing can help you understand what is happening in what you read. It can also help you draw conclusions about what is happening and why.

Write to Read

1. Read "How to Do a Cartwheel." Use a graphic organizer like the one above to draw a conclusion about which way to start a cartwheel.

2. Describe how to do a handstand, a somersault, or some other action without naming it. Exchange papers with a classmate. Try to visualize and draw a conclusion about what your classmate is describing.

484

Strategic Intervention

Draw Conclusions Read "How to Do a Cartwheel" with students. Stop at several points in the article to have students draw conclusions. Use a graphic organizer like the one on p. 484 to help students record the evidence that leads to their conclusions.

ELL

Access Content

Beginning/Intermediate For a Picture It! lesson on draw conclusions, see ELL Teaching Guide, pp. 134–135.

Advanced Before students read "How to Do a Cartwheel," ask for a volunteer to model doing a cartwheel. Point out the student's starting position and where the hands are placed as the feet are lifted off the ground.

How to Do a Cartwheel

To begin a cartwheel, stand erect with one foot slightly in front of you. Use the foot of the side you feel is stronger. Let's assume you're doing a right-sided cartwheel. (To perform a left-sided cartwheel, reverse these directions. Use left for right and right for left.)

Raise both arms and lift your right foot. As you put it back down, reach to your right side and down toward the ground with your right arm. Begin lifting your left leg. Touch your right hand to the ground. Almost immediately, turn your upper body to touch your left hand to the ground beside your right hand. Your right leg should now be off the ground too. For a moment, you will be in a handstand—both hands down, both legs up.

Now bring your left foot down on the other side, lifting your right hand off the ground. Then bring your right foot down, lifting your left hand. You should be standing erect again.

The trick to performing a cartwheel is to keep your back and legs straight up, not out to the side. It sounds easy but it's not. Learning to cartwheel takes practice, practice, practice.

1 Skill Why do you think it's important to start out with the side you feel is stronger? (Think how you would feel starting on your weaker side.)

2 Strategy Visualize how you start out doing a cartwheel and what comes next.

3 Skill Why do you think this action is called a cartwheel?

4 Strategy Picture what someone looks like doing a cartwheel. Then picture the actual wheel of a cart. That can help you understand the name *cartwheel*.

485

Available as **Skill Transparency** 20

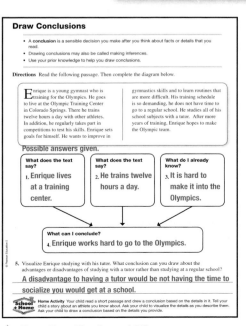

TEACH

1 SKILL Model how to draw conclusions.

Think Aloud **MODEL** I see in the text that to do a cartwheel, you have to put one arm down on the ground to support your body as you begin the cartwheel. I know that the first arm down will bear the most weight. Therefore, it makes sense that you should begin with your stronger side.

2 STRATEGY Visualize the action described.

Think Aloud **MODEL** As I read the text, I make a picture in my mind of what's happening. I see that when you start a cartwheel, you raise both arms and lift one foot off the ground. You start the motion by placing the raised foot on the ground. As you place your hands on the ground one at a time, your legs go up in the air one at a time. As your legs come down one at a time, your hands come up off the ground and into the air one at a time.

PRACTICE AND ASSESS

3 SKILL Possible response: Your body turns like a wheel on a cart.

4 STRATEGY Have a volunteer draw a picture of a wheel that is found on a cart. Have students compare this picture to a person doing a cartwheel.

WRITE Have students complete steps 1 and 2 of the Write to Read activity. You might consider using this as a whole-class activity.

Monitor Progress

Draw Conclusions

If... students are unable to complete **Write to Read** on p. 484,	then... use Practice Book p. 193 to provide additional practice.

The Gymnast   **485**

ONLINE

Have students use a student-friendly search engine and the keywords *USA Gymnastics* to find up-to-date information about gymnastics in the United States. Be sure to follow classroom guidelines for Internet use.

ELL

Build Background Use ELL Poster 20 to build background and vocabulary for the lesson concept of individual development and identity.

▲ **ELL Poster** 20

Build Background

ACTIVATE PRIOR KNOWLEDGE

BEGIN A KWL CHART about gymnastics.

- Give students a few minutes to write what they know about gymnastics. Prompt by asking students to recall a gymnastics competition they may have watched or participated in. Record what students know on a KWL chart.

- Give students two minutes to write two or three questions about the topic. Record questions on the KWL chart. Add a question of your own.

- Tell students that, as they read, they should look for the answers to their questions and note any new information to add to the chart.

Topic		Gymnastics	
K	**W**	**L**	
Gymnastics is a difficult sport.	What does it take to be a gymnast?		
It takes a lot of practice.	Why would someone want to be a gymnast?		

▲ **Graphic Organizer** 4

BACKGROUND BUILDING AUDIO This week's audio explores the topic of gymnastics. After students listen, discuss the challenges of learning the sport. Lead students to a general discussion of learning something new and working hard to meet one's goals.

 **Background Building Audio**

Introduce Vocabulary

WORD RATING CHART

Create word rating charts using the categories *Know*, *Have Seen*, and *Don't Know*. Use the word rating chart.

Word Rating Chart

Word	Know	Have Seen	Don't Know
bluish		✓	
cartwheels	✓		
gymnastics	✓		
hesitation	✓		
limelight			✓
skidded		✓	
somersault			
throbbing			
wincing			

▲ **Graphic Organizer** 5

Read aloud the lesson vocabulary. Then have students sort the words into the three categories: *Know* (know and can use); *Have Seen* (have seen or heard the word; don't know meaning); *Don't Know* (don't know the word). ***Activate Prior Knowledge***

Invite students to share their work. Explain that two of this week's words are compound words. Have students identify the two words. *(limelight and cartwheels)* Write the words on the board. Have a volunteer point out the two smaller words in each compound word. ***Compound Words***

As a class, return to students' word rating charts after they finish reading and have students make changes to their ratings.

Use the Multisyllabic Word Routine on p. DI·1 to help students read multisyllabic words.

Lesson Vocabulary

WORDS TO KNOW

T bluish somewhat blue

T cartwheels sideways handsprings with the legs and arms kept straight

T gymnastics a sport in which very difficult exercises are performed

T hesitation act of failing to act promptly

T limelight center of public attention and interest

T skidded slipped or slid sideways while moving

T somersault to run or jump, turning the heels over the head

T throbbing beating rapidly or strongly

T wincing drawing back suddenly

MORE WORDS TO KNOW

backflips backwards somersaults performed in the air

solitary without companions

spindly very long and slender

T = Tested Word

Vocabulary

Directions Choose the word from the box that best matches each definition below. Write the word on the line.

somersault   1. to run or jump, turning the heels over the head

gymnastics   2. a sport in which very difficult exercises are performed

hesitation   3. act of failing to act promptly

bluish   4. somewhat blue

cartwheels   5. sideways handsprings with the legs and arms kept straight

Check the Words You Know
___bluish
___cartwheels
___gymnastics
___hesitation
___limelight
___skidded
___somersault
___throbbing
___wincing

Directions Choose the word from the box that matches the clues and complete the crossword puzzle.

DOWN
6. the pain I felt when I broke my toe
7. the color of a pale sky
8. the place the stars want to be

ACROSS
9. what my bicycle did when I slammed on the brakes
10. what I am doing when I eat food I don't like

Write a News Report
Imagine you're a sports reporter covering a gymnastics meet. On a separate sheet of paper write a news report. Use as many vocabulary words as you can.
News reports should include words from the vocabulary list and basic facts about a gymnastics meet.

Home Activity Your child identified and used vocabulary words from *The Gymnast*. Skim the articles about a single sport in the sports section of a newspaper. Point out and define the vocabulary that is used to describe each type of sport.

▲ **Practice Book** p. 194

Vocabulary Strategy

OBJECTIVE

Use word structure and suffixes to determine word meaning.

INTRODUCE

Discuss the strategy for word structure using the steps on p. 486.

TEACH

- Have students read "It's Easier in Daydreams," noting any words with suffixes.
- Model using word structure to determine the meaning of *hesitation*.

Think Aloud **MODEL** I recognize the base word *hesitate*, even though the final *e* is dropped. *Hesitate* means "to pause." I also see the suffix *-ion*. I know this suffix means "state of being," so I can guess that *hesitation* means "in a state of hesitation," or "in a state of pausing."

Words to Know

limelight
hesitation
somersault
gymnastics
cartwheels
throbbing
wincing
skidded
bluish

Remember

Try the strategy. Then, if you need more help, use your glossary or dictionary.

Vocabulary Strategy
for Suffixes

Word Structure A suffix is a syllable added to the end of a base word that changes the base word's meaning. The spelling of the base word may also change when the suffix is added. For example, when the suffix *-ion* is added to *appreciate*, the final *e* is dropped: *appreciation*. Adding this suffix adds the meaning "the act or state of being ___." The suffix *-ish* adds the meaning "somewhat" or "like," as in *brownish*. Recognizing a suffix can help you figure out the meaning of an unknown word.

1. Look at the unknown word. See if you recognize a base word in it.

2. Check to see if the suffix *-ion*, *-tion*, or *-ish* has been added to the base word.

3. Ask yourself how the suffix changes the meaning of the base word.

4. Try the new meaning in the sentence to see if it makes sense.

As you read "It's Easier in Daydreams," look for words that end with suffixes. Analyze the base words and the suffixes to figure out the meanings of words you do not know.

486

DAY 2 Grouping Options

Reading
Whole Group Discuss the Question of the Day. Then use pp. 486–489.

Group Time Differentiated Instruction
Read "The Gymnast." See pp. 484f–484g for the small group lesson plan.

Whole Group Use p. 503a.

Language Arts
Use pp. 503e–503k.

Strategic Intervention

Word Structure Review meanings for the common suffixes *-ish* ("somewhat") and *-like* ("resembling") by discussing the meanings of the words *childish* and *childlike*.

Access Content Use ELL Poster 20 to preteach vocabulary. Choose from the following to meet language proficiency levels.

Beginning Use the Multilingual Lesson Vocabulary list that begins on p. 272 of the ELL Teaching Guide, as well as other home-language resources to provide translations of the tested words.

Intermediate After reading, have students create a semantic web with words related to gymnastics.

Advanced Teach the lesson on pp. 486–487. Have students return to the word rating chart and make appropriate changes to their ratings.

Resources for home-language words may include parents, bilingual staff members, bilingual dictionaries, or online translation sources.

It's Easier in Daydreams

I love to watch Olympic gymnasts. In fact, I hope to be one myself one day. In my daydreams, I am already a star. The audience roars as I step into the limelight. Without any hesitation, I somersault across the gym. I move with terrific speed and grace. The judges smile and nod and hold up score cards with perfect 10.0's on them.

So you can understand why I was so upset after what happened. I signed up for a gymnastics class offered by the park district. The teacher showed us how to do cartwheels. "This is easy!" I thought, so

I didn't pay attention. When it was my turn, I ran to the mat, closed my eyes, and threw myself at it. The next thing I knew, I was flat on my back. My head and knees were throbbing. I couldn't help wincing in pain as I got up. On the next try, I lost my nerve and put on the brakes. I skidded several feet into a wall and thumped my shoulder. There's a nice bluish bruise there to remind me. I have a long way to go to reach the Olympics.

Words to Write

Imagine that you are a sports writer. Write an article about a gymnastics competition or some other sporting event you just watched. Use words from the Words to Know list and as many words connected with the sport as you can.

487

BEFORE READING

PRACTICE AND ASSESS

- Have students work with partners to determine the base word, suffix, and meaning of the remaining Words to Know.
- Remind students that sometimes the suffix changes the meaning of the base word.
- If you began a word rating chart on p. 486b, have students reassess their ratings.
- Have students complete Practice Book p. 195.

WRITE Students should use the Words to Know and other words with suffixes in their writing.

Monitor Progress

Word Structure

| If... students need more practice with the lesson vocabulary, | then... use Tested Vocabulary Cards. |

▲ **Practice Book** p. 195

Prereading Strategies

OBJECTIVES

- Draw conclusions using information in the text and prior knowledge.
- Visualize to draw conclusions about a selection.

GENRE STUDY

Autobiography

"The Gymnast" is an autobiography. Explain that an autobiography is a story about a person's life and is written by the person who lived it. An autobiography can be about the person's whole life, part of that person's life, or a single event.

PREVIEW AND PREDICT

Have students read the opening question and the title on pp. 488–489. Then ask them to do a picture walk through the selection. When they finish, have students identify the subject of the selection. Ask, "What do you think the 'The Gymnast' is about?" Students should use lesson vocabulary words in their discussion.

Strategy Response Log

Graphic Organizer Have students close their eyes and picture a gymnast performing. Then ask them to divide a page in half in their strategy response logs to make a two-column chart. On the left, have them draw what they "see" when they visualize a gymnast performing. Students will review their notes and drawings in the Strategy Response Log activity on p. 493.

Will *Gary* succeed in becoming the person he wants to be?

488

 ELL

Access Content Ask students to turn to the picture on p. 491 and choose a volunteer to read the words aloud. Repeat this with the words and pictures on pp. 492, 495, and 496.

Consider having students read the selection summary in English or in students' home languages. See the Multilingual Summaries in the ELL Teaching Guide, pp. 138–140.

The Gymnast

by Gary Soto

Genre

Autobiography is the story of a person's life or of a single event in it, told by the person who lived it. As you read, notice how the author looks back at himself from a humorous point of view.

489

SET PURPOSE

Read the first page of the selection aloud to students. Have them recall what they "saw" when they pictured a gymnast performing. Have them read to find out what Gary Soto has to say about gymnasts.

Remind students to visualize the people, places, and actions as they read. In addition, have them keep track of key details that they can use when drawing conclusions about the selection.

STRATEGY RECALL

Students have now used these before-reading strategies:

- preview the selection to be aware of its genre, features, and possible content;
- activate prior knowledge about that content and what to expect of that genre;
- make predictions;
- set a purpose for reading.

Remind students to be aware of and flexibly use the during-reading strategies they have learned:

- link prior knowledge to new information;
- summarize text they have read so far;
- ask clarifying questions;
- answer questions they or others pose;
- check their predictions and either refine them or make new predictions;
- recognize the text structure the author is using, and use that knowledge to make predictions and increase comprehension;
- visualize what the author is describing;
- monitor their comprehension and use fix-up strategies.

After reading, students will use these strategies:

- summarize or retell the text;
- answer questions they or others pose;
- reflect to make new information become part of their prior knowledge.

Audio CD **AudioText**

Guiding Comprehension

1 ◎ **Draw Conclusions • Inferential**

Reread p. 490, paragraph 1. What makes Gary feel jealous?

Gary's mother is proud of Gary's cousin, Isaac. She is always talking about Isaac. Gary knows that people admire gymnasts.

Monitor Progress	
◎ **Draw Conclusions**	
If... students are unable to draw conclusions about the author's feelings,	**then...** use the skill and strategy instruction on p. 491.

2 **Point of View • Inferential**

From whose point of view is "The Gymnast" told? How do you know?

It's told from Gary's point of view. We know this because the selection is an autobiography. Gary uses first-person narration and tells about events from his own life.

ONLINE

Students who have access to the Internet can use a student-friendly search engine and the keywords *Olympic gymnasts* to learn about top international gymnasts who have participated in the Olympic games. Be sure to follow classroom guidelines for Internet use.

For three days of my eleventh summer I listened to my mother yap about my cousin, Isaac, who was taking gymnastics. She was proud of him, she said one evening at the stove as she pounded a round steak into carne asada and crushed a heap of beans into refritos. I was jealous because I had watched my share of *Wide World of Sports* and knew that people admired an athlete who could **somersault** without hurting himself. I pushed aside my solitary game of Chinese checkers and spent a few minutes rolling around the backyard until I was dizzy and itchy with grass.

That Saturday, I went to Isaac's house where I ate plums and sat under an aluminum arbor watching my cousin, dressed in gymnastic shorts and top, do spindly **cartwheels** and back flips in his backyard while he instructed, "This is the correct way." He breathed in the grassy air, leaped, and came up smiling the straightest teeth in the world.

I followed him to the front lawn. When a car passed he did a **back flip** and looked out the side of his eyes to see if any of the passengers were looking. Some pointed while others looked ahead dully at the road.

2

490

ELL

Extend Language Point to the word "yap." Explain that "yap" has two meanings. Help students name the more common meaning (the sharp barking sound a dog makes). Tell them that "yap" can also mean to talk a lot. Ask students why Gary's mother was yapping about his cousin.

I . . . spent a few minutes rolling around the backyard until I was dizzy and itchy with grass.

491

Draw Conclusions

TEACH

- Remind students that drawing conclusions means making a sensible decision after they think about facts or details in a selection.

- Point out that keeping track of their conclusions as they read can make it easier to understand and respond to the text.

- Explain that self-questioning will help them draw conclusions as they read. Model the process for students.

 Think Aloud **MODEL** As I read the first paragraph, I ask myself, "What does Gary recall about his eleventh summer? What does Gary know from watching *Wide World of Sports?*" I use my answers to these questions to draw the conclusion that Gary's mother's comments about Isaac and Gary's knowledge that people admire gymnasts makes him jealous.

PRACTICE AND ASSESS

Have students reread the sentence, "When a car passed he did a back flip and looked out the side of his eyes to see if any of the passengers were looking." Then ask, "Which of these is a sensible conclusion to draw about Isaac?" *(Choice a)*

a) Isaac likes an audience.

b) Isaac is shy.

c) Isaac is embarrassed to be a gymnast.

Gymnastics

Time for **SOCIAL STUDIES**

Modern gymnastics was introduced to Europe in the early 1800s and to the United States in the 1830s. Some 65 years later, the first major gymnastics competition was held at the 1896 Olympics in Athens, Greece.

Guiding Comprehension

But when I did a cartwheel, the shoes flew off, along with the tape.

492

3 **Generalize • Inferential**

Make a generalization about gymnasts based on what you read about Issac.

Possible response: Gymnasts spend a lot of time practicing.

Monitor Progress
REVIEW **Generalize**

If... students have difficulty generalizing,	**then...** use the skill and strategy lesson on page 493.

4 **Details and Facts • Inferential**

What does Gary seem to think is most interesting about gymnastics?

Possible response: He likes the equipment—the tape, shoes, chalk.

5 **Characters • Critical**

Text to Self **Does Gary remind you of anyone in your own life? Explain why.**

Answers will vary but should be supported by details from the selection.

ELL

Access Content Gary thinks his cousin is a *show-off*. Explain that a *show-off* is someone who behaves in a way that calls attention to him or herself.

My cousin was a show-off, but I figured he was allowed the limelight before one appreciative dog who had come over to look. I envied him and his cloth gymnast shoes. I liked the way they looked, slim, black, and cool. They seemed special, something I could never slip onto my feet.

I ate the plums and watched him until he was sweaty and out of breath. When he was finished, I begged him to let me wear his cloth shoes. **Drops of sweat** fell at his feet. He looked at me with disdain, ran a yellow towel across his face, and patted his neck dry. He tore the white tape from his wrists—I liked the tape as well and tried to paste it around my wrists. He washed off his hands. I asked him about the white powder, and he said it kept his hands dry. I asked him why he needed **dry hands** to do cartwheels and back flips. He said that all gymnasts kept their hands dry, then drank from a bottle of greenish water he said was filled with nutrients.

I asked him again if I could wear his shoes. He slipped them off and said, "OK, just for a while." The shoes were loose, but I liked them. I went to the front yard with my **wrists dripping tape** and my hands white as gloves. I smiled slyly and thought I looked neat. But when I did a cartwheel, the shoes flew off, along with the tape, and my cousin yelled and stomped the grass.

493

Develop Vocabulary

PRACTICE LESSON VOCABULARY

Have students respond true or false to each statement and give reasons.

1. Gymnastics is easy to learn. (False; gymnastics requires many years of practice.)

2. Cartwheels don't involve using your hands. (False; cartwheels involve using your hands to turn end over end).

3. Someone would be *wincing* in pain if he had fallen off his bike. (True; someone might wince with pain if he fell off his bike).

BUILD CONCEPT VOCABULARY

Review previous concept words with students. Ask if students have come across any words today in their reading or elsewhere that they would like to add to the Improving Ourselves Concept Web, such as *appreciative*.

Generalize REVIEW

TEACH

- Generalizations are broad statements or rules that apply to many examples.
- Model how to form a generalization about gymnasts.

 Think Aloud **MODEL** In this story, Isaac practices a lot. I know that gymnastics is very hard. I can generalize that gymnasts spend a lot of time practicing.

PRACTICE AND ASSESS

- Have students reread the second paragraph on p. 493. What generalization does Issac make about gymnasts? *(They all keep their hands dry.)*
- To assess, use Practice Book p. 196.

Visualize Have students review their two-column chart and drawings. (See p. 488.) Have them continue to add to the chart as they read.

Generalize
Directions Read the passage. Then answer the questions below.

Many schools require every student to play at least one sport. By playing sports, many young people say that they meet new friends. By being on a team, a young person can learn cooperation and fair play. Playing a sport can build strength, flexibility, and endurance, and improve fitness. Many experts say young people get a boost in self-confidence as they succeed with new skills they learn through playing sports. Finally, for most young athletes, playing sports is simply a lot of fun.

Possible answers given.
1. Based on the passage, what is a generalization you can make about playing sports?
   Playing sports has many advantages.

2. Which detail from the passage supports this generalization?
   Playing sports can build friendships.

3. What other detail supports this generalization?
   Playing sports can increase fitness and strength.

4. What is a generalization that is stated in the passage?
   For most young athletes, playing sports is a lot of fun.

5. Write a generalization of your own about sports. Write at least one detail to back it up.
   Playing sports can be difficult if you are not very athletic. A slow runner has trouble keeping up during a soccer game.

School + Home **Home Activity** Your child read a short passage and made a generalization based on the passage. Tell your child some specific details about a subject you think is important. Ask him or her to make a generalization about the subject.

▲ **Practice Book** p. 196

If you want to teach this selection in two sessions, stop here.

Guiding Comprehension

If you are teaching the selection in two days, discuss any conclusions so far and review the vocabulary.

6 Predict • Critical

How do you think the selection will end? What helped you make your prediction?

Answers will vary but should be supported with evidence from the selection.

7 Vocabulary • Word Structure

What is the base word in *hesitation*? What suffix has been added to the base word? What does the word mean?

The base word is *hesitate*. The suffix is *-ion*. *Hesitation* means "the state of failing to act promptly."

Monitor Progress	
Word Structure	
If... students need help understanding word structure and identifying suffixes,	**then...** use the vocabulary strategy instruction on page 495.

DAY 3   Grouping Options

Reading

Whole Group Discuss the Question of the Day.

Group Time Differentiated Instruction
Read "The Gymnast." See pp. 484f–484g for the small group lesson plan.

Whole Group Discuss the Reader Response questions on p. 498. Then use p. 503a.

Language Arts
Use pp. 503e–503k.

I was glad to get home. I was jealous and miserable, but the next day I found a pair of old vinyl slippers in the closet that were sort of like gymnastic shoes. I pushed my feet into them, tugging and wincing because they were too small. I took a few steps, admiring my feet, which looked like bloated water balloons, and went outside to do cartwheels on the front lawn. A friend skidded to a stop on his bike, one cheek fat with sunflower seeds. His mouth churned to a stop. He asked why I was wearing slippers on a hot day. I made a face at him and said that they were gymnastic shoes, not slippers. He watched me do *cartwheels*

6 for a while, then rode away doing a wheelie.

I returned inside. I looked for tape to wrap my wrists, but could find only circle bandages in the medicine cabinet. I dipped my hands in flour to keep them dry and went back outside to do cartwheels and, finally, after much

7 hesitation, a *back flip* that nearly cost me my life when I landed on my head. I crawled to the shade, stars of pain pulsating in my shoulder and neck.

My brother glided by on his bike, smooth as a kite. He stared at me and asked why I was wearing slippers. I didn't answer him. My neck still hurt. He asked about the flour on my hands, and I told him to leave me alone. I turned on the hose and drank cool water.

494

ELL

Build Background Point to the word *wheelie*. Help students recognize the word *wheel* in *wheelie*. Explain that a wheelie is a stunt done on a bicycle by raising the front wheel up in the air while riding. Ask students why they think Gary's friend rode away doing a wheelie.

. . . and, finally, after much hesitation, a back flip that nearly cost me my life . . .

VOCABULARY STRATEGY

Word Structure

TEACH

Read aloud p. 495. Model how to use word parts to figure out the meaning of *hesitation*.

Think Aloud **MODEL** On page 495, I see the word *hesitation*. I'm not sure about that word, so I'll look for familiar word parts. I see the base word *hesitate* and the suffix *-ion*, which I know means "state of." I know *hesitate* means "fail to act promptly." So *hesitation* must mean "in a state of failing to act promptly."

PRACTICE AND ASSESS

Have students use word parts to determine the meaning of *bluish* in the first paragraph on p. 497. (The suffix *-ish* means "somewhat" or "like." *Bluish* means "somewhat blue.")

Nadia Comaneci

Time for SOCIAL STUDIES

One of the most famous gymnasts of all time is Nadia Comaneci. At the age of fourteen, she was the first gymnast to score a perfect 10 in Olympic competition. This occurred during her first event, the uneven parallel bars, at the 1976 Olympics. She then went on to receive three gold medals, one silver, and one bronze. Four years later, she won two gold medals and two silver medals at the Olympic Games in Moscow. Comaneci retired from competition in 1984.

EXTEND SKILLS

Personal Essay

A personal essay is a brief discussion of a topic, using first-person pronouns and often revealing the personality of the author. It may include humor and usually supports a relaxed tone. The main purpose of a personal essay is to entertain. Although "The Gymnast" is an autobiography, what features in the selection might lead someone to say that this is a personal essay?

Guiding Comprehension

8 🔵 **Visualize • Inferential**

What details on p. 497 help you visualize the scene?

Possible responses: Throbbing feet, toes cooling on the summery grass, bluish ankles, chill up the back, piranha-like eating, cartwheels by the dizzy dozen, smoke of a barbecue, orange burst, pinpoints of unfortunate light.

9 **Author's Purpose • Inferential**

Question the Author **What is the author trying to tell you when he says, "I ate a plum and pictured my cousin, who was probably cartwheeling to the audience of one sleeping dog"?**

Possible response: He is saying that he realized at that point that gymnastics might not be great as he first thought it was.

10 **Visualize • Critical**

Text to Text **Does this autobiography remind you of any other nonfiction selections you've read? Think about events, characters, and the point of view from which it's told.**

Students' responses should include a comparison to another autobiography they've read. They may mention the first-person point of view, the challenge the author faces, etc.

Strategy Response Log

Summarize When students finish reading the selection, provide this prompt: Imagine that a friend has asked you to tell what happens in "The Gymnast." Summarize the selection in four or five sentences.

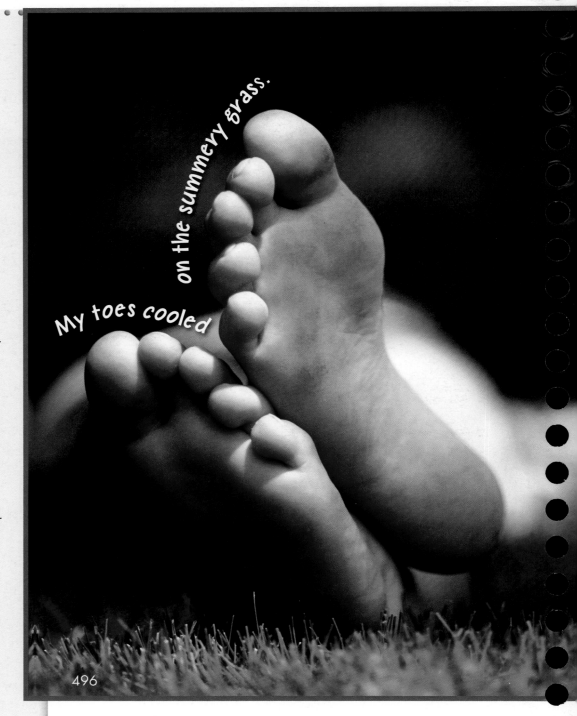

My toes cooled on the summery grass.

496

ⒺⓁⓁ

Access Content Reread aloud the sentence "Dinner was a ten-minute affair of piranha-like eating and thirty minutes of washing dishes." Explain that a piranha is a meat-eating fish known for consuming large amounts of food very fast. *A ten-minute affair* means that it took them ten minutes to eat. Ask students to use this information to describe the family dinner.

I walked to Romain playground where I played Chinese checkers and was asked a dozen times why I was wearing slippers. I'm taking gymnastics, I lied, and these are the kind of shoes you wear. When one kid asked why I had white powder on my hands and in my hair, I gave up on Chinese checkers and returned home, my feet throbbing. But before I went inside, I took off the slippers. My toes cooled on the summery grass. I ran a garden hose on my feet and bluish ankles, and a chill ran up my back.

Dinner was a ten-minute affair of piranha-like eating and thirty minutes of washing dishes. Once finished, I returned to the backyard, where I again stuffed my feet into the slippers and did **cartwheels by the dizzy dozens.** After a while they were easy, I had to move on. I sucked in the summer air, along with the smoke of a faraway barbecue, and tried a back flip. I landed on my neck again, this time I saw an orange burst behind my eyes. I lay on the grass, tired and sweaty, my feet squeezed in the vise of cruel slippers. **8**

I watched the dusk settle and the first stars, pinpoints of unfortunate light tangled in telephone wires. I ate a plum and pictured my cousin, who was probably cartwheeling to the audience of one sleeping dog. **9** **10**

497

Develop Vocabulary

PRACTICE LESSON VOCABULARY

As a class, have students complete the following sentences orally.

1. As he walked in the slippers, Gary's feet were *(throbbing)*.

2. Gary's ankles turned *(bluish)* in color.

3. Gary's first *(somersault)* made him feel a little dizzy.

4. Issac loved the *(limelight)*, so he looked around for an audience.

5. Gary was nervous, but he finally tried a back flip after much *(hesitation)*.

BUILD CONCEPT VOCABULARY

Review previous concept words with students. Ask if students have come across any words today in their reading or elsewhere that they would like to add to the Improving Ourselves Concept Web, such as *tired* and *sweaty*.

⊙ STRATEGY SELF-CHECK

Visualize

Remind students that visualizing means using imagery and sensory details to create pictures in your mind as you read. Visualizing can help readers understand what they read and draw conclusions about events and characters. Use Practice Book p. 197.

SELF-CHECK

Students can ask themselves these questions to assess understanding of the selection.

- Can I visualize what the author describes?
- Does visualizing help me draw conclusions about events and characters?
- Can I use the strategy to help me better understand and enjoy what I'm reading?

Monitor Progress

⊙ **Draw Conclusions**

If... students have difficulty visualizing and drawing conclusions,	**then...** use the Reteach lesson on p. 503b.

Draw Conclusions

- A **conclusion** is a sensible decision you make after you think about facts or details that you read.
- Drawing conclusions may also be called making inferences.
- Use your prior knowledge to help you draw conclusions.

Directions Read the following passage. Then answer the questions below.

When Lance Armstrong was 20, he made the U.S. Olympic cycling team. Three years later, he won an important cycling race, the Tour Du Pont, a premier U.S. cycling event. In 1996, he made the U.S. Olympic team again. That same year, he was diagnosed with cancer. He suffered terrible pain during his treatments and fought hard to get back to cycling. Five months after his diagnosis, he was training again determined to return to the sport he loved. Even though he was weakened from the disease, he wouldn't give up. In 1998, he finally returned to professional cycling. In 1999 he won the Tour de France. In 2005, he became the first seven-time winner of the Tour de France. Lance Armstrong inspires many people with his courage and abilities.

Possible answers given.
1. What conclusion can you draw about Lance Armstrong's character?
   Lance Armstrong is persistent and dedicated to cycling.

2. What is one detail from the passage that supports your conclusion?
   He was cycling five months after his cancer diagnosis.
3. What is another detail from the passage to support your conclusion?
   He won the Tour de France seven times.
4. What conclusion can you draw about how Lance Armstrong inspired other people?
   Lance Armstrong probably inspires people to work to overcome tragedy.
5. How does visualizing help you understand what you read about Lance Armstrong?
   Visualizing him first as sick, then as a champion makes his accomplishments seem more significant.

Home Activity Your child read a short passage and drew conclusions based on details in the passage. Read a newspaper or magazine article about a famous athlete with your child. Ask your child to visualize the details. Afterwards, ask your child to draw a conclusion about this sports star.

▲ **Practice Book** p. 197

Reader Response

Open for Discussion **Personal Response**

 MODEL I'd begin by thinking about how the narrator's jealousy made him pretend he was a gymnast too. This will help me think of other similar instances.

Comprehension Check **Critical Response**

1. Possible responses: "dizzy and itchy with grass"; "skidded to a stop on his bike." Yes. The words describe Gary's experiences and can describe our own. **Author's Purpose**

2. Possible response: Isaac looks to see if people driving by notice his flips. **Draw Conclusions**

3. Responses will vary but should include details such as Isaac's shoes were "slim, black, and cool," while Gary's feet looked like "bloated water balloons" in his slippers. **Visualize**

4. Responses will vary but could include *limelight* and *gymnastics*. **Vocabulary**

 Look Back and Write For test practice, assign a 10–15 minute time limit. For assessment, see the Scoring Rubric at the right.

Retell

Have students retell "The Gymnast."

Monitor Progress

Check Retelling Rubric 4 3 2 1

If... students have difficulty retelling the selection,	then... use the Retelling Cards and the Scoring Rubric for Retelling on p. 499 to assist fluent retelling.

SUCCESS PREDICTOR

 **ELL**

Check Retelling Model retelling by talking about the first photograph. Then have students use photos and other text features to guide their retellings. For more ideas on assessing students' retellings, see the ELL and Transition Handbook.

Reader Response

Open for Discussion The narrator of "The Gymnast" says, "I was jealous and miserable." Why was he jealous? What did his jealousy make him do? Do you know anyone who has had an experience like his? What was the outcome?

1. Gary Soto has taken an incident from his childhood and packed it with sensory details to bring it to life. Find details that tell how things looked and sounded and felt. Do these details bring the incident to life? Explain. **Think Like an Author**

2. Young Gary draws the conclusion that his cousin Isaac is a showoff. Find details from the selection that support this conclusion. **Draw Conclusions**

3. Find passages that show how Gary looks in his gymnastics outfit and how his cousin looks. Discuss how the visual details help make them two very different people. **Visualize**

4. *Somersault* and *cartwheels* are names for gymnastic feats. What other words from the Words to Know list would go into a web with *gymnast* at the center? **Vocabulary**

 Look Back and Write The dog in "The Gymnast" acts as an audience. Find the dog on pages 493 and 497. How does the dog-as-audience change, and what does this change tell you about the gymnast? Write your answer.

Meet author Gary Soto on page 763.

498

Scoring Rubric **Look Back and Write**

Top-Score Response A top-score response will contrast the attitude of the dog toward the practicing gymnast on pp. 493–497 and relate it to the narrator's view.

Example of a Top-Score Response The dog watches the gymnast with interest at first, then goes to sleep. This change matches the change in the narrator, who goes from strong interest to lack of interest. Now that he is more realistic, the narrator does not envy his cousin as much.

For additional rubrics, see p. WA10.

Write Now

Descriptive Writing

Prompt

In "The Gymnast," a boy learns that he can't be anybody but himself.

Think about an important lesson you have learned.

Now write a description of the lesson and how you learned it.

Student Model

Paragraphs separate events that take place at two different times. Phrases signal time shifts.

Not long ago, my classmate Rena invited me to her birthday party. In the invitation, she included a pink printout with exact directions to her house. When I told Mom about the party, she quizzed me about the directions, and I said, "It's cool, Mom. I have them."

Precise nouns, verbs, and adjectives rather than vague ones show effective word choice.

Mom often scolds me about the chaos in my room, so I guess she wasn't surprised when on the day of the party I couldn't find Rena's directions. Together we excavated the piles on my desk and found the printout. I arrived at the party late, but I learned a lesson about why I need to keep my room in better order.

Last sentence describes lesson that was learned.

Use the model to help you write your own description.

499

Write Now

Look at the Prompt Explain that each sentence in the prompt has a purpose.

- Sentence 1 presents a topic.
- Sentence 2 suggests students think about the topic.
- Sentence 3 tells what to write—a description.

Strategies to Develop Word Choice

Have students

- use strong, precise nouns and verbs.

NO: Move things on my desk.

YES: Sort magazines on my desk.

- add vivid adjectives or adverbs to make clearer pictures in readers' minds.

NO: I held the vase.

YES: I held the fragile vase nervously.

For additional suggestions and rubric, see pp. 503g–503h.

Writer's Checklist

☑ **Focus** Do all sentences tell about the lesson?

☑ **Organization** Is the lesson clearly stated?

☑ **Support** Are readers given adequate details?

☑ **Conventions** Are indefinite pronouns used correctly?

Scoring Rubric — Expository Retelling

Rubric 4 3 2 1	4	3	2	1
Connections	Makes connections and generalizes beyond the text	Makes connections to other events, texts, or experiences	Makes a limited connection to another event, text, or experience	Makes no connection to another event, text, or experience
Author's Purpose	Elaborates on author's purpose	Tells author's purpose with some clarity	Makes some connection to author's purpose	Makes no connection to author's purpose
Topic	Describes the main topic	Identifies the main topic with some details early in retelling	Identifies the main topic	Retelling has no sense of topic
Important Ideas	Gives accurate information about events, steps, and ideas using details and key vocabulary	Gives accurate information about events, steps, and ideas with some detail and key vocabulary	Gives limited or inaccurate information about events, steps, and ideas	Gives no information about events, steps, and ideas
Conclusions	Draws conclusions and makes inferences to generalize beyond the text	Draws conclusions about the text	Is able to draw few conclusions about the text	Is unable to draw conclusions or make inferences about the text

Retelling Plan

☑ **Week 1** Assess Strategic Intervention students.

☑ **Week 2** Assess Advanced students.

☑ **Week 3** Assess Strategic Intervention students.

☑ **Week 4** Assess On-Level students.

☑ **This week assess any students you have not yet checked during this unit.**

Use the Retelling Chart on p. TR17 to record retelling.

Selection Test To assess with "The Gymnast," use Selection Tests, pp. 77–80.

Fresh Reads for Differentiated Test Practice For weekly leveled practice, use pp. 115–120.

SUCCESS PREDICTOR

Reading Online

OBJECTIVES

- Examine the features of online reference sources.
- Compare and contrast across texts.

PREVIEW/USE TEXT FEATURES

Have students preview "All About Gymnastics." Ask:

- **How does Alice get from the search result screen to the encyclopedia entry for gymnastics?** *(She clicks on the gymnastics encyclopedia link.)*

- **How are the dictionary entries on pp. 502–503 like an entry in a printed dictionary?** *(Each entry word is in bold; there is a pronunciation and definition.)*

If students have trouble understanding how to use online reference sources, use the Technology Tools Box below.

Link to Social Studies

Have students work in pairs or groups to brainstorm topic ideas. Before they begin their searches, have them predict which online sources will be the most useful for their topics.

DAY 4 Grouping Options

Reading

Whole Group Discuss the Question of the Day.

Group Time Differentiated Instruction
Read "All About Gymnastics." See pp. 484f–484g for the small group lesson plan.

Whole Group Use p. 503a.

Language Arts
Use pp. 503e–503k.

Reading Online
New Literacies: **PearsonSuccessNet.com**

All About Gymnastics

Online Reference Sources

Genre
- You can find reference sources, such as almanacs and dictionaries, on Internet Web sites.
- Some Web sites give you several different reference sources all in one place.

Text Features
- These electronic reference sources look a lot like printed sources, and they're organized the same way.
- Instead of turning pages by hand, you click through them with a mouse.

Link to Social Studies
Explore a topic you like. Use an encyclopedia, dictionary, and other reference sources. Write down facts you find.

After reading Gary Soto's "The Gymnast," Alice decides she might want to do gymnastics. So she goes to an online reference Web site.

For more practice
Take It to the Net
PearsonSuccessNet.com

500

TECHNOLOGY TOOLS

Online Reference Sources

Search Window The search window is where you type the keyword or phrase you want to find information about. In some search engines, you may need to click on the box before typing. To start the search, click on a word like *Search* or *Go,* or press *Enter.*

Search Results The results of a search are displayed in a list below the search window. This list includes links to Web sites that contain the keywords you typed into the search window. Clicking on a link will bring you to a Web site.

 Instead of turning pages, online researchers use these features. The *Back* arrow takes you to the previous page you saw on the screen. The *Forward* arrow returns you to the page you were on before hitting *Back.*

 The home page of any online reference is the first page users see when accessing the site. Other pages usually have the word *Home* or an icon like this. Clicking on it will return you to the home page.

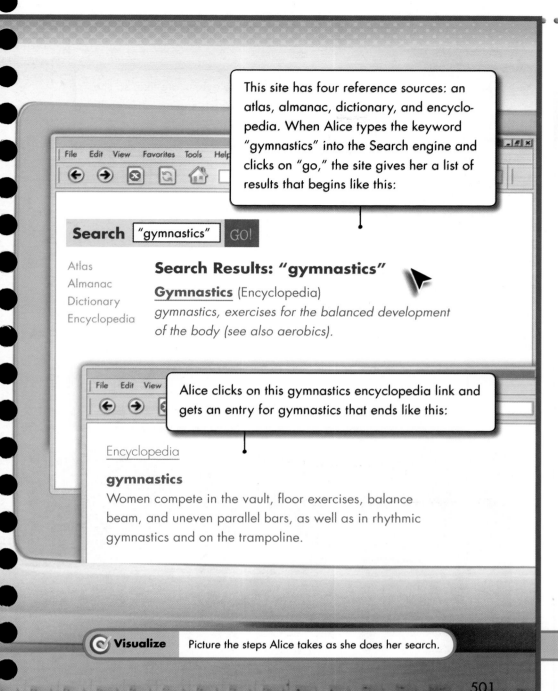

This site has four reference sources: an atlas, almanac, dictionary, and encyclopedia. When Alice types the keyword "gymnastics" into the Search engine and clicks on "go," the site gives her a list of results that begins like this:

Search "gymnastics" GO!

Atlas
Almanac
Dictionary
Encyclopedia

Search Results: "gymnastics"

Gymnastics (Encyclopedia)
gymnastics, exercises for the balanced development of the body (see also aerobics).

Alice clicks on this gymnastics encyclopedia link and gets an entry for gymnastics that ends like this:

Encyclopedia

gymnastics
Women compete in the vault, floor exercises, balance beam, and uneven parallel bars, as well as in rhythmic gymnastics and on the trampoline.

Visualize Picture the steps Alice takes as she does her search.

501

WEB-IQUETTE

Online Reference Sources

Tell students that, while online reference sources are a quick and efficient way to find information, there are rules of etiquette they should follow:

- Check to be sure that you've spelled keywords correctly. If words are misspelled, the search engine may not be able to find the information you need.
- Remember that you will need to record the source of any information you use in a report. This usually means printing out a page or cutting and pasting the Web address into a document. If you record the address by hand, be very careful. Every letter and symbol must be exactly the same as it is on your screen.
- Be sure to follow the classroom rules for saving files, printing pages, and bookmarking Web sites.

NEW LITERACIES: ONLINE REFERENCE SOURCES

Use the sidebar on p. 500 to guide discussion.

- Point out that online reference sources are informational sources, such as almanacs, dictionaries, and encyclopedias.
- Tell students that some online resources have their own search engines. Information can be accessed by typing a keyword or phrase in the search window and then clicking a word like *Search* or *Go,* or pressing *Enter.*
- Discuss with students the similarities and differences between online sources and print sources, and the possible benefits and drawbacks of using each.

AudioText

Visualize

Students should visualize the different steps that Alice needs to take in order to use the online reference source. Students should picture her reading text on the screen and using the mouse to click on links.

Access Content Lead a picture walk to reinforce gymnastics-related vocabulary, such as *gymnastics* (p. 500), *vault, floor exercises* (p. 501) and *pommel horse* (p. 502). Point to the dictionary entries and help students use them to confirm the meanings of these words.

Strategies for Navigation

USE GRAPHIC SOURCES Remind students that using graphic sources can help them visualize what they are reading and make information more clear. Graphic sources include maps, pictures, captions, charts, time lines, and video clips.

Use the Strategy

1. The next time you use an online encyclopedia, look for any graphics that may be related to the entry you are reading. Additional information may be supplied by maps, diagrams, pictures, and captions.

2. Try clicking on any graphics-related links that appear. You may be able to enlarge graphics that are shown by positioning your cursor on them and clicking.

3. After you've explored the graphics related to a topic, think about how they enhance the information you've gathered on your topic.

PRACTICE Think about the ways you use graphic sources at home and at school.

Use a printed reference source, such as an encyclopedia, to search for information on a topic. Think about the ways that an online reference source might use graphics to enhance your understanding of the topic.

The next time you access the Internet, try using an online reference source to find out more about your topic.

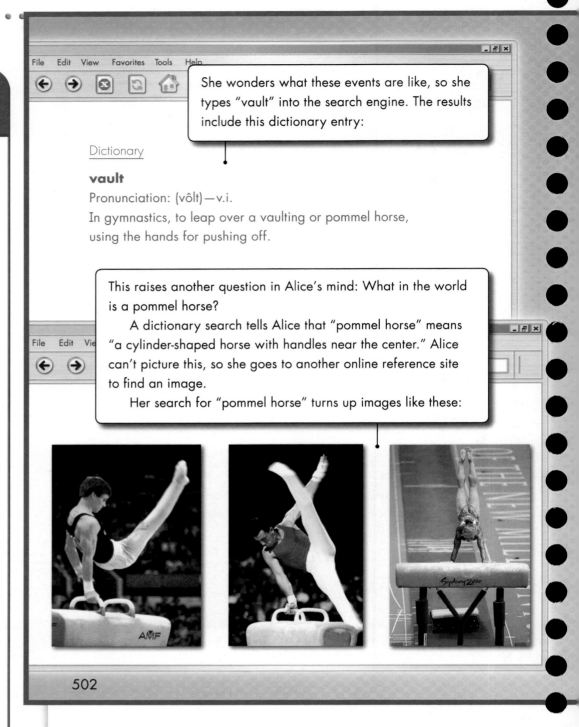

She wonders what these events are like, so she types "vault" into the search engine. The results include this dictionary entry:

Dictionary

vault
Pronunciation: (vôlt)—v.i.
In gymnastics, to leap over a vaulting or pommel horse, using the hands for pushing off.

This raises another question in Alice's mind: What in the world is a pommel horse?

A dictionary search tells Alice that "pommel horse" means "a cylinder-shaped horse with handles near the center." Alice can't picture this, so she goes to another online reference site to find an image.

Her search for "pommel horse" turns up images like these:

502

ELL

Guided Practice If there is time, have students log onto the Internet. Show them how to search for information in an online encyclopedia and access its graphic sources. Help students make connections between the steps they are doing and related vocabulary terms.

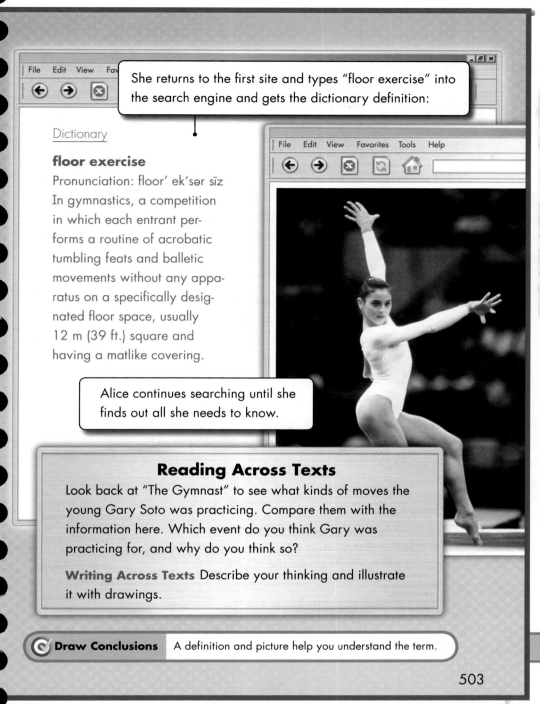

She returns to the first site and types "floor exercise" into the search engine and gets the dictionary definition:

Dictionary

floor exercise

Pronunciation: floor' ek'sər sīz
In gymnastics, a competition in which each entrant performs a routine of acrobatic tumbling feats and balletic movements without any apparatus on a specifically designated floor space, usually 12 m (39 ft.) square and having a matlike covering.

Alice continues searching until she finds out all she needs to know.

Reading Across Texts

Look back at "The Gymnast" to see what kinds of moves the young Gary Soto was practicing. Compare them with the information here. Which event do you think Gary was practicing for, and why do you think so?

Writing Across Texts Describe your thinking and illustrate it with drawings.

Draw Conclusions A definition and picture help you understand the term.

CONNECT TEXT TO TEXT
Reading Across Texts

Locate the descriptions of the different moves that young Gary Soto was practicing in "The Gymnast." Discuss the clues that tell you which event he might have been practicing for.

Writing Across Texts Have students visualize Gary practicing his moves and then make a list of adjectives that describe him as he practices. Students can use the list to describe and illustrate their thinking.

Draw Conclusions

A definition and a photograph provide enough information for a reader to make a sensible decision about the meaning of a term.

Fluency Assessment Plan

- ☑ **Week 1** Assess Advanced students.
- ☑ **Week 2** Assess Strategic Intervention students.
- ☑ **Week 3** Assess On-Level students.
- ☑ **Week 4** Assess Strategic Intervention students.
- ☑ **This week assess any students you have not yet checked during this unit.**

Set individual goals for students to enable them to reach the year-end goal.

- Current Goal: 120–128 wcpm
- Year-End Goal: 140 wcpm

Provide opportunities for English language learners to read aloud to younger children. This allows them to practice their oral reading and improve their fluency.

To develop fluent readers, use Fluency Coach.

DAY 5   Grouping Options

Reading
Whole Group
Revisit the Question of the Week.

Group Time
Differentiated Instruction
Reread this week's Leveled Readers. See pp. 484f–484g for the small group lesson plan.

Whole Group
Use p. 503b–503c.

Language Arts
Use pp. 503d–503l.

PUNCTUATION CLUES
Fluency

DAY 1

Model Reread "The Winning Stroke" on p. 484m. Explain that you will use punctuation as a guide to pause at certain places or raise your voice in excitement. Model for students as you read.

DAY 2

Echo Reading Read aloud the first two paragraphs on p. 493. Have students notice how you pause at commas, dashes, and periods. After you read each sentence, have students repeat after you, doing three echo readings.

DAY 3

Model Read aloud the first paragraph on p. 497. Have students notice how you pause slightly at the commas, and longer at periods. Practice as a class by doing three echo readings.

DAY 4

Partner Reading Partners practice reading aloud paragraph one on p. 497, three times. Students should read using punctuation to pause at appropriate points and offer each other feedback.

Monitor Progress   Check Fluency WCPM

As students reread, monitor their progress toward their individual fluency goals. Current Goal: 120–128 words correct per minute. End-of-Year Goal: 140 words correct per minute.

If… students cannot read fluently at a rate of 120–128 words correct per minute,
then… make sure students practice with text at their independent level. Provide additional fluency practice, pairing nonfluent readers with fluent readers.

If… students already read at 140 words correct per minute,
then… they do not need to reread three to four times.

SUCCESS PREDICTOR

DAY 5

Assessment
Individual Reading Rate Use the Fluency Assessment Plan and do a one-minute timed reading of either selection from this week to assess students in Week 5. Pay special attention to this week's skill, punctuation clues. Provide corrective feedback for each student.

RETEACH

🎯 Draw Conclusions

TEACH

Review the definition of *draw conclusions* on p. 484. Students can complete Practice Book p. 198 on their own, or you can complete it as a class. Explain to students that they will need to read the passage about gymnastics carefully and answer items 1–5 to complete the graphic organizer.

ASSESS

Have students reread p. 497 and work with partners to draw conclusions about why Gary decides to stop practicing gymnastics. Students should identify the facts that led them to this conclusion. *(Possible response: The back flip scared him and he was afraid of getting really hurt. He saw an orange burst behind his eyes after he landed on his neck trying to do one.)*

For additional instruction on drawing conclusions, see DI·56.

EXTEND SKILLS

Simile

TEACH

A simile is a comparison of two unlike things that are alike in at least one way.

- In a simile, words of comparison such as *like* or *as* are used.
- Simile is a kind of figurative language.

Point out the simile on p. 494, paragraph 1, "...admiring my feet, which looked like bloated water balloons. " Have students write the simile in their notebooks, as well as an explanation of the two things being compared *(feet and water balloons)*.

ASSESS

Have students find another simile in "The Gymnast" on p. 493, paragraph 3. Ask them to write the simile (my hands as white as gloves) and answer these questions.

1. **What comparison word is used in the simile?**
2. **What two things are being compared?**
3. **What other items could have been used to compare the two things?**

OBJECTIVES

- 🎯 Draw conclusions.
- ● Recognize simile.

Skills Trace

🎯 Draw Conclusions

Introduce/Teach	TE: 5.4 392–393, 484–485; 5.6 634–635
Practice	Practice Book: 153, 157, 158, 186, 193, 197, 198, 253, 257, 258, 286, 296
Reteach/Review	**TE: 5.4 411b, 467, 503b, DI•52, DI•56; 5.6 653b, 683, 687, 735, 745, DI•52**
Test	Selection Test: 61–64, 77–80, 101–104; Benchmark Test: Units 4, 6

ELL

Access Content Reteach the skill by reviewing the Picture It! lesson on author's purpose in the ELL Teaching Guide, pp. 134–135.

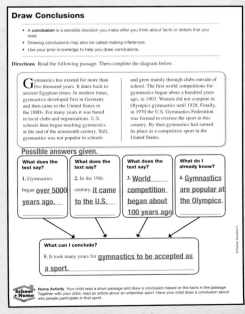

▲ **Practice Book** p. 198

- Formulate an inquiry question that is connected to this week's lesson focus.
- Effectively and efficiently find, evaluate, and communicate information related to an inquiry question using electronic sources.

New Literacies	
Day 1	Identify Questions
Day 2	Navigate/Search
Day 3	Analyze
Day 4	Synthesize
Day 5	Communicate

NEW LITERACIES
Internet Inquiry Activity
EXPLORE GYMNASTICS

Use the following 5-day plan to help students conduct this week's Internet inquiry activity about gymnastics. Remind students to follow classroom rules when using the Internet.

DAY 1

Identify Questions Discuss the lesson focus question: *Why do people try to change themselves?* Remind students that Gary wishes to learn gymnastics because his mother is proud of his cousin's involvement in the sport. Brainstorm ideas for inquiry questions about the sport of gymnastics. For example, students might want to learn about specific gymnastic events, such as the balance beam or parallel bars. Have students work individually, in pairs, or in small groups to write inquiry questions they want to answer.

DAY 2

Navigate/Search Tell students to skim the selection for keywords before using a student-friendly search engine for sources to answer their inquiry questions. Remind them to select keywords specific to their topic. Have students scan the blurbs of the "hits" to decide if the site is relevant and a good source of information.

DAY 3

Analyze Have students use the Web sites they identified on Day 2. Tell them to scan each site for information that helps them with their inquiry questions. Students can take notes from the sites or, if appropriate, print out and highlight relevant information.

DAY 4

Synthesize Have students synthesize information from Day 3 by combining the highlighted information or notes they have taken. Ask them to think about the best methods for sharing what they've learned with the class.

DAY 5

Communicate Have students decide how they want to share their inquiry results. They might use a word processing program to create reports, presentation software to create slide shows, or drawing tools to illustrate the key points.

The Drum

by Nikki Giovanni

daddy says the world is
1 a drum tight and hard
and i told him
i'm gonna beat
2 out my own rhythm

505

WRITING POETRY

Have students write their own poems about a time when they felt they didn't fit in.

Read "The Drum" aloud. Tell students to listen for which words you stress. Point out that by emphasizing key words, the reader can help make the poem more meaningful.

Discuss the Poem

1 Metaphor • Inferential

What metaphor does the father use to describe the world? Why do you think he does so?

Possible response: The father says "the world is a drum tight and hard." Perhaps he has faced hardships in his life, making him feel the need to warn his child about the troubles to come.

2 Character • Inferential

What does this poem tell you about the speaker?

Possible response: The speaker is a child because he or she mentions "daddy." You can also tell that the speaker is strong and independent. He or she plans to face the world described by the father and "beat out my own rhythm."

Unit 4
Reading Poetry

Model Fluent Reading

Read "Desert Tortoise" aloud. Tell students to listen to the way you vary your rate, or tempo, to match the meaning of the poem.

Discuss the Poem

1 Compare and Contrast • Inferential

How are the desert tortoise and the other animals in the poem alike? How are they different?

Possible responses: All of the animals live in the desert. The tortoise stays around for a long time, while the other animals "come and go." The tortoise has a better understanding of how the world works.

2 Draw Conclusions • Inferential

Why does the tortoise think that the desert is "a good place for an old tortoise to walk"?

Possible responses: The tortoise seems to enjoy its life. It refers to feeling safe, warm, and well fed.

EXTEND SKILLS

Imagery

Imagery, or sensory language, is the use of words that help the reader experience the way things look, sound, smell, taste, or feel. Metaphors and similes also add to the reader's experience. Explain that there are several sensory images in "Desert Tortoise." The reader can feel the warm sun and taste *the ripe juicy cactus fruit.* Point out that the word *"jigsaw"* is used to illustrate a metaphor in the poem "Which Lunch Table?" on p. 504. Explain that it helps the reader get a better sense of how fitting in at a school is like piecing a puzzle together.

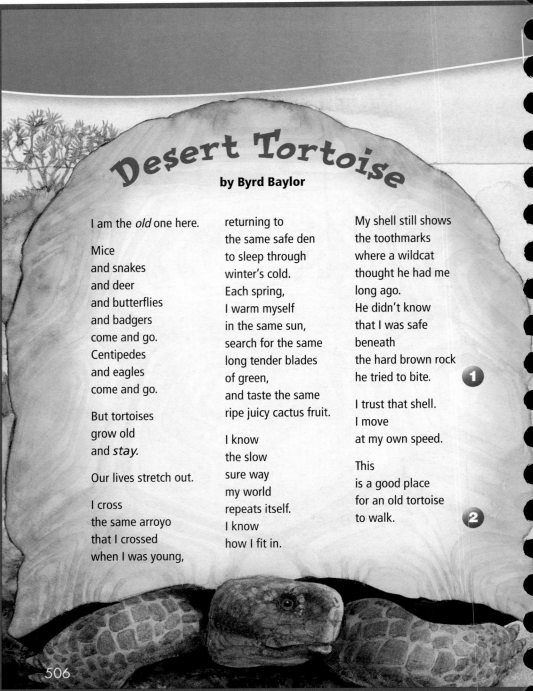

Desert Tortoise
by Byrd Baylor

I am the *old* one here.

Mice
and snakes
and deer
and butterflies
and badgers
come and go.
Centipedes
and eagles
come and go.

But tortoises
grow old
and *stay.*

Our lives stretch out.

I cross
the same arroyo
that I crossed
when I was young,

returning to
the same safe den
to sleep through
winter's cold.
Each spring,
I warm myself
in the same sun,
search for the same
long tender blades
of green,
and taste the same
ripe juicy cactus fruit.

I know
the slow
sure way
my world
repeats itself.
I know
how I fit in.

My shell still shows
the toothmarks
where a wildcat
thought he had me
long ago.
He didn't know
that I was safe
beneath
the hard brown rock
he tried to bite.

I trust that shell.
I move
at my own speed.

This
is a good place
for an old tortoise
to walk.

506

Practice Fluent Reading

Have partners alternate reading sections of "Desert Tortoise" aloud. Tell students to read each section at a rate that matches the meaning. Then ask students to switch parts and read again. Tell them to listen for differences between their readings.

AudioText

Camel

by Lillian M. Fisher

A camel is a mammal,
A most extraordinary animal
Whose appearance is a wee bit odd.
His body is lumpy,
Knees calloused and bumpy,
And his feet are naturally shod.
His humps are fantastical,
His manner bombastical,
Due to his proud ancient past.
He feasts upon brambles
And ploddingly ambles.
His gait is not very fast.
But he carries great loads
On long dusty roads
Where many a beast cannot.
He's a tireless walker
And goes without water
In weather increasingly hot. **1**
This strange-looking beast
Who resides in the East
And in far-off places West
Is found at the zoo
Where he's happy, it's true,
But—
Deep inside—desert is best. **2**

507

✎ WRITING POETRY

Have students write a poem about an animal that adapts well to its environment. What physical traits or behaviors help the animal survive?

Model Fluent Reading

Read "Camel" aloud. Be sure to pause after punctuation marks, not at line breaks. Point out that it is easy to hear the rhymes in this poem and that it has a steady rhythm pattern.

Discuss the Poem

1 **Draw Conclusions • Inferential**
Why do you think the speaker thinks the desert is the best place for the camel?

Possible responses: The camel is suited to life in the hot desert. It eats brambles, walks slowly but steadily, and can go without water for long periods of time.

2 **Tone • Inferential**
What is the tone of the poem? Explain.

The rhymes and the swinging rhythm contribute to a lighthearted tone. The poem is amusing, and the tone reflects that.

Connect Ideas and Themes

Remind students that this unit deals with how people and animals adapt to different situations. Ask students to discuss how each poem relates to this idea. Then have them recall times when they have had to adapt to a new situation.

EXTEND SKILLS

Tone

Tone is the author's attitude toward the subject or the audience. By recognizing tone, the reader can better understand the poem's intended emotional meaning. Students can identify the poem's tone by looking for clue words that illustrate the author's viewpoint, such as those that convey sympathy or humor.

Unit 4
Wrap-Up

OBJECTIVES

- Critically analyze unit theme.
- Connect content across selections.
- Combine content and skills in meaningful activities that build literacy.
- Respond to unit selections through a variety of modalities.

ADAPTING

Discuss the Big Idea

How do people and animals adapt to different situations?

Write the unit theme and Big Idea question on the board. Ask students to think about the selections they have read in the unit. Discuss how each selection and lesson concept can help them answer the Big Idea question from this unit.

Model this for students by choosing a selection and explaining how the selection and lesson concept address the Big Idea.

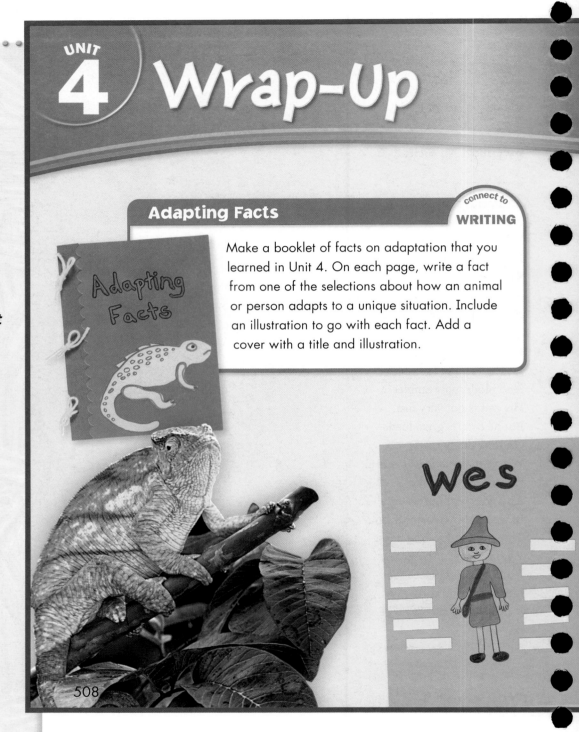

UNIT **4** Wrap-Up

Adapting Facts

connect to WRITING

Make a booklet of facts on adaptation that you learned in Unit 4. On each page, write a fact from one of the selections about how an animal or person adapts to a unique situation. Include an illustration to go with each fact. Add a cover with a title and illustration.

Adapting Facts

Wes

508

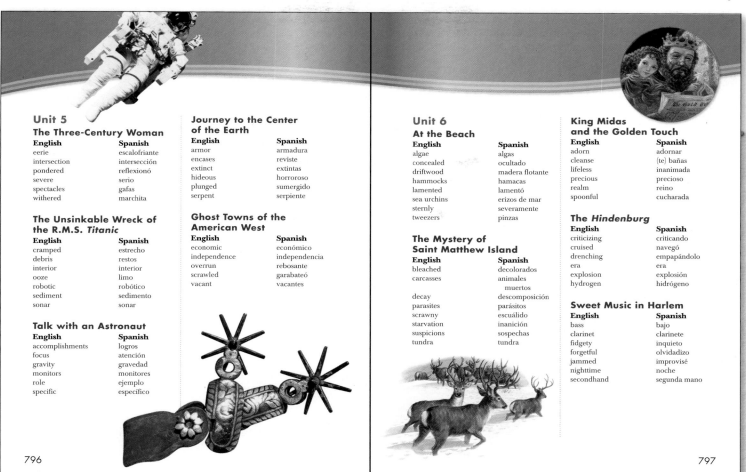

Unit 5

The Three-Century Woman

English	Spanish
eerie	escalofriante
intersection	intersección
pondered	reflexionó
severe	serio
spectacles	gafas
withered	marchita

The Unsinkable Wreck of the R.M.S. *Titanic*

English	Spanish
cramped	estrecho
debris	restos
interior	interior
ooze	limo
robotic	robótico
sediment	sedimento
sonar	sonar

Talk with an Astronaut

English	Spanish
accomplishments	logros
focus	atención
gravity	gravedad
monitors	monitores
role	ejemplo
specific	específico

Journey to the Center of the Earth

English	Spanish
armor	armadura
encases	reviste
extinct	extintas
hideous	horroroso
plunged	sumergido
serpent	serpiente

Ghost Towns of the American West

English	Spanish
economic	económico
independence	independencia
overrun	rebosante
scrawled	garabateó
vacant	vacantes

Unit 6

At the Beach

English	Spanish
algae	algas
concealed	ocultado
driftwood	madera flotante
hammocks	hamacas
lamented	lamentó
sea urchins	erizos de mar
sternly	severamente
tweezers	pinzas

The Mystery of Saint Matthew Island

English	Spanish
bleached	decolorados
carcasses	animales muertos
decay	descomposición
parasites	parásitos
scrawny	escuálido
starvation	inanición
suspicions	sospechas
tundra	tundra

King Midas and the Golden Touch

English	Spanish
adorn	adornar
cleanse	(te) bañas
lifeless	inanimada
precious	precioso
realm	reino
spoonful	cucharada

The *Hindenburg*

English	Spanish
criticizing	criticando
cruised	navegó
drenching	empapándolo
era	era
explosion	explosión
hydrogen	hidrógeno

Sweet Music in Harlem

English	Spanish
bass	bajo
clarinet	clarinete
fidgety	inquieto
forgetful	olvidadizo
jammed	improvisé
nighttime	noche
secondhand	segunda mano

796

797

Acknowledgments

Acknowledgments

Text

22: From *Frindle* by Andrew Clements. Text ©1996 by Andrew Clements. Reprinted by permission of Simon & Schuster Books for Young Readers, an imprint of Simon & Schuster Children's Publishing Division; **36:** *Punctuation Takes a Vacation* by Robin Pulver. Text ©2003 by Robin Pulver. All rights reserved. Reprinted by permission of Holiday House, Inc.; **46:** *Thunder Rose*, text ©2003 by Jerdine Nolen. Illustrations ©2003 by Kadir Nelson. Reprinted by permission of Harcourt, Inc.; **66:** "Measuring Tornadoes" from *Storm Chasers* by Trudi Strain Trueit. ©2002 Franklin Watts, a Division of Scholastic, Inc. Used by permission of Scholastic Library Publishing; **72:** From *Island of the Blue Dolphins*. ©1960, renewed 1988 by Scott O'Dell. Reprinted by permission of Houghton Mifflin Company. All rights reserved; **86:** "7 Survival Questions," by Buck Tilton. Used with permission of Buck Tilton and *Boys' Life*, April 2001. Published by the Boy Scouts of America; **94:** From *Satchel Paige* by Lesa Cline-Ransome, paintings by James E. Ransome. Text ©2000 Lesa Cline-Ransome. Illustrations ©2000 James E. Ransome. Reprinted with the permission of Simon & Schuster Books for Young Readers, an imprint of Simon & Schuster Children's Publishing Division; **110:** From "The Girls of Summer" by Ellen Klages. Adapted with permission, © Exploratorium, www.exploratorium.edu. Used by permission; **116:** From *Shutting Out the Sky* by Deborah Hopkinson. Published by Orchard Books, a division of Scholastic Inc. ©2003 by Deborah Hopkinson. Reprinted by permission of Scholastic Inc.; **130:** "The Immigrant Experience" from *Tenement Tid-Bits*, e-mail newsletter of The Lower East Side Tenement Museum, November 2003. Reprinted by permission of The Lower East Side Tenement Museum at www.tenement.org/immigrantexperience; **134:** "The Microscope" by Maxine W. Kumin. ©1968 by Maxine W. Kumin. Used by permission of The Anderson Literary Agency Inc; **136:** "Full Day" from *Come With Me: Poems For A Journey* by Naomi Shihab Nye. Text ©2000 by Naomi Shihab Nye, Greenwillow Books. Used by permission of HarperCollins Publishers; **146:** From "Inside Out," from *The Circuit* by Francisco Jiménez. ©1997 by Francisco Jiménez. Reprinted by permission of the University of New Mexico Press; **160:** "Random Acts of Kindness" from the Random Acts of Kindness Web site. Reprinted by permission of The Random Acts of Kindness Foundation at www.actsofkindness.org; **166:** *Passage to Freedom: The Sugihara Story*. Text ©1997 by Ken Mochizuki. Illustrations ©1997 by Dom Lee. Afterword ©1997 by Hiroki Sugihara. Permission arranged with Lee & Low Books Inc., New York, NY 10016; **180:** From "I Wanted My Mother," from *Hiding to Survive: Stories of Jewish Children Rescued from the Holocaust*. ©1994 by Maxine B. Rosenberg. Reprinted by permission of Clarion Books/Houghton Mifflin Company. All rights reserved; **190:** "The Ch'i-lin Purse" from *The Ch'i-lin Purse* by Linda Fang. ©1963 by Linda Fang. Reprinted by permission of Farrar, Straus & Giroux, LLC; **206:** "Lion and the Mouse" from *The Fables of Aesop* retold by Ruth Spriggs. ©1975 by Eurobook Limited, Oxfordshire, England. Used by permission; **212:** "Jane Goodall's 10 Ways to Help Save Wildlife," from *National Geographic KIDS*, April 2003. ©2003 National Geographic Society. Reprinted by permission; **226:** "Why Some Animals Are Considered 'Bad' or 'Scary'" from SanDiegoZoo.org. Used by permission of the Zoological Society of San Diego; **234:** Illustrations from *The Midnight Ride of Paul Revere* by Henry Wadsworth Longfellow, graved and painted by Christopher Bing, ©2001 Christopher Bing. Reproduced with permission of the publisher, Handprint Books, Inc.; **250:** "Deborah Sampson" by Michael Zullo from www2.1hric.org. Used by permission of Michael Zullo; **254:** "For Peace Sake" by Cedric McClester ©1990 by Cedric McClester. Used by permission of the author; **256:** "Two People I Want to Be Like" from *If Only I Could Tell You* by Eve Merriam. ©1983 Eve Merriam. Used by permission of Marian Reiner; **257:** "Strangers" from *Good Luck Gold and Other Poems* by Janet S. Wong. ©1994 by Janet S. Wong. Reprinted with the permission of Margaret K. McElderry Books, an imprint of Simon & Schuster Children's Publishing Division. All rights reserved; **266:** From *Wings for the King* by Anne Sroda from *Plays*, November 2000, Vol. 60, No.2. Reproduced with permission of Sterling Partners, Inc./PLAYS, P. O. Box 600160, Newton, MA 02460; **282:** "Becky Schroeder: Enlightened Thinker" from *Brainstorm! The Stories of Twenty American Kid Inventors* by Tom Tucker, illustrated by Richard Loehle. ©1996 by Tom Tucker. Reprinted by permission of Farrar, Straus & Giroux, LLC; **292:** *Leonardo's Horse* by Jean Fritz and illustrated by Hudson Talbott. Text ©Jean Fritz, 2001. Illustrations ©Hudson Talbott, 2001. Published by arrangement with G. P. Putnam's Sons, a division of Penguin Young Readers Group, a member of Penguin Group (USA) Inc. All rights reserved; **312:** "Humans with Wings," from *HumanPower* by Roger Yepsen. ©1992 Roger Yepsen. Reprinted with the permission of Simon & Schuster Books for Young Readers, an imprint of Simon & Schuster Children's Publishing Division; **320:** From *The Dinosaurs of Waterhouse Hawkins* by Barbara Kerley Kelly. Text ©2001 by Barbara Kerley Kelly. Illustrations ©2001 by Brian Selznick. Reprinted by permission of Scholastic, Inc; **340:** "A Model Scientist" adapted from *OWL Magazine*, Oct. 2002. Used by permission of Bayard Canada Inc.; **350:** "Mahalia Jackson" from *The Blues Singers* by Julius Lester. ©2001 Julius Lester. Illustrated by Lisa Cohen. Reprinted by permission of Hyperion Books for Children; **360:** From *Perfect Harmony* by Charles Smith. ©2002 Charles Smith. Reprinted by permission of Hyperion Books For Children; **368:** From *Special Effects in Film and Television* by Jake Hamilton. ©1998 Dorling Kindersley. Reprinted by permission; **380:** Adaptation of "A Trick of the Eye" by Brian Sibley from http://ww.bfi.org.uk. Used by permission of Sheil Land Associates Ltd.; **384:** "Chemistry 101" from *Carver: A Life In Poems* by Marilyn Nelson. ©2001 by Marilyn Nelson. Used by permission of Front Street, a division of Boyds Mill Press, Inc; **385:** "The Bronze Horse" by Beverly McLoughland, *Cricket*, November 1990. Used by permission of the author; **386:** "The Termites" from *Insectlopedia*, ©1998 by Douglas Florian, reprinted by permission of Harcourt, Inc. This material may not be reproduced in any form or by any means without the prior written permission of the publisher; **387:** "Stairs" from *Excuse It Please* by Oliver Herford, J. B. Lippincott Company, 1929; **396:** *Weslandia* by Paul Fleischman. Text ©1999 by Paul Fleischman. Illustrations ©1999 by Kevin Hawkes. Reproduced by the publisher Candlewick Press, Inc., Cambridge, MA; **410:** "Under the Back Porch" by Virginia Hamilton. ©1992, 2004 by Virginia Hamilton. Reprinted by permission of Arnold Adoff, 750 Union St., Yellow Springs, OH 45387; **411:** "Keziah," from *Bronzeville Boys and Girls* by Gwendolyn Brooks. ©1956 by Gwendolyn Brooks Blakely. Used by permission of HarperCollins Publishers; **416:** From *Stretching Ourselves* by Alden R. Carter, Photographs by Carol S. Carter. ©2000 Alden R. Carter. Reprinted by permission of John Hawkins & Associates, Inc.; **434:** "Helpful Tools" from *Do You Remember the Color Blue?* by Sally Hobart Alexander, ©2000 by Sally Hobart Alexander. Used by permission of Viking Children's Books, A Division of Penguin Young Readers Group, A Member of Penguin Group (USA) Inc., 345 Hudson Street, New York, NY 10014, the Author and BookStop Literary Agency. All rights reserved; **440:** From *Exploding Ants* by Joanne Settel, Ph.D. Text ©1999 by Joanne Settel. Reprinted with the permission of Atheneum Books for Young Readers, an imprint of Simon & Schuster Children's Publishing Division; **480:** "Think Dress Codes Are a Drag?" by Emilie Ostrander from the *Chicago Tribune*, April 15, 2003. Copyrighted 4/15/2003, Chicago Tribune Company. All rights reserved. Used with permission; **488:** "The Gymnast" by Gary Soto from *A Summer Life* ©1990 by University Press of New England. Reprinted with permission; **501:** From "Gymnastics" from *The Columbia Electronic Encyclopedia, 6th ed.* ©2003, Columbia University Press. Used by permission; **502:** *Random House Webster's Unabridged Dictionary*. New York: Random House, 1991. **504:** "the drum" from *Spin A Soft Black Song* by Nikki Giovanni. ©1971, 1985 by Nikki Giovanni. Reprinted by permission of Hill and Wang, a division of Farrar, Straus & Giroux, LLC; **505:** "Which Lunch Table?" from *Swimming Upstream: Middle Grade Poems* by Kristine O'Connell George. Text ©2002 by Kristine O'Connell

798

George. Reprinted by permission of Clarion Books, an imprint of Houghton Mifflin Company. All rights reserved; **506:** "Desert Tortoise" from *Desert Voices* by Byrd Baylor. Text ©1981 by Byrd Baylor. Reprinted with the permission of Atheneum Books for Young Readers, an imprint of Simon & Schuster Children's Publishing Division; **507:** "Camel" by Lillian M. Fisher. All other rights reserved, ©Lillian M. Fisher 2004. Used by permission of the author, Lillian M. Fisher; **516:** "The Three-Century Woman" ©1996 by Richard Peck. First published in *Second Sight: Stories for a New Millennium*, Philomel Books. All rights reserved. Used by permission of Sheldon Fogelman Agency, Inc; **540:** "The Unsinkable Wreck of the R.M.S. Titanic" from *Ghost Liners: Exploring the World's Greatest Lost Ships* by Robert D. Ballard and Rick Archbold, illustrations by Ken Marschall. Text ©1998 by Odyssey Corporation and Ken Marschall, from *Ghost Liners*, a Little Brown Madison Press Book. Used by permission; **554:** Excerpt from *Shipwreck Season* by Donna Hill. ©1998 by Donna Hill. Reprinted by permission of Clarion Books, an imprint of Houghton Mifflin Company. All rights reserved; **564:** "Talk with an Astronaut" from "Meet Famous Latinos: Ellen Ochoa" from scholastic.com. ©2004 by Scholastic Inc. Reprinted by permission of Scholastic Inc; **578:** "Crust, Mantle, Core," from Scott Foresman *Science for Texas* by Dr. Timothy Cooney, Michael Anthony DiSpezio, et al. ©2000, Addison-Wesley Educational Publishers, Inc. All Rights Reserved; **608:** Text and Photographs from *Ghost Towns of the American West* by Raymond Bial. ©2001 by Raymond Bial. Reprinted by permission of Houghton Mifflin Company. All rights reserved; **622:** "Dame Shirley Goes to the Gold Rush" from *Journeys in Time: A New Atlas of American History* by Elspeth Leacock and Susan Buckley. Text ©2001 by Elspeth Leacock and Susan Washburn Buckley. Reprinted with permission of Houghton Mifflin Company. All rights reserved; **626:** "Your World" from *The Selected Works of Georgia Douglas Johnson*, by Georgia Douglas Johnson, G. K. Hall ©1997, G. K. Hall. Reprinted by permission of The Gale Group; **627:** "Share the Adventure" ©1993 by Patricia and Fredrick McKissack. First appeared as a National Children's Book Week Poem by The Children's Book Council, Curtis Brown, Ltd., 1993; **628:** "A Path to the Moon," *Giants, Moosequakes and Other Disasters* by bp Nichol, Black Moss Press, 1985. Used by permission of the Estate of bp Nichol; **638:** "At the Beach," from *Salsa Stories* by Lulu Delacre. ©2000 Lulu Delacre. Reprinted by permission of Scholastic, Inc; **652:** "The Eagle and the Bat" from *The Sound of Flutes and Other Indian Legends* by Richard Erdoes and illustrated by Paul Goble, ©1976 by Richard Erdoes. Illustrations ©1976 by Paul Goble. Used by permission of Random House Children's Books, a division of Random House, Inc.; **658:** "The Mystery of Saint Matthew Island" from *The Case of the Mummified Pigs and Other Mysteries in Nature*, written by Susan E. Quinlan, illustrated by Jennifer Owings Dewey. Text ©1995 by Susan E. Quinlan; Illustrations ©1995 by Jennifer Owings Dewey. Published by Caroline House, Boyds Mills Press, Inc. Reprinted by permission; **670:** "Get the Lead Out" from *The Sky's the Limit: Stories of Discovery by Women and Girls* by Catherine Thimmesh, illustrated by Melissa Sweet. Text ©2002 by Catherine Thimmesh. Illustrations ©2002 by Melissa Sweet. Reprinted by permission of Houghton Mifflin Company. All rights reserved; **678:** *King Midas and the Golden Touch* as told by Charlotte Craft, illustrated by K. Y. Craft. Text ©1999 by Charlotte Craft. Illustrations ©1999 Kinuko Y. Craft. Used by permission of HarperCollins Publishers; **698:** "Jimmy Jet and His TV Set" from *Where the Sidewalk Ends* by Shel Silverstein. ©2004 by Evil Eye Music. Used by permission of HarperCollins Publishers; **705:** Adaptation of *The Hindenburg* by Patrick O'Brien, ©2000 by Patrick O'Brien. Reprinted by permission of Henry Holt and Company, LLC; **730:** *Sweet Music in Harlem*. Text ©2004 by Debbie A. Taylor. Illustrations ©2004 by Frank Morrison. Permission arranged with Lee & Low Books, Inc., New York, NY 10016; **754:** "A Sinister Spider Named Ruth" from *Pocketful of Nonsense* by James Marshall, Golden Books, Western Publishing Company, Inc., 1992; **755:** "Sunflakes" from *Country Pie* by Frank Asch, HarperCollins Publishers, 1979; **756:** "Almost Human" from *Earth Lines: Poems for the Green Age* by Pat Moon. ©1993 by Pat Moon. Used by permission of Greenwillow Books and HarperCollins Publishers; **757:** "The Bat", from *The Collected Poems of Theodore Roethke* by Theodore Roethke. ©1938 by Theodore Roethke. Used by permission of Doubleday, a division of Random House, Inc.

Illustrations

Cover: Greg Newbold; **12, 510, 630** Steven Adler; **22-34** James Bernardin; **37-41, 161, 749** Laura Huliska-Beith; **44-45** Jason Wolff; **45-46, 49-64, 792** Kadir Nelson; **46-48** Darryl Ligasan; **69-85** E. B. Lewis; **86-88, 317** Maryjo Koch; **93-108, 792** James Ransome; **110** Charles Pyle; **134-136** Greg Newbold; **146-158** Raul Colon; **160, 206-207** Vladimir Radunsky; **164-179** Dom Lee; **181-185** John Sandford; **190-205** Ed Young; **226-229, 263-265** John Manders; **233-248, 793** Christopher Bing; **260, 388** Melissa Sweet; **266-281, 454, 546, 794** Franklin Hammond; **282-286** Leslie Cober-Gentry; **291-311, 389** Hudson Talbott; **312-315** Dahl Taylor; **317, 340-344** Phil Wilson; **318-338** Brian Selznick; **349-356** Lisa Cohen; **395-409, 795** Kevin Hawkes; **410** Jui Ishida; **437-451, 795** Robert Mancini; **462-478** Gregory Christie; **480-482** Robert Wagt; **504-506, 630** Bob Dacey; **513-531** Matt Faulkner; **532-534** Janan Cain; **554-558** Francis Livingston; **586-598** Marc Sasso; **601** Matt Zang; **622-625** Rodica Prato; **626-628** Shelly Hehenberger; **637-650** Michael Steirnagle; **652** Amanda Hall; **657-665, 797** Tom McNeely; **666** John Burgoyne; **678-697, 797** Kinuko Craft; **698-699** Shel Silverstein; **704-721** Patrick O'Brien; **754-756** Laura Ovresat.

Photographs

Every effort has been made to secure permission and provide appropriate credit for photographic material. The publisher deeply regrets any omission and pledges to correct errors called to its attention in subsequent editions.

Unless otherwise acknowledged, all photographs are the property of Scott Foresman, a division of Pearson Education.

Photo locators denoted as follows: **Top (T), Center (C), Bottom (B), Left (L), Right (R), Background (Bkgd).**

4 ©Sean Murphy/Getty Images; **6, 10** ©Gary Braasch/Corbis; **16** ©Sean Murphy/Getty Images; **17** ©Bettmann/Corbis; **19, 35, 93** Getty Images; **20** ©Jutta Klee/Corbis; **21** ©Corbis; **66** International Stock Photography/Taxi/Getty Images; **67** (CL) ©Jim Reed/Corbis; **91** ©Vintage Military; **92** ©Stephen Dunn/Getty Images; **95** Legends Archive; **113-115, 121** Corbis; **116** ©Bettmann/Corbis; **118** (TL, CL) Bettmann/Corbis; (TR) Prints & Photographs Division/Library of Congress; (CR) Corbis; **120** ©Bettmann/Corbis; **122** Brown Brothers; **123** (TL) Getty Images, (TR) New York Public Library/Art Resource, NY; **124** Museum of the City of New York; **125** Getty Images; **126** Photo Collection Alexander Alland, Sr./Corbis; **127, 129-130, 132** Corbis; **128** ©Tony Linck/Time Life Pictures/Getty Images; **133** ©Joseph Sohm/ChromoSohm Inc./Corbis; **138** ©Sean Murphy/Getty Images; **139** (TR) Sports Icons/©Comstock, Inc., (CR) ©Brad Yeo Collection/the i spot; **140** ©Gary Braasch/Corbis; **141** ©Michael Nichols/NGS Image Collection; **143** ©Larry Dale Gordon/Getty Images; **144** ©Tony Cordoza/Getty Images; **145** (T) ©Geoff Du Feu/Getty Images, (BR) ©Stephen Dalton/NHPA Limited; **159** ©Stephen Dalton/NHPA Limited; **163** Corbis; **164** ©Ken Davies/Masterfile Corporation; **165** Getty Images; **168** (Bkgd) ©Anne Frank House/Getty Images, (C) Courtesy of Joseph Shadur/United States Holocaust Museum; **170, 172, 174, 176** (C) Courtesy of Joseph Shadur/United States Holocaust Museum, (Bkgd) ©Anne Frank House/Getty Images; **171** Bonhams, London, UK/Bridgeman Art Library; **179** Courtesy of Joseph Shadur/United States Holocaust Museum; **187** Illustration Works, Inc.; **188-189** ©2000 Kinuko Y. Craft; **205** ©Linda Fang; **209**

799

(BL) ©Anup Shah/Nature Picture Library, (TR) ©Renee Lynn/Corbis; **210** ©Lori Adamski Peek/Getty Images/Stone; **211** (BR) Melanie Acevedo/FoodPix, (BC, CC) ©Photodisc Green/Getty Images; **212** (TC, TL) ©Roger Eritja/Alamy, (C) ©Michael Nichols/NGS Image Collection; **214** (TC) ©JH Pete Carmichael/Getty Images, (R) ©David Fleetham/Mira; **216** (BR) ©Gay Bumgarner/Stone/Getty Images, (R) ©Anup Shah/Nature Picture Library; **218** ©Ariel Skelley/Corbis; **219** (CL, CC) © Photodisc Green/Getty Images, (BC) ©Melanie Acevedo/FoodPix; **220** (BR) ©Ken J. Howard/Sea Images, (R) ©Michael & Patricia Fogden/Corbis; **222** ©Paco Feria/Peter Arnold, Inc.; **223** ©Bob Hallinen/Anchorage Daily News; **224** ©David Fleetham/Mira; **225** (TR) ©Roger Eritja/Alamy, (CR) ©Pallava Bagla/Corbis; **231** (BR) ©Freelance Photography Guild/Corbis, (BR) ©Comstock Inc.; **232-233** ©Kevin Fleming/Corbis; **240-241** (TR, BR, BL) ©Hans Neleman/Getty Images; **249** (BR) ©Hans Neleman/Getty Images, (TL) ©Michael Nicholson/Corbis, (BR) ©Handprint Books; **250, 253** ©Bettmann/Corbis; **252** (TR) The Granger Collection, NY, (B) Corbis; **254, 256** ©Images/Corbis; **258** ©Gary Braasch/Corbis; **259** (TR) ©David A. Northcott/Corbis, (CR) Getty Images, (BL) ©Gavin Wickham/Eye Ubiquitous/Corbis; **261** ©Jim Henson's Creature Shop/DK Images; **289** ©State Museum of Georgia/AKG London Ltd.; **290** ©Marc Moritsch/NGS Image Collection; **292** ©Royalty-Free/Corbis; **310** ©Leonardo da Vinci's Horse, Inc.; **311** ©William Philpott/Reuters America, Inc.; **341** ©Kevin Kelly; **347** ©Andy Warhol Foundation/Corbis; **348** ©Lewis W. Hine/Getty Images; **356, 360, 363** ©Charles R. Smith, Jr.; **359** ©Milan Sabatini; **361** The Boys Choir of Harlem, Inc.; **365** ©Tom Wagner/Corbis; **366** ©Richard Cummins/Corbis; **367** ©Mitchell Gerber/Corbis; **368** ©Jim Henson's Creature Shop/DK Images; **369, 371-372, 373** (TL)**, 374-376, 378** ©Millenium FX Ltd/DK Images; **370** ©Mike Valentine (BSC)/DK Images; **373** (R) ©Turbo Squid, Inc.; **377** ©Paramount/Everett Collection, Inc.; **381** Getty Images; **382** (CL, TR) ©American Artist, (BL) ©Matthias Kulka/Corbis; **384** (TR) Getty Images, (Bkgd) ©Steve Drake/Veer, Inc.; **385** ©Stuart McClymont/Getty Images; **386** ©Walter Bibikow/Index Stock Imagery; **387** ©Pete Turner/Getty Images; **389** ©Richard T. Nowitz/Corbis; **390** Digital Vision; **391, 416-432** ©Carol Carter; **393** ©PBNJ Productions/Corbis; **413-414** ©Tom Stewart/Corbis; **415** ©Royalty-Free/Corbis; **437** ©Hans Neleman/Getty Images; **438** (TL) ©1984 Defense Mechanisms in Social Insects, Hermann. Reproduced with permission of Greenwood Publishing Group, Inc., Westport, CT., (BL, BC) ©BSIP Agency/Index Stock Imagery; **439** ©BSIP Agency/Index Stock Imagery; **442** (BL) ©Steven Hunt/Getty Images, (TR) ©Oliver Strewe/Getty Images; **443** (TL) ©Fred Bavendam/Minden Pictures, (TR) ©Bob Elsdale/Getty Images; **444** (CL) ©Tim Flach/Getty Images, (BL) ©Ant Photo Library/NHPA Limited; **445** ©Studio Carlo Dani/Animals Animals/Earth Scenes; **446** (TL) ©Tim Flach/Getty Images, (TC) ©Premaphotos/Animals Animals/Earth Scenes; **447** (TL) ©Scott Camazine, (TR) ©Mitsuaki Iwago/Minden Pictures; **448** (TL) ©Tim Flach/Getty Images, (BL) ©Art Wolfe/Getty Images, (BR) ©David Tipling/Photographer's Choice/Getty Images; **450** (CL) ©Tim Flach/Getty Images, (T) ©Joe McDonald/Corbis, (BL) ©Michael & Patricia Fogden/Minden Pictures; **451** ©Michael & Patricia Fogden/Corbis; **453** ©Steven Hunt/Getty Images; **459-461** ©Illustration Works, Inc.; **485, 498** ©Rubberball Productions; **487** ©Reuters/Jeff J. Mitchell/Corbis; **490** Brand X Pictures; **493** Veer, Inc.; **500** ©Don Mason/Corbis; **502** (BL) Corbis, (BC) ©Jon Feingersh/Corbis, (BR) ©Caron P./Corbis; **503** ©Dave Black/Corbis; **508** Digital Vision; **509** ©Stuart Westmorland/Corbis; **514** ©Paul Barton/Corbis; **515** ©Royalty-Free/Corbis; **531** (TL) ©Comstock Inc., (TL) AP/Wide World Photos; **537** (B, BC) Getty Images; **538** ©Ralph White/Corbis; **539-542** ©1998 from Ghost Liners/Little Brown Madison Press Books; **543** (CR) The Granger Collection, NY, **543** (BL) **-546, 548-550, 552** ©1998 from Ghost Liners/Little Brown Madison Press Books; **546-547** Woods Hole Oceanographic Institution; **551** (TL, TR) Woods Hole Oceanographic Institution, (Inset) Michael Freeman/Corbis; **553** (TR, TL) Getty Images, (TL) ©UPP/Topham/The Image Works, Inc.; **562-563** Corbis; **564** ©World Perspectives/Getty Images; **566** Getty Images; **567** ©Mark M. Lawrence/Corbis; **569** Corbis; **570** NASA; **573** NASA; **574** Digital image ©1996 Corbis; Original image courtesy of NASA/Corbis; **576** ©Digital image ©1996 Corbis; Original image courtesy of NASA/Corbis; **577** AP/Wide World Photos; **578** (TC) Getty Images, (CR) Corbis; **579** ©Premium Stock/Corbis; **580** ©Time Life Pictures/NASA/Getty Images; **581** ©NASA/Roger Ressmeyer/Corbis; **583** ©DK Images; **585** ©Illustration Works, Inc.; **599** (TR) Corbis, (TL) Lebrecht Collection; **602** (TL) ©DK Images, (CL) Colin Keates/©DK Images, (TC, CC, TR, CR) Harry Taylor/©DK Images; **605** ©Bettmann/Corbis; **606** ©K.D. Swan/Corbis; **607** (T) ©Joseph Sohm/Visions of America/Corbis, (CC) ©Lester Lefkowitz/Corbis; **608** ©James Nazz/Corbis; **609** ©Chris Collins/Corbis; **610** (L) ©DK Images, (C) ©Raymond Bial; **611** ©John Cancalosi/Peter Arnold, Inc.; **612** ©Bettmann/Corbis; **613** ©Western History Department/Denver Public Library, Western History Collection; **614** (T) Museum of History & Industry/Corbis, **614** (BL)**, 616-617** (BL) ©Raymond Bial, (BR) David Stoecklein/Corbis; **619** (T) ©Lynn Radeka/SuperStock, (BR) ©Western History Department/Denver Public Library/Denver Public Library, Western History Collection; **620** ©Bettmann/Corbis; **621** (TC) ©DK Images, (TL) ©Sarah Bial; **630** NASA; **632** ©Jerry Lofaro/Courtesy of Konica Minolta Business Solutions/American Artists Represents; **633** ©Natalie Fobes/Corbis; **635** (TC) Getty Image, (BL) Brand X Pictures/Getty Images; **636** ©Pat O'Hara/Corbis; **637** ©Martin Harvey/Peter Arnold, Inc.; **651** Getty Images; **655** ©Paul Chinn/San Francisco Chronicle/Corbis; **656** ©Simon Battersby/DK Images; **658** ©Natalie Fobes/Corbis; **663** ©David Klein; **664** (TC) ©Darrell Gulin/Corbis, (TL) ©David Muench/Corbis, (CR) ©Steve Austin/Papilio/Corbis; **667** (TR) ©David Roseneau, (CL) ©David Klein/George Allez; **668** ©David Klein; **669** (TL) ©Susan E. Quinlan, (TL) ©Comstock Inc., (BR) Brand X Pictures; **670** (CR) ©Kathleen Murray, **670-** (TR)**, 671** ©Royalty-Free/Corbis; **672** (BL) ©Kathleen Murray, (L, TR) ©Royalty-Free/Corbis; **673** Christine M. Douglas/©DK Images; **675** (BL) ©Images/Corbis, (TR) ©Royalty-Free/Corbis; **677** Brand X Pictures; **697** ©Charlotte Craft; **701** ©Tim Hawkins/Eye Ubiquitous/Corbis; **702** (BL) ©Lake County Museum/Corbis, (BC) ©Bettmann/Corbis; **703, 729** ©Bettmann/Corbis; **722** ©Owen Franken/Corbis; **724** (CR) Corbis, (B) The Granger Collection, NY; **725** (TR, C) Corbis; **727** ©Underwood & Underwood/Corbis; **728** Corbis; **749** (BL) Courtesy, Lee & Low Books, (BR) Brand X Pictures; **752** ©Art Kane Archives; **758** (CL) ©Werner Dieterich/Getty Images, (CR) Corbis, (BL) ©Jerry Lofaro/Courtesy of Konica Minolta Business Solutions/American Artists Represents; **761** Getty Images; **763** Digital Vision; **765** ©Anthony Redpath/Corbis; **766** ©Richard Price/Getty Images; **767** Corbis; **769** (BR) ©World Perspectives/Getty Images, (TR) ©Getty Images; **770** ©Anthony Redpath/Corbis; **771** ©Royalty-Free/Corbis; **772** (CR) ©Royalty-Free/Corbis, (BL, CL) ©Lake County Museum/Corbis; **773** (BC) ©Mark M. Lawrence/Corbis, (BR) Getty Images; **774** (TR) ©Anthony Redpath/Corbis, (BL) ©Joseph Sohm/Visions of America/Corbis; **775** ©Michael S. Yamashita/Corbis; **794** ©Millenium FX Ltd/DK Images; **796** (TL) ©Corbis/Corbis, (BR) ©David Stoecklein/Corbis.

Glossary

The contents of this glossary have been adapted from *Thorndike Barnhart Advanced Dictionary*. Copyright ©1997, Pearson Education, Inc.

777 (C) Art Resource, NY, (Bkgd) SuperStock, (Insert) SuperStock; 778 Daemmrich Photography; 779 ©Tom McHugh/Photo Researchers, Inc.; 782 Planet Art; 786 SuperStock; 789 ©1996 Grant Wood/VAGA/SuperStock

800

Writing

Assessment

Student Tips for Making Top Scores in Writing Tests

❶ Use transitions such as those below to relate ideas, sentences, or paragraphs.

in addition	nevertheless	finally	however
then	instead	therefore	as a result
for example	in particular	first	such as

❷ Write a good beginning. Make readers want to continue.
- I shouldn't have opened that green box.
- Imagine being locked in a crate at the bottom of the sea.
- When I was four, I saw a purple dog.
- Have you ever heard of a talking tree?

❸ Focus on the topic.
If a word or detail is off-topic, get rid of it. If a sentence is unrelated or loosely related to the topic, drop it or connect it more closely.

❹ Organize your ideas.
Have a plan in mind before you start writing. Your plan can be a list, bulleted items, or a graphic organizer. Five minutes spent planning your work will make the actual writing go much faster and smoother.

❺ Support your ideas.
- Develop your ideas with fully elaborated examples and details.
- Make ideas clear to readers by choosing vivid words that create pictures.
- Avoid dull (get, go, say), vague (thing, stuff, lots of), or overused (really, very) words.
- Use a voice that is appropriate to your audience.

❻ Make writing conventions as error-free as possible.
Proofread your work line by line, sentence by sentence. Read for correct punctuation, then again for correct capitalization, and finally for correct spelling.

❼ Write a conclusion that wraps things up but is more than a repeating of ideas or "The end."
- After all, he was my brother, weird or not.
- The Internet has changed our lives for better and for worse.
- It's not the largest planet but the one I'd choose to live on.
- Now tell me you don't believe in a sixth sense.

Rubric
4 3 2 1

Focus/Ideas

Organization/ Paragraphs

Voice

Word Choice

Sentences

Conventions

Writing Traits

Focus/Ideas refers to the main purpose for writing and the details that make the subject clear and interesting. It includes development of ideas through support and elaboration.

Organization/Paragraphs refers to the overall structure of a piece of writing that guides readers. Within that structure, transitions show how ideas, sentences, and paragraphs are connected.

Voice shows the writer's unique personality and establishes a connection between writer and reader. Voice, which contributes to style, should be suited to the audience and the purpose for writing.

Word Choice is the use of precise, vivid words to communicate effectively and naturally. It helps create style through the use of specific nouns, lively verbs and adjectives, and accurate, well-placed modifiers.

Sentences covers strong, well-built sentences that vary in length and type. Skillfully written sentences have pleasing rhythms and flow fluently.

Conventions refers to mechanical correctness and includes grammar, usage, spelling, punctuation, capitalization, and paragraphing.

WRITING Workshop

Story

OBJECTIVES

- Develop an understanding of a story.
- Create a particular mood in your story.
- Use pronouns and antecedents correctly.
- Establish criteria for evaluating a story.

Key Features
Story

▶ **In a story, a writer spins a real or imagined tale.**

- Has a beginning, middle, and end
- Focuses on one incident or event
- Uses time-order words to show the sequence of events
- Has characters, plot, and a setting

Writing Prompt: **Adapting**

Tell a story about a character who succeeds by adapting to a new situation. Focus on an event that shows this person's resourcefulness. Your story may be real or imagined.

Purpose: Entertain the reader

Audience: Your classmates

READ LIKE A WRITER

Ask students to look back at *Weslandia.* Point out several passages with dialogue, or spoken words between characters. Explain that the author of a story includes dialogue to help bring the story characters to life. Characters' words can also help create mood and humor. Tell students that they will write a **story** using dialogue and other story elements to create a mood.

EXAMINE THE MODEL AND RUBRIC

GUIDED WRITING Read the model aloud. Point out that the writer grabs the reader's attention in the first sentence by asking a question. Discuss how the model reflects traits of good writing.

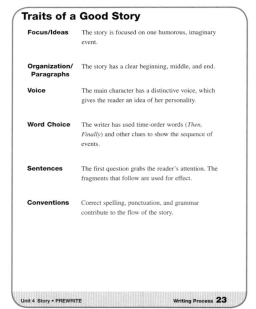

Secret Student Superhero

Was it something I ate? Something I drank? A wish upon a star? You won't believe what happened to me yesterday. I woke up with superpowers.

That's right, superpowers. Don't ask me what caused it. All I know is that I felt different as soon as I put my feet on the floor yesterday morning. Lighter. Smarter. Stronger.

I realized my powers on the playground right before the first bell. Lisa was complaining that she hadn't finished the math homework because it had been too hard. I asked to see her paper and blinked at it. Suddenly the answers were all filled in!

"Awesome! Thank you, Sara," Lisa shouted.

I handed her paper back, feeling totally confused. Then, when I got to my classroom, things turned even weirder. I had X-ray vision—but only for the teacher's edition of our textbook. I didn't participate in the class discussion because it wouldn't have been fair. I could see all the answers! Red words floated right in front of my teacher.

Finally, at lunchtime recess, my superpower secret was revealed. We played our usual basketball game, boys against the girls. I was unstoppable! Usually, I can't score a single basket. But with superpowers I was getting some serious air on my slam dunk.

That's how I learned what happens when you're a superpower showoff. You lose those superpowers. After lunch I returned to my classroom and couldn't see any answers from the teacher's edition. And we had a pop quiz!

It was fun while it lasted, but it sure didn't last long. I had been looking forward to flying home too.

Unit 4 Story • PREWRITE — Writing Process **22**

Traits of a Good Story

Focus/Ideas	The story is focused on one humorous, imaginary event.
Organization/ Paragraphs	The story has a clear beginning, middle, and end.
Voice	The main character has a distinctive voice, which gives the reader an idea of her personality.
Word Choice	The writer has used time-order words (*Then, Finally*) and other clues to show the sequence of events.
Sentences	The first question grabs the reader's attention. The fragments that follow are used for effect.
Conventions	Correct spelling, punctuation, and grammar contribute to the flow of the story.

Unit 4 Story • PREWRITE — Writing Process **23**

▲ **Writing Transparency** WP22   ▲ **Writing Transparency** WP23

Connect to Weekly Writing

Week 1	E-mail 411g–411h
Week 2	Journal Entry 435g–435h
Week 3	Story About an Animal 457g–457h
Week 4	Advice 483g–483h
Week 5	Describe How You Achieved a Goal 503g–503h

Strategic Intervention
See Differentiated Instruction p. WA8.

Advanced
See Differentiated Instruction p. WA9.

ELL
See Differentiated Instruction p. WA9.

Additional Resources for Writing
Writing Rubrics and Anchor Papers, pp. 62–68

FINDING A TOPIC

- Have students discuss times when they had to adapt to a new situation. Tell them that a real event can be the basis for a fictional story.
- Ask students to think of people they know about, such as historical figures, celebrities, or family members. Tell students that a writer may borrow characteristics from real people to create a believable fictional character.
- Share classic stories. Have students answer the following questions about a few favorites: Who is the story about? What is the problem, or conflict? Tell them to consider those same questions when coming up with their own idea.

NARROW A TOPIC Have students jot down topics and ideas.

Molly bakes a cake What is the problem, or conflict?
Transferring to a new school I've never done this, so I lack information.
A boy gets lost on a bike ride I have firsthand knowledge of this.

PREWRITING STRATEGY

GUIDED WRITING Display Writing Transparency WP24. Model how to complete a story chart.

Think Aloud

MODEL This student will write a story about a boy who gets lost on a bike ride with his dad. The main character is also the narrator. The setting is a specific place: country roads. In a short story, be specific with the setting and events and keep characters to a minimum. If you think of a better solution while writing, use it.

PREWRITING ACTIVITIES

- Have students use Grammar and Writing Practice Book p. 172 to map out the characters, setting, events, and solution for their story.
- Students can brainstorm how to adapt to a new situation.

Adapting to something new

Real	Imagined
going to a new school	falling into an underground world
getting my first job	winning the lottery
advancing on swim team	being selected for the Olympics

Story Chart

Directions Fill in the story chart with the characters, setting, events, and solution for your story.

Title

The Bike Ride

Characters

the narrator and his dad

Setting

country roads.

Events

Narrator goes on a long bike ride with his dad.
↓
Narrator gets separated from his dad on the ride.
↓
Narrator must get over his fears and find his way home.

Solution

Narrator retraces his route and returns to the starting point.

Unit 4 Story • PREWRITE   Writing Process **24**

▲ **Writing Transparency** WP24

Monitor Progress

Differentiated Instruction

If... students have trouble deciding on a story idea,	then... ask them to tell you a story they've heard about a family member.

Story Chart

Directions Fill in the story chart with the characters, setting, events, and solution for your story.

Title

Characters

Answers should include details on character, setting, plot, and solution.

Setting

Events

↓
↓
↓

Solution

▲ **Grammar and Writing Practice Book** p. 172

Adapting **WA3**

Think Like a Writer

Create a Fictional World An engaging story draws the reader in by painting a picture of the setting and providing details. Sensory details show your reader what the setting looks, smells, tastes, sounds, and feels like. Include sensory details, and the reader will fully experience your fictional world.

Support Writing If students include home-language words in their drafts, help them find replacement words in English.
Resources can include
• conversations with you
• other home-language speakers
• bilingual dictionaries, if available
• online translation sources

Good Beginnings

Directions Practice writing sentences that will grab your reader's attention. Using your story idea as the topic, write one sentence for each strategy. You can use one of the sentences to start your first draft.

1. Ask a question.
   Answers should be based on the provided strategies and should be complete sentences
2. Use an exclamation. with correct capitalization and punctuation.

3. Use a sound word.

4. Hint at the ending.

5. Use a simile.

6. Make a list.

7. Set the scene.

▲ **Grammar and Writing Practice Book** p. 173

WRITING THE FIRST DRAFT

GUIDED WRITING Use Writing Transparency WP25 to practice writing good beginnings.

• Discuss why a good beginning is essential to a story. Have students read the strategies for writing a good beginning.

• Read through the sample sentences and have students identify which strategy the writer used in each sentence.

 MODEL Read these sentences and think about the strategies for writing a good beginning. How does each beginning sentence really grab the reader's attention? Let's identify the strategy used for each. You will choose one of these when writing your own stories.

Good Beginnings

Every story must have a beginning, middle, and an end, but a good beginning is most important. If your story beginning does not grab the reader, he or she may not continue reading to the middle and the end.

Strategies for Writing a Good Beginning	
Ask a question	Use a simile
Use an exclamation	Use a sound word
Make a list	Set the scene
Hint at the ending	

Directions Read the beginning sentences below and identify which strategy the author uses in each sentence.

1. Crack! Sometimes you know it's a home run the moment the bat strikes the ball.
   Use a sound word.

2. Kate's knees felt like water as she walked onstage.
   Use a simile.

3. Did anyone ask me if I wanted to transfer schools?
   Ask a question.

4. Swimsuit, swim cap, goggles, nose clips. Grace checked her bag one last time before leaving for the swim meet.
   Make a list.

5. Hooray! I finally got my first job, a paper route.
   Use an exclamation.

6. Jack always said he wanted a little sister, but he hadn't thought his wish would be doubled.
   Hint at the ending.

7. The sun warmed the back of my neck, and a gentle breeze cooled the sweat on my forehead as I pedaled along the country road.
   Set the scene.

Unit 4 Story • DRAFT   Writing Process **25**

▲ **Writing Transparency** WP25

WRITER'S CRAFT Mood

Here are some ways writers can create mood:
• Include sensory details.
• Use descriptive language.
• Create characters who fit the tone of the story.

DRAFTING STRATEGIES

• Have students review their story chart before they write.
• Students should use one strategy for writing a good beginning.
• Remind students to keep their audience and purpose in mind.
• Students should reread their story to see where they might add sensory details to support the mood.
• Have students use Grammar and Writing Practice Book p. 173 to practice writing good beginnings.

WRITER'S CRAFT Elaboration

PRONOUNS AND ANTECEDENTS Explain that one way to elaborate is to use pronouns and antecedents correctly. Antecedents, or referents, are the noun each pronoun refers back to. With pronouns, writers can avoid repeating nouns.

Needs a Pronoun
Bill looked for his homework, but he couldn't find <u>his homework</u>.
Bill looked for his homework, but he couldn't find <u>it</u>.

Needs an Antecedent
I looked for <u>them</u> at the park, but I couldn't find them.
I looked for <u>Jessica and Ann</u> at the park, but I couldn't find them.

Use Grammar and Writing Practice Book p. 174 to practice using pronouns and antecedents correctly.

REVISING STRATEGIES

GUIDED WRITING Use Writing Transparency WP26 to model revising. Point out the Revising Marks, which students should use when they revise their work.

Think Aloud

MODEL This is part of the story about a boy who gets separated from his dad on a bike ride. The first sentence has been replaced with a sentence that uses one of the strategies for good beginnings. *It was sunny and breezy* doesn't grab the reader's eye the way setting the scene does. In the second paragraph, the writer has deleted the words *and trains,* which are not necessary to the story. The writer has also taken out a lengthy description about asking his dad to ride and replaced it with a shorter sentence. The writer does not want to give too much information in the first paragraph.

PEER REVISION Write the Revising Checklist on the board or make copies to distribute. Students can use this checklist to revise their stories. Have partners read each other's first drafts. Remind them to be courteous and specific with suggestions.

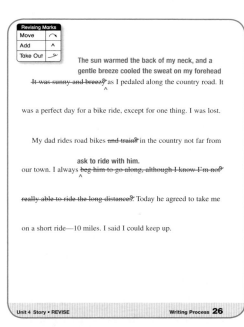

▲ **Writing Transparency** WP26

Elaboration
Pronouns
Directions The sentences below need a pronoun or an antecedent. Replace the underlined word or words with an appropriate pronoun or antecedent. **Possible answers:**

1. It is so useful. Did you ever wonder who invented it?
<u>A calculator is so useful. Did you ever wonder who invented it?</u>

2. I've had my skateboard for so long, my skateboard is covered in stickers.
<u>I've had my skateboard for so long, it is covered in stickers.</u>

3. Beth is such a great singer because <u>Beth</u> has been taking lessons since <u>Beth</u> was five years old.
<u>Beth is such a great singer because she has been taking lessons since she was five years old.</u>

4. <u>She</u> is the best runner in class. No one can beat her in the 50-yard dash.
<u>Susie is the best runner in class. No one can beat her in the 50-yard dash.</u>

5. Dan left for school without <u>it</u>, and he had to call home and ask his mom to bring it to him.
<u>Dan left for school without his backpack, and he had to call home and ask his mom to bring it to him.</u>

6. John asked if <u>John</u> could go to the movies Friday night.
<u>John asked if he could go to the movies Friday night.</u>

▲ **Grammar and Writing Practice Book** p. 174

Writing Workshop

Editing Checklist

- ✔ Did I spell all homophones correctly?
- ✔ Did I use subject and object pronouns correctly?
- ✔ Did I check the punctuation and capitalization of every sentence?
- ✔ Did I check words with suffixes and prefixes?

Support Writing Invite students to read their drafts aloud to you. Observe whether they seem to note any spelling or grammatical errors by stumbling or self-correcting. Return to those errors and explain how to correct them. Use the appropriate Grammar Transition Lessons in the ELL Resource Handbook to explicitly teach the English conventions.

EDITING STRATEGY

READ YOUR WORK ALOUD Suggest that students use an editing strategy. Have them read their stories aloud with a partner. Students should consider the following questions as they listen to the stories: Whose story is it? What is the problem? Is the solution clear?

GUIDED WRITING Use Writing Transparency WP27 to model the process of editing by reading work aloud. Indicate the Proofreading Marks, which students should use when they edit their work. Write the Editing Checklist on the board or make copies to distribute. Students can use this checklist to edit their work.

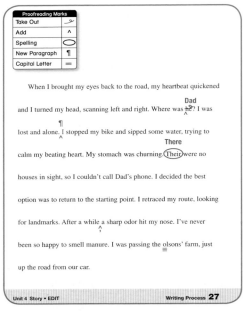

▲ **Writing Transparency** WP27

 MODEL The second sentence says *Where was he?* The writer has used a pronoun without an antecedent, so *he* has been changed to *Dad.* A new paragraph starts with the words *I stopped my bike.* A new paragraph is necessary because this section of the story is when the character thinks about a solution. The word *Their* has been replaced with *There.* The writer had confused these homophones. Finally, the writer needs a comma following the phrase *After a while* and a capital *o* for the proper possessive noun *Olsons'.*

 USING TECHNOLOGY Students who have written or revised their stories on computers should keep these points in mind as they edit:

- Select a special font for your final draft to give your story a professional look. Choose script or a style that matches the mood of your story.

- If your program has a print preview or a page layout feature, you may wish to use it when you are done typing your work. It will show you how the work will appear on your page before it is printed.

- When you have questions about how to do something, check with a friend or use the Help menu.

SELF-EVALUATION

Prepare students to fill out a Self-Evaluation Guide. Display Writing Transparency WP28 to model the self-evaluation process.

Think Aloud

MODEL I would give the story a *4.*

Focus/Ideas This story focuses on how a character adapts to an event.

Organization/Paragraphs The story has a clear beginning, middle, and end.

Voice The narrator's voice contributes to the mood of suspense.

Word Choice The writer has included details that build suspense, such as *heartbeat quickened.*

Sentences Writer uses a variety of sentence types and lengths.

Conventions Grammar, capitalization, and spelling are used correctly.

EVALUATION Assign Grammar and Writing Practice Book p. 175. Tell students that when they evaluate their own stories, assigning a score of 3, 2, or even 1 does not necessarily indicate a bad paper. The ability to identify areas for improvement in future writing is a valuable skill.

The Bike Ride

The sun warmed the back of my neck, and a gentle breeze cooled the sweat on my forehead as I pedaled along the country road. It was a perfect day for a bike ride, except for one thing. I was lost.

My dad rides road bikes in the country not far from our town. I always ask to ride with him. Today he agreed to take me on a short ride—10 miles. I said I could keep up.

My muscles burned as I pumped up hills, right behind my dad. He told me to ride in his "draft." That way he cut the oncoming wind for me. On the wide open road, I didn't need to ride so close. The surface was flat, and I pedaled along slowly as I looked out at fields of grain, horses, a white barn with black trim.

When I brought my eyes back to the road, my heartbeat quickened, and I turned my head, scanning left and right. Where was Dad? I was lost and alone.

I stopped my bike and sipped some water, trying to calm my beating heart. My stomach was churning. There were no houses in sight, so I couldn't call Dad's cell phone. I decided the best option was to return to the starting point. I retraced my route, looking for landmarks. After a while, a sharp odor hit my nose. I've never been so happy to smell manure. I was passing the Olsons' farm, just up the road from our car.

As I turned the final corner, I saw Dad, standing by the car, talking on his cell phone. He threw his arms around me and congratulated me on finding my way back to our starting point. I'm glad Dad gave me a chance to ride with him, but for now, I think I'll stick to neighborhood bike rides.

Unit 4 Story • PUBLISH   Writing Process **28**

▲ **Writing Transparency** WP28

Ideas for Publishing

Class Storybook Bind students' stories into a class book. Have students design a cover that reflects the theme of the unit.

Act It Out Choose a few of the students' stories and have those students act them out for the class, incorporating mood and dialogue.

Self-Evaluation Guide
Story

Directions Think about the final draft of your story. Then rate yourself on a scale of from 4 to 1 (4 is the highest) on each writing trait. After you fill out the chart, answer the questions.

Writing Traits	4	3	2	1
Focus/Ideas				
Organization/Paragraphs				
Voice				
Word Choice				
Sentences				
Conventions				

1. What is the best part of your story?
   <u>Students' responses should show that they have given thought to the stories they have written.</u>

2. Write one thing you would change about this story if you had the chance to write it again.

▲ **Grammar and Writing Practice Book** p. 175

Scoring Rubric Story

Rubric 4 3 2 1	4	3	2	1
Focus/Ideas	Story well focused on one event	Story generally focused on one event	Story without clear focus	Story without focus
Organization/ Paragraphs	Well organized; clear beginning, middle, end	Organized, with a beginning, middle, end	Lacking clear beginning, middle, end	Not organized
Voice	Voice of character or narrator believable	Voice of character or narrator somewhat believable	Character or narrator lacking distinct voice	Character or narrator's voice not believable
Word Choice	Uses words to show sequence of events and support mood	Uses some words to show sequence and support mood	Sequence of events unclear; no mood	No attempt to show sequence of events
Sentences	Varied and well-constructed sentences	Most sentences varied and well constructed	Some sentences well constructed	Contains fragments or run-ons
Conventions	Few, if any, errors	Several minor errors	Frequent errors	Many errors that distract from the story

For 6-, 5-, and 3-point Scoring Rubrics, see pp. WA11–WA14.

WRITING Workshop

Story Differentiated Instruction

WRITING PROMPT: Adapting

Tell a story about a character who succeeds by adapting to a new situation. Focus on an event that shows this person's resourcefulness. Your story may be real or imagined.

Purpose: Entertain the reader

Audience: Your classmates

Pick One

MODIFY INSTRUCTION

ALTERNATIVE PROMPTS

ALTERNATIVE PROMPTS: Narrative Writing

Strategic Intervention Think of a familiar tale about a character who changes. Retell this story in your own words. Begin your story with a sentence that shows one of the ideas for a good beginning.

On-Level A resourceful character deals well with problems. Write your story about a main character who finds a particularly clever way to solve his or her problem.

Advanced Your real or imagined story should include at least three characters. How do your characters work together to solve the problem? Develop a clear obstacle that they must overcome.

Strategic Intervention

MODIFY THE PROMPT

Help emerging writers organize their ideas by transferring their story chart into three paragraphs. Write the headings *Beginning, Middle,* and *End.* Have students write several sentences under each heading.

PREWRITING SUPPORT

- Invite a guest speaker or storyteller to come to your class to generate interest in storytelling and demonstrate the power of story.

- Work with your students to narrow their story ideas, focusing on only one event.

- Interview students to get details about their characters, setting, and plot. Make suggestions about any elements they may be missing.

OPTIONS

- Give students the option of writing a group story under your supervision.

CHECK PROGRESS Segment the assignment into manageable pieces. Check work at intervals, such as graphic organizers and first drafts, to make sure writing is on track.

MODIFY THE PROMPT

Expect advanced writers to target a problem and solution in their story. Encourage them to incorporate sensory details to create a mood. Their stories should include a larger cast of characters and possibly dialogue.

APPLY SKILLS

- As students revise their work, have them consider some ways to improve it.

  Begin with a question, a sound word, or one of the other strategies for writing a good beginning.

  Use sensory details to enhance your story.

  Look for opportunities to use time-order words.

OPTIONS

- Students can follow these steps to create their own class rubrics.

  1. Read examples of class stories and rank them 1–4, with 4 the highest.

  2. Discuss how they arrived at each rank.

  3. Isolate the six traits and make a rubric based on them.

CHECK PROGRESS Discuss students' Self-Evaluation Guides. Work with students to monitor their growth and identify their strengths and weaknesses as writers.

MODIFY THE PROMPT

Allow beginning speakers to dictate their stories to you or a classmate to record. In the revising step, have students copy the story they have dictated.

BUILD BACKGROUND

- Write the word *Story* on the board. Ask students to think about the earliest stories. How were stories passed down before people had a written language? Ask for examples of early stories and famous oral storytellers. *(Aesop, Homer)* Discuss the list of Key Features of a story that appears in the left column of p. WA2.

OPTIONS

- As students write their stories, guide them toward books, magazines, or Web sites that provide comprehension support through features such as the following.

  strong picture/text correspondence

  text in the home language

  detailed photographs or illustrations

- For more suggestions on scaffolding the Writing Workshop, see the ELL and Transition Handbook.

CHECK PROGRESS You may need to explain certain traits and help students fill out their Self-Evaluation Guides. Downplay conventions and focus more on ideas. Recognize examples of vocabulary growth and efforts to use language in more complex ways.

Scoring Rubric | Look Back and Write

2 points The response indicates that the student has a complete understanding of the reading concept embodied in the task. The response is accurate, complete, and fulfills all the requirements of the task. Necessary support and/or examples are included, and the information given is clearly text-based.

1 point The response indicates that the student has a partial understanding of the reading concept embodied in the task. The response includes information that is essentially correct and text-based, but the information is too general or too simplistic. Some of the support and/or examples may be incomplete or omitted.

0 points The response indicates that the student does not demonstrate an understanding of the reading concept embodied in the task. The student has either failed to respond or has provided a response that is inaccurate or has insufficient information.

Scoring Rubric | Look Back and Write

4 points The response indicates that the student has a thorough understanding of the reading concept embodied in the task. The response is accurate, complete, and fulfills all the requirements of the task. Necessary support and/or examples are included, and the information is clearly text-based.

3 points The response indicates that the student has an understanding of the reading concept embodied in the task. The response is accurate and fulfills all the requirements of the task, but the required support and/or details are not complete or clearly text-based.

2 points The response indicates that the student has a partial understanding of the reading concept embodied in the task. The response that includes information is essentially correct and text-based, but the information is too general or too simplistic. Some of the support and/or examples and requirements of the task may be incomplete or omitted.

1 point The response indicates that the student has a very limited understanding of the reading concept embodied in the task. The response is incomplete, may exhibit many flaws, and may not address all requirements of the task.

0 points The response indicates that the student does not demonstrate an understanding of the reading concept embodied in the task. The student has either failed to respond or has provided a response that is inaccurate or has insufficient information.

Scoring Rubric — Narrative Writing

Rubric 4 3 2 1	6	5	4	3	2	1
Focus/Ideas	Excellent, focused narrative; well elaborated with quality details	Good, focused narrative; elaborated with telling details	Narrative focused; adequate elaboration	Generally focused narrative; some supporting details	Sometimes unfocused narrative; needs more supporting details	Rambling narrative; lacks development and detail
Organization/ Paragraphs	Strong beginning, middle, and end; appropriate order words	Coherent beginning, middle, and end; some order words	Beginning, middle, and end easily identifiable	Recognizable beginning, middle, and end; some order words	Little direction from beginning to end; few order words	Lacks beginning, middle, end; incorrect or no order words
Voice	Writer closely involved; engaging personality	Reveals personality	Pleasant but not compelling voice	Sincere voice but not fully engaged	Little writer involvement, personality	Careless writing with no feeling
Word Choice	Vivid, precise words that bring story to life	Clear words to bring story to life	Some specific word pictures	Language adequate but lacks color	Generally limited or redundant language	Vague, dull, or misused words
Sentences	Excellent variety of sentences; natural rhythm	Varied lengths, styles; generally smooth	Correct sentences with some variations in style	Correctly constructed sentences; some variety	May have simple, awkward, or wordy sentences; little variety	Choppy; many incomplete or run-on sentences
Conventions	Excellent control; few or no errors	No serious errors to affect understanding	General mastery of conventions but some errors	Reasonable control; few distracting errors	Weak control; enough errors to affect understanding	Many errors that prevent understanding

Scoring Rubric — Narrative Writing

Rubric 4 3 2 1	5	4	3	2	1
Focus/Ideas	Excellent, focused narrative; well elaborated with quality details	Good, focused narrative; elaborated with telling details	Generally focused narrative; some supporting details	Sometimes unfocused narrative; needs more supporting details	Rambling narrative; lacks development and detail
Organization/ Paragraphs	Strong beginning, middle, and end; appropriate order words	Coherent beginning, middle, and end; some order words	Recognizable beginning, middle, and end; some order words	Little direction from beginning to end; few order words	Lacks beginning, middle, end; incorrect or no order words
Voice	Writer closely involved; engaging personality	Reveals personality	Sincere voice but not fully engaged	Little writer involvement, personality	Careless writing with no feeling
Word Choice	Vivid, precise words that bring story to life	Clear words to bring story to life	Language adequate but lacks color	Generally limited or redundant language	Vague, dull, or misused words
Sentences	Excellent variety of sentences; natural rhythm	Varied lengths, styles; generally smooth	Correctly constructed sentences; some variety	May have simple, awkward, or wordy sentences; little variety	Choppy; many incomplete or run-on sentences
Conventions	Excellent control; few or no errors	No serious errors to affect understanding	Reasonable control; few distracting errors	Weak control; enough errors to affect understanding	Many errors that prevent understanding

Scoring Rubric — Narrative Writing

Rubric 4 3 2 1	3	2	1
Focus/Ideas	Excellent, focused narrative; well elaborated with quality details	Generally focused narrative; some supporting details	Rambling narrative; lacks development and detail
Organization/ Paragraphs	Strong beginning, middle, and end; appropriate order words	Recognizable beginning, middle, and end; some order words	Lacks beginning, middle, end; incorrect or no order words
Voice	Writer closely involved; engaging personality	Sincere voice but not fully engaged	Careless writing with no feeling
Word Choice	Vivid, precise words that bring story to life	Language adequate but lacks color	Vague, dull, or misused words
Sentences	Excellent variety of sentences; natural rhythm	Correctly constructed sentences; some variety	Choppy; many incomplete or run-on sentences
Conventions	Excellent control; few or no errors	Reasonable control; few distracting errors	Many errors that prevent understanding

Scoring Rubric — Descriptive Writing

Rubric 4 3 2 1	6	5	4	3	2	1
Focus/Ideas	Excellent, focused description; well elaborated with quality details	Good, focused description; elaborated with telling details	Description focused; good elaboration	Generally focused description; some supporting details	Sometimes unfocused description; needs more supporting details	Rambling description; lacks development and detail
Organization/Paragraphs	Compelling ideas enhanced by order, structure, and transitions	Appealing order, structure, and transitions	Structure identifiable and suitable; transitions used	Adequate order, structure, and some transitions to guide reader	Little direction from beginning to end; few transitions	Lacks direction and identifiable structure; no transitions
Voice	Writer closely involved; engaging personality	Reveals personality	Pleasant but not compelling voice	Sincere voice but not fully engaged	Little writer involvement, personality	Careless writing with no feeling
Word Choice	Vivid, precise words that create memorable pictures	Clear, interesting words to bring description to life	Some specific word pictures	Language adequate; appeals to senses	Generally limited or redundant language	Vague, dull, or misused words
Sentences	Excellent variety of sentences; natural rhythm	Varied lengths, styles; generally smooth	Correct sentences with variations in style	Correctly constructed sentences; some variety	May have simple, awkward, or wordy sentences; little variety	Choppy; many incomplete or run-on sentences
Conventions	Excellent control; few or no errors	No serious errors to affect understanding	General mastery of conventions but some errors	Reasonable control; few distracting errors	Weak control; enough errors to affect understanding	Many errors that prevent understanding

Scoring Rubric — Descriptive Writing

Rubric 4 3 2 1	5	4	3	2	1
Focus/Ideas	Excellent, focused description; well elaborated with quality details	Good, focused description; elaborated with telling details	Generally focused description; some supporting details	Sometimes unfocused description; needs more supporting details	Rambling description; lacks development and detail
Organization/Paragraphs	Compelling ideas enhanced by order, structure, and transitions	Appealing order, structure, and transitions	Adequate order, structure, and some transitions to guide reader	Little direction from beginning to end; few transitions	Lacks direction and identifiable structure; no transitions
Voice	Writer closely involved; engaging personality	Reveals personality	Sincere voice but not fully engaged	Little writer involvement, personality	Careless writing with no feeling
Word Choice	Vivid, precise words that create memorable pictures	Clear, interesting words to bring description to life	Language adequate; appeals to senses	Generally limited or redundant language	Vague, dull, or misused words
Sentences	Excellent variety of sentences; natural rhythm	Varied lengths, styles; generally smooth	Correctly constructed sentences; some variety	May have simple, awkward, or wordy sentences; little variety	Choppy; many incomplete or run-on sentences
Conventions	Excellent control; few or no errors	No serious errors to affect understanding	Reasonable control; few distracting errors	Weak control; enough errors to affect understanding	Many errors that prevent understanding

Scoring Rubric — Descriptive Writing

Rubric 4 3 2 1	3	2	1
Focus/Ideas	Excellent, focused description; well elaborated with quality details	Generally focused description; some supporting details	Rambling description; lacks development and detail
Organization/Paragraphs	Compelling ideas enhanced by order, structure, and transitions	Adequate order, structure, and some transitions to guide reader	Lacks direction and identifiable structure; no transitions
Voice	Writer closely involved; engaging personality	Sincere voice but not fully engaged	Careless writing with no feeling
Word Choice	Vivid, precise words that create memorable pictures	Language adequate; appeals to senses	Vague, dull, or misused words
Sentences	Excellent variety of sentences; natural rhythm	Correctly constructed sentences; some variety	Choppy; many incomplete or run-on sentences
Conventions	Excellent control; few or no errors	Reasonable control; few distracting errors	Many errors that prevent understanding

Scoring Rubric — Persuasive Writing

Rubric 4 3 2 1	6	5	4	3	2	1
Focus/Ideas	Persuasive argument carefully built with quality details	Persuasive argument well supported with details	Persuasive argument focused; good elaboration	Persuasive argument with one or two convincing details	Persuasive piece sometimes unfocused; needs more support	Rambling persuasive argument; lacks development and detail
Organization/ Paragraphs	Information chosen and arranged for maximum effect	Evident progression of persuasive ideas	Progression and structure evident	Information arranged in a logical way with some lapses	Little structure or direction	No identifiable structure
Voice	Writer closely involved; persuasive but not overbearing	Maintains persuasive tone	Persuasive but not compelling voice	Sometimes uses persuasive voice	Little writer involvement, personality	Shows little conviction
Word Choice	Persuasive words carefully chosen for impact	Argument supported by persuasive language	Uses some persuasive words	Occasional persuasive language	Generally limited or redundant language	Vague, dull, or misused words; no persuasive words
Sentences	Excellent variety of sentences; natural rhythm	Varied lengths, styles; generally smooth	Correct sentences with variations in style	Carefully constructed sentences; some variety	Simple, awkward, or wordy sentences; little variety	Choppy; many incomplete or run-on sentences
Conventions	Excellent control; few or no errors	No serious errors to affect understanding	General mastery of conventions but some errors	Reasonable control; few distracting errors	Weak control; enough errors to affect understanding	Many errors that prevent understanding

Scoring Rubric — Persuasive Writing

Rubric 4 3 2 1	5	4	3	2	1
Focus/Ideas	Persuasive argument carefully built with quality details	Persuasive argument well supported with details	Persuasive argument with one or two convincing details	Persuasive piece sometimes unfocused; needs more support	Rambling persuasive argument; lacks development and detail
Organization/ Paragraphs	Information chosen and arranged for maximum effect	Evident progression of persuasive ideas	Information arranged in a logical way with some lapses	Little structure or direction	No identifiable structure
Voice	Writer closely involved; persuasive but not overbearing	Maintains persuasive tone	Sometimes uses persuasive voice	Little writer involvement, personality	Shows little conviction
Word Choice	Persuasive words carefully chosen for impact	Argument supported by persuasive language	Occasional persuasive language	Generally limited or redundant language	Vague, dull, or misused words; no persuasive words
Sentences	Excellent variety of sentences; natural rhythm	Varied lengths, styles; generally smooth	Carefully constructed sentences; some variety	Simple, awkward, or wordy sentences; little variety	Choppy; many incomplete or run-on sentences
Conventions	Excellent control; few or no errors	No serious errors to affect understanding	Reasonable control; few distracting errors	Weak control; enough errors to affect understanding	Many errors that prevent understanding

Scoring Rubric — Persuasive Writing

Rubric 4 3 2 1	3	2	1
Focus/Ideas	Persuasive argument carefully built with quality details	Persuasive argument with one or two convincing details	Rambling persuasive argument; lacks development and detail
Organization/ Paragraphs	Information chosen and arranged for maximum effect	Information arranged in a logical way with some lapses	No identifiable structure
Voice	Writer closely involved; persuasive but not overbearing	Sometimes uses persuasive voice	Shows little conviction
Word Choice	Persuasive words carefully chosen for impact	Occasional persuasive language	Vague, dull, or misused words; no persuasive words
Sentences	Excellent variety of sentences; natural rhythm	Carefully constructed sentences; some variety	Choppy; many incomplete or run-on sentences
Conventions	Excellent control; few or no errors	Reasonable control; few distracting errors	Many errors that prevent understanding

Scoring Rubric — Expository Writing

Rubric 4 3 2 1	6	5	4	3	2	1
Focus/Ideas	Insightful, focused exposition; well elaborated with quality details	Informed, focused exposition; elaborated with telling details	Exposition focused, good elaboration	Generally focused exposition; some supporting details	Sometimes unfocused exposition needs more supporting details	Rambling exposition; lacks development and detail
Organization/ Paragraphs	Logical, consistent flow of ideas; good transitions	Logical sequencing of ideas; uses transitions	Ideas sequenced with some transitions	Sequenced ideas with some transitions	Little direction from beginning to end; few order words	Lacks structure and transitions
Voice	Writer closely involved; informative voice well suited to topic	Reveals personality; voice suited to topic	Pleasant but not compelling voice	Sincere voice suited to topic	Little writer involvement, personality	Careless writing with no feeling
Word Choice	Vivid, precise words to express ideas	Clear words to express ideas	Words correct and adequate	Language adequate but may lack precision	Generally limited or redundant language	Vague, dull, or misused words
Sentences	Strong topic sentence; fluent, varied structures	Good topic sentence; smooth sentence structure	Correct sentences that are sometimes fluent	Topic sentence correctly constructed; some sentence variety	Topic sentence unclear or missing; wordy, awkward sentences	No topic sentence; many incomplete or run-on sentences
Conventions	Excellent control; few or no errors	No serious errors to affect understanding	General mastery of conventions but some errors	Reasonable control; few distracting errors	Weak control; enough errors to affect understanding	Many errors that prevent understanding

Scoring Rubric — Expository Writing

Rubric 4 3 2 1	5	4	3	2	1
Focus/Ideas	Insightful, focused exposition; well elaborated with quality details	Informed, focused exposition; elaborated with telling details	Generally focused exposition; some supporting details	Sometimes unfocused exposition needs more supporting details	Rambling exposition; lacks development and detail
Organization/ Paragraphs	Logical, consistent flow of ideas; good transitions	Logical sequencing of ideas; uses transitions	Sequenced ideas with some transitions	Little direction from beginning to end; few order words	Lacks structure and transitions
Voice	Writer closely involved; informative voice well suited to topic	Reveals personality; voice suited to topic	Language adequate but may lack precision	Little writer involvement, personality	Careless writing with no feeling
Word Choice	Vivid, precise words to express ideas	Clear words to express ideas	Topic sentence correctly constructed; some sentence variety	Generally limited or redundant language	Vague, dull, or misused words
Sentences	Strong topic sentence; fluent, varied structures	Good topic sentence; smooth sentence structure	Sincere voice suited to topic	Topic sentence unclear or missing; wordy, awkward sentences	No topic sentence; many incomplete or run-on sentences
Conventions	Excellent control; few or no errors	No serious errors to affect understanding	Reasonable control; few distracting errors	Weak control; enough errors to affect understanding	Many errors that prevent understanding

Scoring Rubric — Expository Writing

Rubric 4 3 2 1	3	2	1
Focus/Ideas	Insightful, focused exposition; well elaborated with quality details	Generally focused exposition; some supporting details	Rambling exposition; lacks development and detail
Organization/ Paragraphs	Logical, consistent flow of ideas; good transitions	Sequenced ideas with some transitions	Lacks structure and transitions
Voice	Writer closely involved; informative voice well suited to topic	Sincere voice suited to topic	Careless writing with no feeling
Word Choice	Vivid, precise words to express ideas	Language adequate but may lack precision	Vague, dull, or misused words
Sentences	Strong topic sentence; fluent, varied structures	Topic sentence correctly constructed; some sentence variety	No topic sentence; many incomplete or run-on sentences
Conventions	Excellent control; few or no errors	Reasonable control; few distracting errors	Many errors that prevent understanding

Unit 4
Monitoring Fluency

Ongoing assessment of student reading fluency is one of the most valuable measures we have of students' reading skills. One of the most effective ways to assess fluency is taking timed samples of students' oral reading and measuring the number of words correct per minute (WCPM).

How to Measure Words Correct Per Minute—WCPM

Choose a Text
Start by choosing a text for the student to read. The text should be:
- narrative
- unfamiliar
- on grade level

Make a copy of the text for yourself and have one for the student.

Timed Reading of the Text
Tell the student: As you read this aloud, I want you to do your best reading and to read as quickly as you can. That doesn't mean it's a race. Just do your best, fast reading. When I say *begin*, start reading.

As the student reads, follow along in your copy. Mark words that are read incorrectly.

Incorrect	Correct
• omissions	• self-corrections within 3 seconds
• substitutions	• repeated words
• mispronunciations	
• reversals	

After One Minute
At the end of one minute, draw a line after the last word that was read. Have the student finish reading but don't count any words beyond one minute. Arrive at the words correct per minute—WCPM—by counting the total number of words that the student read correctly in one minute.

Fluency Goals
Grade 5 End-of-Year Goal = 140 WCPM

Target goals by unit

Unit 1 105 to 110 WCPM	**Unit 4** 120 to 128 WCPM
Unit 2 110 to 116 WCPM	**Unit 5** 125 to 134 WCPM
Unit 3 115 to 122 WCPM	**Unit 6** 130 to 140 WCPM

More Frequent Monitoring
You may want to monitor some students more frequently because they are falling far below grade-level benchmarks or they have a result that doesn't seem to align with their previous performance. Follow the same steps above, but choose 2 or 3 additional texts.

Fluency Progress Chart Copy the chart on the next page. Use it to record each student's progress across the year.

Unit 4
Assess and Regroup

FYI In Grade 5 there are opportunities for regrouping every five weeks—at the end of Units 2, 3, 4, and 5. These options offer sensitivity to each student's progress, although some teachers may prefer to regroup less frequently.

Regroup for Unit 5
To make regrouping decisions at the end of Unit 4, consider student's end-of-unit scores for
- Unit 4 Retelling
- Fluency (WCPM)
- Unit 4 Benchmark Test

Group Time

On-Level	Strategic Intervention	Advanced
To continue On-Level or to move into the On-Level group, students should	**Students would benefit from Strategic Intervention if they**	**To move to the Advanced group, students should**
• score 3 or better on their cumulative unit rubric scores for Retelling	• score 2 or lower on their cumulative unit rubric scores for Retelling	• score 4 on their cumulative unit rubric scores for Retelling and demonstrate expansive vocabulary and ease of language in their retellings
• meet the current benchmark for fluency (120–128 WCPM), reading On-Level text such as Student Edition selections	• do not meet the current benchmark for fluency (120–128 WCPM)	• score 95% on the Unit 4 Benchmark Test
• score 80% or better on the Unit 4 Benchmark Tests	• score below 60% on the Unit 4 Benchmark Tests	• read above-grade-level material fluently (120–128 WCPM)
• be capable of working in the On-Level group based on teacher judgment	• are struggling to keep up with the On-Level group based on teacher judgment	• be capable of handling the problem solving and investigative work of the Advanced group based on teacher judgment

QUESTIONS TO CONSIDER
- What types of test questions did the student miss? Are they specific to a particular skill or strategy?
- Does the student have adequate background knowledge to understand the test passages or selections for retelling?

- Has the student's performance met expectations for daily lessons and assessments with little or no reteaching?
- Is the student performing more like students in another group?
- Does the student read for enjoyment, different purposes, and varied interests?

Benchmark Fluency Scores
Current Goal: **120–128 WCPM**

End-of-Year Goal: **140 WCPM**

Leveled Readers

Table of Contents

Learning to Play the Game

Learning to Play the Game
by Adam McClellan
illustrated by Dan Grant

◉ **DRAW CONCLUSIONS**

◉ **ANSWER QUESTIONS**

LESSON VOCABULARY blunders, civilization, complex, envy, fleeing, inspired, rustling, strategy

SUMMARY The author tells a story about a brother and sister who have just moved to a new town. The story focuses on their adjustment to a new group of friends and a school environment. At first, things seem difficult, but soon they become more comfortable.

INTRODUCE THE BOOK

BUILD BACKGROUND Discuss with students what they know about moving from one place to another. Ask: Have you moved to a new town? What were some of the differences between your new town and your old community? Discuss how it is sometimes difficult at first to make new friends.

PREVIEW Invite students to look at the cover of the book. Discuss what you can tell about the book just from looking at this illustration. Ask: What can you guess about how these children feel? Where are they? Discuss what students might already be able to predict about the story they are about to read.

TEACH/REVIEW VOCABULARY Use one of the vocabulary words in a sentence that shows its meaning in context, such as "I felt *envy* when my best friend got new sneakers before I did." Then invite students to give another sentence that uses the vocabulary word. Repeat this process with each vocabulary word.

TARGET SKILL AND STRATEGY

◉ **DRAW CONCLUSIONS** Remind students that when we *draw conclusions,* we read with the idea that we will make a decision based on our reading. Suggest that as they go through this book, they try to draw conclusions about how Ella and Pete are going to adjust to their new home.

◉ **ANSWER QUESTIONS** Remind students that *answering questions* about their reading helps them to remember important information. Suggest that as they read, they think about questions the teacher may ask about their reading and try to take notes about what their answers will be.

READ THE BOOK

Use the following questions to support comprehension.

PAGES 4–5 Look at the illustrations. What are some of the things Ella and Pete will see in their new neighborhood? *(They will see unfinished houses and a park.)*

PAGE 8 Based on the illustration, what conclusions can you draw about what is happening to Pete and Ella? *(They are waiting to be chosen for teams to play a game.)*

PAGE 24 Why do you think the author may have included a page explaining what goes on at festivals in different towns? *(The author is trying to suggest a way to become more comfortable in a new place.)*

TALK ABOUT THE BOOK

READER RESPONSE

1. Possible response: new attitude about their move because they are making friends
2. Possible response: ask Mom, read books, talk to friends
3. Possible response: *simple, easy, basic*
4. Possible response: assembly and lunch routines, location of important places in school

RESPONSE OPTIONS

WRITING Invite students to write a paragraph about the first thing they would do to get comfortable in a new place.

CONTENT CONNECTIONS

SOCIAL STUDIES Suggest that students go to the library to look for books about friendship.

🅔🅛🅛 Show students a picture of someone from another culture or country that they are not familiar with. Discuss how it might feel for that person to move to the United States.

Draw Conclusions

- When we **draw conclusions**, we make a decision based on what we have read. We use details and facts to help us.

Directions Reread the following excerpt from *Learning to Play the Game* and answer the following questions.

> "Hi," said Ella. The sudden silence made her nervous. "Ummm . . . we just moved in. I'm Ella, and this is my brother Pete. Pete, say hello to everyone."
> "Ummm, hello?" was all Pete could say. Ella could tell that her brother was as nervous as she was!
> A tall girl with blond hair nodded. "OK, Ella and Pete," she said. "I'm Tiffany. We're going to play Two Bases. Want to play?"
> "Sure," Ella nodded. "Is it like baseball?"

1. What conclusion can you draw about how well Pete and Ella know the other children?

_____

2. Which detail helped you reach the conclusion for question #1?

_____

3. What conclusion can you draw about who the leader is among the group of children?

_____

4. Which detail helped you reach the conclusion for question #3?

_____

5. What conclusion can you draw about Ella's knowledge of the game Two Bases?

_____

© Pearson Education 5

74

Name_____

Vocabulary

Directions Review the meanings of these words.

blunders	mistakes
civilization	society; a group of people who follow rules
complex	complicated; not simple
envy	jealousy
fleeing	running away
inspired	hopeful; interested
rustling	shuffling; moving in a noisy way
strategy	approach

Check the Words You Know

____blunders
____civilization
____complex
____envy
____fleeing
____inspired
____rustling
____strategy

Directions Read the sentence. Then write your own sentence using each vocabulary word.

1. I hope I didn't make too many *blunders* on my spelling test.

_____

2. Our *civilization* may end if we keep polluting.

_____

3. Understanding how budgets work is a *complex* idea.

_____

4. I felt *envy* when I saw their new car.

_____

5. The mouse was *fleeing* as the cat chased it.

_____

6. Hearing your new song, I became *inspired* to write my own song.

_____

7. There was a *rustling* in the leaves as my cat came near.

_____

8. Our team needed a new *strategy* if we were going to win the game.

_____

75

Name_____

Graphic Sources

Graphic sources are graphs, maps, pictures, photographs, and diagrams that help strengthen one's understanding of text.

Directions On the map below, mark where the world's different habitats are found, including the Arctic, temperate areas, grasslands, deserts, and tropical rain forests. Show the animals that live in each area. Remember to include a title for your map and a key.

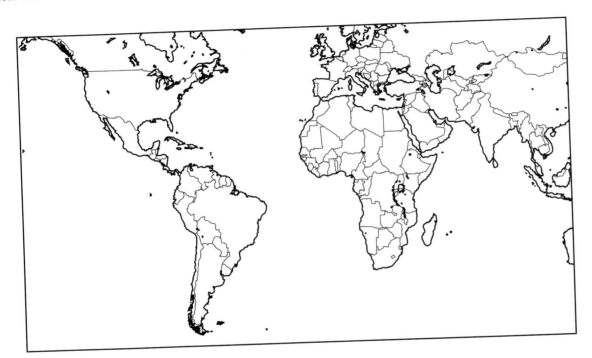

82

Vocabulary

Directions Choose the word from the box that best matches each clue. Write the word on the line.

Check the Words You Know

___critical
___enables
___mucus
___scarce
___specialize
___sterile

_____ **1.** If a person does this, he or she helps make something possible.

_____ **2.** This is something slippery that comes from the body of an animal.

_____ **3.** This means you are referring to something that is very important.

_____ **4.** This refers to a place that cannot sustain life.

_____ **5.** This is when there aren't very many of a certain thing.

_____ **6.** When an animal does this, it changes to suit its habitat.

Directions Write a brief paragraph about *Surviving the Weather: Animals in Their Environments* using each of the words in the box above.

_____

_____

_____

_____

_____

_____

© Pearson Education 5

83

Vocabulary

Directions Fill in the missing spaces in each sentence below with the correct word from the "Words to Know" box and an appropriate word from the "Birds to Know" box. You may refer to your reader for information about the birds.

Check the Words You Know	Birds to Know
___critical ___enable ___mucus ___scarce ___specialize ___sterile	penguins pelican woodpeckers ostriches

1. _____ have a special _____ on their tongues for snatching up insects to eat.

2. _____ live in an environment where food is _____.
They have to walk a long way in search of food.

3. _____ have adapted flippers in place of wings that _____ them
to swim underwater.

4. The _____ has the longest beak of any bird. It allows it to _____
in fishing by scooping fish from the water.

5. Scientists who work with baby birds keep them in a _____ environment so they
stay healthy.

6. When birds are endangered, bird conservationists feel it is _____ to help save
them.

83

A Home for Humans...

 **GRAPHIC SOURCES**

 **MONITOR AND FIX UP**

LESSON VOCABULARY asteroids, astronomically, contend, cycle, deflect, extraterrestrial, vegetation

---

SUMMARY This book presents information about research on deep-space travel and the adaptations humans would have to make to sustain long voyages.

INTRODUCE THE BOOK

BUILD BACKGROUND Ask students to share what interests them about space and space travel. Ask what they think it would be like to live in outer space.

ELL Build background for English language learners by using a map of the solar system to introduce and talk about space and space travel.

PREVIEW/USE TEXT FEATURES Have students look at the photos, captions, and headings. How do these text features help them know how this book is organized?

TEACH/REVIEW VOCABULARY Have students locate the vocabulary words in the text. Have them define each word using context clues, the glossary, and a dictionary. Then invite students to list for each word as many words as possible that have similar meanings or are related in some way.

TARGET SKILL AND STRATEGY

GRAPHIC SOURCES Remind students that *graphic sources* are graphs, maps, photographs, and diagrams that help strengthen their understanding of the text. Students may also use graphic sources before reading to predict and preview information. Have students read page 18 and then look at the chart. Ask: What information is in the chart? How does the chart add to what they read in the text?

MONITOR AND FIX UP Remind students that good readers constantly *monitor,* or check, comprehension as they read. If the text isn't making sense, they can use *fix-up* strategies, such as adjusting reading rate, reading on, or rereading and reviewing. Have students read pages 6–7. Encourage them check their comprehension by working with a partner to ask each other questions and review the text.

READ THE BOOK

Use the following questions to support comprehension.

PAGE 8 Why do scientists think Mars is the most likely planet to support life? *(A meteorite that fell to Earth from Mars 13,000 years ago appeared to have bacteria in it. Mars has, or once had, water.)*

PAGES 10–11 Why is zero gravity a problem for humans? *(People lose muscle and bone strength, heart becomes inefficient)*

PAGE 14 Name some benefits of a space colony. *(Helpful to have experiments done in zero gravity; develop vaccines; conversion of solar power)*

TALK ABOUT THE BOOK

READER RESPONSE
1. Oil
2. Responses will very but should show an understanding of centripetal force and use common examples such as spinning a bucket of water in a circle.
3. Possible response: *performed*
4. Student questions will vary. Possible response: Possible source could include International Energy Agency.

RESPONSE OPTIONS

WRITING Ask students what their opinions are about space travel. Have students write a persuasive paper about whether we should or shouldn't pursue space travel. Be sure students include facts they learned from the book to support their main idea.

CONTENT CONNECTIONS

SCIENCE Have students explore space by looking on the internet.

TIME FOR Science

Graphic Sources

Graphic sources are graphs, maps, pictures, photographs, and diagrams that help strengthen understanding of text.

Directions Using information you learned from the book, show the distance between Earth and the moon and Earth and Mars. On the lines provided below the diagram write what scientists are learning about life in space and questions they still have. Add questions that you have.

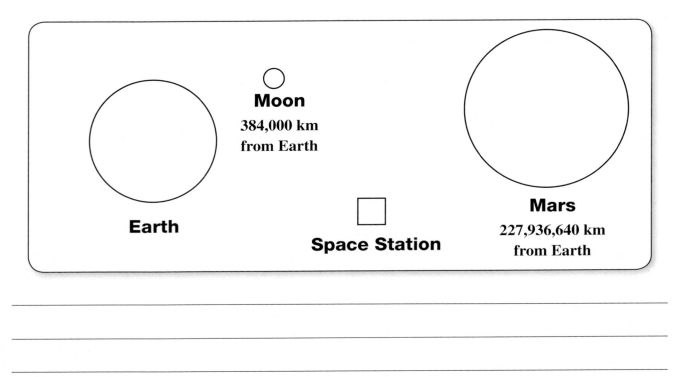

_____

_____

_____

_____

_____

_____

_____

_____

_____

82

Vocabulary

Directions Complete each sentence with a word from the box.

> ### Check the Words You Know
>
> ___ cavities   ___ combination
> ___ demonstrates   ___ episode
> ___ profile   ___ strict

1. Marcus was afraid that his teacher would be _____ .

2. The teacher told them to watch tonight's _____ of *Star Trek*.

3. Marcus's new school was a _____ of old and new.

4. The bulletin board in art class _____ the students' artistic talents.

5. Marcus had not had _____ for three years.

6. The art teacher traced his _____ on a piece of paper.

Directions Write a brief paragraph discussing Marcus's first day at school, using as many vocabulary words as possible.

_____

_____

_____

_____

_____

_____

_____

_____

_____

_____

© Pearson Education 5

87

Nathaniel Comes to Town

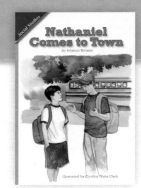

🔾 **GENERALIZE**

🔾 **STORY SEQUENCE**

LESSON VOCABULARY annoyingly, foreboding, gallantly, humiliation, jostling, skeptically

---

SUMMARY Drew hates school and has very few friends. Then Nathaniel, a boy he met at the beach the summer before, moves to town. Drew and Nathaniel become friends, although there are some bumps in their relationship. By the end of the story, their friendship is patched and Drew feels better about school.

INTRODUCE THE BOOK

BUILD BACKGROUND Ask students if any of them have ever had trouble finding friends in school. What did they do to make new friends?

PREVIEW/USE TEXT FEATURES Encourage students to look at the chapter headings and illustrations to guess what happens in this book.

ELL Give ELL students a list of vocabulary definitions and have them match the definition with the correct vocabulary word.

TEACH/PREVIEW VOCABULARY Go over the vocabulary words with students. Have them note that all the words have one or more endings. Have students tell the base word, the definition, and how the ending affects the word's meaning.

TARGET SKILL AND STRATEGY

🔾 **GENERALIZE** Remind students that a *generalization* is a broad statement or rule that applies to many examples. There are several different examples of friendship in the story. Have the students try to generalize what friendship means based on the examples in the story.

🔾 **STORY SEQUENCE** Tell students that authors sometimes write stories that trace a character's change of heart through the story. Have students look at the story in this light.

READ THE BOOK

Use the following questions to support comprehension.

PAGES 4–6 List all of the reasons you can find in the first chapter that Drew doesn't like school. *(no friends, former friends, feeling sick)*

PAGE 8 What did Drew think of Nathaniel after spending time with him at the beach? *(He thought he was annoyingly smart.)*

PAGES 24–27 What happens between Drew and Nathaniel while they are playing basketball? *(They become friends again.)*

TALK ABOUT THE BOOK

READER RESPONSE
1. Possible response: Moving to a new school can be difficult.
2. Responses will vary.
3. Responses will vary.
4. Possible responses: Nathaniel makes friends by actively trying and not being easily defeated. Drew takes longer to make friends.

RESPONSE OPTIONS

WRITING Have students think back to their first day in grammar school. Have them write about how they felt and if they made any new friends that day.

CONTENT CONNECTIONS

SOCIAL STUDIES Have students read about the Three Famous Failures on p. 32. Have them choose one of the three and research that person on the Internet or in the library.

Time for SOCIAL STUDIES

Generalize

- A **generalization** is a broad statement or rule that applies to many examples. A generalization is made after thinking about a number of examples or facts and what they have in common.

Directions What are some of the difficulties faced by Nathaniel as a new student? What can you generalize about the difficulties that all new students face?

1-5.

_____

_____

_____

_____

_____

Directions Based on Drew's experiences, what can you generalize about how difficult it is to help a new student find his way?

6-10.

_____

_____

_____

_____

_____

_____

_____

© Pearson Education 5

86

Vocabulary

Directions Fill in the blank with the word from the box that fits best.

Check the Words You Know

___ annoyingly	___ foreboding
___ gallantly	___ humiliation
___ jostling	___ skeptically

1. Drew viewed going to school with _____ and dread.

2. Nathaniel _____ tried to make friends at his new school.

3. The color of Drew's basketball caused him _____ .

4. In gym class, Nathaniel tried _____ for the ball.

5. Drew's sister liked to tease him _____ .

6. Drew reacted _____ to his teacher's cheerful greeting.

Directions Write a brief paragraph discussing Nathaniel's first day at school, using as many vocabulary words as possible.

_____

_____

_____

_____

_____

_____

_____

_____

_____

_____

87

Let the Games Begin

Let the Games Begin: History of the Olympics

Unit 4 Week 5

👁 **DRAW CONCLUSIONS**

👁 **VISUALIZE**

LESSON VOCABULARY bluish, cartwheels, gymnastics, hesitation, limelight, skidded, somersault, throbbing, wincing

SUMMARY This book describes the history of the Olympic Games and how the games have changed through the years. It focuses on the historic 1904 Olympics and its memorable athletes like Felix Carvajal.

INTRODUCE THE BOOK

BUILD BACKGROUND Discuss what students know about the Olympics. If they have watched the Olympic Games, ask them to describe the events. Prompt them to discuss which event they would most like to try.

PREVIEW/USE TEXT FEATURES As students preview the book, have them look at the photographs and read the captions. Ask them to point to specific photographs that give them clues about what the book will teach them. Have them explain their choices.

TEACH/REVIEW VOCABULARY Have students write each vocabulary word on a sheet of paper and look for words with suffixes. Have them circle the suffixes and write a new word containing each suffix.

ELL Have students write each vocabulary word on a sheet of paper and look for words with suffixes. Have them circle the suffixes. Then have them look up the meaning of each suffix in a dictionary and write their answers on a sheet of paper. If time permits, ask students to write a new word using each suffix.

TARGET SKILL AND STRATEGY

👁 **DRAW CONCLUSIONS** Remind students that a *conclusion* is a sensible decision reached after thinking about details or facts in what is read. As they read, have them ask themselves this question: What facts tell me that Felix Carvajal was a strong-minded man? Have them write the facts on a sheet of paper as they read.

👁 **VISUALIZE** Remind students that to *visualize* is to create a picture in the mind. As students read, suggest that they visualize what it was like to compete in the early Olympics.

READ THE BOOK

Use the following questions to support comprehension.

PAGES 11 AND 13 What conclusions can you draw about Felix Carvajal? *(He didn't give up on reaching his goal.)*

PAGES 14 AND 15 What made the 1904 marathon difficult? *(Roads were unpaved, runners had no water.)*

PAGE 18 Why was it amazing that Ray Ewry competed in the Olympics? *(He had polio as a child and the doctors said he would never walk again.)*

TALK ABOUT THE BOOK

TALK ABOUT IT
1. Responses will vary.
2. dirt road, no water, hot weather, dust in their eyes
3. Responses will vary.
4. Possible response: He had a wooden leg and yet medaled in these events.

RESPONSE OPTIONS

WRITING Suggest that students write about one of the sports in this book and what it would be like to play it in the Olympics.

CONTENT CONNECTIONS

SOCIAL STUDIES Students can learn more about these and other interesting sports through Internet and library research.

Time for SOCIAL STUDIES

Draw Conclusions

A **conclusion** is a sensible decision reached after thinking about details or facts in what is read.

Directions Read the following paragraph and answer the questions.

The most amazing athlete of the 1904 Olympics was Ray Ewry. He was a track athlete from America. He had polio when he was a child and the doctors said he would never walk again. The young boy wanted to make his legs stronger, so he began jumping. Ewry's legs got so strong that when he went to the 1900 Games in Paris, he won first place three times! His medals were for the standing long jump, the standing high jump, and the standing triple jump. He won gold medals in the same events in the 1904 Olympics. The crowds loved him and cheered for him. He must have enjoyed being in the limelight.

1-5. What conclusions can you draw about the kind of person Ray Ewry was?

_____

_____

_____

_____

6-10. What details about him helped you come to these conclusions?

_____

_____

_____

_____

© Pearson Education 5

90

Vocabulary

Directions Write the word from the box that best matches each definition.

> **Check the Words You Know**
>
> ___bluish   ___cartwheels
> ___gymnastics   ___hesitation
> ___limelight   ___skidded
> ___somersault   ___throbbing
> ___wincing

1. the focus of attention _____

2. having a blue tint _____

3. exercises that use strength, agility, and coordination _____

4. shrinking one's face or body in pain or disgust _____

5. slid _____

6. rolling over by turning heels over head _____

7. a pause _____

8. sideways handsprings _____

9. pulsating or beating strongly _____

10. Write a sentence using any vocabulary word from the box.

_____

_____

© Pearson Education 5

91

Answer Key for Below-Level Reader Practice

Learning to Play the Game   LR1

Draw Conclusions, LR2

Possible responses given. **1.** They don't know them at all. **2.** Ella introduces herself and her brother. **3.** Tiffany seems to be the leader. **4.** Tiffany talks to the children and invites them to play the game. **5.** She doesn't know how to play the game.

Vocabulary, LR3

Possible responses given. **1.** Her blunders cost us the game. **2.** The president made a great contribution to civilization. **3.** Some people find geometry to be very complex. **4.** We should not feel any envy toward others. **5.** As the school bell rang, the students started fleeing the building. **6.** Your good grades have inspired me to study harder. **7.** The rustling of the blankets told me the puppy was in my bed. **8.** The strategy I use with homework is to do it when I get home.

A New Girl in Class   LR10

Generalize, LR11

Generalization: Possible responses: Cerebral palsy makes it difficult for a person to develop motor skills. Supporting Facts: Support: Babies born with it often have a hard time learning to roll over, sit up, stand, or walk. Support: Physical therapy is usually required for muscle control and development. Support: People with cerebral palsy can't participate normally in regular sports.

Vocabulary, LR12

1. abdomen—the section of the body that holds the intestines and stomach; the belly **2.** artificial—produced by humans, not nature **3.** gait—a particular way of walking, stepping, or running **4.** handicapped—people who have a mental or physical disability **5.** therapist—a specialist who provides treatment or healing of an illness or disability **6.** wheelchair—a chair equipped with large wheels for the use of a disabled person. Responses will vary.

Surviving the Weather   LR19

Graphic Sources, LR20

Responses will vary.

Vocabulary, LR21

1. enables **2.** mucus **3.** critical **4.** sterile **5.** scarce **6.** specialize. Responses will vary.

Moving   LR28

Generalize, LR29

Responses will vary. Supporting Details: Several were on the coast. Joey went to school in each city. Joey made new friends in each city. Supporting Details: He learned to be less shy. He got involved in sports. He listened to his mother's advice.

Vocabulary, LR30

1. strict **2.** combination **3.** cavities **4.** demonstrates **5.** episode **6.** profile **7–10.** Responses will vary.

Let the Games Begin   LR37

Draw Conclusions, LR38

Possible responses given. **1–5.** He was determined, worked hard to reach his goals, never gave up, didn't let obstacles get in his way. **6–10.** He had polio, but was determined to be in the Olympics. He practiced jumping. He didn't listen to people who said he couldn't do it.

Vocabulary, LR39

1. limelight **2.** bluish **3.** gymnastics **4.** wincing **5.** skidded **6.** somersault **7.** hesitation **8.** cartwheels **9.** throbbing **10.** Responses will vary.

Answer Key for On-Level Reader Practice

Adventure to the New World — LR4

Draw Conclusions, LR5

Possible responses given. **1.** They expected to find the colony guarded by soldiers. **2.** English soldiers had been sent to guard the settlement. Roanoke leaders wouldn't allow the island to be totally abandoned. **3.** They had trouble growing food and were not able to make friends with the local inhabitants. **4.** They ran low on supplies and they encountered difficulties with local Indians. **5.** Jane and her family might likely have decided not to go to the New World if they had known that they would find the soldiers vanished and the fort in ruins.

Vocabulary, LR6

1. fleeing **2.** inspired **3.** strategy **4.** complex **5.** civilization **6.** blunders **7.** envy **8.** inspired **9.** strategy **10.** rustling

Everybody Wins! The Story of Special Olympics — LR13

Generalize, LR14

Generalize/The Special Olympics have grown considerably. Supporting Facts/In the first year, 1,000 people competed. Two years later, more than twice as many athletes competed. The first winter games attracted 500 athletes; in 1993, more than 1,600 athletes competed. **5.** Possible response: The success of the Special Olympics proves that intellectually disabled people can play sports.

Vocabulary, LR15

1. therapist **2.** handicapped **3.** abdomen **4.** wheelchair **5.** gait **6.** artificial **7–10.** Responses will vary.

Changing to Survive: Bird Adaptations — LR22

Graphic Sources, LR23

Responses may vary.

Vocabulary, LR24

1. Woodpeckers, mucus **2.** Ostriches, scarce **3.** Penguins, enable **4.** Pelican, specialize **5.** Sterile **6.** critical

The New Kid at School — LR31

Generalize, LR32

Possible answers given. **1.** that they will be mean to him **2.** that he will never make new friends **3.** He's afraid of getting lost. **4.** He's afraid his teacher may be strict. **5.** that they will be nice to him **6.** that he will easily make new friends **7.** That he won't get lost, or if he does, he can ask for directions. **8.** That his teacher may be nice

Vocabulary, LR33

1. strict **2.** episode **3.** combination **4.** demonstrates **5.** cavities **6.** profile **7–10.** Responses will vary.

Strange Sports with Weird Gear — LR40

Draw Conclusions, LR41

Possible responses given. **1.** Yes, because the equipment is heavy and difficult to move **2.** No, because they don't need to wear protective gear **3.** Yes, because the players wear protective head and hand gear **4.** to make their routine more exciting **5.** rhythmic gymnastics because I like to dance

Vocabulary, LR42

1. limelight **2.** bluish **3.** gymnastics **4.** wincing **5.** skidded **6.** somersault **7.** hesitation **8.** cartwheels **9.** throbbing **10.** Responses will vary.

Group Time

ROUTINE

Strategic Intervention

DAY 1

Learning to Play the Game

by Adam McClellan
illustrated by Dan Grant

Leveled Reader **Database**

ONLINE

PearsonSuccessNet.com

1 Build Background

REINFORCE CONCEPTS Display the People Adapting Concept Web. This week's concept is *people adapting*. People adapt by changing to fit different conditions and situations. Discuss the meaning of each word on the web, using the definitions on p. 392l and the Concept Vocabulary Routine on p. DI·1.

CONNECT TO READING This week you will read about ways people adapt in difficult situations. Using what you know can help you adapt to a different situation. In "The Black Stallion," Alec used what he knew from biology class to survive on the island by eating carragheen.

2 Read Leveled Reader *Learning to Play the Game*

BEFORE READING Using the Picture Walk Routine on p. DI·1, guide students through the text focusing on key concepts and vocabulary. Ask questions such as:

pp. 4–5 What do Ella and Pete see in their new neighborhood? *(a park, an unfinished house)* How do you think they feel?

pp. 14–15 How do you think Ella and Pete feel in these pictures? *(possibly sad, frustrated)*

DURING READING Read pp. 3–5 aloud, while students track the print. Do a choral reading of pp. 6–9. If students are capable, have them read and discuss the remainder of the book with a partner. Ask: How did Ella and Pete adapt to their new neighborhood? What did Ella and Pete do when they played with the other kids in the park?

AFTER READING Have pairs of students discuss the ways to adapt to a new neighborhood. We read *Learning to Play the Game* to learn about how Ella and Pete adapted to their new neighborhood. Understanding how people adapt will help us as we read *Weslandia*.

Monitor Progress

Selection Reading and Comprehension

If... students have difficulty reading the selection with a partner,	**then...** have them follow along as they listen to the Online Leveled Reader Audio.
If... students have trouble understanding ways Ella and Pete adapted to the new game,	**then...** reread pp. 20–23 and discuss these pages together.

Differentiated Instruction

Table of Contents

Routine Cards

Routine Card

Fluent Word Reading Routine

Teach students to read words fluently using this Routine.

1 Connect Write an example word. Isolate the sound-spelling or word structure element you will focus on and ask students to demonstrate their understanding.

2 Model When you come to a new word, look at all the letters in the word and think about its vowel sound. Say the sounds in the word to yourself and then read the word. Model reading the example words in this way. When you come to a new word, what are you going to do?

3 Group Practice Write other similar words. Let's read these words. Look at the letters, think about the vowel sounds, and say the sounds to yourself. When I point to the word, let's read it together. Allow 2-3 seconds previewing time for each word.

Routine Card

Oral Rereading Routine

Use this Routine when students read orally.

1 Read Have students read the entire book orally.

2 Reread For optimal fluency, students should reread the text three or four times.

3 Provide Feedback Listen as students read and provide corrective feedback regarding their oral reading and their use of decoding strategies.

Routine Card

Paired Reading Routine

Use this Routine when students read in pairs.

1 Reader 1 Begins Students read the entire book, switching readers at the end of each page.

2 Reader 2 Begins Have partners reread; now the other partner begins.

3 Reread For optimal fluency, students should reread three or four times.

4 Provide Feedback Listen as students read. Provide corrective feedback regarding their oral reading and their use of decoding strategies.

Routine Card

Choral Reading Routine

Use this Routine when students read chorally.

1 Select a Passage Choose an appropriate passage from the selection.

2 Divide into Groups Assign each group a part to read.

3 Model Have students track the print as you read.

4 Read Together Have students read along with you.

5 Independent Reading Have the groups read aloud without you. Monitor progress and provide feedback. For optimal fluency, students should reread three to four times.

For alternate Leveled Reader lesson plans that teach 🌑 **Draw Conclusions,** 🌑 **Answer Questions,** and **Lesson Vocabulary,** see pp. LR1–LR9.

DAY 1

On-Level

ROUTINE

1 Build Background

DEVELOP VOCABULARY Write the word *island* and ask students to define it in their own words. *(a small piece of land, land surrounded by water)* Have you ever been on an island? How did you get there? Repeat this activity with the word *wharf* and other words from the Leveled Reader *Adventure to the New World.* Use the Concept Vocabulary Routine on p. DI•1 as needed.

2 Read Leveled Reader *Adventure to the New World*

BEFORE READING Have students create a web with the label *Starting a New Settlement.* This book tells about the adventure that Jane and her family had as they moved to Virginia. As you read, look for key words that relate to Jane's new home. Record them in your web.

DURING READING Have students follow along as you read pp. 4–10. Then let them complete the book on their own. Remind students to add words to their web as they read.

AFTER READING Have students compare the words on their web. Point out the words that describe doing something in a new situation that will help them as they read tomorrow's story *Weslandia.*

Advanced

ROUTINE

1 Read Leveled Reader *Cheaper, Faster, Better*

BEFORE READING Recall the Read Aloud "The Black Stallion." How did Alec adapt to his surroundings? *(He remembered what he learned in biology class and ate carrageen.)* Today you will read about how people adapted to changes in technology.

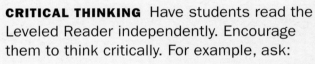

CRITICAL THINKING Have students read the Leveled Reader independently. Encourage them to think critically. For example, ask:

• What does the word *adapt* mean, and how can you apply that to technology?

• How did your parents adapt to changes in technology? Do they think their lives are better or worse for it?

AFTER READING Have students review the selection to find five or more unfamiliar words and determine their meanings by using context clues or by consulting a dictionary. Then ask them to write statements or questions that both include the words and convey their meanings. Have students meet with you to discuss the selection and the statements or questions they wrote.

2 Independent Extension Activity

NOW TRY THIS Assign "Now Try This" on pp. 22–23 of *Cheaper, Faster, Better* for students to work on throughout the week.

DAY 1

Weslandia

Group Time

Audio CD **AudioText**

① Word Study/Phonics

LESSON VOCABULARY Use p. 394b to review the meanings of *blunders, civilization, complex, envy, fleeing, inspired, rustling,* and *strategy.* Have individuals practice reading the words from word cards.

DECODING MULTISYLLABIC WORDS Write *outcast,* saying the word as you write it. Then model how to use meaningful parts to read longer words. First I ask myself if I see any parts that I know. I see *out* at the beginning of the word, and *cast* at the end. I know that the *out* is "away" and that *cast* is "throw." So I think an *outcast* is "something that is thrown away." Use the multisyllabic Word Routine on p. DI·1 to help students read these other words from *Weslandia: miserable, disliked, alarming, tormentors, snapping, mumbled, almighty.* Be sure students understand the meanings of words such as *tormentors* and *almighty.*

Use *Strategies for Word Analysis*, Lesson 16, with students who have difficulty mastering word analysis and need practice with decodable text.

② Read *Weslandia,* pp. 396–403

BEFORE READING *Learning to Play the Game* explained how Ella and Pete adapted to their new neighborhood. Think about this as you read *Weslandia.*

Using the Picture Walk Routine on p. DI·1, guide students through the text asking questions such as those listed below. Read the question on p. 396. Together, set a purpose for reading.

pp. 398–399 What do the illustrations show Wesley doing? *(In one picture he is standing on a pogo stick in a room full of things, and in the other picture, he seems to be running away from young people with odd haircuts.)*

pp. 402–403 Why do you think the two boys are spying on Wesley?

DURING READING Follow the Guiding Comprehension routine on pp. 398–403. Have students read along with you while tracking the print or do a choral reading. Stop every two pages to ask what has happened so far. Prompt as necessary.

- What was the idea Wes came up with for his summer project?
- Why did Wes decide to wear a robe?

AFTER READING What has happened in the selection so far? What do you think will happen next? Reread passages with students for comprehension as needed.

Monitor Progress

Word and Story Reading

If... students have difficulty reading multisyllabic words in the selection,	**then...** have them look for and read meaningful parts in the words or have them chunk words with no recognizable parts.
If... students need practice reading words fluently,	**then...** use the Fluent Word Reading Routine on the DI tab.
If... students have difficulty reading along with the group,	**then...** have them follow along as they listen to the AudioText.

Advanced

ROUTINE

1 Extend Vocabulary

WORD STRUCTURE Choose a word, such as the word *engaging* from p. 10 of *Cheaper, Faster, Better:* "Whether you're checking movie times, looking for blouses, doing literary research, or engaging in any other activity..." What does the word *engaging* mean? *(Engaging is participating.)* How did you determine the word's meaning? *(I checked to see if an ending has been added to the base word. Then I determined how the ending changed the meaning of the word.)* Discuss why word structure is helpful, and remind students to use the strategy as they read *Weslandia*.

2 Read *Weslandia,* pp. 396–403

BEFORE READING Today you will read a fiction story about a boy who creates his own world to adapt to his surroundings. As you read, think about other selections you have read in which people adapted to new situations.

For their Strategy Response Log (p. 396), have students make a list of questions they have about the selection based on the artwork. Encourage students to review and answer their questions as they read.

PROBLEM SOLVING Have students read pp. 398–403 independently. Have them list difficult situations that people their age can face, such as having an argument with a friend, not getting invited to a party, or not having anyone to be with at recess, and think about ways to meet or adapt to those situations.

AFTER READING Have partners discuss the selection and share their Strategy Response Log entries. Have students select three or four difficult situations that they wrote about previously. Then have the students write a short paragraph providing someone with advice to help deal with each situation.

Weslandia
Group Time

Audio CD **AudioText**

Monitor Progress

Word and Story Reading

If... students have difficulty reading multisyllabic words in the selection,	then... have them look for and read meaningful parts in the words or have them chunk words with no recognizable parts.
If... students have difficulty reading along with the group,	then... have them follow along as they listen to the AudioText.

Strategic Intervention

ROUTINE

1 Reinforce Comprehension

⊙ **SKILL DRAW CONCLUSIONS** Have students tell what drawing conclusions is *(a decision you make after thinking about the details in a story)*. If necessary, review the meaning and provide a model. Conclusions are decisions you make after thinking about the details in a story. One example of drawing a conclusion is deciding that Wes sticks out from other boys, as his mother says. Using the details in the story, that he dislikes pizza, soda, and football, doesn't shave his head, and is good at fleeing, or running away, helps me draw that conclusion.

Ask students what they can conclude about Wes when he doesn't plant vegetables but is thrilled about the plant seeds that blow into his garden. *(He likes surprises.)*

2 Read *Weslandia*, pp. 404–407

BEFORE READING Have students retell what happened in the story so far. Ask: What was the idea that Wes came up with for his summer project? Reread p. 400 and model how to answer the question. As I read I use the answer to the question to help me draw a conclusion. Wesley turned over a plot of ground so I think Wes is going to grow his own crop. Remind them to think about their own experiences and the answers to questions that were raised about the rest of *Weslandia*. ⊙ **STRATEGY Answer Questions**

DURING READING Follow the Guiding Comprehension routine on pp. 404–407. Have students read along with you while tracking print or do a choral reading. Stop every two pages to ask students what has happened so far. Prompt as necessary.

- Why did Wesley's schoolmates become curious about what he was doing?
- What did Wesley call his plant?

AFTER READING How does Wesley adapt his environment when he doesn't have friends? Reread with students for comprehension as needed. Tell them that tomorrow they will read two poems, "Under the Back Porch" and "Keziah," that explain how children adapt in their own way.

Advanced

ROUTINE

1 Extend Comprehension

SKILL DRAW CONCLUSIONS Have the students draw a conclusion about a friend they think might have characteristics similar to Wesley. Tell the students to give several reasons for their conclusion.

STRATEGY ANSWER QUESTIONS Have students write questions about Wesley that are not in the story. They should give their questions to a partner and answer each other's questions. Ask questions such as:

- What kind of student do you think Wesley is?
- What would Wesley be like as an adult?

2 Read *Weslandia,* pp. 404–407

BEFORE READING Have students recall what has happened in the selection so far. Remind them to draw conclusions and to answer questions they have as they read the remainder of the story.

CRITICAL THINKING Have students read pp. 404–407 independently. Encourage them to think critically. For example, ask:

- Were Wesley's ways of dealing with his situation good ways? Are there better ways he could have handled it?

AFTER READING Have students complete the Strategy Response Log activity (p. 406). Then have the students review the story to find descriptions of an unfamiliar setting. Tell students to make a list of words or phrases the author uses that help them imagine this setting. Students can circle the images on their list that best help them picture what the author is describing.

DAY 3

AudioText

Group Time

Poetry

Under the Back Porch

Keziah

Audio CD   AudioText

ROUTINE

1 Practice Retelling

REVIEW STORY ELEMENTS Help students identify the main character, minor characters, and the setting of *Weslandia*. Then guide them in using the Retelling Cards to list story events in sequence. Prompt students to include important details.

RETELL Using the Retelling Cards, have students work in pairs to retell *Weslandia*. Monitor retelling and prompt students as needed. For example, ask:

- Tell me what this story is about in a few sentences.
- What is the main character in this story like?
- Why do you think the author wrote this story?

If students struggle, model a fluent retelling.

Grade 5
Retelling Cards
PEARSON
Scott Foresman

2 Read Poetry

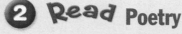

BEFORE READING Read the genre information on p. 410. Have students share what they know about poetry. Then explain that "Under the Back Porch" and "Keziah" are written in the first person, but *Weslandia* is not. This means that a speaker is saying the poems, using the word *I*, whereas in *Weslandia* a storyteller or narrator told the story.

DURING READING Have students read along with you while tracking the print or do a choral reading of the poems. Stop to discuss imagery, pointing out that images in the lines are used to express thoughts and feelings. As you read, think about the image in this sentence about the speaker's house: *There is a yard stretched around it and in back.*

AFTER READING Have students share their reactions to the poems. Then guide them through the Reading Across Texts and Writing Across Texts activities, prompting if necessary.

- How would you describe Weslandia?
- Which details about Weslandia do you find interesting?
- How could you put them into a poem?

Monitor Progress

Word and Poem Reading

If... students have difficulty reading multisyllabic words in the selection,	**then...** have them look for and read meaningful parts in the words or have them chunk words with no recognizable parts.
If... students have difficulty reading along with the group,	**then...** have them follow along as they listen to the AudioText.

Advanced

1 Read Poetry

CREATIVE THINKING Have students make a list of different literary genres, such as fantasy, fiction, biography, poetry, expository nonfiction, and so on. Tell students to pick one literary genre, identify its genre, and choose a passage to rewrite in a different genre. Students can share their writing with a partner.

AFTER READING Discuss Reading Across Texts. Have students do Writing Across Texts independently.

2 Extend Genre Study

RESEARCH Have students research other forms of poetry. Have them make a list of different forms of poetry, such as haiku, limericks, and acrostics.

WRITE Have students rewrite either "Under the Back Porch" or "Keziah" in different forms of poetry. Have students share their poems in small groups.

AudioText

Weslandia

Group Time

DAY 5

Leveled Reader Database
ONLINE
PearsonSuccessNet.com

ROUTINE

① Reread for Fluency

MODEL Read aloud pp. 4–5 of the Leveled Reader *Learning to Play the Game,* emphasizing observing punctuation marks. Have students notice how you pause at commas and raise your voice slightly to indicate a question. Then read pp. 6–7 word-by-word without pausing in sentences. Have students tell you which model sounded better. Discuss how reading and observing punctuation with the tone of voice creates expression.

PRACTICE Have students reread passages from *Learning to Play the Game* with a partner or individually. For optimal fluency, they should reread three or four times. As students read, monitor fluency and provide corrective feedback. Students in this group are assessed in Weeks 2 and 4.

② Retell Leveled Reader *Learning to Play the Game*

Model how to skim the book, retelling as you skim. Then ask students to retell the book, using the pictures to help them retell each event. Prompt them as needed.

- When and where does this story take place?
- What happened next in the story?

Monitor Progress

Fluency

If... students have difficulty reading fluently,	**then...** provide additional fluency practice by pairing nonfluent readers with fluent ones.

For alternate Leveled Reader lesson plans that teach
Draw Conclusions, Answer Questions,
and **Lesson Vocabulary,** see pp. LR1–LR9.

On-Level

DAY 5

1 Reread for Fluency   ROUTINE

MODEL Read aloud p. 4 of the Leveled Reader *Adventure to the New World,* emphasizing observing punctuation marks. Have students note that you pause at commas and you raise your voice slightly to indicate a question. Discuss how observing punctuation by the tone of voice creates better expression.

PRACTICE Have students reread passages from *Adventure to the New World* with a partner or individually. For optimal fluency, they should reread three or four times. As students read, monitor fluency and provide corrective feedback. Students in this group are assessed in Week 3.

2 Retell Leveled Reader *Adventure to the New World*

Have students use chapter titles and illustrations as a guide to retell the story. Prompt as needed.

- Tell me what this story is about in a few sentences.
- What is Jane like in the story?
- How does this story remind you of other stories?

Advanced

DAY 5

1 Reread for Fluency   ROUTINE

PRACTICE Have students reread passages from the Leveled Reader *Cheaper, Faster, Better* with a partner or individually. As students read, monitor fluency and provide corrective feedback. If students read fluently on the first reading, they do not need to reread three to four times. Assess the fluency of students in this group using p. 411a.

2 Revisit Leveled Reader *Cheaper, Faster, Better*

RETELL Have students retell the Leveled Reader *Cheaper, Faster, Better.*

NOW TRY THIS Have students complete their projects. You may wish to explore with them their ideas of life without familiar technology.

Group Time

Leveled Reader Database
ONLINE
PearsonSuccessNet.com

ROUTINE

DAY 1

❶ Build Background

REINFORCE CONCEPTS Display the Overcoming Physical Limitations Concept Web. This week's concept is *overcoming physical limitations.* Overcoming physical limitations is one way of adapting. Discuss the meaning of each word on the web, using the definitions on p. 412l and the Concept Vocabulary Routine on p. DI·1.

CONNECT TO READING This week you will read about ways people with cerebral palsy have met challenges and overcome their physical limitations. You will learn how their lives are like and unlike your own. What did Wilma Rudolph in "Wilma Unlimited" have to do to overcome her physical limitations and finally represent the United States in the Olympic Games? *(She was dedicated, worked hard, and didn't give up.)*

❷ Read Leveled Reader *A New Girl in Class*

BEFORE READING Using the Picture Walk Routine on p. DI·1, guide students through the text focusing on key concepts and vocabulary. Ask questions such as:

pp. 4–5 This selection is about a new class member who has cerebral palsy and about how the class reacts to her arrival. How do the students prepare for her? *(They look as if they're researching cerebral palsy.)* Research is one way to learn new information.

p. 10 This picture shows Lisa, the new student, and her physical therapist. What do you think a physical therapist does? *(helps physically handicapped people move)* What objects help Lisa walk? *(leg braces and bars)*

DURING READING Read pp. 3–5 aloud, while students track the print. Do a choral reading of pp. 6–9. If students are capable, have them read and discuss the remainder of the book with a partner. Ask: What do some scientists believe causes cerebral palsy? What does the class decide to do to support research on cerebral palsy?

AFTER READING Encourage pairs of students to discuss what they have learned about cerebral palsy. We read *A New Girl in Class* to learn about the causes of cerebral palsy and how people can work to overcome this physical limitation. Understanding cerebral palsy will help us as we read *Stretching Ourselves.*

Monitor Progress

Selection Reading and Comprehension

If... students have difficulty reading the selection with a partner,	**then...** have them follow along as they listen to the Online Leveled Reader Audio.
If... students have trouble understanding the causes of cerebral palsy,	**then...** reread pp. 6, 8, and 9 and discuss the importance of getting oxygen to the brain.

For alternate Leveled Reader lesson plans that teach 🔵 **Generalize,** 🔵 **Predict,** and **Lesson Vocabulary,** see pp. LR10–LR18.

On-Level

ROUTINE

1 Build Background

DEVELOP VOCABULARY Write the word *dedication* and ask students to define it in their own words. *(When you feel dedication to something, you feel loyalty or devotion to it.)* Where or when would you expect to find dedication? *(anytime someone is committed or devoted to something or somebody)* Whom do you know who has shown dedication? Repeat this activity with the word *therapist* and other words from the Leveled Reader *Everybody Wins!* Use the Concept Vocabulary Routine on p. DI·1 as needed.

2 Read Leveled Reader *Everybody Wins!*

BEFORE READING Have students create a time line starting with the 1960s and continuing to the present. This book tells about people who have overcome physical limitations to become participants in the Special Olympics. We will learn how the Special Olympics began and how it expanded to the present. As you read, look for important dates. Record these dates, along with labels of what happened, on your time line.

DURING READING Have students follow along as you read pp. 3–9. Then let them complete the book on their own. Remind students to add facts to their time lines as they read.

AFTER READING Have students compare the facts on their time lines. Point out that knowing about overcoming physical limitations will help them as they read tomorrow's story *Stretching Ourselves.*

Advanced

ROUTINE

1 Read Leveled Reader *Feel, Think, Move*

BEFORE READING Recall the Read Aloud selection "Wilma Unlimited." Why do you think athletes and people who have physical limitations may need physical therapists? *(to help strengthen and mend damaged bones and muscles)* Today you will read about how the brain communicates with muscles and bones to enable the human body to move.

CREATIVE THINKING Have students read the Leveled Reader independently. Encourage them to think creatively. For example, ask:

- How would you explain a growth spurt to a teenager who is afraid of growing too fast?
- Imagine you are writing a job description for a therapist. What qualities are important for this line of work?

AFTER READING Have students review the meanings of the following words in the Glossary on p. 22: *cerebral hemispheres, coordination, musculoskeletal, neurons, therapists.* Then ask them to write a summary of *Feel, Think, Move* that includes the words and uses context to convey their meanings. Encourage students to meet with you and discuss the summaries they wrote.

2 Independent Extension Activity

NOW TRY THIS Assign "Now Try This" on pp. 20–21 of *Feel, Think, Move* for students to work on throughout the week.

Group Time

Audio CD AudioText

DAY **2**

① Word Study/Phonics

LESSON VOCABULARY Use p. 414b to review the meanings of *abdomen, artificial, gait, handicapped, therapist,* and *wheelchair.* Have individuals practice reading the words from word cards.

DECODING MULTISYLLABIC WORDS Write *abdomen,* saying the word as you write it. Then model how to use chunking to read longer words. I see a chunk at the beginning of the word: *ab.* I see a part in the middle: *do,* and another part: *men.* I say each chunk slowly: *ab do men.* I say the chunks fast to make a whole word: *abdomen.* Is it a real word? Yes, I know the word *abdomen.*

Use the Multisyllabic Word Routine on p. DI·1 to help students read these other words from *Stretching Ourselves: medicine, cerebral, tendons, muscles, oxygen, impatiently, especially,* and *particularly.* Make sure students understand the meanings of words such as *tendons* and *impatient.*

Use *Strategies for Word Analysis,* Lesson 17, with students who have difficulty mastering word analysis and need practice with decodable text.

② Read *Stretching Ourselves,* pp. 416–423

BEFORE READING *A New Girl in Class* explained what causes cerebral palsy and how a girl with CP learned to overcome her physical limitations. Remember what you have learned as you read *Stretching Ourselves.*

Using the Picture Walk Routine on p. DI·1, guide students through the text asking questions such as those listed below. Read the question on p. 417. Together, set a purpose for reading.

pp. 416–419 How is the girl stretching in each picture?

pp. 420–423 What are these children doing? *(looking into a machine, playing with dogs, painting, using a computer)* Do they seem interested in these activities? Do they seem handicapped?

DURING READING Follow the Guiding Comprehension Routine on pp. 418–423. Have students read along with you while tracking the print or do a choral reading. Stop every two pages to ask what has happened so far. Prompt as necessary.

- What did you learn about cerebral palsy?
- What do you learn about Nic on p. 422?

AFTER READING What have you learned in the selection so far? What do you think you will learn about tomorrow? Reread passages with students for comprehension as needed.

Monitor Progress

Word and Selection Reading

If… students have difficulty reading multisyllabic words in the selection,	**then…** have them look for and read meaningful parts in the words or have them chunk words with no recognizable parts.
If… students need practice reading words fluently,	**then…** use the Fluent Word Reading Routine on the DI tab.
If… students have difficulty reading along with the group,	**then…** have them follow along as they listen to the AudioText.

Advanced

ROUTINE

1 Extend Vocabulary

CONTEXT CLUES Choose and read a sentence or passage containing a difficult word, such as this passage from p. 3 of *Feel, Think, Move:* "Your muscles and bones make up an amazing system known as the musculoskeletal system. Working together, muscles and bones enable the body to move." What does the word *musculo-skeletal* mean? *(a system of muscles and bones that enables the body to move)* How did you determine the word's meaning? *(I used the context clues* system, muscles and bones, enable the body to move.*)* Discuss why context clues are helpful, and remind students to use the strategy as they read *Stretching Ourselves*.

2 Read *Stretching Ourselves*, pp. 416–423

BEFORE READING Today you will read a selection about people with cerebral palsy and how they work with family and therapists to overcome their physical limitations. As you read, think about what causes cerebral palsy and how it affects muscles.

Have students continue to ask questions for their Strategy Response Log (p. 416). Encourage them to write answers to their questions as they read.

CREATIVE THINKING Have students read pp. 416–423 independently. Encourage them to think critically and creatively. For example, ask:

• On p. 421, it says that Emily calms herself down when she's upset by mothering her dolls and caring for her dogs. What are some other things Emily could do to relax when she is upset or tired?

AFTER READING Have partners discuss the selection and share their Strategy Response Log entries. Encourage them to discuss how computers can be used to help students with disabilities. Have students research ways computers can help these students.

DAY **2**

Audio CD AudioText

Group Time

AudioText

DAY
4

Strategic Intervention

ROUTINE

1 Practice Retelling

REVIEW MAIN IDEAS Help students identify the main ideas in *Stretching Ourselves.* List the ideas students mention. Then ask questions to help students differentiate between essential and nonessential information.

RETELL Using the Retelling Cards, have students work with partners to retell the important ideas. Show partners how to summarize in as few words as possible. Monitor retelling and prompt students as needed. For example, ask:

Grade 5
Retelling Cards
PEARSON
Scott Foresman

- What was this selection mostly about?
- Why do you think the author wrote this selection?
- What was the author trying to tell us or teach us?

If students struggle, model a fluent retelling.

2 Read "Helpful Tools"

BEFORE READING Read the genre information on p. 434. Expository nonfiction provides information or an explanation. *Stretching Ourselves* is expository nonfiction. You find this kind of writing everywhere, including encyclopedias and magazines. It is often divided into sections with headings to make it easier to read. As we read "Helpful Tools," think about what it explains.

Read the rest of the panel on p. 434. Then have students scan the pages looking for headings and illustrations.

DURING READING Have students read along with you while tracking the print or do a choral reading of the selection. Reread the last sentence of paragraph one to make sure that students understand that Braille helps blind people read through the sense of touch—with a system of raised dots that stand for letters and numbers.

AFTER READING Have students share their reactions to the selection. Then guide them through the Reading Across Texts and Writing Across Texts activities, prompting if necessary.

- What are three inventions or devices that help people with physical limitations?
- How does each tool help these people?

Monitor Progress

Word and Selection Reading

If...	then...
If... students have difficulty reading multisyllabic words in the selection,	**then...** have them look for and read meaningful parts in the words or have them chunk words with no recognizable parts.
If... students have difficulty reading along with the group,	**then...** have them follow along as they listen to the AudioText.

Advanced

ROUTINE

1 Read "Helpful Tools"

CREATIVE THINKING Have students read pp. 434–435 independently. Encourage them to think creatively. For example, ask:

- This article mentions Braille clothing tags. What kinds of tags would be useful in the kitchen or bathroom of someone without sight?
- Imagine someone who cannot talk or someone who cannot hear. Think of one invention that would make his or her life easier.

AFTER READING Discuss Reading Across Texts. Have students do Writing Across Texts independently.

2 Extend Genre Study

RESEARCH Have students use online or print resources to find other expository nonfiction articles about new inventions. Have them make a list of inventions they find interesting.

WRITE Have students choose one of the inventions on their lists and write an article explaining the invention to a second grader. Add labels and pictures to help break up text and explain it.

Audio CD **AudioText**

DAY 5

Leveled Reader Database ONLINE

PearsonSuccessNet.com

ROUTINE

1 Reread for Fluency

MODEL Read aloud p. 15 of the Leveled Reader *A New Girl in Class* using your voice to show the emotion in the characters' speeches. Have students notice how you read the first paragraph to indicate Mr. Forgle's friendly, welcoming tone. Read the speeches of Karen and Dave in tones that show their interest and respect. Read the final paragraph to show Mr. Forgle's enthusiastic support of the students' idea. Then read p. 17 in an unemotional monotone voice. Have students tell you which model sounded better. Discuss how reading aloud with emotion can make the characters seem alive.

PRACTICE Have students reread passages from *A New Girl in Class* with a partner or individually. For optimal fluency, they should reread three or four times. As students read, monitor fluency and provide corrective feedback. Assess the fluency of students in this group using p. 435a.

2 Retell Leveled Reader *A New Girl in Class*

Model how to skim the book, retelling as you skim. Then ask students to retell the book, one incident at a time, using the pictures to help them retell. Prompt them as needed.

- What are these pages mostly about?
- What did the characters do?
- What else happened in this story?

Monitor Progress

Fluency

If... students have difficulty reading fluently,	**then...** provide additional fluency practice by pairing nonfluent readers with fluent ones.

For alternate Leveled Reader lesson plans that teach ◑**Generalize,** ◑**Predict,** and **Lesson Vocabulary,** see pp. LR10–LR18.

On-Level

DAY 5

① Reread for Fluency ◢ROUTINE

MODEL Read aloud p. 15 of the Leveled Reader *Everybody Wins!* Have students note the rhythmic patterns in Liinah's quote and the determination in your voice as you read the quote. Have them note the rise of your voice in the exclamatory sentences. Discuss how reading people's direct quotes should communicate their feelings, and illustrate further by reading aloud quotes on pp. 12, 17, and 18.

PRACTICE Have students reread passages from *Everybody Wins!* with a partner or individually. For optimal fluency, they should reread three or four times. As students read, monitor fluency and provide corrective feedback. Students in this group are assessed in Week 3.

② Retell Leveled Reader *Everybody Wins!*

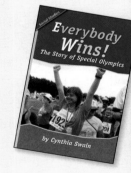

Have students use section heads and illustrations as a guide to summarize the important facts they learned from each section of the book. Prompt as needed.

- What did you learn from reading this selection?
- Why do you think the author wrote this selection?
- What was the author trying to teach us?

Advanced

DAY 5

① Reread for Fluency ◢ROUTINE

PRACTICE Have students reread passages from the Leveled Reader *Feel, Think, Move* with a partner or individually. As students read, monitor fluency and provide corrective feedback. If students read fluently on the first reading, they do not need to reread three to four times. Students in this group were assessed in Week 1.

② Revisit Leveled Reader *Feel, Think, Move*

RETELL Have students retell the Leveled Reader *Feel, Think, Move.*

NOW TRY THIS Have students complete their projects. You may wish to review their sources and see whether they need any additional diagrams, information, or resources. Have them present their projects.

Group Time

DAY 1

Strategic Intervention

ROUTINE

1 Build Background

REINFORCE CONCEPTS Display the Animal Adaptations Concept Web. This week's concept is *animal adaptations.* Animals, people—even plants—have to adapt, or change, in order to survive in their environments. Discuss the meaning of each word on the web, using the definitions on p. 436l and the Concept Vocabulary Routine on p. DI·1.

CONNECT TO READING This week you will read about many different kinds of animals that have adapted to their environments in order to survive. For instance, you already learned that snakes have learned to "hear" by sensing vibrations through their jawbones. Can you think of other ways animals have adapted in order to survive? *(Answers will vary.)*

2 Read Leveled Reader *Surviving the Weather*

BEFORE READING Using the Picture Walk Routine on p. DI·1, guide students through the text, focusing on key concepts and vocabulary. Ask questions such as:

pp. 4–5 This selection describes how animals have adapted to many different environments. Which of these photographs shows an animal using a special physical trait in order to survive? *(the giraffe)*

pp. 8–9 The images on pp. 8–9 show a harsh habitat, the Arctic tundra. The Arctic tundra has a layer of permafrost. *Permafrost* is ground that stays frozen all year. How do these animals look as if they have adapted to permafrost and very cold weather?

DURING READING Read pp. 4–5 aloud, while students track the print. Do a choral reading of pp. 6–14. If students are capable, have them read and discuss the remainder of the book with a partner. Ask: In what ways have animals adapted to survive in the Arctic tundra? (Possible responses: *The polar bear and musk ox have thick coats. The brown bear hibernates.*) How have animals adapted to survive in savannas? (Possible response: *Elephants get water from the baobab tree, and lions live in prides.*) How have animals adapted to survive in rain forests? *(Animals such as monkeys live in trees to protect themselves from animals that would eat them.)*

AFTER READING Have pairs of students discuss the different ways animals have adapted in order to survive. We read *Surviving the Weather* to learn about how animals adapt to their environments to survive. Understanding animal adaptation will help us as we read *Exploding Ants.*

Monitor Progress

Selection Reading and Comprehension

If... students have difficulty reading the selection with a partner,	then... have them follow along as they listen to the Online Leveled Reader Audio.
If... students have trouble understanding how animals specialize,	then... reread p. 16 and discuss how elephants are specialists in getting water from baobab trees.

For alternate Leveled Reader lesson plans that teach **Graphic Sources,** **Monitor and Fix Up,** and **Lesson Vocabulary,** see pp. LR19–LR27.

On-Level

ROUTINE

DAY 1

1 Build Background

DEVELOP VOCABULARY Write the word *reptiles* and ask students to define the word and list all the reptiles they can think of. *(cold-blooded animals with backbone and lungs, usually covered with horny plates or scales; alligators, caimans, crocodiles, lizards, snakes, turtles)* Then have students define and discuss *flamingo* and other bird names from the Leveled Reader *Changing to Survive.* Use the Concept Vocabulary Routine on p. DI•1 as needed.

2 Read Leveled Reader *Changing to Survive*

BEFORE READING Have students create a KWL chart with the topic head *Birds.* Have them fill out the columns for What I **K**now and What I **W**ant to Know. This book tells about different types of birds. As you read, look for facts you can add to the third column of your chart.

DURING READING Have students follow along as you read pp. 3–9. Then let them complete the book on their own. Remind students to add facts to the What I **L**earned column as they read.

AFTER READING Have students compare information from columns 2 and 3 of their KWL charts. Point out that understanding how different animals adapt to survive will help them as they read tomorrow's selection, *Exploding Ants.*

Advanced

ROUTINE

DAY 1

1 Read Leveled Reader *A Home for Humans in Outer Space*

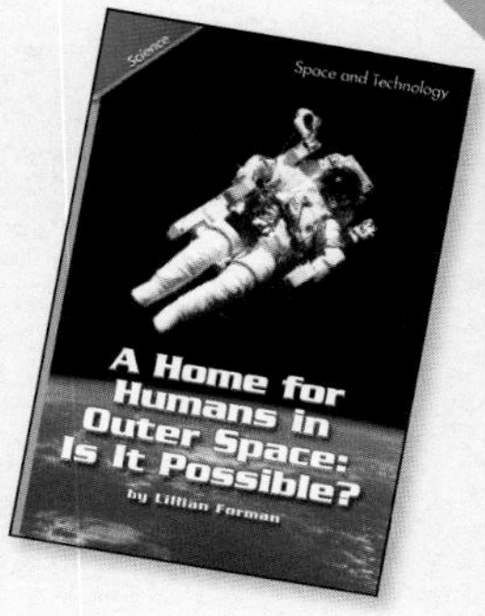

BEFORE READING Recall the Read Aloud "Snake Scientist." How can you tell that snakes adapted to their surroundings better than their cousins, the dinosaurs? *(Snakes have survived, whereas dinosaurs are extinct.)* Today you will read a selection that describes how humans may have to adapt themselves right off the planet in order to survive.

PROBLEM SOLVING Have students read the Leveled Reader independently. Encourage them to think analytically. For example, ask:

- What are some other ways scientists could try to prevent an asteroid from crashing into Earth?
- Do you think space colonization will be possible in your lifetime? Why or why not?

AFTER READING Have students review the selection to find words that relate to the idea of adaptation. They can use a web or other graphic organizer to categorize the words and show how they are related. Students can put a star next to the words they like best and explain why the words appeal to them. Have students meet as a group or with you to discuss the selection and the word web.

2 Independent Extension Activity

NOW TRY THIS Assign "Now Try This" on pp. 18–19 of *A Home for Humans in Outer Space* for students to work on throughout the week.

Exploding Ants
Group Time

Audio CD AudioText

Monitor Progress

Word and Selection Reading

If... students have difficulty reading multisyllabic words in the selection,	**then...** have them look for and read meaningful parts in the words or have them chunk words with no recognizable parts.
If... students need practice reading words fluently,	**then...** use the Fluent Word Reading Routine on the DI tab.
If... students have difficulty reading along with the group,	**then...** have them follow along as they listen to the AudioText.

Strategic Intervention

ROUTINE

1 Word Study/Phonics

LESSON VOCABULARY Use p. 438b to review the meanings of *critical, enables, mucus, scarce, specialize,* and *sterile.* Have individuals practice reading the words from word cards.

DECODING MULTISYLLABIC WORDS Write *similarly,* saying the word as you write it. Then model how to use meaningful parts to read longer words. This is a four-syllable word formed from the base word *similar* and the suffix *-ly.* First I cover the suffix and sound out the base word: *sim-ə-lər, similar,* which means "alike" or "much the same." I already know that the suffix *-ly* means "in a _____ way." So *similarly* must mean "in an alike way" or "in much the same way."

Use the Multisyllabic Word Routine on p. DI·1 to help students read these other words from *Exploding Ants: aborigines, nectar, nutrients, nutritious, opponents, predators, predigested,* and *regurgitated.* Be sure students understand words such as *nutrients* and *predators.*

Use *Strategies for Word Analysis,* Lesson 18, with students who have difficulty mastering word analysis and need practice with decodable text.

2 Read *Exploding Ants,* pp. 440–447

BEFORE READING *Surviving the Weather* described how animals adapt to a wide range of habitats. The selection you are going to read today also shows how animals adapt—in rather unusual ways.

Using the Picture Walk Routine on p. DI·1, guide students through the text, asking questions such as those listed below. Read the question on p. 441. Together, set a purpose for reading.

pp. 444–445 Look at the images on these two pages. What do you think this part of the selection will be about? *(ants that live in a very dry climate and how they adapt to survive)*

pp. 446–447 What is happening in this drawing? *(Ants and a scorpion seem to be fighting each other.)* Which do you think would be the winner?

DURING READING Follow the Guiding Comprehension routine on pp. 442–447. Have students read along with you while tracking the print, or do a choral reading. Stop every two pages to ask what has happened so far. Prompt as necessary.

• What did you learn about honey ants?
• What did you learn that you didn't already know about how animals specialize in order to survive?

AFTER READING What have you learned so far? What do you think you will learn about tomorrow? Reread passages as needed.

Advanced

ROUTINE

1 Extend Vocabulary

CONTEXT CLUES Choose and read a sentence or passage containing a difficult word, such as this passage from p. 10 of *A Home for Humans in Outer Space:* "One of the most critical issues scientists are investigating is how people can survive for long periods in zero gravity." In this context, what does the word *critical* mean? *(of a crisis; important)* How did you determine the word's meaning? (Possible response: *The selection is about making homes for people in outer space. The heading for this section is "Space and the Human Body." Therefore, investigating how people can survive in zero gravity sounds as if it would be a very important issue.)* Discuss why context clues are helpful, and remind students to use the strategy as they read *Exploding Ants.*

2 Read *Exploding Ants,* pp. 440–447

BEFORE READING Recall the Read Aloud selection "Snake Scientist" and how the author marvels at how fascinating snakes are in the ways they have adapted. Today you will read a selection that describes some other unusual ways animals have adapted in order to survive.

Have students write some animal adaptation facts for their Strategy Response Logs (p. 440).

CRITICAL THINKING Have students read pp. 442–447 independently. Have them think critically. For example, ask:

- How would your understanding have been different if there were no art or photographs on these pages?

AFTER READING Have partners discuss the selection, add information about animal adaptation to their Strategy Response Logs, and share their Strategy Response Log entries. Then have students draw pictures illustrating one or more of their adaptation facts.

DAY 2

Audio CD — AudioText

Exploding Ants
Group Time

ROUTINE

Audio CD AudioText

Monitor Progress

Word and Selection Reading

If... students have difficulty reading multisyllabic words in the selection,	**then...** have them look for and read meaningful parts in the words or have them chunk words with no recognizable parts.
If... students have difficulty reading along with the group,	**then...** have them follow along as they listen to the AudioText.

1 Reinforce Comprehension

SKILL GRAPHIC SOURCES Have students explain what graphic sources are *(charts, diagrams, pictures and photographs with captions, graphs, and maps, among other things, that can help strengthen students' understanding of what they read)*. If necessary, review the meaning and provide a model. Graphic sources are ways of showing information visually. The drawings and photographs in *Exploding Ants* are all examples of graphic sources. They help increase your understanding of what you read in the selection.

If students have trouble explaining how a graphic source clarifies or adds to the text, have them identify each graphic source on pp. 442–443. Then, working in pairs, have students tell what each picture shows and explain how it relates to the text. Help students as needed.

2 Read *Exploding Ants*, pp. 448–451

BEFORE READING Have students retell what they have learned in the selection so far. Then ask: What could you do if you didn't understand how the replete ants provide food for the honey ant colony? Reread the second paragraph on p. 445 and model the monitor and fix-up strategy. I read on page 445 that the *repletes regurgitate big drops of golden honey*. I'm not sure what *regurgitate* means, but I remember seeing a similar word earlier in the selection, so I'm going to reread a few paragraphs to see if I can figure it out. Read the third paragraph on p. 444. Here it says that the replete *receives regurgitated, or spit up, food*, so it sounds as if the replete "spits up" food to feed the other ants. The author is right: that *is* gross. **STRATEGY Monitor and Fix Up**

DURING READING Follow the Guiding Comprehension routine on pp. 448–451. Have students read along with you while tracking the print, or do a choral reading. Stop every two pages to ask what has happened so far. Prompt as necessary.

- What did you learn about owls' eating habits that you didn't already know?
- What was the last paragraph on page 451 about?

AFTER READING What did reading *Exploding Ants* help you learn about how animals have to adapt in order to survive? Reread passages with students for comprehension as needed. Tell them that tomorrow they will read "The Creature from the Adapting Lagoon," a science experiment that will further help them understand the concept of how animals adapt to survive.

ROUTINE

1 Extend Comprehension

SKILL GRAPHIC SOURCES Have students choose at least three images from *Exploding Ants* and write captions for them. They should glean information from the selection, as well as from print or online resources, to provide information that will enhance and strengthen readers' understanding of the selection.

STRATEGY MONITOR AND FIX UP Read or have a volunteer read the second paragraph on p. 446. Ask:

- What could you do if you didn't understand some of the words in this paragraph?
- What could you do if some of the information is confusing?

2 Read *Exploding Ants*, pp. 448–451

BEFORE READING Have students recall what they have learned from the selection so far. Remind them to use graphic sources and monitor and fix-up strategies as they read the rest of the selection.

CREATIVE THINKING Have students read pp. 448–451 independently. Have them think creatively. For example, ask:

- What would you do if you were a scientist studying the animals on these pages?

AFTER READING Have students complete the Strategy Response Log activity on p. 450. Then have students use online or print resources to find information about some careers available in a zoo or another facility or in conservation that focuses on working with animals. Tell students to write down a few details about each career on the list. Students can note which careers, if any, appeal to them and why.

DAY 3

Audio CD AudioText

Group Time

ONLINE

PearsonSuccessNet.com

ROUTINE

1 Reread for Fluency

MODEL Read aloud pp. 4–5 of the Leveled Reader *Surviving the Weather*, emphasizing your tempo and rate. Read the selection slowly and carefully, paying special attention to scientific words such as *specialize* and *habitats*. Then read pp. 6–7 in a fast-paced, clipped rate. Have students tell you which model sounded better. Discuss how reading at a tempo appropriate to the material will help the listener to understand what is being read more easily. Point out that the reader is also less likely to make mistakes.

PRACTICE Have students reread passages from *Surviving the Weather* with a partner or individually. For optimal fluency, they should reread three or four times. As students read, monitor fluency and provide corrective feedback. Students in this group are assessed in Weeks 2 and 4.

2 Retell Leveled Reader *Surviving the Weather*

Model how to skim the book, retelling as you skim. Then ask students to retell the book, one chapter at a time. Prompt them as needed.

- What is this chapter mostly about?
- What did you learn from reading this chapter?

Monitor Progress

Fluency

If... students have difficulty reading fluently,	**then...** provide additional fluency practice by pairing nonfluent readers with fluent ones.

For alternate Leveled Reader lesson plans that teach
 Graphic Sources, **Monitor and Fix Up,**
and **Lesson Vocabulary,** see pp. LR19–LR27.

On-Level

1 Reread for Fluency ROUTINE

MODEL Read aloud pp. 4–5 of the Leveled Reader *Changing to Survive*, emphasizing your tempo and rate. Read the selection slowly and carefully, paying special attention to scientific words such as *Archaeopteryx*. Discuss how reading at a tempo appropriate to the material will help the listener to understand what is being read more easily. Point out that the reader is also less likely to make mistakes.

PRACTICE Have students reread passages from *Changing to Survive* with a partner or individually. For optimal fluency, they should reread three or four times. As students read, monitor fluency and provide corrective feedback. Assess the fluency of students in this group using p. 457a.

2 Retell Leveled Reader *Changing to Survive*

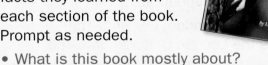

Have students use subheads and photographs as a guide to summarize the important facts they learned from each section of the book. Prompt as needed.

- What is this book mostly about?
- What did you learn from reading this book?

Advanced

1 Reread for Fluency ROUTINE

PRACTICE Have students reread passages from the Leveled Reader *A Home for Humans in Outer Space* with a partner or individually. As students read, monitor fluency and provide corrective feedback. If students read fluently on the first reading, they do not need to reread three to four times. Students in this group were assessed on Week 1.

2 Revisit Leveled Reader *A Home for Humans in Outer Space*

NOW TRY THIS Have students complete their projects. You may wish to review their ideas and drawings to see whether they need any additional suggestions. Have them present their projects.

Group Time

Strategic Intervention

DAY 2

Audio CD AudioText

1 Word Study/Phonics

LESSON VOCABULARY Use p. 460b to review the meanings of *cavities, combination, demonstrates, episode, profile,* and *strict.* Have individuals practice reading the words from word cards.

DECODING MULTISYLLABIC WORDS Write *guaranteed,* saying the word as you write it. Then model how to use meaningful parts to read longer words. First I ask myself if I see any parts I know. If I see a part I know, like *-ed,* I look at the base word. The base word is long, so I will read the chunks. I see *-an* and *-tee.* The *u* in *guar-* is confusing, but I try reading the chunks several ways and realize the *u* is silent. I add the *-ed* and say the chunks fast to read the whole word: *guar an teed.* I read the word again faster: *guaranteed.* It means "promised or made certain."

Use the multisyllabic word routine on p. DI·1 to help students read these words from *The Stormi Giovanni Club: professors, philosophers, distressed, digressed, gestures, examining, promises, scintillating,* and *designing.* Be sure students understand the meanings of words such as *distressed, digressed,* and *scintillating.*

Use *Strategies for Word Analysis,* Lesson 19, with students who have difficulty mastering word analysis and need practice with decodable text.

2 Read *The Stormi Giovanni Club,* pp. 462–469

BEFORE READING *Moving* explained the pluses and minuses of moving to new places and the differences and similarities between places. Think about this as you read the play *The Stormi Giovanni Club.*

Using the Picture Walk Routine on p. DI·1, guide students through the text asking questions such as those listed below. Read the question on p. 463. Together, set a purpose for reading.

pp. 464–465 What do these illustrations show? How do you know?

pp. 466–468 What kinds of situations do you see? How are these pictures related?

DURING READING Follow the Guiding Comprehension routine on pp. 464–469. Have students read along with you while tracking the print or do a choral reading. Stop every two pages to ask what has happened so far. Prompt as necessary.

• Why does Stormi decide to form the Stormi Giovanni Club?
• How does Stormi feel about making new friends? How do you know?

AFTER READING What has happened in the play so far? What do you think will happen next? Reread passages as needed.

Monitor Progress

Word and Play Reading

If... students have difficulty reading multisyllabic words in the selection,	**then...** have them look for and read meaningful parts in the words or have them chunk words with no recognizable parts.
If... students need practice reading words fluently,	**then...** use the Fluent Word Reading Routine on the DI tab.
If... students have difficulty reading along with the group,	**then...** have them follow along as they listen to the AudioText.

Advanced

ROUTINE

1 Extend Vocabulary

CONTEXT CLUES Choose and read a sentence or passage containing a difficult word, such as this sentence from p. 23 of *Nathaniel Comes to Town*: "My dad's voice reverberates from inside the oven, where he's scraping at something from Julie's cooking mishap." What does the word *reverberates* mean? *(echoes)* How did you determine the word's meaning? *(I used the context clues* voice, inside, *and* oven *and imagined sound bouncing around inside the oven.)* Discuss why context clues are helpful, and remind students to use the strategy as they read the *The Stormi Giovanni Club*.

2 Read *The Stormi Giovanni Club*, pp. 462–469

BEFORE READING Today you will read a play called *The Stormi Giovanni Club*. It tells the experience of a girl who has to adapt to a new city and school and make new friends. As you read, think about other ways people adapt to new cities or schools that you have read about.

Have students write predictions in their Strategy Response Log (p. 462). Encourage students to revise predictions as they read.

PROBLEM SOLVING Have students read pp. 464–469 independently. Encourage them to use problem-solving skills and strategies. For example, ask:

- When have you had to adapt to a new place? How did you feel about it?
- What advice can you give to others who are experiencing the same situation?

AFTER READING Have partners discuss the selection and share their Strategy Response Log predictions and how accurate they were. Then have students write about a time when they had to adapt to a new place, such as a new town or new school or new classroom, perhaps even an entirely different country. Tell students to include what it was like to leave old friends and make new ones and how they had to adjust in order to fit in. Have students meet with you to discuss the selection and their writings.

DAY 2

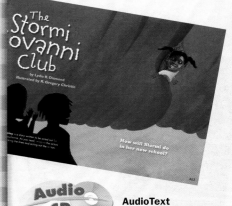

AudioText

Group Time

Strategic Intervention

DAY 4

Audio CD AudioText

1 Practice Retelling

REVIEW STORY ELEMENTS Have students identify the main characters and the setting of *The Stormi Giovanni Club*. Then guide them in using the Retelling Cards to list the play's events in sequence. Prompt students to include important details.

RETELL Using the Retelling Cards, have students work in pairs to retell *The Stormi Giovanni Club*. Monitor retelling and prompt students as needed. For example, ask:

- What is the problem in the play?
- How was the problem solved?
- Has anything like this happened to you?

2 Read "Think Dress Codes Are a Drag?"

BEFORE READING Read the genre information on p. 480. Discuss the features of newspaper articles such as datelines, headlines, bylines, lead paragraphs, and bodies. Help with students' understanding by identifying the features of newspaper articles using a sample article from a newspaper that contains all of these features. Emphasize to students the purposes of newspaper articles. As we read "Think Dress Codes Are a Drag?" think about the features of the article as well as what information or issue it presents.

Read the rest of the panel on p. 480. Then have students scan the pages, identifying the features of the newspaper article and the pictures used to support the ideas.

DURING READING Have students read along with you while tracking the print or do a choral reading of the selection. Stop to discuss difficult vocabulary. Also, discuss words related to clothing styles or types of clothing mentioned in the selection.

AFTER READING Have students share their reactions to the selection. Then guide them through the Reading Across Texts and Writing Across Texts activities, prompting if necessary.

- What problems did the students in *The Stormi Giovanni Club* and the newspaper article have?
- How did the students handle their problems?
- How would you have handled these problems?

Monitor Progress

Word and Selection Reading

If... students have difficulty reading multisyllabic words in the selection,	**then...** have them look for and read meaningful parts in the words or have them chunk words with no recognizable parts.
If... students have difficulty reading along with the group,	**then...** have them follow along as they listen to the AudioText.

For alternate Leveled Reader lesson plans that teach **Draw Conclusions,** **Visualize,** and **Lesson Vocabulary,** see pp. LR37–LR45.

On-Level

DAY 1

1 Build Background

DEVELOP VOCABULARY Write the word *competitive* and ask students to define it in their own words. *(trying to win something)* When might you be competitive? *(during a race, playing basketball or some other game)* Repeat this activity with the word *accuracy* and other words from the Leveled Reader *Strange Sports with Weird Gear.* Use the Concept Vocabulary Routine on p. DI·1 as needed.

2 Read Leveled Reader *Strange Sports with Weird Gear*

BEFORE READING Have students create three-column charts with the labels Sport, Gear, and Physical Traits. This book tells about sports and what it takes to play them. As you read, look for facts about each sport, the gear needed to play it, and the physical traits players should have. Record them in your three-column chart.

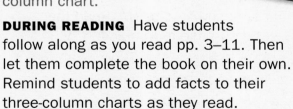

DURING READING Have students follow along as you read pp. 3–11. Then let them complete the book on their own. Remind students to add facts to their three-column charts as they read.

AFTER READING Have students compare the facts on their three-column charts. Point out that facts about what it takes to be an athlete will help them as they read tomorrow's story "The Gymnast."

Advanced

DAY 1

1 Read Leveled Reader *What Makes Great Athletes?*

BEFORE READING Recall the Read Aloud "The Winning Stroke." What did Jerry do to improve his swimming? *(He practiced his strokes until he got them right.)* Today you will read about what it takes to be a great athlete.

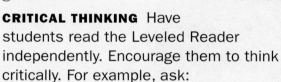

CRITICAL THINKING Have students read the Leveled Reader independently. Encourage them to think critically. For example, ask:

- How can athletes encourage us to make changes in ourselves?
- How can people prepare to compete in challenging sports?

AFTER READING Have students review the selection to find words that describe great athletes. Then ask them to use these words to write sentences that describe athletes. Have students meet with you or as a group and discuss the selection and the sentences they wrote.

2 Independent Extension Activity

NOW TRY THIS Assign "Now Try This" on pp. 18–19 of *What Makes Great Athletes?* for students to work on throughout the week.

Group Time

AudioText

ROUTINE

1 Word Study/Phonics

LESSON VOCABULARY Use p. 486b to review the meanings of *bluish, cartwheels, gymnastics, hesitation, limelight, skidded, somersault, throbbing,* and *wincing.* Have individuals practice reading the words from word cards.

DECODING MULTISYLLABIC WORDS Write *solitary,* saying the word as you write it. Then model how to use chunking to read longer words. *I see a chunk at the beginning of the word, sol. I see a chunk in the middle, i, and another chunk, tar. I see a chunk at the end, y. I say each chunk slowly, sol i tar y. I say the chunks fast to make a whole word: solitary. Is it a real word? Yes, I know the word solitary.*

Use the Multisyllabic Word Routine on p. DI·1 to help students read these other words from "The Gymnast": *aluminum, instructed, dully, appreciative, disdain,* and *nutrients.* Be sure students understand the meanings of words such as *disdain* and *nutrients.*

Use *Strategies for Word Analysis,* Lesson 20, with students who have difficulty mastering word analysis and need practice with decodable text.

2 Read "The Gymnast," pp. 488–493

BEFORE READING *Let the Games Begin* explained how athletes improved themselves to compete in the Olympics. Think about these athletes as you read "The Gymnast."

Using the Picture Walk Routine on p. DI·1, guide students through the text asking questions such as those listed below. Read the question on p. 488. Together, set a purpose for reading.

pp. 488–489 What is this boy doing? Why do you think he's doing this? *(a cartwheel; he wants to improve his gymnastics)*

pp. 490–493 What do you see on these pages? *(someone's legs, someone doing a cartwheel)* Why do you think there are pictures of cartwheels? *(The boy needs more practice to do cartwheels correctly.)*

DURING READING Follow the Guiding Comprehension routine on pp. 490–493. Have students read along with you while tracking the print or do a choral reading. Stop every two pages to ask what has happened so far. Prompt as necessary.

- What is Gary's problem?
- Who is Isaac? What does Gary think of Isaac?

AFTER READING What has happened in the selection so far? What do you think will happen next? Reread passages with students for comprehension as needed.

Monitor Progress

Word and Selection Reading

If... students have difficulty reading multisyllabic words in the selection,	then... have them look for and read meaningful parts in the words or have them chunk words with no recognizable parts.
If... students need practice reading words fluently,	then... use the Fluent Word Reading Routine on the DI tab.
If... students have difficulty reading along with the group,	then... have them follow along as they listen to the AudioText.

Advanced

ROUTINE

1 Extend Vocabulary

WORD STRUCTURE Read this sentence from p. 3 of *What Makes Great Athletes?*: "We can smile with admiration at the height, grace, and form of a ballplayer's jump as he makes a catch." What does the word admiration mean? *(a feeling of wonder, pleasure, and approval)* How could you use word structure to determine the word's meaning? *(I recognize the base word admire, even though the final e is dropped. I know what admire means, and I know the suffix -tion means the state of being, so I determined the meaning.)* Discuss why suffixes are helpful, and remind students to use the strategy as they read "The Gymnast."

2 Read "The Gymnast," pp. 488–493

BEFORE READING Today you will read about a boy who wants to become a great athlete. As you read, think about what you have read about great athletes.

Have students create a T-chart for their Strategy Response Log (p. 488). Students should add to it as they read.

CRITICAL THINKING Have students read pp. 490–493 independently. Encourage them to think critically and creatively. For example, ask:

• Which sport do you think is the most challenging? How can athletes prepare for it?

AFTER READING Have partners discuss the selection and share their Strategy Response Log entries and the images they have visualized. Have students write sentences in the right column of their charts explaining their images. Then have students choose the one image that best describes the selection so far.

AudioText

The Gymnast
Group Time

DAY
3

Audio CD AudioText

ROUTINE

1 Reinforce Comprehension

◉ SKILL DRAW CONCLUSIONS Have students explain what a conclusion is *(a sensible decision you make after you think about facts or details that you read)*. If necessary, review the meaning and provide a model.

Drawing a conclusion means making a sensible decision after you have the facts or details about something. For example, if the sky suddenly turned dark, that probably means it's going to rain. I can draw this conclusion based on my prior knowledge of this happening.

Ask students to draw conclusions using the following examples.

I did well on my last math test because I studied for it. I have another test tomorrow. *(I should study for tomorrow's test.)*

Ralph always has everything he needs when it's time to start class. He has all of his assignments completed on time. *(Ralph is a very organized student.)*

2 Read "The Gymnast," pp. 494–497

BEFORE READING Have students retell what happened in the selection so far. Ask: What seems to interest Gary the most about gymnastics? Reread the last paragraph on p. 493 and model how to draw a conclusion. As I read I try to picture what Gary looks like. He is wearing his cousin's shoes and has tape wrapped around his wrists. Gary must really like the gymnastics gear. Remind students to visualize as they read the rest of "The Gymnast." **◉ STRATEGY Visualize**

DURING READING Follow the Guiding Comprehension routine on pp. 494–497. Have students read along with you while tracking the print or do a choral reading. Stop every two pages to ask what has happened so far. Prompt as necessary.

- What does Gary do the next day to improve his gymnastics?
- How does Gary feel about gymnastics at the end of the selection?

AFTER READING How does Gary try to improve himself? Reread with students for comprehension as needed. Tell them that tomorrow they will read "All About Gymnastics," a selection about using online reference sources to find information about doing gymnastics.

Monitor Progress

Word and Selection Reading

If... students have difficulty reading multisyllabic words in the selection,	**then...** have them look for and read meaningful parts in the words or have them chunk words with no recognizable parts.
If... students have difficulty reading along with the group,	**then...** have them follow along as they listen to the AudioText.

Advanced

DAY 3

1 Extend Comprehension

⏺ **SKILL DRAW CONCLUSIONS** Have students discuss Gary and Isaac. Have students draw conclusions about the motives and characteristics behind the cousins' actions.

⏺ **STRATEGY VISUALIZE** Have a volunteer reread p. 493 while others close their eyes. Ask students which words or phrases help them visualize Gary and Isaac. Ask questions such as:

• What does Gary look like compared to his cousin?
• Why does Gary want to try on the gymnastic gear?

2 Read "The Gymnast," pp. 494–497

BEFORE READING Have students recall what has happened in the selection so far. Remind them to draw conclusions and to visualize as they read the remainder of the selection.

CRITICAL THINKING Have students read pp. 494–497 independently. Encourage them to think critically. For example, ask:

• Why is Gary pushing himself so hard?

AFTER READING Have students complete the Strategy Response Log activity (p. 496). Then have them list other sports and visualize the movements or plays associated with those sports. Tell students to write descriptive sentences about the sports. Have students read their sentences aloud to the group while the others close their eyes and visualize.

Audio CD **AudioText**

Group Time

DAY 4

ROUTINE

① Practice Retelling

REVIEW MAIN IDEAS Help students identify the main ideas in "The Gymnast." List the main events in this selection from the autobiography. Then ask questions to help students differentiate between essential and nonessential information.

RETELL Using the Retelling Cards, have students work with partners to retell the important ideas from "The Gymnast." Monitor retelling and prompt students as needed. For example, ask:

- What was the selection mostly about?
- Why do you think the author wrote this selection?

If students struggle, model a fluent retelling.

② Read "All About Gymnastics"

BEFORE READING Read the genre information on p. 500. Recall the Read Aloud "The Winning Stroke," rereading portions of the text as needed. We have read several selections about how athletes improve themselves for their sports. What did Jerry do to improve his swimming in "The Winning Stroke"? *(He practiced his swimming strokes until he got them right.)* As we read "All About Gymnastics," think about what other information about gymnastics you could find by using online reference sources.

Read the rest of the panel on p. 500. Then have students scan the pages looking for images of online resources.

DURING READING Have students read along with you while tracking the print or do a choral reading of the selection. Stop to discuss the search windows and the search results. Make sure students understand the difference between the window and the results.

AFTER READING Have students share their reactions to the selection. Then guide them through the Reading Across Texts and Writing Across Texts activities, prompting if necessary.

- What gymnastic moves was Gary practicing?
- What would Gary look like while doing these moves?
- Which gymnastic event would he most likely be practicing for?

Audio CD **AudioText**

Monitor Progress

Word and Selection Reading

If... students have difficulty reading multisyllabic words in the selection,	**then...** have them look for and read meaningful parts in the words or have them chunk words with no recognizable parts.
If... students have difficulty reading along with the group,	**then...** have them follow along as they listen to the AudioText.

ROUTINE

1 Read "All About Gymnastics"

CRITICAL THINKING Have students read pp. 500–503 independently. Encourage them to think critically. For example, ask:

- Are there any other possible online reference sources not listed here?
- What other key words might you use to find information about gymnastics?

AFTER READING Discuss the selection and Reading Across Texts with students. Have students do Writing Across Texts independently.

2 Extend Genre Study

RESEARCH Have students locate print sources for information about gymnastics. Have them compare the information found in these sources to the information that would be found using online sources. Discuss which sources provide the best or most reliable information.

WRITING Have students write online dictionary entries for plays or moves from other sports. Have them list key words that would link online search engines to their entries.

DAY 4

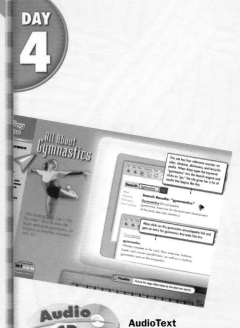

AudioText

The Gymnast

Group Time

DAY 5

Let the Games Begin: History of the Olympics

Leveled Reader Database

ONLINE

PearsonSuccessNet.com

ROUTINE

1 Reread for Fluency

MODEL Read aloud pp. 3–4 of the Leveled Reader *Let the Games Begin,* emphasizing how you use punctuation clues. Have students note the changes in your intonation for question marks and exclamation marks. Also point out how you pause after commas and periods. Then reread pp. 3–4 in a monotone voice. Do not pause for commas or stop for periods. Have students tell you which model made more sense. Discuss how using punctuation clues helps you understand what you are reading.

PRACTICE Have students reread passages from *Let the Games Begin* with a partner or individually. For optimal fluency, they should reread three or four times. As students read, monitor fluency and provide corrective feedback. Assess any students you have not yet checked during this unit.

2 Retell Leveled Reader *Let the Games Begin*

Model how to use heads and photographs to retell. Then ask students to retell the book, one section at a time. Prompt them as needed.

- What are these pages mostly about?
- What did you learn from reading these pages?

Monitor Progress

Fluency

If... students have difficulty reading fluently,	**then...** provide additional fluency practice by pairing nonfluent readers with fluent ones.

For alternate Leveled Reader lesson plans that teach 🔵 **Draw Conclusions,** 🔵 **Visualize,** and **Lesson Vocabulary,** see pp. LR37–LR45.

On-Level

1 Reread for Fluency — ROUTINE

MODEL Read aloud p. 3 of the Leveled Reader *Strange Sports with Weird Gear,* emphasizing how you use punctuation clues. Have students note the rise of your voice for questions and how you pause a little longer for the dash. Discuss how changing your intonation helps listeners understand better what you are reading.

PRACTICE Have students reread passages from *Strange Sports with Weird Gear* with a partner or individually. For optimal fluency, they should reread three or four times. As students read, monitor fluency and provide corrective feedback. Assess any students you have not yet checked during this unit.

2 Retell Leveled Reader *Strange Sports with Weird Gear*

Have students use heads and photographs as a guide to summarize the important facts they learned from each section of the book. Prompt as needed.

- What is this book mostly about?
- What did you learn from reading this book?
- Why do you think the author wrote this book?

Advanced

1 Reread for Fluency — ROUTINE

PRACTICE Have students reread passages from the Leveled Reader *What Makes Great Athletes?* with a partner or individually. As students read, monitor fluency and provide corrective feedback. If students read fluently on the first reading, they do not need to reread three or four times. Assess any students you have not yet checked during this unit.

2 Revisit Leveled Reader *What Makes Great Athletes?*

RETELL Have students retell the Leveled Reader *What Makes Great Athletes?*

NOW TRY THIS Have students complete their projects. You may wish to review their writing and see whether they need any additional ideas. Have them present their projects.

Draw Conclusions

When students move beyond the literal meaning of a text to draw conclusions, they get more ideas from what they read and understand better the points an author is trying to make. Use the following routine to guide students in drawing conclusions.

1 DISCUSS DRAWING CONCLUSIONS

Tell students a conclusion is a sensible decision they reach based on details or facts in a story or an article. Explain when they draw conclusions, they think about information in the text and what they already know.

2 MODEL DRAWING A CONCLUSION

Model using your own experiences to draw a conclusion.

 Think Aloud

MODEL The smell of peanuts and cotton candy filled the air. I heard clapping, I even heard loud bellows that sounded like elephants. I knew a circus was going on.

Discuss how you combined what you already knew with details (smell of peanuts and cotton candy, clapping, loud bellows) to draw a conclusion.

3 ASK QUESTIONS

Read aloud a passage and ask questions that foster drawing conclusions. For example: *What kind of person is the main character? How can you tell? Why do you think the character acts this way?*

4 USE A GRAPHIC ORGANIZER

Have partners read both fiction and nonfiction passages. Students can ask each other questions that lead to drawing conclusions. Suggest that they use webs or charts to show the facts or details that support their conclusions.

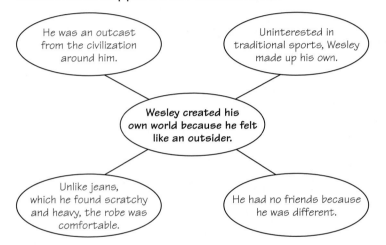

He was an outcast from the civilization around him.

Uninterested in traditional sports, Wesley made up his own.

Wesley created his own world because he felt like an outsider.

Unlike jeans, which he found scratchy and heavy, the robe was comfortable.

He had no friends because he was different.

▲ **Graphic Organizer** 15

Research on Drawing Conclusions

FOCUS ON RESEARCH

"Inference is a mosaic, a dazzling constellation of thinking processes, but the tiles available to form each mosaic are limited, circumscribed. There must be a fusion of words on a page—and constraints of meaning they impose—and the experience and knowledge of the reader."

Ellin Oliver Keene and Susan Zimmerman,
Mosaic of Thought

Keen, Ellin Oliver, and Susan Zimmermann. *Mosaic of Thought: Teaching Comprehension in a Reader's Workshop.* Heinemann, 1997, p. 154; 1992, p. 238.

Generalize

Recognizing generalizations helps students judge the validity of an argument. Making their own generalizations helps students understand and summarize texts. Use this routine to teach generalizing.

1 DEFINE GENERALIZATION

Explain that a *generalization* is a broad statement or rule that applies to many examples. A *valid generalization* is well supported by facts and logic. A *faulty* one is not well supported.

2 DISCUSS CLUE WORDS

Students should look for clue words that signal generalizations as they read. List words on the board:

all	none
most	few
always	never
generally	in general

3 MODEL GENERALIZING

Explain that when readers generalize, they think about a number of examples and decide what they have in common. After reading a passage containing several facts, model how to generalize.

4 SCAFFOLD GENERALIZING

Before students write their own generalizations, have them choose from several the one most valid for a paragraph. You may also ask them to complete stems, such as: *The climate in the Arctic is generally _____ .*

5 PRACTICE GENERALIZING

Have students record a generalization and examples in a web.

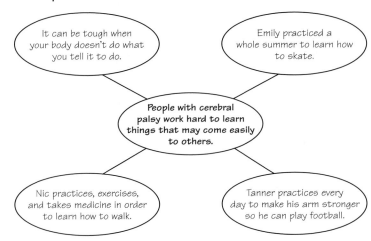

It can be tough when your body doesn't do what you tell it to do.

Emily practiced a whole summer to learn how to skate.

People with cerebral palsy work hard to learn things that may come easily to others.

Nic practices, exercises, and takes medicine in order to learn how to walk.

Tanner practices every day to make his arm stronger so he can play football.

▲ **Graphic Organizer** 15

Research on Generalizing

"To be able to create a summary of what one has just read, one must discern the most central and important ideas in the text. One also must be able to generalize from examples or from things that are repeated. In addition, one has to ignore irrelevant details."

National Reading Panel,
Teaching Children to Read

National Reading Panel. *Teaching Children to Read: Reports of the Subgroups.* National Institute of Child Health & Human Development, National Institutes of Health, 2000, p. 4-92.

Graphic Sources

Graphic sources can be a valuable aid to readers in previewing and comprehending text. When students interpret and create graphics as they read, they often strengthen their understanding of the text. Use this routine to teach graphic sources.

1 DISCUSS GRAPHIC SOURCES

Explain that a graphic is a way of showing information visually. Graphics can include pictures, charts, graphs, maps, diagrams, schedules, and so on. Graphics often show information from the text in a visual way. They can organize many facts or ideas.

2 USE GRAPHICS TO PREVIEW

Remind students to look for graphics when they preview. Graphics are often a good way to discover what the story or article is about.

3 COMPARE GRAPHICS TO TEXT

Have students compare a selection with graphics and discuss the author's purpose for including graphics. Captions, charts, diagrams, and maps may present information that is not found elsewhere in the article. They may also help the reader better understand text information.

4 CREATE GRAPHICS

Give students opportunities to create their own pictures, charts, and other graphics to help them organize and understand text information.

5 USE A GRAPHIC ORGANIZER

Have students create a chart from information in a selection. Depending on the content, they may use a two-, three-, four-, or five-column chart.

Ways Animals Adapt to Find Food	Ways Animals Adapt to Find Shelter	Ways Animals Adapt to Find Safety
• When food is scarce, worker ants called "repletes" feed honey stored in their bodies to their fellow ants. • Large pythons can swallow big prey, like a pig, and go for more than a year without any other food.	• Holes and organs inside the body of a bigger animal can provide a warm, safe home for a smaller animal like an insect.	• When other insects invade their colony, soldier ants explode, spraying a deadly chemical at their enemies.

▲ **Graphic Organizer** 26

Research on Graphic Sources

"Teaching students to organize the ideas that they are reading about in a systematic, visual graph benefits the ability of the students to remember what they read and may transfer, in general, to better comprehension and achievement in Social Studies and Science content areas."

National Reading Panel,
Teaching Children to Read

National Reading Panel. *Teaching Children to Read: Reports of the Subgroups.* National Institute of Child Health & Human Development, National Institutes of Health, 2000, p. 4-45.

Generalize

Recognizing generalizations helps students judge the validity of an argument. Making their own generalizations helps students understand and summarize texts. Use this routine to teach generalizing.

1 DEFINE GENERALIZATION

Explain that a *generalization* is a broad statement or rule that applies to many examples. A *valid generalization* is well supported by facts and logic. A *faulty* one is not well supported.

2 DISCUSS CLUE WORDS

Students should look for clue words that signal generalizations as they read. List words on the board:

all	none
most	few
always	never
generally	in general

3 MODEL GENERALIZING

Explain that when readers generalize, they think about a number of examples and decide what they have in common. After reading a passage containing several facts, model how to generalize.

4 SCAFFOLD GENERALIZING

Before students write their own generalizations, have them choose from several the one most valid for a paragraph. You may also ask them to complete stems, such as: *The climate in the Arctic is generally _____ .*

5 PRACTICE GENERALIZING

Have students record a generalization and examples in a web.

▲ **Graphic Organizer** 15

Research on Generalizing

"To be able to create a summary of what one has just read, one must discern the most central and important ideas in the text. One also must be able to generalize from examples or from things that are repeated. In addition, one has to ignore irrelevant details."

National Reading Panel,
Teaching Children to Read

National Reading Panel. *Teaching Children to Read: Reports of the Subgroups.* National Institute of Child Health & Human Development, National Institutes of Health, 2000, p. 4-92.

Draw Conclusions

When students move beyond the literal meaning of a text to draw conclusions, they get more ideas from what they read and understand better the points an author is trying to make. Use the following routine to guide students in drawing conclusions.

1 DISCUSS DRAWING CONCLUSIONS

Tell students a conclusion is a sensible decision they reach based on details or facts in a story or an article. Explain when they draw conclusions, they think about information in the text and what they already know.

2 MODEL DRAWING A CONCLUSION

Model using your own experiences to draw a conclusion.

 Think Aloud **MODEL** The smell of peanuts and cotton candy filled the air. I heard clapping, I even heard loud bellows that sounded like elephants. I knew a circus was going on.

Discuss how you combined what you already knew with details (smell of peanuts and cotton candy, clapping, loud bellows) to draw a conclusion.

3 ASK QUESTIONS

Read aloud a passage and ask questions that foster drawing conclusions. For example: *What kind of person is the main character? How can you tell? Why do you think the character acts this way?*

4 USE A GRAPHIC ORGANIZER

Have partners read both fiction and nonfiction passages. Students can ask each other questions that lead to drawing conclusions. Suggest that they use webs or charts to show the facts or details that support their conclusions.

▲ **Graphic Organizer** 15

Research on Drawing Conclusions

"Inference is a mosaic, a dazzling constellation of thinking processes, but the tiles available to form each mosaic are limited, circumscribed. There must be a fusion of words on a page—and constraints of meaning they impose—and the experience and knowledge of the reader."

Ellin Oliver Keene and Susan Zimmerman,
Mosaic of Thought

Keen, Ellin Oliver, and Susan Zimmermann. *Mosaic of Thought: Teaching Comprehension in a Reader's Workshop.* Heinemann, 1997, p. 154; 1992, p. 238.

Providing students with reading materials they can and want to read is an important step toward developing fluent readers. A running record allows you to determine each student's instructional and independent reading level. Information on how to take a running record is provided on pp. DI·59–DI·60.

Instructional Reading Level

Only approximately 1 in 10 words will be difficult when reading a selection from the Student Edition for students who are at grade level. (A typical fifth-grader reads approximately 120–140 words correct per minute.)

- Students reading at grade level should read regularly from the Student Edition and On-Level Leveled Readers, with teacher support as suggested in the Teacher's Editions.
- Students reading below grade level can read the Strategic Intervention Leveled Readers. Instructional plans can be found in the Teacher's Edition and the Leveled Reader Teaching Guide.
- Students who are reading above grade level can read the Advanced Leveled Readers. Instructional plans can be found in the Teacher's Edition and the Leveled Reader Teaching Guide.

Independent Reading Level

Students should read regularly in independent-level texts in which no more than approximately 1 in 20 words is difficult for the reader. Other factors that make a book easy to read include the student's interest in the topic, the amount of text on a page, how well illustrations support meaning, and the complexity and familiarity of the concepts. Suggested books for self-selected reading are provided for each lesson on p. TR14 in this Teacher's Edition.

Guide students in learning how to self-select books at their independent reading level. As you talk about a book with students, discuss the challenging concepts in it, list new words students find in sampling the book, and ask students about their familiarity with the topic. A blackline master to help students evaluate books for independent reading is provided on p. DI·58.

Self-Selected/Independent Reading

While oral reading allows you to assess students' reading level and fluency, independent reading is of crucial importance to students' futures as readers and learners. Students need to develop their ability to read independently for increasing amounts of time.

- Schedule a regular time for sustained independent reading in your classroom. During the year, gradually increase the amount of time devoted to independent reading.
- Encourage students to track the amount of time they read independently and the number of pages they read in a given amount of time. Tracking will help motivate them to gradually increase their duration and speed. Blackline masters for tracking independent reading are provided on pp. DI·58 and TR15.

Choosing a Book for Independent Reading

When choosing a book, story, or article for independent reading, consider these questions:

_____ 1. Do I know something about this topic?

_____ 2. Am I interested in this topic?

_____ 3. Do I like reading this kind of book (fiction, fantasy, biography, or whatever)?

_____ 4. Have I read other things by this author? Do I like this author?

If you say "yes" to at least one of the questions above, continue:

_____ 5. In reading the first page, was only about 1 of every 20 words hard?

If you say "yes," continue:

_____ 6. Does the number of words on a page look about right to me?

If you say "yes," the book or article is probably at the right level for you.

Silent Reading

Record the date, the title of the book or article you read, the amount of time you spent reading, and the number of pages you read during that time.

Date	Title	Minutes	Pages

Taking a Running Record

A running record is an assessment of a student's oral reading accuracy and oral reading fluency. Reading accuracy is based on the number of words read correctly. Reading fluency is based on the reading rate (the number of words correct per minute) and the degree to which a student reads with a "natural flow."

How to Measure Reading Accuracy

1. Choose a grade-level text of about 80 to 120 words that is unfamiliar to the student.
2. Make a copy of the text for yourself. Make a copy for the student or have the student read aloud from a book.
3. Give the student the text and have the student read aloud. (You may wish to record the student's reading for later evaluation.)
4. On your copy of the text, mark any miscues or errors the student makes while reading. See the running record sample on page DI·60, which shows how to identify and mark miscues.
5. Count the total number of words in the text and the total number of errors made by the student. Note: If a student makes the same error more than once, such as mispronouncing the same word multiple times, count it as one error. Self-corrections do not count as actual errors. Use the following formula to calculate the percentage score, or accuracy rate:

$$\frac{\text{Total Number of Words} - \text{Total Number of Errors}}{\text{Total Number of Words}} \times 100 = \text{percentage score}$$

Interpreting the Results

- A student who reads **95–100%** of the words correctly is reading at an **independent level** and may need more challenging text.
- A student who reads **90–94%** of the words correctly is reading at an **instructional level** and will likely benefit from guided instruction.
- A student who reads **89%** or fewer of the words correctly is reading at a **frustrational level** and may benefit most from targeted instruction with lower-level texts and intervention.

How to Measure Reading Rate (WCPM)

1. Follow Steps 1–3 above.
2. Note the exact times when the student begins and finishes reading.
3. Use the following formula to calculate the number of words correct per minute (WCPM):

$$\frac{\text{Total Number of Words Read Correctly}}{\text{Total Number of Seconds}} \times 60 = \text{words correct per minute}$$

Interpreting the Results

An appropriate reading rate for a fifth-grader is 120–140 (WCPM).

Running Record Sample

Running Record Sample

Symbols

Did you know that every day in cities across the United States, students like you are helping others?

Each year in Louisiana, [H.] a young student and her younger brother have gone around collecting stuffed animals for [the] children who live in a homeless shelter.

In New York City, seventy-(six) students from Harlem teamed up with four Olympic athletes to transform a run-down park into a playground featuring a daffodil garden.

And ~~each~~ [every] year in Indiana, a young student has gone around collecting hundreds of bundles of [sc] baby clothes and other baby items. In the fall she delivers them to a home for mothers who are having [/tof/] tough times.

—From *Using Special Talents*
On-Level Reader 5.2.1

Accurate Reading
The student reads a word correctly.

Hesitation
The student hesitates over a word, and the teacher provides the word. Wait several seconds before telling the student what the word is.

Insertion
The student inserts words or parts of words that are not in the text.

Omission
The student omits words or word parts.

Substitution
The student substitutes words or parts of words for the words in the text.

Self-Correction
The student reads a word incorrectly but then corrects the error. Do not count self-corrections as actual errors. However, noting self-corrections will help you identify words the student finds difficult.

Mispronunciation/Misreading
The student pronounces or reads a word incorrectly.

Running Record Results
Total Number of Words: **107**
Number of Errors: **5**

Reading Time: **51 seconds**

▶ **Reading Accuracy**

$\dfrac{107 - 5}{107}$ x 100 = 95.327 = 95%

Accuracy Percentage Score: **95%**

▶ **Reading Rate—WCPM**

$\dfrac{102}{51}$ x 60 = 120 = 120 words correct per minute

Reading Rate: **120 WCPM**

Teacher Resources

Table of Contents

Unit 1 · Vocabulary Words · Spelling Words

Frindle

Vocabulary Words

acquainted	guaranteed
assignment	procedures
essential	reputation
expanded	worshipped

Short vowel VCCV, VCV

distance	enjoy	husband	regular
method	perhaps	tissue	denim
anger	figure	mustard	
problem	channel	shuttle	
butter	admire	advance	
petals	comedy	drummer	

Thunder Rose

Vocabulary Words

branded	pitch
constructed	resourceful
daintily	thieving
devastation	veins
lullaby	

Long vowel VCV

fever	native	agent	legal
broken	silent	motive	solo
climate	labor	vital	
hotel	spider	acorn	
basic	label	item	
vocal	icon	aroma	

Island of the Blue Dolphins

Vocabulary Words

gnawed	ravine
headland	shellfish
kelp	sinew
lair	

Long vowel digraphs

coast	arrow	crease	complain
feast	needle	groan	sneeze
speech	charcoal	breeze	
wheat	praise	willow	
Spain	faint	appeal	
paint	maintain	bowling	

Satchel Paige

Vocabulary Words

confidence	unique
fastball	weakness
mocking	windup
outfield	

Adding -ed, -ing

supplied	included	qualified	satisfied
supplying	including	qualifying	satisfying
denied	admitted	identified	
denying	admitting	identifying	
decided	occurred	delayed	
deciding	occurring	delaying	

Shutting Out the Sky

Vocabulary Words

advice	immigrants
advised	luxury
circumstanc-es	newcomer
elbow	peddler
hustled	

Contractions

they're	what'll	wouldn't
you've	doesn't	who've
weren't	hadn't	shouldn't
needn't	could've	who'd
there'd	would've	this'll
they've	should've	couldn't
mustn't	might've	

Unit 2 | Vocabulary Words | Spelling Words

Inside Out

Vocabulary Words

caterpillar	migrant
cocoon	sketched
disrespect	unscrewed
emerge	

Spelling Words

Digraphs *th, sh, ch, ph*

shovel	establish	shatter	attach
southern	although	ethnic	ostrich
northern	challenge	shiver	
chapter	approach	pharmacy	
hyphen	astonish	charity	
chosen	python	china	

Passage to Freedom

Vocabulary Words

agreement	refugees
cable	representa-tives
diplomat	superiors
issue	visa

Spelling Words

Irregular plurals

staffs	chiefs	quizzes	chefs
ourselves	buffaloes	sheriffs	pianos
pants	flamingos	dominoes	
scissors	beliefs	thieves	
loaves	echoes	measles	
volcanoes	shelves	avocados	

The Ch'i-lin Purse

Vocabulary Words

astonished	procession
behavior	recommend
benefactor	sacred
distribution	traditions
gratitude	

Spelling Words

Vowel sounds with *r*

snore	report	repair	volunteer
tornado	prepare	sword	declare
spare	pioneer	ignore	
appear	chair	order	
career	beware	engineer	
square	smear	resort	

Jane Goodall's 10 Ways to Help Save Wildlife

Vocabulary Words

conservation
contribute
enthusiastic
environment
investigation

Spelling Words

Final Syllables *-en, -an, -el, -le, -il*

example	oxygen	fossil	sudden
level	wooden	toboggan	beagle
human	double	veteran	
quarrel	travel	chisel	
scramble	cancel	suburban	
evil	chuckle	single	

The Midnight Ride of Paul Revere

Vocabulary Words

fate	magnified
fearless	somber
glimmer	steed
lingers	

Spelling Words

Final Syllables *-er, -ar, -or*

danger	surrender	caterpillar
wander	solar	rumor
tractor	sticker	glimmer
dollar	locker	linger
harbor	helicopter	sensor
eager	pillar	alligator
eraser	refrigerator	

Unit 3 — Vocabulary Words — Spelling Words

Wings for the King

Vocabulary Words

admiringly	subject
permit	worthless
scoundrel	

Spelling Words

Schwas

jewel	pajamas	carnival	operate
kingdom	estimate	illustrate	celery
gasoline	tomorrow	elegant	
factory	humidity	census	
garage	Chicago	terrific	
tropical	bulletin	celebrate	

Leonardo's Horse

Vocabulary Words

achieved	fashioned
architect	midst
bronze	philosopher
cannon	rival
depressed	

Spelling Words

Compound words

waterproof	earthquake	spotlight	postcard
teaspoon	rowboat	blindfold	humming-bird
grasshopper	scrapbook	whirlpool	thumbtack
homesick	countryside	tablespoon	
barefoot	lightweight	greenhouse	
courthouse	fishhook		

The Dinosaurs of Waterhouse Hawkins

Vocabulary Words

erected	proportion
foundations	tidied
mold	workshop
occasion	

Spelling Words

Consonant sounds /j/, /ks/, /sk/, and /s/

excuse	science	exclaim	smudge
scene	schedule	fascinate	schooner
muscle	gigantic	ginger	
explore	scheme	scholar	
pledge	Japan	scent	
journal	excellent	dodge	

Mahalia Jackson

Vocabulary Words

appreciate	religious
barber	slavery
choir	teenager
released	

Spelling Words

One consonant or two

address	Mississippi	Tennessee	allowance
college	immediate	gallop	zucchini
mirror	command	opponent	
recess	appreciate	barricade	
committee	announce	broccoli	
collect	possess	accomplish	

Special Effects in Film and Television

Vocabulary Words

background
landscape
miniature
prehistoric
reassembled

Spelling Words

Prefixes un-, de-, dis

uncover	disability	unpredict-able	disqualify
defrost	discomfort	disapprove	undecided
uncomfortable	deodorant	disappoint	
discourage	unemployed	unpleasant	
disadvantage	deflate	dehydrated	
unfortunate	disbelief		
unfamiliar			

Unit 4

Weslandia

Vocabulary Words

blunders   fleeing
civilization   inspired
complex   rustling
envy   strategy

Spelling Words

Words from many cultures

khaki	vanilla	cobra	karate
hula	canyon	koala	kiosk
banana	yogurt	barbecue	
ballet	banquet	safari	
waltz	macaroni	buffet	
tomato	polka	stampede	

Stretching Ourselves: Kids with Cerebral Palsy

Vocabulary Words

abdomen
artificial
gait
handicapped
therapist
wheelchair

Prefixes over-, under-, sub-, super-, out-

overlook	underground	submarine	subdivision
underline	overboard	undercover	subhead
subway	undercurrent	overcast	
subset	superstar	outfield	
supermarket	overtime	output	
outlet	supersonic	supernatural	

Exploding Ants: Amazing Facts About How Animals Adapt

Vocabulary Words

critical
enables
mucus
scarce
specialize
sterile

Homophones

cent	whether	tide	course
sent	their	tied	coarse
scent	there	pale	
threw	they're	pail	
through	chili	aloud	
weather	chilly	allowed	

The Stormi Giovanni Club

Vocabulary Words

cavities
combination
demonstrates
episode
profile
strict

Suffixes -ible, -able

sensible	flexible	laughable	responsible
washable	reasonable	sociable	tolerable
available	favorable	allowable	
agreeable	breakable	divisible	
fashionable	convertible	hospitable	
valuable	forgettable	reversible	

The Gymnast

Vocabulary Words

bluish   skidded
cartwheels   somersault
gymnastics   throbbing
hesitation   wincing
limelight

Negative prefixes

invisible	impatient	illogical
illiterate	independent	indefinite
irregular	incorrect	imperfect
irresistible	inactive	immobile
impossible	imperfect	irresponsible
informal	impolite	inexpensive
illegal	immature	

Unit 5	Vocabulary Words		Spelling Words			
The Three-Century Woman	eerie intersection pondered severe spectacles withered		**Multisyllabic words**			
			elementary vehicle miniature probability definition substitute	variety literature elevator Pennsylvania ravioli cafeteria	mosaic tuxedo meteorite fascination cylinder intermediate	centennial curiosity
The Unsinkable Wreck of the R.M.S. *Titanic*	cramped debris interior ooze	robotic sediment sonar	**Unusual spellings**			
			league sergeant yacht doubt fatigue debt	blood vague anxious foreign bargain condemn	intrigue villain cantaloupe flood depot cordial	subtle disguise
Talk with an Astronaut	accomplish- ments focus gravity	monitors role specific	**Greek word parts**			
			geology thermometer astronaut atmosphere biology thermal	disaster meteorology technology hemisphere zoology sociology	biosphere thermos asterisk thermostat astronomy spherical	ecology mythology
Journey to the Center of the Earth	armor encases extinct	hideous plunged serpent	**Latin roots**			
			project audience decade territory auditorium terrier	decimal injection December reject eject terrace	audit decimeter audition audible decathlon terrarium	dejected terrain
Ghost Towns of the American West	economic independence overrun	scrawled vacant	**Related words**			
			politics political major majority equal equation sign	signature arrive arrival inspire inspiration human humanity	clean cleanse resign resignation unite unity	

Unit 6

	Vocabulary Words		Spelling Words			

At the Beach

algae	lamented
concealed	sea urchins
driftwood	sternly
hammocks	tweezers

Suffixes -ous, -sion, -ion, -ation

famous	nervous	tension	occupation
invention	explanation	humorous	destination
election	various	exhibition	
furious	decision	attraction	
imagination	relaxation	invasion	
education	conversation	creation	

The Mystery of Saint Matthew Island

bleached	scrawny
carcasses	starvation
decay	suspicions
parasites	tundra

Final Syllable -ant, -ent, -ance, -ence

important	absence	confidence	excellence
experience	appearance	conference	persistent
ignorant	intelligent	insurance	
entrance	evidence	ambulance	
difference	pollutant	hesitant	
instance	clearance	consistent	

King Midas and the Golden Touch

adorn	precious
cleanse	realm
lifeless	spoonful

Words with ei and ie

brief	seize	yield	shield
believe	ceiling	deceive	conceited
receive	field	achieve	
leisure	neither	grief	
piece	apiece	niece	
relief	receipt	protein	

The Hindenburg

criticizing	era
cruised	explosion
drenching	hydrogen

Compound words

ice cream	textbook	dead end	cartwheel
a lot	guidelines	password	root beer
keyboard	newspaper	teenager	fingerprint
fairy tale	space shuttle	skateboard	
horseshoe		everything	
piggy bank	hay fever	barbed wire	

Sweet Music in Harlem

bass
clarinet
fidgety
forgetful
jammed
nighttime
secondhand

Easily confused words

quiet	than	from	medal
quite	then	form	metal
finely	since	later	
finally	sense	latter	
except	affect	adapt	
accept	effect	adopt	

Grade 4 Vocabulary

Use this list of fourth grade tested vocabulary words for review and leveled activities.

A

aboard
affords
amazed
amphibians
ancestors
ancient
anticipation
appeared
aquarium
astronauts
atlas
aviator
avoided
awkward

B

bargain
bawling
bewildered
biologist
bluff
boarding school
bow
brilliant
brisk
bustling

C

canopy
capable
capsule
cargo
celestial
chant
chorus
cockpit
colonel
conducted
Constitution
continent
convergence
cord

coward
coyote
cradle
crime
crumbled
curiosity

D

dangle
dappled
daring
depart
destruction
dignified
dismay
docks
dolphins
dormitory
draft
drag
dudes
duke
dungeon

E

elegant
enchanted
endurance
escape
etched
exhibit
expected

F

fascinated
favor
flex
flexible
forbidding
forecasts
fouled
fragrant

frost
furiously

G

generations
genius
glacier
gleamed
glider
glimpses
glint
glorious
grand
granite
grizzly

H

hangars
hatch
heaves
homeland
hoop
horizon
howling
humble

I

icebergs
immense
impressive
inland

J

jersey

L

lagoon
lassoed
link
lizard
longed
loomed

lunar
lurking

M

magician
majesty
manual
marveled
massive
mechanical
memorial
migrating
minister
miracle
module
monument

N

naturalist
navigation
noble
numerous

O

offended
outspoken

P

palettes
parlor
payroll
peasant
peculiar
politics
pollen
pollinate
porridge
positive
prairie
preserve
prideful
pulpit
pulses

Q

quaint
quarantine
quivered

R

recalls
reference
reptiles
reseats
resemblance
reservation
responsibility
rille
rim
riverbed
roundup
rudder
ruins
rumbling
runt

S

salamander
scan
scent
scholars
sculptures
seeker
selecting
shatter
shielding
shimmering
shrieked
slithered
slopes
society
solemnly
solo
species
speechless
spurs

staggered
stalled
stern
still
stumped
summoning
surface
surge
swatted

T

taunted
temple
terraced
terror
thickets
timid
torrent
towering
trench
triumph
tropical
trudged

U

unbelievable
uncover

V

vain
vanished
vehicle

W

wharf
wilderness
wondrous

Y

yearned

Grade 6 Vocabulary

Use this list of sixth grade tested vocabulary words for leveled activities.

A

absurd
abundant
access
accustomed
aggressive
aliens
apparently
application
architecture
artifacts
astronomers
authority

B

barge
basin
beacon
behalf
benefits
bondage
burden

C

campaigns
candidate
captive
caravans
characteristic
charities
collapse
collide
combustion
commissioned
compact
companionship
comrades
confidently
conformed
conquer
converts
corridors
corrode

counselor
customary

D

dean
decline
decrees
delirious
democracy
densest
destination
destiny
detect
devise
dingy
diploma
disgraced
dismounted
distressed
dramatic
dubiously

E

earthen
eaves
efficiency
emphasized
empire
encounter
engulfed
enraged
enrich
equator
erosion
eternity
evaporates
existence
expanse
expedition
exploit
exported
extract

F

fixtures
flimsy
flourish
foreigners
formal
former
fragile
frantic
frustration
fulfill

G

galaxy
generated
groping

H

hatchet
hoard
homesteaders
hospitable
hovers

I

ideal
identity
ignite
immortal
imprinted
incident
industrial
insulated
invaders
isolation

L

lance
legacy
leisure
lunging
lush

M

maintenance
manuscripts
materialize
medieval
menacing
migration
misfortune
moisture
molten
momentous
mongrel
mythology

N

navigator
negotiate
nub

O

obedient
observatory
obstacle
opera
ordeal
ore

P

painstaking
particles
patron
percentage
permission
persisted
physical
pleas
poisonous
prejudice
presence
prey
primitive
privileged
proclaimed

progress
promoted
provisions

Q

quests
quill

R

receded
recital
recycled
refrain
registered
reigned
reject
relish
renewed
renowned
repay
reproduce
resound
retreat
revolting
romping
rowdy
rural

S

sanctuaries
secretive
settlement
sluggish
slung
smoldered
specimens
speckled
squire
stiffened
stimulating
stunned
subscribe
sufficient

surplus
survive

T

technology
tolerated
toll
torment
transmitted
traversed
treacherous
treaded
tropics

U

unaccompanied
unison
universal
urban

V

ventured
verify
version
vigorously
volcanic

W

waft
waning
wilt

Legibility

When handwriting is legible, letters, words, and numbers can be read easily. Handwriting that is not legible can cause problems for the reader and make communication difficult. Legibility can be improved if students are able to identify what is causing legibility problems in their handwriting. Focus instruction on the following five elements of legible handwriting.

Size

Letters need to be a consistent size. Students should focus on three things related to size: letters that reach to the top line, letters that reach halfway between the top and bottom line, and letters that extend below the bottom line. Writing letters the correct size can improve legibility. Often the letters that sit halfway between the top and bottom line cause the most problems. When students are writing on notebook paper, there is no middle line to help them size letters such as *m, a, i,* and *r* correctly. If students are having trouble, have them draw middle lines on their notebook paper.

Shape

Some of the most common handwriting problems are caused by forming letters incorrectly. These are the most common types of handwriting problems:

- Round letters such as *a, o,* and *g* are not closed.
- Looped letters such as *l, e,* and *b* have no loops.
- Letters such as *i, t,* and *d* have loops that shouldn't be there.

Have students examine one another's writing to indicate which words are hard to read, and then discuss which letters aren't formed correctly. They can then practice those particular letters.

Spacing

Letters within words should be evenly spaced. Too much or too little space can make writing difficult to read. A consistent amount of space should also be used between words in a sentence and between sentences. Suggest that students use the tip of their pencil to check the spacing between words and the width of their pencil to check the spacing between sentences.

Slant

Correct writing slant can be to the right or to the left, or there may be no slant at all. Slant becomes a legibility problem when letters are slanted in different directions. Suggest that students use a ruler to draw lines to determine if their slant is consistent.

Smoothness

Written letters should be produced with a line weight that is not too dark and not too light. The line should be smooth without any shaky or jagged edges. If students' writing is too dark, they are pressing too hard. If the writing is too light, they are not pressing hard enough. Usually shaky or jagged lines occur if students are unsure of how to form letters or if they are trying to draw letters rather than using a flowing motion.

D'Nealian™ Cursive Alphabet

D'Nealian™ Alphabet

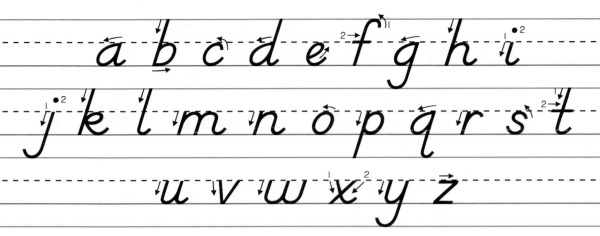

a b c d e f g h i
j k l m n o p q r s t
u v w x y z

A B C D E F G
H I J K L M N O
P Q R S T U V
W X Y Z . , ' ?

1 2 3 4 5 6
7 8 9 10

Manuscript Alphabet

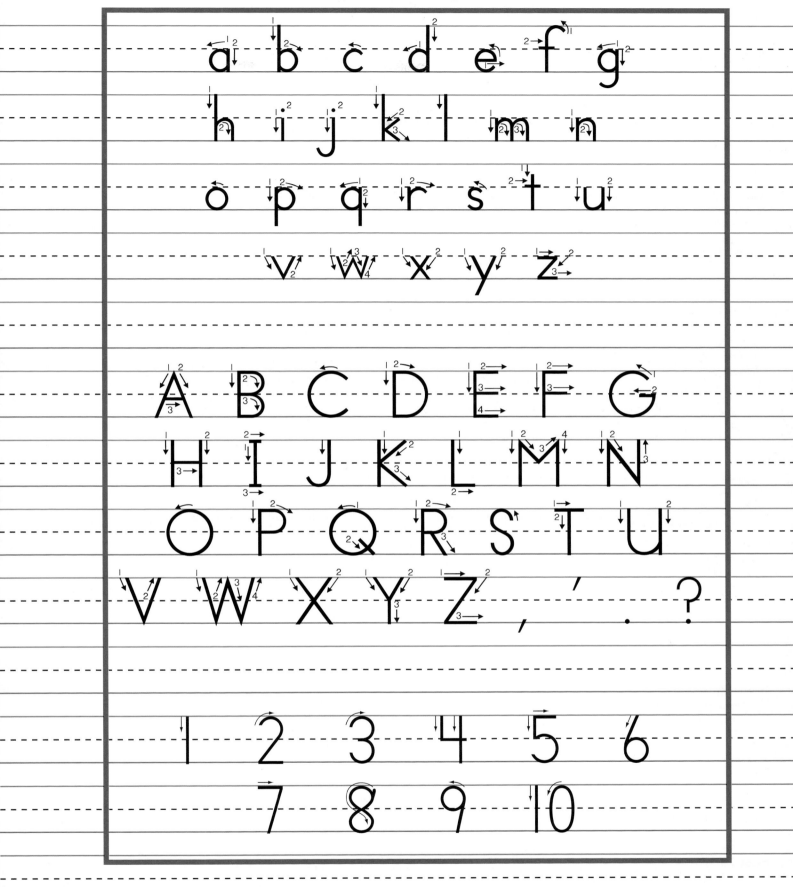

Unit 4 *Adapting*

	Below-Level	On-Level	Advanced

Weslandia

To Read Aloud!
The Magic of the Glits
by Carole Adler (MacMillan, 1979) A summer becomes enchanted and unforgettable when Jeremy creates a world of magical beach creatures to comfort a young orphan girl.

Martin's Mice
by Dick King-Smith (Knopf, 1988) A farm cat does not want to catch mice and decides to keep them as pets instead in this delightful tale about difference and self-esteem.

Loser
by Jerry Spinelli (HarperCollins, 2002) An exuberant, eccentric boy, labeled a loser by his classmates, eventually shows the power of the human spirit and that anyone can become a hero.

Seedfolks
by Paul Fleischman (HarperCollins, 1997) In this story of a girl planting a garden in a trash-filled vacant lot, the author shows us a community born and nurtured in an urban environment.

Stretching Ourselves

To Read Aloud!
Teens with Physical Disabilities
by Glen Alan Cheney (Enslow; 1995) Eight teenagers tell of the challenges they face in their everyday lives.

What's Wrong with Timmy?
by Maria Shriver (Warner, 2001) As Kate and Timmy, a boy with Down Syndrome, become friends, Kate realizes that they have a lot in common, despite their differences.

Sparks
By Graham McNamee (Yearling, 2003) When Todd is moved from Special Education to a regular fifth grade class, he struggles to keep up, but eventually finds his own special gift.

Petey
by Ben Mikaelsen (Hyperion, 1998) Petey, an elderly man with cerebral palsy, befriends a boy and shares with him the joy of life.

Exploding Ants: Amazing Facts About How Animals Adapt

To Read Aloud!
Hiding Out: Camouflage in the Wild
by James Martin and Art Wolfe (Random House, 1993) Text and photographs explore why and how animals use camouflage for adaptation.

Animals in Motion
by Pamela Hickman and Pat Stephens (Kids Can Press, 2000) This book contains facts, activities and easy experiments that show kids the amazing ways animals move.

One Day in the Desert
by Jean Craighead George (HarperCollins, 1983) The animals and people of the Sonoran Desert in Arizona adapt to cruel living conditions.

The Case of the Monkeys That Fell From the Trees: And Other Mysteries in Tropical Nature
by Susan Quinlan (Boyd Mills, 2003) Eleven scientific investigations reveal the interdependence between plants, animals and insects.

The Stormi Giovanni Club

To Read Aloud!
Dear Mr. Henshaw
by Beverly Cleary (HarperCollins, 1994) In letters to his favorite author, ten-year-old Leigh reveals his problems with his parents' divorce, being the new boy in school and finding his place in the world.

Alexander, Who's Not (Do You Hear Me! I Mean It!) Going to Move
by Judith Viorst (Atheneum, 1995) Alexander is horrified at the prospect of moving 1,000 miles away in this raucous picture book.

P.S. Longer Letter Later
by Paula Danziger and A.M. Martin (Scholastic, 1998) When Tara Starr moves away she and her best friend work hard to continue their friendship through letters.

The Ballad of Lucy Whipple
by Karen Cushman (Houghton Mifflin, 1996) When California Morning Whipple moves with her family to a rugged California mining town, she is unhappy until she begins to feel at home.

The Gymnast

To Read Aloud!
Pool Party
by Gary Soto (Yearling Books, 1995) Rudy is worried when he's invited to a pool party hosted by the most popular girl at school.

The Skirt
by Gary Soto (Doubleday, 1992) Miata leaves her precious folkorico skirt on the bus and she and her friend Ana must figure out how to get it back.

Fearless Fernie: Hanging Out with Fernie and Me
by Gary Soto (Putnam, 2002) These poems tell about the lives of two best friends and will speak to any child who has ever faced embarrassing moments at school.

Baseball in April and Other Stories
by Gary Soto (Harcourt, 1990) These stories feature young people whose joys and pain are brought to life through daily events that reveal love, friendship, growing up, success and failure.

See also Assessment Handbook, p. 119

Unit 4 Reading Log

Name _____

Dates Read	Title and Author	What is it about?	How would you rate it?	Explain your rating.
From ____ to ____			Great 5 4 3 2 1 Awful	
From ____ to ____			Great 5 4 3 2 1 Awful	
From ____ to ____			Great 5 4 3 2 1 Awful	
From ____ to ____			Great 5 4 3 2 1 Awful	
From ____ to ____			Great 5 4 3 2 1 Awful	

© Pearson Education

Unit 4 Narrative Retelling Chart

Selection Title ——————

Name ——————

Date ——————

Retelling Criteria/Teacher Prompt	Teacher-Aided Response	Student-Generated Response	Rubric Score (Circle one.)
Connections Has anything like this happened to you? How does this story remind you of other stories?			4　3　2　1
Author's Purpose Why do you think the author wrote this story? What was the author trying to tell us?			4　3　2　1
Characters Describe _____ (character's name) at the beginning and end of the story.			4　3　2　1
Setting Where and when did the story happen?			4　3　2　1
Plot Tell me what the story was about in a few sentences.			4　3　2　1

Summative Retelling Score　4　3　2　1

Comments

_____

_____

_____

Unit 4 Expository Retelling Chart

Selection Title _____ **Name** _____ **Date** _____

Retelling Criteria/Teacher Prompt	Teacher-Aided Response	Student-Generated Response	Rubric Score (Circle one.)
Connections Did this selection make you think about something else you have read? What did you learn about as you read this selection?			4 3 2 1
Author's Purpose Why do you think the author wrote this selection?			4 3 2 1
Topic What was the selection mostly about?			4 3 2 1
Important Ideas What is important for me to know about _____ (topic)?			4 3 2 1
Conclusions What did you learn from reading this selection?			4 3 2 1

Summative Retelling Score 4 3 2 1

Comments _____

Reading

Concepts of Print and Print Awareness	Pre-K	K	1	2	3	4	5	6
Develop awareness that print represents spoken language and conveys and preserves meaning	•	•	•					
Recognize familiar books by their covers; hold book right side up	•	•						
Identify parts of a book and their functions (front cover, title page/title, back cover, page numbers)	•	•	•					
Understand the concepts of letter, word, sentence, paragraph, and story	•	•	•					
Track print (front to back of book, top to bottom of page, left to right on line, sweep back left for next line)	•	•	•					
Match spoken to printed words	•	•	•					
Know capital and lowercase letter names and match them	•	•T	•					
Know the order of the alphabet	•	•	•					
Recognize first name in print	•	•	•					
Recognize the uses of capitalization and punctuation			•	•				
Value print as a means of gaining information	•	•	•					

Phonological and Phonemic Awareness	Pre-K	K	1	2	3	4	5	6
Phonological Awareness								
Recognize and produce rhyming words	•	•	•					
Track and count each word in a spoken sentence and each syllable in a spoken word	•	•	•					
Segment and blend syllables in spoken words			•					
Segment and blend onset and rime in one-syllable words		•	•					
Recognize and produce words beginning with the same sound	•	•	•					
Identify beginning, middle, and/or ending sounds that are the same or different	•	•	•					
Understand that spoken words are made of sequences of sounds	•	•	•					
Phonemic Awareness								
Identify the position of sounds in words			•	•				
Identify and isolate initial, final, and medial sounds in spoken words	•	•	•					
Blend sounds orally to make words or syllables			•	•				
Segment a word or syllable into sounds; count phonemes in spoken words or syllables			•	•				
Manipulate sounds in words (add, delete, and/or substitute phonemes)	•	•	•					

Phonics and Decoding	Pre-K	K	1	2	3	4	5	6
Phonics								
Understand and apply the *alphabetic principle* that spoken words are composed of sounds that are represented by letters	•	•	•					
Know letter-sound relationships		•T	•T	•T				
Blend sounds of letters to decode		•	•T	•T	•T			
Consonants, consonant blends, and consonant digraphs		•	•T	•T	•T			
Short, long, and r-controlled vowels; vowel digraphs; diphthongs; common vowel patterns			•T	•T	•T			
Phonograms/word families		•	•	•	•			
Word Structure								
Decode words with common word parts		•	•T	•T	•T	•	•	•
Base words and inflected endings			•T	•T	•	•	•	•
Contractions and compound words			•T	•T	•T	•	•	•
Suffixes and prefixes			•T	•T	•T	•	•	•
Greek and Latin roots						•	•	•
Blend syllables to decode words			•T	•T	•T	•	•	•
Decoding Strategies								
Blending strategy: Apply knowledge of letter-sound relationships to decode unfamiliar words		•	•	•	•			
Apply knowledge of word structure to decode unfamiliar words		•	•	•	•	•	•	•
Use context and syntax along with letter-sound relationships and word structure to decode	•	•	•	•	•	•	•	•
Self-correct			•	•	•	•	•	•

Fluency	Pre-K	K	1	2	3	4	5	6
Read aloud fluently with accuracy, comprehension, appropriate pace/rate; with expression/intonation (prosody); with attention to punctuation and appropriate phrasing			•T	•T	•T	•T	•T	•T
Practice fluency in a variety of ways, including choral reading, partner/paired reading, Readers' Theater, repeated oral reading, and tape-assisted reading		•	•	•	•	•	•	•

• instructional opportunity   **T** tested in standardized test format

	Pre-K	K	1	2	3	4	5	6
Work toward appropriate fluency goals by the end of each grade			•T	•T	•T	•T	•T	•T
Read regularly in independent-level material			•	•	•	•	•	•
Read silently for increasing periods of time			•	•	•	•	•	•

Vocabulary (Oral and Written)

	Pre-K	K	1	2	3	4	5	6
Word Recognition								
Recognize regular and irregular high-frequency words	•	•	•T	•T				
Recognize and understand selection vocabulary		•	•	•T	•	•	•	•
Understand content-area vocabulary and specialized, technical, or topical words			•	•	•	•	•	•
Word Learning Strategies								
Develop vocabulary through direct instruction, concrete experiences, reading, listening to text read aloud	•	•	•	•	•	•	•	•
Use knowledge of word structure to figure out meanings of words			•	•T	•T	•T	•T	•T
Use context clues for meanings of unfamiliar words, multiple-meaning words, homonyms, homographs			•	•T	•T	•T	•T	•T
Use grade-appropriate reference sources to learn word meanings	•	•	•	•	•T	•T	•T	•T
Use picture clues to help determine word meanings	•	•	•					
Use new words in a variety of contexts	•	•	•	•	•	•	•	•
Examine word usage and effectiveness		•	•	•	•	•	•	•
Create and use graphic organizers to group, study, and retain vocabulary			•	•	•	•	•	•
Extend Concepts and Word Knowledge								
Academic language	•	•	•	•	•	•	•	•
Classify and categorize	•	•	•	•	•	•	•	•
Antonyms and synonyms			•	•T	•T	•T	•T	•T
Homographs, homonyms, and homophones				•	•T	•T	•T	•T
Multiple-meaning words			•	•	•T	•T	•T	•T
Related words and derivations					•	•	•	•
Analogies					•		•	
Connotation/denotation						•	•	•
Figurative language and idioms			•	•	•	•	•	•
Descriptive words (location, size, color, shape, number, ideas, feelings)	•	•	•	•	•	•	•	•
High-utility words (shapes, colors, question words, position/directional words, and so on)	•	•	•	•				
Time and order words	•	•	•	•	•	•	•	•
Transition words						•	•	•
Word origins: Etymologies/word histories; words from other languages, regions, or cultures						•	•	•
Shortened forms: abbreviations, acronyms, clipped words			•	•	•	•	•T	

Text Comprehension

	Pre-K	K	1	2	3	4	5	6
Comprehension Strategies								
Preview the text and formulate questions	•	•	•	•	•	•	•	•
Set and monitor purpose for reading and listening	•	•	•	•	•	•	•	•
Activate and use prior knowledge	•	•	•	•	•	•	•	•
Make predictions	•	•	•	•	•	•	•	•
Monitor comprehension and use fix-up strategies to resolve difficulties in meaning: adjust reading rate, reread and read on, seek help from reference sources and/or other people, skim and scan, summarize, use text features								
Create and use graphic and semantic organizers		•	•	•	•	•	•	•
Answer questions (text explicit, text implicit, scriptal), including *who, what, when, where, why, what if, how*	•	•	•	•	•	•	•	•
Look back in text for answers			•	•	•	•	•	•
Answer test-like questions			•	•	•	•	•	•
Generate clarifying questions, including *who, what, where, when, how, why,* and *what if*	•	•	•	•	•	•	•	•
Recognize text structure: story and informational (cause/effect, chronological, compare/contrast, description, problem/solution, proposition/support)	•	•	•	•	•	•	•	•
Summarize text		•	•	•	•	•	•	•
Recall and retell stories	•	•	•	•	•	•	•	•
Identify and retell important/main ideas (nonfiction)	•	•	•	•	•	•	•	•
Identify and retell new information			•	•	•	•	•	•
Visualize; use mental imagery		•	•	•	•	•	•	•
Use strategies flexibly and in combination			•	•	•	•	•	•

Comprehension Skills

	Pre-K	K	1	2	3	4	5	6
Author's purpose			• T	• T	• T	• T	• T	• T
Author's viewpoint/bias/perspective					•	•	•	• T
Categorize and classify	•	•	•	•				
Cause and effect		•	• T	• T	• T	• T	• T	• T
Compare and contrast	•	•	• T	• T	• T	• T	• T	• T
Details and facts		•	•	•	•	•	•	•
Draw conclusions		•	• T	• T	• T	• T	• T	• T
Fact and opinion			• T	• T	• T	• T	• T	• T
Follow directions/steps in a process	•	•	•	•	•	•	•	•
Generalize					• T	• T	• T	• T
Graphic sources		•	•	•	•	• T	• T	• T
Main idea and supporting details		• T	• T	• T	• T	• T	• T	• T
Paraphrase			•	•	•	•	•	•
Persuasive devices and propaganda			•	•	•	•	•	•
Realism/fantasy	•	•	• T	• T	• T	•	•	•
Sequence of events	•	• T	• T	• T	• T	• T	• T	• T

Higher Order Thinking Skills

	Pre-K	K	1	2	3	4	5	6
Analyze				•	•	•	•	•
Describe and connect the essential ideas, arguments, and perspectives of a text			•	•	•	•	•	•
Draw inferences, conclusions, or generalizations, support them with textual evidence and prior knowledge		•	•	•	•	•	•	•
Evaluate and critique ideas and text			•	•	•	•	•	•
Hypothesize						•	•	•
Make judgments about ideas and text			•	•	•	•	•	•
Organize and synthesize ideas and information			•			•	•	•

Literary Analysis, Response, & Appreciation

Genre and Its Characteristics

	Pre-K	K	1	2	3	4	5	6
Recognize characteristics of a variety of genre	•	•	•	•	•	•	•	•
Distinguish fiction from nonfiction	•	•	•	•	•	•	•	•
Identify characteristics of literary texts, including drama, fantasy, traditional tales		•	•	•	•	•	•	•
Identify characteristics of nonfiction texts, including biography, interviews, newspaper articles		•	•	•	•	•	•	•
Identify characteristics of poetry and song, including nursery rhymes, limericks, blank verse	•	•	•	•	•	•	•	•

Literary Elements and Story Structure

	Pre-K	K	1	2	3	4	5	6
Character	•	• T	• T	• T	• T	• T	• T	•
Recognize and describe traits, actions, feelings, and motives of characters		•	•	•	•	•	•	•
Analyze characters' relationships, changes, and points of view		•	•	•	•	•	•	•
Analyze characters' conflicts				•	•	•	•	•
Plot and plot structure	•	• T	• T	• T	• T	• T	• T	•
Beginning, middle, end	•	•	•	•	•			
Goal and outcome or problem and solution/resolution		•	•	•	•	•	•	•
Rising action, climax, and falling action/denouement; setbacks						•	•	•
Setting	•	• T	• T	• T	• T	• T	•	•
Relate setting to problem/solution						•	•	•
Explain ways setting contributes to mood						•	•	•
Theme		•	• T	• T	•	•	•	•
Use Literary Elements and Story Structure	•	•	•	•	•	•	•	•
Analyze and evaluate author's use of setting, plot, character				•	•	•	•	•
Identify similarities and differences of characters, events, and settings within or across selections/cultures		•	•	•	•	•	•	•

Literary Devices

	Pre-K	K	1	2	3	4	5	6
Allusion								•
Dialect						•	•	•
Dialogue and narration	•	•	•	•	•	•	•	•
Exaggeration/hyperbole						•	•	•
Figurative language: idiom, jargon, metaphor, simile, slang			•	•	•	•	•	•

• instructional opportunity   **T** tested in standardized test format

	Pre-K	K	1	2	3	4	5	6
Flashback						•	•	•
Foreshadowing							•	•
Formal and informal language				•	•	•	•	•
Humor					•	•	•	•
Imagery and sensory words				•	•	•	•	•
Mood				•	•	•	•	•
Personification				•	•	•	•	•
Point of view (first person, third person, omniscient)					•	•	•	•
Puns and word play				•	•	•	•	•
Sound devices and poetic elements	•	•	•	•	•	•	•	•
Alliteration, assonance, onomatopoeia	•	•	•	•	•	•	•	•
Rhyme, rhythm, repetition, and cadence	•	•	•	•	•	•	•	•
Word choice				•	•	•	•	•
Symbolism				•	•	•	•	•
Tone							•	•

Author's and Illustrator's Craft

	Pre-K	K	1	2	3	4	5	6
Distinguish the roles of author and illustrator	•	•	•	•				
Recognize/analyze author's and illustrator's craft or style				•	•	•	•	•

Literary Response

	Pre-K	K	1	2	3	4	5	6
Recollect, talk, and write about books	•	•	•	•	•	•	•	•
Reflect on reading and respond (through talk, movement, art, and so on)	•	•	•	•	•	•	•	•
Ask and answer questions about text	•	•	•	•	•	•	•	•
Write about what is read	•	•	•	•	•	•	•	•
Use evidence from the text to support opinions, interpretations, or conclusions				•	•	•	•	•
Support ideas through reference to other texts and personal knowledge				•	•	•	•	•
Locate materials on related topic, theme, or idea				•	•	•	•	•
Generate alternative endings to plots and identify the reason for, and the impact of, the alternatives	•	•	•	•	•	•	•	•
Synthesize and extend the literary experience through creative responses	•	•	•	•	•	•	•	•
Make connections: text to self, text to text, text to world	•	•	•	•	•	•	•	•
Evaluate and critique the quality of the literary experience				•	•	•	•	•
Offer observations, react, speculate in response to text				•	•	•	•	•

Literary Appreciation/Motivation

	Pre-K	K	1	2	3	4	5	6
Show an interest in books and reading; engage voluntarily in social interaction about books	•	•	•	•	•	•	•	•
Choose text by drawing on personal interests, relying on knowledge of authors and genres, estimating text difficulty, and using recommendations of others	•	•	•	•	•	•	•	•
Read a variety of grade-level appropriate narrative and expository texts			•	•	•	•	•	•
Read from a wide variety of genres for a variety of purposes	•	•	•	•	•	•	•	•
Read independently			•	•	•	•	•	•
Establish familiarity with a topic			•	•	•	•	•	•

Cultural Awareness

	Pre-K	K	1	2	3	4	5	6
Develop attitudes and abilities to interact with diverse groups and cultures	•	•	•	•	•	•	•	•
Connect experiences and ideas with those from a variety of languages, cultures, customs, perspectives	•	•	•	•	•	•	•	•
Understand how attitudes and values in a culture or during a period in time affect the writing from that culture or time period						•	•	•
Compare language and oral traditions (family stories) that reflect customs, regions, and cultures	•	•	•	•	•	•	•	•
Recognize themes that cross cultures and bind them together in their common humanness						•	•	•

Language Arts

Writing	Pre-K	K	1	2	3	4	5	6
Concepts of Print for Writing								
Develop gross and fine motor skills and hand/eye coordination	•	•	•					
Print own name and other important words	•	•	•					
Write using pictures, some letters, and transitional spelling to convey meaning	•	•	•					
Dictate messages or stories for others to write	•	•	•					

	Pre-K	K	1	2	3	4	5	6
Create own written texts for others to read; write left to right on a line and top to bottom on a page	•	•	•					
Participate in shared and interactive writing	•	•	•					

Traits of Writing

Focus/Ideas

	Pre-K	K	1	2	3	4	5	6
Maintain focus and sharpen ideas		•	•	•	•	•	•	•
Use sensory details and concrete examples; elaborate		•	•	•	•	•	•	•
Delete extraneous information			•	•	•	•	•	•
Rearrange words and sentences to improve meaning and focus				•	•	•	•	•
Use strategies, such as tone, style, consistent point of view, to achieve a sense of completeness						•	•	•

Organization/Paragraphs

	Pre-K	K	1	2	3	4	5	6
Use graphic organizers to group ideas		•	•	•	•	•	•	•
Write coherent paragraphs that develop a central idea			•	•	•	•	•	•
Use transitions to connect sentences and paragraphs			•	•	•	•	•	•
Select an organizational structure based on purpose, audience, length						•	•	•
Organize ideas in a logical progression, such as chronological order or by order of importance		•	•	•	•	•	•	•
Write introductory, supporting, and concluding paragraphs						•	•	•
Write a multi-paragraph paper				•	•	•	•	•

Voice

	Pre-K	K	1	2	3	4	5	6
Develop personal, identifiable voice and an individual tone/style			•	•	•	•	•	•
Maintain consistent voice and point of view						•	•	•
Use voice appropriate to audience, message, and purpose						•	•	•

Word Choice

	Pre-K	K	1	2	3	4	5	6
Use clear, precise, appropriate language		•	•	•	•	•	•	•
Use figurative language and vivid words				•	•	•	•	•
Select effective vocabulary using word walls, dictionary, or thesaurus		•	•	•	•	•	•	•

Sentences

	Pre-K	K	1	2	3	4	5	6
Combine, elaborate, and vary sentences		•	•	•	•	•	•	•
Write topic sentence, supporting sentences with facts and details, and concluding sentence			•	•	•	•	•	•
Use correct word order			•	•	•	•	•	•
Use parallel structure in a sentence							•	•

Conventions

	Pre-K	K	1	2	3	4	5	6
Use correct spelling and grammar; capitalize and punctuate correctly		•	•	•	•	•	•	•
Correct sentence fragments and run-ons					•	•	•	•
Use correct paragraph indention				•	•	•	•	•

The Writing Process

	Pre-K	K	1	2	3	4	5	6
Prewrite using various strategies	•	•	•	•	•	•	•	•
Develop first drafts of single- and multiple-paragraph compositions		•	•	•	•	•	•	•
Revise drafts for varied purposes, including to clarify and to achieve purpose, sense of audience, precise word choice, vivid images, and elaboration		•	•	•	•	•	•	•
Edit and proofread for correct spelling, grammar, usage, and mechanics		•	•	•	•	•	•	•
Publish own work	•	•	•	•	•	•	•	•

Types of Writing

	Pre-K	K	1	2	3	4	5	6
Narrative writing (such as personal narratives, stories, biographies, autobiographies)	•	•	• T	• T	• T	• T	• T	• T
Expository writing (such as essays, directions, explanations, news stories, research reports, summaries)		•	• T	• T	• T	• T	• T	• T
Descriptive writing (such as labels, captions, lists, plays, poems, response logs, songs)	•	•	• T	• T	• T	• T	• T	• T
Persuasive writing (such as ads, editorials, essays, letters to the editor, opinions, posters)		•	• T	• T	• T	• T	• T	• T

Writing Habits and Practices

	Pre-K	K	1	2	3	4	5	6
Write on a daily basis	•	•	•	•	•	•	•	•
Use writing as a tool for learning and self-discovery			•	•	•	•	•	•
Write independently for extended periods of time		•	•	•	•	•	•	•

ENGLISH LANGUAGE CONVENTIONS in WRITING and SPEAKING

	Pre-K	K	1	2	3	4	5	6
Grammar and Usage in Speaking and Writing								
Sentences								
Types (declarative, interrogative, exclamatory, imperative)	•	•	• T	• T	• T	• T	• T	• T
Structure (simple, compound, complex, compound-complex)	•	•	•	•	•	• T	• T	• T

• instructional opportunity   **T** tested in standardized test format

	Pre-K	K	1	2	3	4	5	6
Parts (subjects/predicates: complete, simple, compound; phrases; clauses)				•T	•	•T	•T	•T
Fragments and run-on sentences		•	•	•	•	•	•	•
Combine sentences, elaborate			•	•	•	•	•	•
Parts of speech: nouns, verbs and verb tenses, adjectives, adverbs, pronouns and antecedents, conjunctions, prepositions, interjections		•	•T	•T	•T	•T	•T	•T
Usage								
Subject-verb agreement		•	•T	•	•	•T	•T	•T
Pronoun agreement/referents			•T	•	•	•T	•T	•T
Misplaced modifiers						•	•T	•T
Misused words					•	•	•	•T
Negatives; avoid double negatives					•	•	•	•

Mechanics in Writing

	Pre-K	K	1	2	3	4	5	6
Capitalization (first word in sentence, proper nouns and adjectives, pronoun *I*, titles, and so on)	•	•	•T	•T	•T	•T	•T	•T
Punctuation (apostrophe, comma, period, question mark, exclamation mark, quotation marks, and so on)		•	•T	•T	•T	•T	•T	•T

Spelling

	Pre-K	K	1	2	3	4	5	6
Spell independently by using pre-phonetic knowledge, knowledge of letter names, sound-letter knowledge	•	•	•	•	•	•	•	•
Use sound-letter knowledge to spell	•	•	•	•	•	•	•	•
Consonants: single, double, blends, digraphs, silent letters, and unusual consonant spellings		•	•	•	•	•	•	•
Vowels: short, long, *r*-controlled, digraphs, diphthongs, less common vowel patterns, schwa		•	•	•	•	•	•	•
Use knowledge of word structure to spell			•	•	•	•	•	•
Base words and affixes (inflections, prefixes, suffixes), possessives, contractions and compound words			•	•	•	•	•	•
Greek and Latin roots, syllable patterns, multisyllabic words			•	•	•	•	•	•
Spell high-frequency, irregular words		•	•	•	•	•	•	•
Spell frequently misspelled words correctly, including homophones or homonyms			•	•	•	•	•	•
Use meaning relationships to spell					•	•	•	•

Handwriting

	Pre-K	K	1	2	3	4	5	6
Gain increasing control of penmanship, including pencil grip, paper position, posture, stroke	•	•	•	•				
Write legibly, with control over letter size and form; letter slant; and letter, word, and sentence spacing		•	•	•	•	•	•	
Write lowercase and capital letters	•	•	•	•				
Manuscript	•	•	•	•	•	•	•	
Cursive				•	•	•	•	•
Write numerals	•	•	•					

Listening and Speaking

	Pre-K	K	1	2	3	4	5	6
Listening Skills and Strategies								
Listen to a variety of presentations attentively and politely	•	•	•	•	•	•	•	•
Self-monitor comprehension while listening, using a variety of skills and strategies	•	•	•	•	•	•	•	•
Listen for a purpose								
For enjoyment and appreciation	•	•	•	•	•	•	•	•
To expand vocabulary and concepts	•	•	•	•	•	•	•	•
To obtain information and ideas	•	•	•	•	•	•	•	•
To follow oral directions	•	•	•	•	•	•	•	•
To answer questions and solve problems	•	•	•	•	•	•	•	•
To participate in group discussions	•	•	•	•	•	•	•	•
To identify and analyze the musical elements of literary language	•	•	•	•	•	•	•	•
To gain knowledge of one's own culture, the culture of others, and the common elements of cultures	•	•	•	•	•	•	•	•
Recognize formal and informal language			•	•	•	•	•	•
Listen critically to distinguish fact from opinion and to analyze and evaluate ideas, information, experiences	•		•	•	•	•	•	•
Evaluate a speaker's delivery				•	•	•	•	•
Interpret a speaker's purpose, perspective, persuasive techniques, verbal and nonverbal messages, and use of rhetorical devices					•	•	•	•
Speaking Skills and Strategies								
Speak clearly, accurately, and fluently, using appropriate delivery for a variety of audiences, and purposes	•	•	•	•	•	•	•	•
Use proper intonation, volume, pitch, modulation, and phrasing		•	•	•	•	•	•	•
Speak with a command of standard English conventions			•	•	•	•	•	•
Use appropriate language for formal and informal settings	•	•	•	•	•	•	•	•

	Pre-K	K	1	2	3	4	5	6
Speak for a purpose								
To ask and answer questions	•	•	•	•	•	•	•	•
To give directions and instructions	•	•	•	•	•	•	•	•
To retell, paraphrase, or explain information			•	•	•	•	•	•
To communicate needs and share ideas and experiences	•	•	•	•	•	•	•	•
To participate in conversations and discussions	•	•	•	•	•	•	•	•
To express an opinion	•	•	•	•	•	•	•	•
To deliver dramatic recitations, interpretations, or performances	•	•	•	•	•	•	•	•
To deliver presentations or oral reports (narrative, descriptive, persuasive, and informational)	•	•	•	•	•	•	•	•
Stay on topic	•	•	•	•	•	•		•
Use appropriate verbal and nonverbal elements (such as facial expression, gestures, eye contact, posture)	•	•	•	•	•	•	•	•
Identify and/or demonstrate methods to manage or overcome communication anxiety						•	•	•

Viewing/Media	Pre-K	K	1	2	3	4	5	6
Interact with and respond to a variety of print and non-print media for a range of purposes	•	•	•	•	•	•	•	•
Compare and contrast print, visual, and electronic media					•	•	•	•
Analyze and evaluate media			•	•	•	•	•	•
Recognize purpose, bias, propaganda, and persuasive techniques in media messages				•	•	•	•	•

Research and Study Skills

Understand and Use Graphic Sources	Pre-K	K	1	2	3	4	5	6
Advertisement			•	•	•	•	•	•
Chart/table	•	•	•	•	•	•	•	•
Diagram/scale drawing			•	•	•	•	•	•
Graph (bar, circle, line, picture)			•	•	•	•	•	•
Illustration, photograph, caption, label	•	•	•	•	•	•	•	•
Map/globe	•	•	•	•	•	•	•	•
Order form/application						•	•	•
Poster/announcement	•	•	•	•	•	•	•	
Schedule						•	•	•
Sign	•	•	•	•		•		
Time line				•	•	•	•	•

Understand and Use Reference Sources	Pre-K	K	1	2	3	4	5	6
Know and use parts of a book to locate information	•	•	•	•	•	•	•	•
Use alphabetical order			•	•	•	•		
Understand purpose, structure, and organization of reference sources (print, electronic, media, Internet)	•	•	•	•	•	•	•	•
Almanac						•	•	•
Atlas		•	•	•	•	•	•	•
Card catalog/library database				•	•	•	•	•
Dictionary/glossary		•		•	• T	• T	• T	• T
Encyclopedia			•	•	•	•	•	•
Magazine/periodical			•	•	•	•	•	•
Newspaper and newsletter			•	•	•	•	•	•
Readers' Guide to Periodical Literature						•	•	•
Technology (computer and non-computer electronic media)		•	•	•	•	•	•	•
Thesaurus				•	•	•	•	•

Study Skills and Strategies	Pre-K	K	1	2	3	4	5	6
Adjust reading rate			•	•	•	•	•	•
Clarify directions	•	•	•	•	•	•	•	•
Outline				•	•	•	•	•
Skim and scan			•	•	•	•	•	•
SQP3R						•	•	•
Summarize		•	•	•	•	•	•	•
Take notes, paraphrase, and synthesize			•	•	•	•	•	•
Use graphic and semantic organizers to organize information		•	•	•	•	•	•	•

• instructional opportunity　　　**T** tested in standardized test format

Test-Taking Skills and Strategies	Pre-K	K	1	2	3	4	5	6
Understand the question, the vocabulary of tests, and key words				•	•	•	•	•
Answer the question; use information from the text (stated or inferred)		•	•	•	•	•	•	•
Write across texts				•	•	•	•	•
Complete the sentence				•	•	•	•	•

Technology/New Literacies	Pre-K	K	1	2	3	4	5	6
Non-Computer Electronic Media								
Audio tapes/CDs, video tapes/DVDs	•	•	•	•	•	•	•	
Film, television, and radio		•	•	•	•	•	•	•
Computer Programs and Services: Basic Operations and Concepts								
Use accurate computer terminology	•	•	•	•	•	•	•	•
Create, name, locate, open, save, delete, and organize files		•	•	•	•	•	•	•
Use input and output devices (such as mouse, keyboard, monitor, printer, touch screen)	•	•	•	•	•	•	•	•
Use basic keyboarding skills		•	•	•	•	•	•	•
Responsible Use of Technology Systems and Software								
Work cooperatively and collaboratively with others; follow acceptable use policies	•	•	•	•	•	•	•	•
Recognize hazards of Internet searches		•	•	•	•	•	•	•
Respect intellectual property					•	•	•	•
Information and Communication Technologies: Information Acquisition								
Use electronic web (non-linear) navigation, online resources, databases, keyword searches			•	•	•	•	•	•
Use visual and non-textual features of online resources	•	•	•	•	•	•	•	•
Internet inquiry			•	•	•	•	•	•
Identify questions			•	•	•	•	•	•
Locate, select, and collect information			•	•	•	•	•	•
Analyze information			•	•	•	•	•	•
Evaluate electronic information sources for accuracy, relevance, bias				•	•	•	•	•
Understand bias/subjectivity of electronic content (about this site, author search, date created)					•	•	•	•
Synthesize information					•	•	•	•
Communicate findings				•	•	•	•	•
Use fix-up strategies (such as clicking *Back, Forward,* or *Undo;* redoing a search; trimming the URL)			•	•	•	•	•	•
Communication								
Collaborate, publish, present, and interact with others		•	•	•	•	•	•	•
Use online resources (e-mail, bulletin boards, newsgroups)			•	•	•	•	•	•
Use a variety of multimedia formats			•	•	•	•	•	•
Problem Solving								
Select the appropriate software for the task	•	•	•	•	•	•	•	•
Use technology resources for solving problems and making informed decisions			•	•	•	•	•	•
Determine when technology is useful				•	•	•	•	•

The Research Process	Pre-K	K	1	2	3	4	5	6
Choose and narrow the topic; frame and revise questions for inquiry		•	•	•	•	•	•	•
Choose and evaluate appropriate reference sources			•	•	•	•	•	•
Locate and collect information	•	•	•	•	•	•	•	•
Take notes/record findings				•	•	•	•	•
Combine and compare information				•	•	•	•	•
Evaluate, interpret, and draw conclusions about key information		•	•	•	•	•	•	•
Summarize information		•	•	•	•	•	•	•
Make an outline				•	•	•	•	•
Organize content systematically		•	•	•	•	•	•	•
Communicate information		•	•	•	•	•	•	•
Write and present a report		•	•	•	•	•	•	•
Include citations						•	•	•
Respect intellectual property/plagiarism						•	•	•
Select and organize visual aids		•	•	•	•	•	•	•

Author's craft/style/language. See **Literary craft.**

Author's note. See **Genres.**

Author's perspective/viewpoint/bias, 5.1 105, 111b, 136, 229b, 5.2 221, 256, 5.6 717. See also **Literary craft.**

Author's possible meanings. See **Author's perspective/viewpoint/bias; Literary craft,** author's perspective/viewpoint/bias; **Theme (as a story element).**

Authors, program, 5.1 xx, 5.2 iv, 5.3 iv, 5.4 iv, 5.5 iv, 5.6 iv

Author's purpose, 5.2 151, 162l–162m, 162–163, 169, 175, 185b, DI·16, DI·17, DI·53, 5.3 262l–262m, 262–263, 269, 277, 283, 287b, 375, DI·6, DI·7, DI·52, 5.4 436l–436m, 445, 481, 5.5 521, 560l–560m, 560–561, 567, 573, 579, 581b, 591, DI·26, DI·27, DI·54

Author study, 5.1 139b–139n

Autobiography. See **Genres.**

B

Background, build. See **Concept development; Prereading strategies,** activate prior knowledge.

Base words with and without spelling changes. See **Spelling,** word structure; **Word structure.**

Bias, 5.1 105, 111b, 5.2 221, 5.6 717

Bibliography
  self-selected reading, 5.1 DI·57–DI·58, TR14–TR17, 5.2 DI·57–DI·58, TR14–TR17, 5.3 DI·57–DI·58, TR14–TR17, 5.4 DI·57–DI·58, TR14–TR17, 5.5 DI·57–DI·58, TR14–TR17, 5.6 DI·57–DI·58, TR14–TR17
  trade book library, 5.1 18i, 42i, 68i, 90i, 112i, 5.2 142i, 162i, 186i, 208i, 230i, 5.3 262i, 288i, 316i, 346i, 364i, 5.4 392i, 412i, 436i, 458i, 484i, 5.5 512i, 536i, 560i, 582i, 604i, 5.6 634i, 654i, 674i, 700i, 726i

Bilingual students. See **ELL (English Language Learners) suggestions.**

Biography. See **Genres.**

Build background. See **Concept development; Prereading strategies,** activate prior knowledge.

C

Capitalization
  nouns, proper, 5.1 133e–133f
  See also **Writing process,** edit.

Card catalog. See **Reference sources.**

Career awareness, 5.3 340–345, 5.5 578–581

Cartoons. See **Genres.**

Case study. See **Genres.**

Categorizing. See **Classifying.**

Cause and effect, 5.1 27, 42l–42m, 42–43, 51, 57, 59, 112l–112m, 112–113, 119, 125, 131, 133b, DI·16, DI·17, DI·46, DI·47, DI·53, DI·56, 5.3 271, 5.5 582l–582m, 582–583, 589, 593, 603, 603b, DI·36, DI·37, DI·55

Central message of text. See **Main idea, Theme (as a story element).**

Character, 5.1 18l–18m, 18–19, 25, 29, 37, 41b, 49, 77, DI·6, DI·7, DI·52, 5.5 512l–512m, 512–513, 519, 525, 533, 535, 535b, DI·6, DI·7, DI·52

Character Counts! See **Character education.**

Character education (as demonstrated in literature selections)
  attentiveness, 5.1 86–89, 5.2 212–223, 5.4 416–431, 5.6 730–747
  caring, 5.2 146–157, 160–161, 190–203, 212–223, 5.4 462–477, 5.5 532–535
  citizenship, 5.2 234–247, 5.5 564–575
  fairness, 5.1 94–107, 110–111
  initiative, 5.1 46–63, 116–127, 5.3 282–287, 5.4 396–407, 5.5 622–625
  patience, 5.1 72–83, 5.3 292–309, 320–337
  respect, 5.1 94–107, 5.2 146–157, 166–177
  responsibility, 5.2 166–177, 212–223, 5.6 670–673
  trustworthiness, 5.2 212–223, 5.5 516–529, 5.6 638–649, 652–653

Choral reading. See **Fluency, reading.**

Chronology. See **Sequence.**

Chunking. See **Word structure,** chunking.

Classifying
  statements of evidence. See **Fact and opinion, statements of.**
  words into groups, 5.1 70b, 5.4 394b, 5.6 702b

Classroom-based assessment. "If/then" assessment occurs throughout lessons and Guiding Comprehension.

Classroom management, 5.1 18d–18e, 18f–18g, 18g-1–18g-4, 42d–42e, 42f–42g, 42g-1–42g-1, 68d–68e, 68f–68g, 68g-1–68g-4, 90d–90e, 90f–90g, 90g-1–90g-4, 112d–112e, 112f–112g, 112g-1–112g-4, 5.2 142d–142e, 142f–142g, 142g-1–142g-4, 162d–162e, 162f–162g, 162g-1–162g-4, 186d–186e, 186f–186g, 186g-1–186g-4, 208d–208e, 208f–208g, 208g-1–208g-4, 230d–230e, 230f–230g, 230g-1–230g-4, DI·52, 5.3 262d–262e, 262f–262g, 262g-1–262g-4, 288d–288e, 288f–288g, 288g-1–288g-4, 316d–316e, 316f–316g, 316g-1–316g-4, 346d–346e, 346f–346g, 346g-1–346g-4, 364d–364e, 364f–364g, 364g-1–364g-4, 5.4 392d–392e, 329f–329g, 329g-1–329g-4, 412d–412e, 412f–412g, 412g-1–412g-4, 436d–436e, 436f–436g, 436g-1–436g-4, 458d–458e, 458f–458g, 458g-1–458g-4, 484d–484e, 484f–484g, 484g-1–484g-4, 5.5 512d–512e, 512f–512g, 512g-1–512g-4, 536d–536e, 536f–536g, 536g-1–536g-4, 560d–560e, 560f–560g, 560g-1–560g-4, 582d–582e, 582f–582g, 582g-1–582g-4, 604d–604e, 604f–604g, 604g-1–604g-4, 5.6 634d–634e, 634f–634g, 634g-1–634g-4, 654d–654e, 654f–654g, 654g-1–654g-4, 674d–674e, 674f–674g, 674g-1–674g-4, 700d–700e, 700f–700g, 700g-1–700g-4, 726d–726e, 726f–726g, 726g-1–726g-4

Clauses
  dependent, 5.1 89e–89f
  independent, 5.1 89e–89f

Colon, 5.1 40, 5.3 333, 5.6 753e–753f

Comma, 5.1 40, 89f, 111e–111f, 5.6 699e–699f

Common word parts. See **Word structure.**

Communication, effective. See **Listening,** tips; **Speaking,** tips.

Community, involvement of. See **School-home connection.**

fluent reading, 5.1 41a, 67a, 89a, 111a, 133a, 5.2 161a, 185a, 207a, 229a, 253a, 5.3 287a, 315a, 345a, 363a, 383a, 5.4 411a, 435a, 457a, 483a, 503a, 5.5 535a, 559a, 581a, 603a, 625a, 5.6 653a, 673a, 699a, 725a, 753a

graphophonic cues, using, 5.1 21, 5.2 233, 5.3 367, 5.4 395, 5.5 607, 5.6 677

monitor and fix up, 5.1 42–43, 55, 57, 63, DI·17, 5.2 162–163, 175, 177, 183, 185, 5.4 436–437, 449, 451, 456, 457, 5.5 560–561, 572, 573, 575, 581

prereading, 5.1 22, 46, 72, 94, 116, 5.2 146, 166, 190, 212, 234, 5.3 266, 292, 320, 350, 368, 5.4 396, 416, 440, 462, 488, 5.5 516, 540, 564, 586, 608, 5.6 638, 658, 678, 704, 730

research, 5.1 41l, 67l, 89l, 111l, 133l, 5.2 161l, 185l, 207l, 229l, 253l, 5.3 287l, 315l, 345l, 363l, 383l, 5.4 411l, 435l, 457l, 483l, 503l, 5.5 535l, 559l, 581l, 603l, 625l, 5.6 653l, 673l, 699l, 725l, 753l

spelling, 5.1 41i–41j, 67i–67j, 89i–89j, 111i–111j, 133i–133j, 5.2 161i–161j, 185i–185j, 207i–207j, 229i–229j, 253i–253j, 5.3 287i–287j, 315i–315j, 345i–345j, 363i–363j, 383i–383j, 5.4 411i–411j, 435i–435j, 457i–457j, 483i–483j, 503i–503j, 5.5 535i–535j, 559i–559j, 581i–581j, 603i–603j, 625i–625j, 5.6 653i–653j, 673i–673j, 699i–699j, 725i–725j, 753i–753j

viewing, 5.1 67d, 5.2 207d, 5.3 315d, 5.4 503d, 5.5 559d

vocabulary. See Vocabulary strategies.

Structural analysis. See **Word structure.**

Study strategies, 5.1 41l, 67l, 89l, 111l, 133l, 5.2 161l, 185l, 207l, 229l, 253l, 5.3 287l, 315l, 345l, 363l, 383l, 5.4 411l, 435l, 457l, 483l, 503l, 5.5 535l, 559l, 581l, 603l, 625l, 5.6 653l, 673l, 699l, 725l, 753l. See also **Assessment,** test-taking strategies; **Content-area texts; Graphic sources; Organizing information; Parts of a book; Reference sources; Textbook-reading techniques.**

Style, author's. See **Literary craft.**

Style, illustrator's. See **Literary craft.**

Subject-verb agreement, 5.2 253e–253f

Suffixes. See **Vocabulary strategies, Word structure.**

Summarizing, 5.1 112–113, 125, 127, 133, DI·46, DI·47, 5.3 288–289, 303, 307, 309, 315, 383, DI·16, DI·17, 5.5 582–583, 593, 597, 601, 625, DI·36, DI·37

Sustained silent reading. See **Self-selected reading.**

Syllables. See **Spelling,** word structure; **Word structure,** chunking, syllabication.

Synonyms, 5.1 20b, 92–93, 5.2 188b, 5.4 394b, 438–439, 447, 5.5 584b. See also **Vocabulary strategies.**

Synthesizing. See **Connections, making; Reading across texts.**

T

Tables. See **Graphic sources,** chart/table.

Taking notes. See **Note-taking.**

Tall tale. See **Genres.**

Target comprehension skills. See **Comprehension skills, explicit/implicit instruction** for a total listing of these skills.

Target comprehension strategies. See **Comprehension strategies, explicit/implicit instruction** for a total listing of these strategies.

Teaching strategies
  informal assessment. See **Running record,** taking a.
  modeling. This strategy is part of every lesson.
  think-aloud. This strategy is part of every lesson.
  See also **Graphic and semantic organizers,** types.

Technology
  e-mail, 5.1 130–133, 5.4 483k
  information and communication technologies. See **Technology,** new literacies.
  Internet article, 5.2 250–253, 5.3 380–383, 5.4 500–503, 5.5 578–581, 5.6 722–725
  Internet/World Wide Web. See **Technology,** new literacies.
  new literacies
    bias, 5.1 111k
    bookmarks, 5.1 67k, 5.2 207k, 253k, 5.4 501, 5.5 579, 625k, 5.6 653k
    documentation of Web sites, 5.1 67, 5.2 161k, 253k, 5.3 287k, 315k, 5.4 411k, 457k, 5.5 535k, 603k, 5.6 673k
    electronic media, 5.1 20a, 41k, 44a, 48, 58, 67k, 70a, 74, 81, 84, 89k, 92a, 96, 111k, 114a, 118, 133k, 5.2 144a, 156, 161k, 164a, 168, 185k, 188a, 192, 207k, 210a, 222, 229k, 232a, 236, 253k, 5.3 264a, 268, 287k, 290a, 294, 315k, 318a, 322, 331, 345k, 348b, 352, 363k, 366a, 370, 383k, 5.4 394a, 402, 411k, 414a, 418, 435k, 438a, 444, 457k, 460a, 466, 483k, 486a, 490, 503k, 5.5 514a, 518, 531, 535k, 538a, 542, 559k, 562a, 566, 581k, 584a, 588, 603k, 606a, 610, 625k, 5.6 636a, 644, 653k, 656a, 664, 673k, 676a, 680, 699k, 702a, 708, 725k, 728a, 732, 753k
    e-mail, 5.1 130–133, 5.2 160, 161, 5.4 483k
    etiquette, 5.1 131, 5.2 251, 5.3 381, 5.4 483k, 501, 5.5 579, 5.6 723
    evaluating Internet information and sources, 5.1 41k, 67k, 89k, 111k, 5.2 161k, 207k, 229k, 251, 253k, 5.3 287k, 315k, 345k, 363k, 381, 382, 383k, 5.4 411k, 435k, 457k, 483k, 500–503, 503k, 5.5 535k, 559k, 579, 581k, 603k, 625k, 5.6 653k, 673k, 699k, 722–725, 725k, 753k
    folder, 5.1 132
    homepage, 5.1 5.4 500, 5.6 722
    Internet article, 5.2 250–253, 5.3 380–383, 5.4 500–503, 5.5 578–581, 5.6 722–725
    Internet inquiry, 5.1 20a, 41k, 44a, 48, 58, 67a, 70a, 74, 81, 84, 89k, 92a, 96, 111k, 114a, 118, 133k, 5.2 144a, 156, 161k, 164a, 168, 185k, 188a, 192, 207k, 210a, 222, 229k, 232a, 236, 253k, 5.3 264a, 268, 287k, 290a, 294, 315k, 318a, 322,

331, 345k, 348b, 352, 363k, 366a, 370, 383k, 5.4 394a, 402, 411k, 414a, 418, 435k, 438a, 444, 457k, 460a, 466, 483k, 486a, 490, 503k, 5.5 514a, 518, 535k, 538a, 542, 559k, 562a, 566, 581k, 584a, 588, 603k, 606a, 610, 625k, 5.6 636a, 644, 653a, 656a, 664, 673k, 676a, 680, 699k, 702a, 708, 725k, 728a, 732, 753k
    keyword, 5.1 20a, 44a, 48, 58, 67k, 70a, 74, 81, 84, 89k, 92a, 96, 114a, 118, 5.2 144a, 156, 161k, 168, 185k, 188a, 192, 210a, 222, 229k, 232a, 236, 250, 252, 253k, 5.3 264a, 268, 290a, 294, 315k, 318a, 331, 348a, 352, 366a, 370, 380, 381, 5.4 394a, 402, 411k, 414a, 418, 432, 435k, 438a, 444, 457k, 460a, 483k, 486a, 490, 501, 503k, 5.5 514a, 535k, 538a, 542, 559k, 562a, 566, 578, 584a, 588, 606a, 610, 625k, 5.6 636a, 644, 653a, 656a, 664, 676a, 680, 699k, 702a, 708, 725k, 728a, 732, 753k
    library catalog, 5.6 749
    links, 5.1 111k, 5.2 250, 5.3 380, 381, 382, 5.4 435k, 500, 501, 502, 5.5 559k, 578–580, 5.6 724, 725k, 753k
    online reference sources and directories, 5.1 5.2 250, 5.3 5.4 500–503, 503k, 5.5 562a, 578–581, 5.6 721
    presentation software, 5.1 41k, 111k, 133k, 5.2 161k, 185k, 207k, 229k, 253k, 5.3 287k, 315k, 363k, 383k, 5.4 411k, 435k, 457k, 483k, 5.5 559k, 581k, 603k, 625k, 5.6 673k, 699k, 725k, 753k
    reference source. See **Reference sources.**
    search engines, 5.1 20a, 41k, 44a, 48, 58, 67k, 74, 81, 84, 89k, 92a, 114a, 118, 5.2 156, 161k, 164a, 168, 185k, 188a, 192, 207k, 210a, 222, 229k, 232a, 236, 250, 253k, 5.3 264a, 268, 287k, 290a, 294, 315k, 318a, 322, 331, 345k, 348a, 352, 363k, 366a, 370, 380–383, 5.4 394a, 402, 411k, 414a, 418, 435k, 438a, 444, 457k, 460a, 466, 486a, 490, 501, 502, 503k, 5.5 514a, 518, 538a, 542, 562a, 566, 580, 581k, 584a, 588, 606a, 610, 5.6 636a, 644, 656a, 664, 673k, 676a, 699k, 702a, 708, 725k, 728a, 732
    searching and navigating the Internet, 5.1 20a, 41k, 44a, 48, 58, 67k, 70a, 74, 81, 84, 89k, 92a, 96, 111k, 114a, 118, 133k, 5.2 144a, 456, 459, 161k, 164a, 168, 185k, 188a, 192, 207k, 210a, 222, 229k, 232a, 236, 253k, 5.3 264a, 268, 287k, 290a, 294, 315k, 318a, 322, 331, 345k, 348b, 352, 363k, 366a, 370, 383k, 5.4 394a, 402, 411k, 414a, 418, 435k, 438a, 444, 457k, 460a, 466, 483k, 486a, 490, 503k, 5.5 514a, 518, 535k, 538a, 542, 559k, 562a, 566, 581k, 584a, 588, 603k, 606a, 610, 625k, 5.6 636a, 644, 653k, 656a, 664, 673k, 676a, 680, 699k, 702a, 708, 725k, 728a, 732, 753k
    technology tools, 5.1 130, 5.2 250, 5.3 380, 5.4 500, 5.5 578, 5.6 722
    URLs, 5.1 67k, 111k, 133k, 5.2 253k, 5.3 287k, 363k, 5.4 435k, 5.5 603k, 625k, 5.6 699k, 722
    use graphic sources, 5.4 502
    use web site features, 5.1 130–131, 5.2 160, 250, 251, 252, 5.3 380, 382, 5.4 500, 5.5 578, 5.6 722, 724, 753k

Teacher's Edition

Text

KWL Strategy: The KWL Interactive Reading Strategy was developed and is used by permission of Donna Ogle, National-Louis University, Evanston, Illinois, co-author of *Reading Today and Tomorrow*, Holt, Rinehart & Winston Publishers, 1988. (See also *The Reading Teacher*, February 1986, pp. 564–570.)

Page 392m: From "At the Water's Edge" from *The Black Stallion* by Walter Farley. © 1941 by Walter Farley. Copyright renewed 1969 by Walter Farley. Used by permission of Random House Children's Books, a division of Random House, Inc.

Page 412m: Excerpt from *Wilma Unlimited: How Wilma Rudolph Became the World's Fastest Woman*. Text © 1996 by Kathleen Krull. Reprinted by permission of Harcourt, Inc.

Page 436m: Text excerpt from "Reptile Superheroes" from *The Snake Scientist* by Cy Montgomery. Text © 1999 by Cy Montgomery. Reprinted by permission of Houghton Mifflin Company. All rights reserved.

Page 458m: From "Count on Fiona" from *Only Fiona* by Beverly Keller. Reprinted by permission of Beverly Keller.

Page 484m: From "Jerry Takes Off" from *The Winning Stroke* by Matt Christopher. © 1994 by Matt Christopher (Text); © 1994 by Karen Lidbeck (Illustration). Used by permission of Little, Brown and Co., Inc.

Artists
Greg Newbold: cover, page i

Photographs
Every effort has been made to secure permission and provide appropriate credit for photographic material. The publisher deeply regrets any omission and pledges to correct errors called to its attention in subsequent editions.

Unless otherwise acknowledged, all photographs are the property of Scott Foresman, a division of Pearson Education.

Photo locators denoted as follows: Top (T), Center (C), Bottom (B), Left (L), Right (R), Background (Bkgd)

18M Getty Images;

42M (Bkgd) (TR) Getty Images; (TC) Hemera Technologies;

87L (BL) ©Royalty-Free/Corbis, (BR) Comstock Images/Getty Images;

88M (T) Getty Images; (BR) Digital Vision;

111L Brand X Pictures/Getty Images;

112M Brand X Pictures;

137N Getty Images;

146M Getty Images;

148J NASA;

160J Digital Wisdom, Inc.;

220M Brand X Pictures;

223N Getty Images;

228I Getty Images;

240J Getty Images;

288M Getty Images;

315L Getty Images;

316M Getty Images;

322M Getty Images;

346M Getty Images;

388K Brand X Pictures;

392M Getty Images;

408M Getty Images;

412M (T) ©Comstock Inc, (Bkgd) Getty Images;

430M Getty Images;

436M ©Dover Publications;

456M Getty Images;

457L Getty Images;

476K Getty Images;

484M ©Image Source Limited;

512M Getty Images;

535L ©Royalty-Free/Corbis;

536M Hemera Technologies;

560M Getty Images;

582M Getty Images;

600M ©Dover Publications;

634M Brand X Pictures;

643M (TC) Brand X Pictures, (Bkgd) Getty Images;

654M Getty Images;

674M ©Dover Publications;

700M (C) ©Dover Publications; (Bkgd) Getty Images;

724M ©Dover Publications;

762M Brand X Pictures.